The Sportsworld of the Hanshin Tigers

SPORT IN WORLD HISTORY

Edited by Susan Brownell, Robert Edelman, Wayne Wilson, and Christopher Young

This University of California Press series explores the story of modern sport from its recognized beginnings in the nineteenth century to the current day. The books present to a wide readership the best new scholarship connecting sport with broad trends in global history. The series delves into sport's intriguing relationship with political and social power, while also capturing the enthusiasm for the subject that makes it so powerful.

The Sportsworld of the Hanshin Tigers

Professional Baseball in Modern Japan

William W. Kelly

UNIVERSITY OF CALIFORNIA PRESS

University of California Press, one of the most
distinguished university presses in the United States,
enriches lives around the world by advancing
scholarship in the humanities, social sciences, and
natural sciences. Its activities are supported by the
UC Press Foundation and by philanthropic
contributions from individuals and institutions.
For more information, visit www.ucpress.edu.

University of California Press
Oakland, California

Library of Congress Cataloging-in-Publication Data

Names: Kelly, William W. (William Wright),
    1946– author.
Title: The sportsworld of the Hanshin
    Tigers : professional baseball in modern Japan /
    William W. Kelly.
Description: Oakland, California : University of
    California Press, [2019] | Series: Sport in world
    history ; 5 | Includes bibliographical references
    and index. |
Identifiers: LCCN 2018020210 (print) | LCCN 2018026682
    (ebook) | ISBN 9780520971141 (ebook) |
    ISBN 9780520299412 (cloth : alk. paper) |
    ISBN 9780520299429 (pbk. : alk. paper)
Subjects: LCSH: Hanshin Taigasu (Baseball team) |
    Baseball—Japan—20th century.
Classification: LCC GV875.H36 (ebook) | LCC GV875.H36
    K45 2019 (print) | DDC 796.357/640952187—dc23
LC record available at https://lccn.loc.gov/2018020210

[Manufactured in the United States of America / Printed
in China]

28   27   26   25   24   23   22   21   20   19
10   9   8   7   6   5   4   3   2   1

Contents

Illustrations

Full-color versions of many of these illustrations as well as other figures and photographs can be found at https://professional.wwkelly.net/ht.

MAPS

Acknowledgments

A baseball game seems very long and excruciatingly slow to many people—as exciting as watching paint dry, some of my closest friends complain. Yet baseball is a horse race compared to the pace of this book's emergence, which began with some initial speculations back in the early 1990s and is based largely on field research conducted in Japan over multiple intervals from 1996 through 2005. I have written many articles since then about Japanese baseball and the Hanshin Tigers in particular, and a bit of this has made its way into passages in this book. But the shape of this book, its argument, and its prose are quite different from my other baseball writing, and as I will note shortly, I was relieved and surprised to find an unexpected value in the long interval between primary fieldwork and its final publication.

The long gestation period has also greatly expanded the number of individuals and institutions that have provided me with all manner of intellectual, financial, and psychological support. I begin by acknowledging the work of Robert Whiting, whose books and articles on Japanese baseball, in English and Japanese, stretch from the 1970s through the present. This may surprise some readers of my previous writings, because I have taken issue with a couple of Whiting's characterizations. It may surprise (though hopefully not annoy) Mr. Whiting himself, who has responded sharply to my criticisms. But it was his earliest work that first showed me—and many others—the mutual significance of sports, baseball in particular, and modern Japanese society, and he continues to inform us with the flair of good journalism and the substance of academic scholarship.

Several persons were instrumental in my initial entry into Kansai area baseball. I am indebted to Andrew Gordon, not only a preeminent Japan historian but also an astute baseball analyst, for introducing me to Ishikawa Masahiko and his editor, Endō Yasuo, at the Osaka Asahi Newspaper Sports Bureau. They were immediately supportive of my project and graciously negotiated access to all three Kansai clubs (Hanshin Tigers, Orix BlueWave, and Kintetsu Buffaloes) and provided me with working space at the stadiums. There were numerous others in the sports media whom I came to rely on for information and insight, most especially Terao Hirokazu, senior feature writer for Nikkan Sports, who has shared his expertise for many years. During my early years of research, I was especially aided by Tominomori Yōsuke of Asahi Shimbun, Kishimoto Chiaki and Hanae Hisashi of Nikkan Sports, and Ueyama Noei of SupoNichi. I am especially grateful to Nikkan Sports News West Japan and to Nakamura Ken, head of its editorial department, for permission to include so many illustrations in this book.

All three Kansai baseball clubs were welcoming in their own ways, and I appreciate the time and resources that they so willingly offered. For reasons that I explain in the book, I ended up spending most of my fieldwork with the Hanshin Tigers club, which bore the burden of my intrusions. Takano Eiichi, Saruki Tadao, Tsunekawa Tatsuzō, and Hamada Tomoaki were especially important in giving me access to all aspects of club life, and I continue to value meetings and discussions with Yoshida Yoshio, the manager in the early years of my fieldwork and still one of Japan's most important ambassadors of baseball to the world. Morikawa Hidetatsu in the Orix BlueWave front office and Sakō Takakzu at Kintetsu were most helpful in introducing me to members of those clubs and teams. I spent hundreds of hours among the fan clubs in the outfield bleachers of multiple stadiums, especially Kōshien. Moritani Kazuo, who was head of the major association of fan clubs at Kōshien, and Fujita Kenji, the force behind the "Roving Tigers Club," ensconced every game along the bleacher bench halfway up the right-field stands, opened up to me the multiple worlds of Hanshin fandom and allowed me to move freely among them.

Throughout those years, dozens of players, coaches, staff, fans, vendors, reporters, and broadcasters tolerated my presence and my often-naive questions and shared their knowledge, perspectives, passions, and anxieties. I was not a reporter seeking a quote for the next morning's edition, and they usually shared their thoughts with the understanding that they would not be identified by name. I have respected that here in the text, although they are indelible to me in my own memory and gratitude.

Japan has small but impressive fields of scholarship in sports history and sports sociology, and I acknowledge some of that work here because it continues to provide me with such a foundation of knowledge. About Hanshin and Kansai baseball, I have drawn particularly from my colleagues Kiku Kōichi, Sugimoto Atsuo, Takahashi Hidesato, Shimizu Satoshi, Takahashi Hidesato, and Nagai Yoshikazu. For the manuscript itself, two of my colleagues, anonymously, provided the University of California Press with some of the most trenchant and helpful readings I have ever received. Dr. Tonoike Yukiko at my home department at Yale expertly rendered the maps and tables, and Sharon Langworthy was the best copyeditor I have ever worked with.

Initial funding for the field research came from the Japan Foundation and from the Social Science Research Council, whose fellowship committee graciously overcame its initial skepticism about the $900 budget line in my proposal for the "purchase of baseball game tickets!" Waseda University, through its generous Asakawa Kan'ichi Fellowship, has provided a comfortable writing environment, and my sponsor there and longtime friend Glenda Roberts has welcomed me for several extended stays at the Graduate School of Asia-Pacific Studies. The Department of Anthropology and the Council on East Asian Studies at Yale have been home for my entire career, and my affection for and my indebtedness to the faculty, staff, graduate students, and undergraduates extend far beyond this project. For almost four decades, they have provided constant stimulation, boundless generosity, and continuing collegiality.

Authors usually end their acknowledgments with appreciation to their partners and families, often as an apology for all the time that the project took from their personal lives together. My wife, Louisa Cunningham, and our daughter Claire did indeed generously indulge me with the time that I have spent on this and my other research over the years, but my deeper gratitude runs in the opposite direction. They are my greatest sources of support and love, and what I most appreciate is that they have never indulged me in taking too much time for this project from our rich life together.

A Note on Terms and Japanese Language

Team is a term used widely and loosely in sportswriting, and *Hanshin Tigers* and just *Hanshin* are heard in everyday and media talk across the Kansai region. Both usages are confusing because they refer to several distinct units. In this book, I distinguish among the team, club, and company in order to understand their connections. The Hanshin Tigers team consists of the players, the manager, and the coaches; they and only they wear the uniform and take the field. The Hanshin Tigers club includes this team and its front office of executives and staff, who directly operate the team. Some of the operational staff (such as the trainers and the media relations staff) may wear club-logo athletic wear, but never the full player uniform; most of the front office staff dress as any regular corporate office employees do. The Hanshin Tigers club, in turn, is a subsidiary of the Hanshin Electric Railroad Company, which is the corporation that owns the club. My point is that the team, the club, and the company are distinct, constituent units in what I formulate as the Hanshin Tigers *sportsworld*.

Two abbreviations appear throughout this book, NPB and MLB. The official English name of the organization of professional baseball is Nippon (for Japan) Professional Baseball, hence NPB. Professional baseball in the United States is incorporated as Major League Baseball, or MLB. For brevity, I refer to the two professional organizations by their official initials throughout the book.

Japanese baseball has an extensive lingo, which I want to communicate because this linguistic grid is vital to the meaning, power, and value of the Hanshin Tigers world. However, Japanese is a foreign language to most readers of this book, and terms in their original form can be off-putting rather than revealing. Thus, I have tried as much as possible to use English glosses for Japanese terms upon their first appearance. The Japanese terms that I introduce in the text are written in Romanized form. Japan specialists who want to know how the terms are actually written in Japanese characters and syllabary may refer to the glossary at the end of the book.

For those in Japan studies who wish to learn even more Japanese baseball lingo, I have made available an extensive glossary of terms in the supplementary online resources, covering every term used in this book and much else as well. This may be found at https://professional. wwkelly.net/ht. It had its origin in the field glossary that I had to create while making my way through the research. I was already quite an advanced speaker and reader of Japanese, but the extensive specialized terms and daily slang of the baseball world formed a baffling and unfamiliar argot. My field glossary started as daily jottings in my notebook as I encountered more and more Japanese terms and phrases that I had never heard before, and it has become over the years a useful adjunct to the research itself.

Finally, throughout the text and bibliography I follow Japanese convention in ordering Japanese personal names with the surname first, followed by the given name. For example, the Hall of Fame shortstop and later Hanshin manager is identified here as Yoshida Yoshio; Yoshida is his surname.

CHAPTER I

Introducing Hanshin Tigers Baseball

"Sports is the toy department of human life," quipped the famous New York City sportswriter Jimmy Cannon (Popick 2012). They are entertaining breaks from the struggles of everyday demands and from the serious business of politics and the economy. Sports are games, and we play them and watch them for fun and relaxation.

We scholars seem to have taken Cannon's remark at face value, judging from how little attention we have paid to sports as an object of study. Perhaps we have failed to notice how firmly his tongue was planted in his cheek. Sports are fun, sports are games, but sports are far more than fun and games, as Cannon and much of the rest of the world have realized for a long time.

Most of the organized sports we play today took their present form in the nineteenth century, and they have shaped and reflected our modern life for 150 years. Sports are big business and patriotic pursuits. They have profoundly influenced our mass media;, our science; our daily language; and our feelings about equality, race, gender, conflict, and character. Sports as activities range from our own daily workouts at the neighborhood gym or friendly matches at the local tennis court to the world's largest gatherings of humanity at the quadrennial Olympics. They are at the heart of what it means to be modern.

Cannon chose an insightful metaphor of sports as life's toy store because just as a toy store is a serious business that indulges our fancy for playthings, sports are profound anomalies. They are serious fun—

pleasurable recreation that can require hard work ("going for the burn" in aerobics, "hitting the wall" in running a marathon, or "maxing out" on a skateboard). Sports are intensely physical activities that also demand mental focus, emotional commitment, and spiritual drive. And professional sports present the starkest contradiction of all: playing for pay seems to violate our cherished distinction between paid labor and leisure play. More than a century of debate about sports and amateurism testifies to our unease about the propriety of professional sports.

This is certainly true for Japan, where one sport—baseball—has been the center of the national sportscape throughout the twentieth century and into the twenty-first. As the premier sport in secondary schools, baseball has been the model for adolescent masculinity. As a staple of media promotion and in huge stadiums of urban leisure, baseball has been among the most popular forms of metropolitan entertainment. As Japan's dominant professional team sport, it has been a template for corporate organization. As a league sport of local teams, it has been a vehicle for regional loyalties and rivalries. And with its imagery of samurai with bats, baseball has fostered a continuing sports nationalism in US-Japanese relations. This book explores the forms of baseball in modern Japan and how and why the sport has held such a central place in the society.

It does so by focusing on the world of a single professional team, the Hanshin Tigers, whose features and fortunes reveal much about baseball in modern Japanese society. For the last half century, the Hanshin Tigers have been the second most popular professional baseball team in Japan. They are based on the edge of the country's second-largest city, Osaka, and over those decades, their rivalry with the Tokyo Yomiuri Giants, the most powerful and popular team in Japan, has carried the frustrations of regional subordination to the national center. The team's corporate owner has been a small parent company that has constantly intruded in team and front office affairs. The team has had the added pressure of playing on the "sacred ground" of Kōshien Stadium, revered throughout Japan as the permanent site of the annual national high school baseball tournaments (see figure 1). The Tigers have long been scrutinized by a voracious, local sports media, even more than the home press attention to the sports teams of New York, Boston, Barcelona, and other passionate sports cities. The team is followed rabidly by organized, independent fan club associations, which rock the stadium at every home game, and by knowledgeable and concerned fans across the Kansai region.

FIGURE 1. A Tigers game at Hanshin Kōshien Stadium in 2014. From Wikimedia Creative Commons.

The Tigers' popularity, however, has not been based on strength and success. In over a half century, from 1950 to 2003, they won only three Central League championships and but a single Japan Series. Most painfully, in the twenty years from 1983 to 2003, they finished in last place ten times and only managed a winning record three times in those two decades. It was in spite of—and in no small way, because of—five decades of loss, frustration, and perennial infighting that they remained the overwhelming sentimental favorite in the Kansai region. This book analyzes the Hanshin Tigers baseball world and offers an account of why it is so compelling and instructive.

This was not quite the book that I thought I would write when I set out on this research back in 1996, over twenty years ago. I knew then that baseball was crucial to understanding the social and cultural significance of sports in modern Japan, and I thought it was important to move away from Tokyo and particularly from the Yomiuri Giants, Japan's most famous professional team, based in the nation's capital and the focus of most Japanese and foreign attention. What was baseball like away from its ground zero? To find out, I chose to go to Japan's second region, Kansai, which is essentially the sprawling tri-city conurbation of Osaka, Kobe, and Kyoto, and which was then home to three of Japan's twelve professional baseball teams. The Kintetsu Buffaloes (Kintetsu Bafarōzu) were based on the east side of Osaka; Hanshin played at Kōshien, just to the west of Osaka city center; and the Orix BlueWave (Orikkusu Burūwēvu) played in Green Stadium, in the northwest corner of Kobe (see map 1).

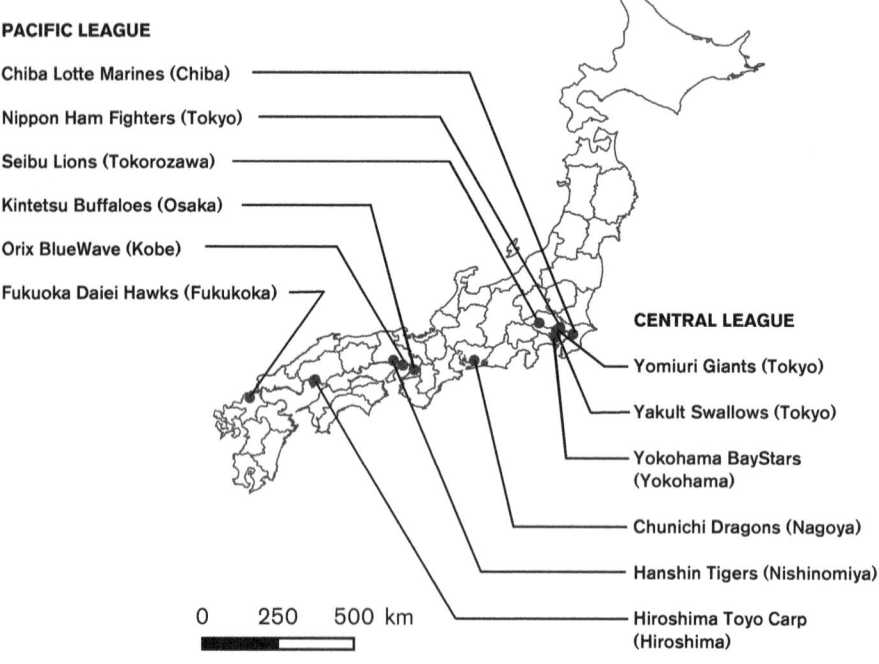

PACIFIC LEAGUE

Chiba Lotte Marines (Chiba)

Nippon Ham Fighters (Tokyo)

Seibu Lions (Tokorozawa)

Kintetsu Buffaloes (Osaka)

Orix BlueWave (Kobe)

Fukuoka Daiei Hawks (Fukukoka)

CENTRAL LEAGUE

Yomiuri Giants (Tokyo)

Yakult Swallows (Tokyo)

Yokohama BayStars (Yokohama)

Chunichi Dragons (Nagoya)

Hanshin Tigers (Nishinomiya)

Hiroshima Toyo Carp (Hiroshima)

0   250   500 km

MAP 1. The home stadium locations of the twelve teams in Nippon Professional Baseball, 1998.

Kansai offered a splendid opportunity for a controlled comparison of three cases in a single region, and during my first month there I went around to all three clubs with introductions and began attending their practices and games. However, I immediately discovered that no one else but me was paying equal attention to the three teams. No matter whom I met—journalists, shopkeepers, fellow public transit passengers, or other ordinary folk—no matter which daily sports newspaper I read, and no matter which television sports show I watched, throughout Kansai, everyone was far more consumed by the Hanshin Tigers than by anything that happened with the Orix or Kintetsu teams. To an outsider, they were playing the same game, fundamentally, in all three stadiums. What was so distinctive about the game at Kōshien that it drew such disproportionate attention? This question, at once quite local and specific, turned out to be conceptually challenging and analytically productive. This book is my answer.

FIRST ENCOUNTERS

Although I did not appreciate it then, hints of Hanshin's exceptionalism revealed themselves to me at the very beginning of my fieldwork. In the space of three months, from July through September 1996, I had three sets of experiences that redefined my research and reshaped its analysis: watching the disciplining of a player and the firing of the team's manager, tracking the club's coverage by the daily sports newspapers, and experiencing the raucous irreverence of the stadium fan clubs.

I arrived in Osaka in July 1996, at a moment of intense club controversy and media scrutiny for the Hanshin Tigers. A firestorm was brewing around a Tigers infielder named Kameyama Tsutomu, who was then in his eighth year with the team. Kameyama had been wildly popular and moderately promising in his first years with Hanshin (he even made the Central League all-star team in 1992), but by the mid-1990s he was plagued by injuries and was bouncing back and forth between the main team and the farm team. His behavior was increasingly erratic, and he had a penchant for attracting sensationalist media coverage as yet another Hanshin "troublemaker" (a translation of *osawagase otoko* and *mondaiji*, which were the Japanese terms used by both the coaching staff and the media). Earlier in the spring of 1996, he had persuaded the club to send him to the United States to be treated for an Achilles tendon problem, but when he returned, the media speculated about whether he had actually gone through with the procedure while he was there. He was then sent down to the farm team to rehabilitate, but throughout May and June he was chronically late for daily practices, failed to show up for several of the team's games, and had a habit of running off to the toilet in the middle of games. The club was concerned enough to have him undergo psychological testing and angry enough to sentence him to a kind of house arrest. These and other developments (e.g., early in the season he separated from his wife, and they began divorce proceedings in July) earned him constant coverage in the daily sports newspapers and special attention from the Tigers main team manager, Fujita Taira. Fujita himself was so hot tempered that he was known as the "devil manager," and by midseason the team's woes left him beleaguered by increasing front office and media criticism.

Matters came to a head just at the moment of my arrival in mid-July, when Kameyama was late yet again for morning practice at the farm team's facility near Kōshien. When he did show up, around noon, he was called out onto the field by the farm team manager, who loudly

FIGURE 2. Front-page headline declaring that manager Fujita's dismissal has been decided. *Nikkan Sports*, Osaka edition, September 4, 1996, 1. Courtesy of Nikkan Sports Newspaper.

berated him in front of everyone. Kameyama was then ordered to sit cross-legged in the middle of the outfield in Zen meditation style for several hours in the withering sun of a brutally hot Osaka July day, while practice continued around him and the media took photographs and filed dispatches.

Trying quickly to learn more about the Hanshin situation, I was brought up to date by the team's beat reporters about other recent turmoil, including the reassignment of the number two executive in the front office (Sawada Kuniaki) in June and Fujita's disciplining of other players, including the team's flamboyant star, Shinjō Tsuyoshi. Fujita had abruptly released the team's two American players in early June, then quickly signed two replacements, neither of whom was contributing successfully by late July. Hanshin languished near the bottom of the standings, and fans began to protest, throwing megaphones onto the field after games, refusing to cheer, taunting the team bus, and accosting players on road trips.

Hanshin's difficulties continued as the season wore on, and Fujita himself came under attack. Kuma Shinjirō, the chairman of the parent company and the longtime designated "owner" of the club, voiced confidence in Fujita in late July, but the team's extended August road trip was a disaster. In a five-hour meeting on September 2, the club's board of directors (dominated by Kuma and other parent company executives) decided informally that Fujita had to go (as reported in the article in figure 2).

The news leaked, and the meeting was headlined in the next morning's sports papers. Lengthy media analyses followed, and the five regional sports dailies immediately began speculating on (and promoting) various candidates for the job—primarily ex-Hanshin players who were then on retainer as commentators to the very sports papers that were pushing their candidacies (see figure 3).

Hanshin management dithered for ten days, until the board made its formal decision on September 13. The baseball club president told the massed media that he would meet with Fujita at 5:00 that evening to accept the latter's resignation and that he would then hold a press conference at 6:00. This proved to be an embarrassing misjudgment. The club expected Fujita, like many before him, to accept the inevitable and to tender his resignation, thus preserving the company's reputation and moving the spotlight back to the team and its prospects for the next season. But Fujita was angry and stubborn. He demanded to be fired, and he held out against the club president in an extraordinary nine-hour, closed-door session (with the press waiting outside). It ended at 2:00 a.m. without resolution—more fodder for the morning editions—but the next day Fujita finally gave in and submitted his resignation.

Such a highly public dispute was unusual, I was told, but it was only one of many well-publicized tensions on the team and among the team, the club, and the parent company that were to continue for some time, and it was a puzzling and unnerving introduction to the project. How

FIGURE 3. Front-page article tracking five probable candidates in the "Hanshin manager race" (all of whom were former Hanshin players), with the headline announcing that two have been eliminated from contention. *Nikkan Sports*, Osaka edition, September 10, 1996, 1. Courtesy of Nikkan Sports Newspaper.

was I to make sense of a confrontation between a seemingly troubled, immature player and a hotheaded and frustrated manager? Why did the question of being fired versus resigning lead to a nine-hour standoff? The personalities seemed larger than life—which is to say, the issues were exaggerated and the emotions blown out of proportion. And every event immediately produced multiple versions and hinted at deeper conflicts of interest lurking below the daily drama. It was like watching a soap opera version of Kurosawa's classic film *Rashomon* every day. What could the sequence of events in those first months mean for my understanding of Hanshin and Japanese baseball?

For some time, I was skeptical of making too much of this. Any anthropologist knows that when we begin fieldwork, we enter ongoing chains of events and sets of interpersonal relationships whose meaning and significance we seldom immediately understand, and as any follower of sports knows, this particular field of study—the stadium of professional sports—is constantly roiled by personnel frictions. By that measure, I thought that what was happening was probably unremarkable even as I stumbled to appreciate the nuances. However, as I continued to reflect back, Kameyama's shenanigans, Fujita's troubles, the club's turmoil, and indeed Hanshin's rather dismal season on the field had introduced me to several recurring themes in Hanshin baseball that became integral to the analysis I offer here and that were reinforced by two other features of Hanshin Tigers baseball that struck me forcefully in those first months: the colorful sports daily newspapers and the boisterous Kōshien fan clubs.

I spent most afternoons before the evening games at the ballpark, watching the media do their work and the teams make their preparations. I began to interview the reporters and photographers, I visited newsrooms, and I spent part of each game in the press box. My introduction to the three baseball clubs had come through the Osaka Sports Department of the *Asahi* newspaper, one of the three major national daily newspapers, along with *Mainichi* and *Yomiuri*. All three had beat reporters and photographers assigned to each of the three clubs, and all three papers had sports sections that reported game results and some brief stories—minimal coverage compared with major papers in the United States and England, for example.

However, I soon recognized that Hanshin received far greater coverage in the five daily sports newspapers, and there was a huge readership for these garish tabloid-style papers, sold at every news kiosk and convenience store in the region. When riding the train and subway, going into coffee shops, or sitting at bars, I realized these daily sports papers were ubiquitous. And despite the presence of three baseball clubs in the region, virtually every issue of all five dailies featured the Tigers on the front page, with Orix, Kintetsu, and teams in other sports relegated to paltry coverage on a few inside pages. What was it about Hanshin that seemed to have monopolized the attention of the daily sports newspapers, and why were these papers, not the prestigious general dailies, the leading sports medium?

Along with the summer's turmoil in the club and the over-the-top media coverage, a third feature that struck me immediately was the intensity of the Kōshien Stadium spectators. I spent a lot of time in all three stadiums that first summer (and continued to do so over the years), viewing games from different locations, and in all the stadiums there was a noisy, collective cheering, especially coming from the outfield bleachers. Everywhere, the continuous chanting, uniformed cheerleaders, blaring trumpets, and waving banners reminded me much more of European professional soccer than of American baseball. However, in this respect also, Kōshien clearly stood out for the total fan involvement, the intricacy of the cheering, the irreverence of the jeers, and, as I probed, the complexity of the fan club organization. Organized fans are the active vanguard of spectators in any professional sport, but my field notes from the first few months contained many remarks on how exceptionally active the Kōshien fans seemed.

In the following year, 1997, when I returned to continue my fieldwork, the controversies of the previous year had been replaced by fresh optimism about a new season, a new manager, and new players. Despite this, the Tigers started sinking in the league standings early in the season, and similar tensions and disputes once again surfaced. Nonetheless, Hanshin remained the center of attention in Kansai region sports, eclipsing the two other teams even as Orix again had a stellar run. By then, the puzzle of the Tigers' preeminence had become a central curiosity to me.

I was especially confused that the Orix BlueWave went virtually unnoticed. In 1996, they had cruised to a Pacific League championship for the second straight year behind another record-setting performance by their superstar player, Suzuki Ichirō, and they were led by a popular, garrulous manager, Ohgi Akira. Their season culminated in late October, when they easily defeated Hanshin's archrivals, the Yomiuri Giants, in the Japan Series. For two years they had provided inspiration to a city, Kobe, that had been devastated by a major earthquake in January 1995. So what was it about Hanshin, and why did it claim such a monopoly on sports reporting and everyday conversation, while the fortunes of the two other Kansai teams were relegated to an occasional press column or a broadcast afterthought? This gradually became a more compelling question than an even-handed, comparative study of the three teams. It is the animating ethnographic question of this book: What was it about the Hanshin Tigers?

To answer this question, I drew upon two concepts and two themes that clarified for me the distinctiveness of the Hanshin Tigers. The concepts are the notion of a *sportsworld*, which I formulate as my analytical unit of study, and the genre of television soap operas, which I use analogously. In the next section I characterize the Hanshin Tigers as a highly instructive example of a sportsworld. In the section after that I discuss how the experience of the Hanshin Tigers, at least over the years when I was studying them closely, was very much like that of a long-running television soap opera, dense with overlapping narratives that unfolded melodramatically and were charged with moral fervor. One can find cases of such sportsworlds in many places, but I argue that the distinctive fascination of the Hanshin Tigers was what their sportsworld displayed about workplace dynamics in an era when the conditions of work were a matter of both national pride and concern, as well as what it symbolized in decades when Osaka and Kansai were feeling the frustrations of sliding into second-city status. The Hanshin Tigers were a compelling melodrama of workplace life and regional rivalry.

THE HANSHIN TIGERS AS A SPORTSWORLD

The preferred strategy of most anthropologists has long been the extended case study. We try to understand the lifeways of people in part of a society by spending a lot of time there, detailing the organization of life and the patterns of meaning among its participants. These can be employees at a regional bank or an automobile manufacturing plant, students and teachers at an elementary school or a junior college, residents of a farm village or a city neighborhood, or denizens of a hostess bar or a public bath, to cite just a few examples from the extensive corpus by anthropologists who have worked in Japan. We come back and write books that we call ethnographies, which are analytical portraits of these bounded and named social units (even if we disguise the names for responsible confidentiality).

What of ethnographies of sports, then? Anthropologists in sports studies have produced very impressive ethnographies of what I would call sports locations as well as situated case studies of sports individuals. Holly Swyers (2010), for instance, through her own intensive participant observation in the bleachers of Chicago's Wrigley Field, showed how the longtime regulars had built a structured community of stadium denizens that generated an experience of effervescence. Another anthropologist, Roger Magazine (2007), highlighted the fan club of a university-sponsored professional soccer team in Mexico City and how it defined itself against other fan clubs and other team identities. Richard Light (1999) detailed the practice routines and dormitory life of a Japanese university rugby club to demonstrate how they created a culturally specific hegemonic masculinity. Laura Spielvogel's (2003) comparative ethnography of two fitness clubs in metropolitan Tokyo revealed the contradictory dispositions of both members and instructors to dominant norms of body, beauty, and fitness. Alan Klein (1997:esp. pt. 3) wrote an ethnographic analysis of forms of nationalism through an ethnography of a semiprofessional baseball team that was based in two adjacent cities on both sides of the US-Mexican border and played in leagues in both countries. George Gmelch (Gmelch 2006; Gmelch and Weiner 1998) and Orin Starn (2012) have given us grounded portraits of individuals at work in professional baseball and professional golf, respectively, that provide broad lessons about the structuring of careers, the business of sports, and sports' capacity to dramatize celebrity and race in the contemporary United States.[1] By focusing on particular locations, organizations, and individuals, these and many other sports ethnographers have been able to address critical questions about socialization, gender ideology, ethnicity, nationalism, ethnopsychology, and more (Besnier, Brownell, and Carter 2017 is a masterful synthesis of this growing field).

I have been much inspired by such work, but my perspective here is somewhat different. Rather than focus analytically on a single location—the stadium, the team in practice and competition, the fans in their clubs—I argue that these places and people necessarily and mutually constitute something larger that brings the Hanshin Tigers into collective being as a sportsworld. Faced with a professional team spectator sport and thinking comparatively about three teams in the same region, it was clear to me that "Hanshin Tigers baseball" was much more than the nine players who take the field for its games and the nine innings of baseball that they play each game. The Hanshin Tigers were a team (*chīmu* is the Japanese borrowing) of players and coaches and manager; Japanese professional baseball teams had quite large rosters, with up to seventy players under contract, only a few of whom were in play and on display at any one time. The Hanshin Tigers were also a baseball club (*kyūdan* is the term), in that behind and above the team was an administrative front office (*furonto*). With upward of one hundred employees, the front consisted of management executives; specialists like scouts, trainers, accountants, marketers, and media handlers; and general office workers. And finally, the Hanshin Tigers were a corporate entity, indeed a wholly owned subsidiary company of the Hanshin Electric Railroad Corporation. In Japanese business lingo, the Tigers were a "child company" (*kogaisha*) of a parent corporation (*oyagaisha*), whose president was the designated owner of the club. Furthermore, there was a spatial topography to Hanshin baseball. It was centered on the diamond within Kōshien Stadium (operated by Hanshin Kōshien Kyūjo, another Hanshin child company), which hosted cacophonous gatherings of tens of thousands of people for sixty or so baseball game days every year. But the Hanshin world extended well beyond that, to staff offices, practice facilities, a player dormitory, stadiums around the league, and spring training camps in several locations.

Surrounding these Hanshin entities were extensive and intrusive media: dozens of beat reporters, photographers, feature writers, desk editors, and television and radio announcers and commentators, who devoted twelve hours every day to reporting on the team, the club, and the corporation. Watching in the stadium and on television, reading the papers, and listening on radio were millions of Hanshin Tigers spectators and fans, following the games and the team with a wide range of passion and knowledge. They were found not just in the stadium but also in bars, homes, and workplaces within and beyond Kansai.

The focal point of Tigers baseball is the action on the field between the baselines—this is a compelling sport to play and watch—but the world of Tigers baseball is composed of the intensive interactions among this extensive cast of characters. It is a world of life and livelihood and identity, of dreams and disappointments, of profits and pleasures. The question was, then, just how might I conceptualize this as an ethnographic space?

It was thinking through this question that led me to the concept of a "social world," which was first proposed by the sociologist Howard S. Becker in the 1970s.[2] At the time he was studying the production and marketing of art, and he formulated what he called the "social world of art" to capture the matrix of diverse actors and interests whose common focus on art objects and diverse contributions created value. In his book, first published in 1982, Becker characterized his line of analysis as follows: "The idea of an art world forms the backbone of my analysis. 'Art world' is commonly used by writers on the arts in a loose and metaphoric way, mostly to refer to the most fashionable people associated with those newsworthy objects and events that command astronomical prices. I have used the term in a more technical way, to denote the network of people whose cooperative activity, organized via their joint knowledge of conventional means of doing things, produces the kind of art works that art world is noted for" (Becker 2008:xxiv). Becker admitted that this was a loosely structured and porously bounded concept—possibly even tautological—but he was correct that the concept has broader application. He continued:

> This tautological definition mirrors the analysis, which is less a logically organized sociological theory of art than an exploration of the potential of the idea of an art world for increasing our understanding of how people produce and consume art works. . . . I think it generally true that sociology does not discover what no one ever knew before, in this differing from the natural sciences. Rather, good social science produces a deeper understanding of things that many people are already pretty much aware of. . . . [W]hatever virtue this analysis has does not come from the discovery of any hitherto unknown facts or relations. Instead, it comes from exploring systematically the implications of the art world concept.
>
> Though the basic idea seems commonplace, many of its implications are not. Thus, it seems obvious to say that if everyone whose work contributes to the finished art work does not do his part, the work will come out differently. But it is not obvious to pursue the implication that it then becomes a problem to decide which of all these people is the artist, while the others are only support personnel. (2008:xxiv)

Like art, sports too can precipitate local worlds of performers and others, who form a direct and mediated social nexus around a team, a place, or a style. Sportsworlds are centered on performance, which gives pride of place to the athletes, but the dynamics of power, the making of meaning, the creation of memory, and the negotiation of value can be distributed across a much wider range of participants. These sportsworlds are loosely bounded, fuzzy sets with elusive material, physical, sensual, social, and ideological dimensions. However, the concept of social world, which I localized here as a sportsworld, nicely captures the collaborative production that is not easily framed by a formal institution (such as a school, a factory, or a fitness club) or the social boundaries of a neighborhood or village.[3]

Nine men take the field and play baseball against nine other men. It is a generic sporting contest, played by a rulebook that is shared across nations and time. But when they take a certain field with certain uniforms, those men become Hanshin Tigers players. This is the crucial point: they are Hanshin Tigers players not because of what they do on the field, but because they are part of a broader production of meaning, a much wider collective action by many people who are not on the field but distributed in positions and locations that generate and sustain the narrative fabric and affective identity of the Hanshin Tigers.

As I experienced very quickly, all those in such a sportsworld are not in direct and stable relationships with one another. The concept of a sportsworld is by no means that of a harmonious Durkheimian solidarity. I found few strong ties and structural affinities among players and their coaching staff; within and between the front office and the parent company; among the various media; and across the intense fans, occasional spectators, and others in the region who felt degrees of concern about Hanshin. The key point is that all of them are essential to producing the events, the practices, and the feelings that constitute the Hanshin Tigers as a recognizable sportsworld and distinctive baseball identity. Much of this book is devoted to exploring these parts of the Hanshin Tigers sportsworld, their relationships to each other, and their roles in defining this sportsworld. To appreciate the Hanshin Tigers as a sportsworld is essential not only to understanding their importance for Japanese society but also to understanding the potential of anthropology to reveal the place of sports in modern life.

THE HANSHIN TIGERS AS SOAP OPERA: NARRATIVES, NUMBERS, MELODRAMA, AND MORALITY

The events that confronted me early on revealed a crisis of authority, a fracture of club harmony, a fascination with breakdown and loss, and a tendency toward emotional and moral melodrama. I mentioned previously that my first impression of the Hanshin Tigers in 1996 was of a soap opera, but I did not really take that seriously, in analytical terms, until much later. I now think that an analogy to the soap opera genre is actually crucial to appreciating the distinctive features of the Tigers sportsworld, and in several respects it is a better exemplar than the television shows that inspired the construction of the genre.

Soap opera as a genre of television is probably not familiar to younger readers of this book because its heyday was decades ago, when broadcast television dominated the airwaves. A soap opera was a daily serial drama of everyday life and interpersonal relationships; episodes were typically thirty minutes in length and shown in an afternoon time slot.[4] "Soap" referred to the soap and detergent companies that advertised on the shows (although most soaps drew a broader set of advertisers), and the tag indicated the primary audience: "housewives" who might seek an entertaining afternoon break between morning domestic chores and their children's return from school later in the day. Soap operas actually began in the 1930s as radio dramas, but they were an especially significant genre of television from its beginnings in the 1950s through the end of the twentieth century. Such US shows as *Days of Our Lives*, *As the World Turns*, and *General Hospital* were iconic in establishing the conventions of soap operas.[5]

Scholars have identified three key elements of the soap opera as a genre. First, the narratives are complex, multiple, and nonepisodic plots that unfold unevenly, with incongruent themes and incomplete outcomes. (This is often phrased as deferring the "satisfaction" of a final resolution, but surely there is as much satisfaction in a never-resolved drama!) Second, these meandering plots are built around multiple interpersonal struggles among long-term characters who evoke viewers' identification and empathy (and sometimes anger). Third, the "structure of feeling" (Williams 1982) that shapes soap opera is not drama but melodrama, an on-your-sleeve, in-your-face, operatic emotional excess. Soap opera characters seldom display subtle modulations of emotion, preferring instead exaggerated displays of feelings.

It is easy to see how spectator sports can be likened to television soap operas, and indeed a number of analysts have made this connection. Ava Rose and James Friedman, for example, observed:

> In sport, both the analysis of the game, and the synthesis of past and present, always point toward the future. The teleological momentum of the game— and of each sport—is reinforced by the commentators' discourse of anticipation and speculation. However, this apparently linear trajectory does not lead to resolution or closure in the classical sense. Like daytime soaps—but unlike the majority of prime-time and weekend programming—television sport is serial: it is ongoing, continuous, and always to-be-continued. As with any serial, the consumption of television sports cannot be defined by the viewing of a single programme. Each game is perceived in relation to the entire season, the history of each sport, and the yearly cycle of sports representation on television. In this way, the outcome of a game is never the end: there is always a next game, the next season, and the next star player. (Rose and Friedman 1994:27)

An analogy between television soap operas and spectator sports has dissenters (e.g., Margaret Morse 1983), but my field research over the years with Hanshin persuaded me of their powerful affinities, and I argue that this provides a central framework for the shape and intensity of the Hanshin Tigers sportsworld. Nonetheless, I want to refine the broad claim of Rose and Friedman that spectator sports are all structured and savored as soap operas. It is not quite that simple.

On the one hand, the claim is too broad; it does not hold for all spectator sports. There are certainly compelling, continuing, and overlapping dramas in professional tennis and skiing, in college and professional basketball, in rugby, and so forth. However, in many sports, the characters are too few, the schedules too intermittent, the stories too underdeveloped, and the attention too localized to warrant an analogy to *Days of Our Lives*, or *The East Enders*, or other such soaps.

On the other hand, soccer in the elite leagues of some European and South American countries, cricket in places like Pakistan, ice hockey in Canada, and other cases of a national central sport may indeed fit the genre. And of all the spectator sports, baseball offers the best potential as a sporting soap opera. The almost daily contests throughout the eight-month MLB and NPB seasons make them the longest seasons in all professional sports. Baseball is a team sport of large rosters and many specialist positions. The nonregulation league format sustains long-standing rivalries, and the well-publicized, multiple levels of baseball careers (in Japan, where national attention is paid even to high school teams and players, who are followed into university and pro ranks) can give longevity to the characters in public attention. And like many soap operas, baseball is set within a well-defined, familiar, almost "domestic" space: the baseball diamond, with much of the action taking place at home plate, around the infield, and in the dugout. The game is marked by emotionally coded music, as in soap operas, and the demonstrative gestures of the players and umpires.

Indeed, baseball actually accentuates the features of television soap operas in three respects—narrative, emotion, and morality—and these features are key to understanding the dynamics of personal experience and interpersonal relations in the Hanshin Tigers sportsworld we enter in the chapters that follow.[6]

First of all, the narrative tapestry of the Tigers world far exceeds that of even the longest-running television soap, across the roster of players, throughout seasons, and over the eighty-year history of the club, and these are stories that connect Tigers players to a club history and also to player-characters and stories of the eleven other NPB teams. However, every player and every team is not only emplotted in overlapping, ongoing stories, they are also equally defined by a dense grid of statistical measures of performance. Record keeping is a defining feature of modern sports (Guttmann 1978), but baseball exceeds all other sports in the dozens of statistical metrics it now maintains for every player, game, and team.

Every player-character is suspended in a matrix of narratives and numbers. Every sports paper, on every day during the season, publishes several dense tables that rank the top twenty or so pitchers and hitters, dissected by almost two dozen statistical indexes (games played, wins, strikeouts, base-on-balls, earned-run-average, etc.). Every year the leading publishers produce even more detailed guidebooks that provide comparative details on all players on every team: their height and weight, sports biographies, key performance statistics, and rising and falling salaries for the last five years. There is no other occupation in the world with such continual public documentation of work performance metrics, and individual and team narratives unfold through a dense statistical grid.

Second, the stories and stats by which we know baseball actions and actors bear even more emotional weight than television soaps, because sports are competitions driven by an unrelenting tension between the predictable and the unpredictable. Knowing much and caring much are mutually conditioning, and television soaps are called operatic precisely because of the melodramatic flourishes by actors and fans alike. Sports, more so than soaps, are agonistic contests between "us" and "them." Soap operas have casts of good guys and bad guys who can elicit fierce audience identification over a long viewing history, but baseball games are competitions that result in a winner and a loser and present an even clearer dramatic choice. The identification of sports fans and their home teams further amplifies their emotional commitment. Gaining a lead, giving up a lead, hitting a home run, striking out, winning the game, losing the game—players and spectators are on a perpetual emotional rollercoaster, expressed in voices and gestures, amplified by photographers and television close-ups.

Moreover, emotion as the outward display of inner feelings is further heightened by the particular construction of suspense in a stop-and-go interval sport like baseball. Suspense is the perpetual tension between the rigid predictability of the rule-governed frame and the utter unpredictability of the outcome of every action. A batter steps into the batter's box to face the pitcher. Everything about the moment is dictated by the rulebook; everyone on the field and in the stands understands the frame of the moment immediately and completely. But what comes next—what will happen when the pitcher delivers the pitch—is entirely unknowable. Will the next instant be a strike, a hit, a foul, a ball? It is true (and important) that even the scriptwriters of television soaps do not know where the various plots and characters are going beyond a near horizon of the next few episodes, and there is even apparently a fair amount of improvisation, day in and day out, as the actors keep up with the fast-paced shooting schedule. However, at every moment in a sporting contest—every pitch, every shot, every run—no one, not the athletes, coaches, or spectators, really knows what will happen next. This perpetual suspense deepens the melodramatic qualities of the multiple and continuous action sequences. The batter may hit the ball through the infield and run safely to first base. That moment is utterly knowable and rulebook governed, but the next moment—the next pitch, the next action—is entirely open ended. That is a defining quality of all sports. They are always tightly framed (made "meaningful") by formal, arbitrary rules (there are nine players on the field, each team has three outs per inning, the pitcher must pitch from a mound that is precisely sixty feet, six inches from the front of the five-sided home plate, and many, many more stipulations). Yet they are also always live contests. Not only do we not know the winner of the game in advance, we do not know the outcome of any of the thousands of actions that make up the game. Suspense in sports is not just not knowing what the next moment will bring. It lies in the sharp contrast of the utter knowability of each frame of action with the unknowability of its outcome.

A third way in which baseball exceeds soap operas as an exemplar of the genre lies in what Rose and Friedman called its "moral Manichaeism," its rigid, exaggerated binary of good and bad:

> Like melodrama, sports narratives highlight personal struggle, social tension, and moral conflict. The extremes of emotion are exaggerated, and opposing forces are pitted against each other in absolute dualisms. Everything in sports representation reiterates this "moral manichaeism": from the clashing of team helmets generated by the opening computer graphics, and the visual contrasts between the teams' colours and opposing movements, to the endless juxtapositions of closeups highlighting the personal inner struggles of coaches and players from the two sides. Even the referees are visually coded as the arbiters of this conflict: wearing the black and white stripes which symbolize their 'objective' position as mediators between opposing forces. (Rose and Friedman 1994:29–30)

Soap opera narratives, to be sure, are given moral coding with "good" characters and "bad" characters, but they fall well short of the starkly contested nature of sports. The contest fuels passionate emotional investment in the actions and the outcomes and invests them with clear-cut moral ambitions. "We want passionately to win" becomes "we normatively should win." We, the good guys, must win, and you, the bad guys, must lose; our honor must be upheld, our effort and talent validated. Players, clubs, spectators, and even parts of the media align in just solidarity.

This is formidable, but also fragile. These solidarities, so densely woven with narratives and numbers, so deeply felt, and so morally charged, are fragile because of a further quality of sports that was especially exposed in the Hanshin sportsworld: the desperate search for accountability in the face of radical indeterminacy. On September 14, 1996, Fujita was forced to resign as manager, with the team facing yet another last-place finish. But was he to blame for the team's performance—or rather, how much and in what ways was he to blame?

The 1996 season had 135 games, and every game was played over three hours with multiple actions by a large cast: more than thirty players usually appeared in any one game, two managers and four umpires made decisions and calls, and there were seventy-five or so player at-bats and upward of two hundred pitches. It obviously matters deeply which team wins and which team loses, but what is so maddeningly opaque is who is responsible for winning and losing. A decisive strike-out, a dramatic home run, an umpire's disputed call—there are moments in every game that players, media, and fans will point to as the turning point, the game changer, the winning moment, or the culprit. But these apparent turning points are, in a sociologist's terms, path-dependent, and they come about only because of a long chain of prior actions and decisions. To this must be added the role of "luck." Was it the weather, the ball catching a bad break in the infield grass, a gust of wind that carried the ball over the fence? No one ever knows for sure, and the debate only dies down as the teams must get ready for the next day's contest, the media begin to write the next day's stories, and the fans return to the ballpark. The certainty of which team has won a baseball contest is as absolute as the uncertainty about why it won.

And yet the stakes in the game—emotional, moral, and financial— make it crucial to determine what fundamentally can never be determined. In the Hanshin sportsworld, we will see, over and over, what the British anthropologist Max Gluckman called the search for the "allocation of responsibility" (1972), for what drew the team, the club, the ownership, the media, and the fans into perpetual, acrimonious, irresolvable debate.

Thus, there were not only contests between "our" Hanshin Tigers and "those" Yomiuri Giants. The Hanshin sportsworld was riven with internal division. One form of this was the persistent rhetorical opposition that the media and the fans made between the "Fierce Tigers" (Mōko) and the "No-Good Tigers" (Dame Tora). No one doubted that for all too long the proud and powerful Mōko had turned into the inept and hapless Dame Tora, but no one could agree on who was at fault.

In short, I am arguing here, drawing affinities to the genre of soap opera, that this was a sportsworld infused with multiple, overlapping narratives. It was a continuous melodrama of overflowing emotions, both felt and displayed, that were heightened by the moral imperative of a contest, the nature of suspense in an interval sport like baseball, and the radical uncertainty of accountability. Even so, not all teams are as embedded within worlds as densely developed as that of the Hanshin Tigers, and not all teams generate such compelling soap opera. This returns me to the puzzle that confronted me in this fieldwork of why the Hanshin Tigers stood out so prominently from the two other Kansai teams, and indeed from all of the other NPB teams.

LOVABLE LOSERS?

It's like when your child is running in a foot race in kindergarten. Even more than winning a first place ribbon, you cheer your kid on fervently hoping that s/he will at least do well and get through without an injury. That's what cheering the Tigers is all about!

—Anonymous "Tiger-crazy" fan, as reported in Rokusaisha (1996:60)

It may seem puzzling that the Hanshin Tigers' preeminence occurred in the decades when the team descended into serial losses and organizational turmoil. The last-place team in a league is known as the cellar dweller, and by the late 1980s, throughout the 1990s, and into the early 2000s, the Hanshin Tigers were the perennial cellar dweller of the Central League (see figure 4). How was it that the least successful team in the region had by far the most robust sportsworld?

For a long time I was fixated on and somewhat blinded by this apparent thematic of failure; it did seem problematic that ineptitude, infighting, and poor performance could really sustain such widespread interest and concern. True, there can be a perverse fascination in watching ineptitude and in following the farces of factional struggles, and there can be a self-aggrandizing moral charge from rooting for the underdog. Indeed, throughout sports there is the archetype of the lovable loser, applied for decades to baseball teams like the Boston Red Sox and the Chicago Cubs. As veteran Boston sports journalist Dan Shaughnessy put it, "They are like your children, these Red Sox. They drive you

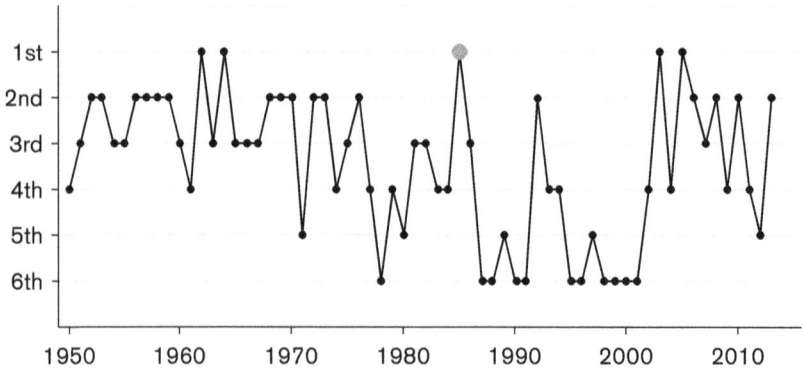

FIGURE 4. The Hanshin Tigers final season standings in the Central League, 1950–2017.

crazy and break your heart, but you still love them and you always take them back" (Shaughnessy 2011).

I had conversations like this with players, press, and fans in Osaka over the years as well. Some expressed feelings very much like Shaughnessy's; a fan mused, "[Hanshin players] have covered a wide swath of less-than-savory characters, short on self-discipline if long on personal charm. He is that stupid brother who dropped out of school and has been causing the family no end of trouble since. Still, you can't disown him because the kids love him and because he's family. So you are stuck with him, and you make the best of it" (field notes, July 1999). Others would with a shrug readily apply the common Japanese sentiment, "It's inevitable and nothing can be done about it" (field notes, August 2001).

I did not doubt these explanations for their resigned but steady affiliation. Nonetheless, I came to think that the sources of fascination and commitment in the Hanshin sportsworld were often more distinctive than those broad sentiments. In this book I draw out and try to substantiate the two major themes that animated this world and its lifeways.

A SOAP OPERA OF WORKPLACE STRUGGLES AND SECOND-CITY ANXIETIES

Central to understanding Hanshin was the fascination of this sportsworld as a workplace to those within it. All professional sports are just that—workplaces of professionals—and the conditions of employment, the forms of ownership, the authority of the manager, and the trajectories of careers are of interest and concern to athletes, media, and fans. This was especially true for the Hanshin Tigers. Hanshin baseball, for many, was savored as a long-running corporate drama. In the second half of the twentieth century in Japan, the corporation—the large organization workplace—emerged as a central institution in the life experiences of Japanese, whether male or female, white collar, blue collar, or pink collar. It shaped aspirations even for those who never made it into the ranks of the top companies and instead found themselves somewhere in the many tiers of workplaces below Toyota and Sumitomo Bank or a prestigious national ministry. Indeed, Osaka was famously a city of smaller companies, often subsidiaries or independent businesses. Similarly, Hanshin was a team within and below the front office, the club within and below that parent company. The fascination with Hanshin was not because it displayed the ideal forms of legitimate authority and smooth workplace relations that burnished the image of Japan, Inc. in those days. Rather, the Hanshin world dramatized the more common reality of rivalries and office politics, of unpredictable and sometimes undeserved success and adversity—in short, conditions of work familiar to the team's followers in their own lives.

Following the Hanshin Tigers, people told me, was like reading the salaryman comics, one of the most popular genres of Japanese comics. With titles like "Tanaka-kun," "Section Chief Shima Kōsaku," and "The Old Osaka Way of Finance," these "office comics" were serialized stories in weekly comic books, variety magazines, and some newspapers, sometimes running for a decade or more, periodically collected and issued in multivolume anthologies.[7] They were humorous, sardonic, cynical narrative pictorials of office rivalries, business dealings, shop floor pressures, water cooler romances, stock market shenanigans, botched promotions, and so forth. They gave pointed, bittersweet expression to life under pretentious, unreasonable, uncaring bosses and the demanding drudgery of day-to-day work.

And that was precisely what the Hanshin Tigers dramatized. Effort, talent, chance, accountability—the ingredients of any worker's lot—were on public display every evening on the baseball diamond and then related in melodramatic detail in the daily sports papers. Individual actions were framed by an organizational grid of authority. Of course, baseball to many fans is an intrinsically fascinating game; it is deceptively difficult to play, intricate to coordinate, and absorbing to watch. I do not want to discount the pleasures (and pains) of the sport itself.

But if we are to appreciate the inordinate attention given to Hanshin over other baseball experiences, we need to identify more particular factors in building an account, and key to this were the workplace dynamics on display.

There was a second source of fascination that complemented Hanshin's features as a workplace, and this constitutes the other major theme in the Hanshin Tigers soap opera. One reason the Osaka regional economy had become so characterized by what Japanese economists call the medium-small business sector is that many of the major corporations that used to be headquartered in Osaka had been moving up to Tokyo since the 1960s. For the first two-thirds of the century, Tokyo and Osaka were relatively balanced in economic power and prestige. Tokyo was the nation's political capital, to be sure, with the government ministries, major universities, and much economic clout. However, it was not until the 1960s—the decade of the Tokyo Olympics, the Shinkansen bullet train (going "up" to Tokyo and "down" to all other cities), and Japan's sudden burst of growth in gross national product (GNP) and export manufacturing—that the center of gravity tipped decisively toward Tokyo. Like France, Greece, Mexico, and many other nations, Japan became decidedly unipolar, and Osaka and the Kansai region more broadly slipped to second-city status—and a second-city mentality.

That, too, is what the Hanshin Tigers came to express. As I detail later, for a decade or so after the two-league system was created in 1950, Osaka area teams were, if anything, stronger than the Tokyo Yomiuri Giants. It was only from 1965, when the Giants began an unprecedented nine-year streak as Japan champions, that professional baseball, like the corporate world, became Tokyo centric. By the 1980s and 1990s, as the only Kansai-area team in the Central League, the Hanshin Tigers had to carry the full weight of Kansai's struggles against the national center throughout the season.

THE CHAPTERS TO COME

Following is a brief description of the broad analytical framework of the book. Against my initial intentions to balance my fieldwork across the three Kansai teams, I was drawn instead to the question of Hanshin's overwhelming claim on the region—even as the Orix BlueWave were playing far better baseball in the other Pacific League with one of the greatest players ever, Ichirō. This led me to see how the team itself was embedded in a wider sportsworld and to appreciate Hanshin Tigers baseball as a coproduction of the players, the management, the ownership, the media, the fans, and others. There was raw action: baseballs were pitched and hit, players ran and caught balls, umpires judged. But all this action was only significant because of who in particular was acting in what fashion at any one moment, and this depended on a deep web of biographies, relationships, records, and strategies—all constantly recorded, narrativized, transmitted, and analyzed to recursively motivate the actions that followed.

The chapters that follow explore the principal sites, temporal rhythms, and human characters in that sportsworld. Chapter 2 begins at the epicenter, game day at home in Kōshien Stadium. Playing in (and defending) Japan's most storied stadium brings immense prestige and unrelenting pressure, but it is crucial to realize that the spatial coordinates of the sportsworld are far wider than Kōshien. Hanshin Tigers baseball is distributed across visiting stadiums, practice facilities, dormitories, newsrooms, sports bars, and home living rooms throughout Kansai. The nightly game itself, nine innings over three hours or so, may be the fundamental unit of time, but baseball at this level is a complex matrix of multiple overlapping temporalities; at-bats, innings, games, series, seasons, and careers are among the units and sequences of action. These times and spaces of baseball action create the most developed matrix of numbers and narratives of all sports, a matrix that underlies the soap opera structure of Hanshin baseball.

Chapter 3 profiles the players. A Japanese professional team like Hanshin has a large roster, more than seventy players at any one time under contract. They are bundles of unique talents and distinctive career narratives, but they also illustrate some of the common life conditions of the professional athlete. The chapter considers selection, training, injury management, contract negotiations, career dynamics, retirement prospects, and other features that constitute complex and sometimes contradictory hierarchies of accomplishment, authority, and compensation, as well as irreconcilable tensions between individual competition and team cohesiveness.

It is the responsibility of the manager to prepare and command this large body of players, and chapter 4 analyzes the fraught and frequently untenable position of Hanshin managers and the coaching staffs they bring in to assist them. Almost all Hanshin managers have been star players themselves, and almost all of them have played for Hanshin. It is the most inbred organization in NPB. Despite this—or probably because of it—there have been twenty-five managerial changes in sixty-seven years of two-league play, stark evidence of the short leash and brief tenure of most men in that job. Becoming the Hanshin manager is one of the most prestigious and precarious positions in Japanese sports.

Much of the pressure felt by the Hanshin manager is placed on him by a large and intrusive management structure, and chapter 5 details its two levels. The Hanshin club is the front office staff that directly manages (some would say micromanages) the team, and it too is based in offices at Kōshien Stadium. The club is itself a direct subsidiary of the parent Hanshin Electrical Railroad Company. The intercity electric line it operates is the shortest among all five Kansai private railroads, and it operates a spectrum of transport, retail, and leisure businesses to compensate for this. The Tigers were not a profit center, but they were the most prominent face of the corporation, and this contradiction was a perpetual anxiety to upper management, most of whom had no baseball experience or acumen. In the contemporary United States we may bemoan helicopter parents; the Hanshin front office and Hanshin railroad company are NPB's version of our familial micromanaging parents.

Kōshien Stadium is not only Japan's most storied stadium but also its most raucous one. Americans coming to watch Hanshin baseball here are fascinated by the spectator garb, chanting, trumpets, banners, balloons, and other elements of the festive atmosphere, but as baseball fans many of them are equally appalled that all of this noisy spectacle makes it difficult to "properly" appreciate the subtleties of the game. This is a rather ethnocentric dismissal by fans who have apparently never been to a European soccer game, or even an American college football game! Hanshin fan behavior at the stadium is passionate, choreographed, and collective, but it is also more complex and variegated than its first assault on the senses. This is the initial subject of chapter 6, which explores the aesthetics and routines of cheering and the elaborate social organization that lies behind it. It would be wrong, however, to treat the stadium fanatics as the limits of spectatorship in the Hanshin sportsworld, and the chapter considers the many ways of being a Hanshin fan and of being aware of and affiliated with Hanshin, from the excitement of the games to the routines of everyday life. The Tigers are hard to ignore in this region, even for those uninterested or even actively antagonistic.

Part of the power of the Yomiuri group in Tokyo is that it controlled its own newspapers and television and radio networks. This the Hanshin parent company lacked, so it found itself in a deeply problematical codependency with the regional and national media. At the center of the regional sports media were the five daily sports papers, which combined the exuberance of tabloid storytelling with the expertise of full-time teams of highly knowledgeable reporters, editors, photographers, and commentators. This Faustian bargain and the genuinely grueling work of sports reporting and broadcasting are the topics of chapter 7.

These seven chapters lay out the parameters of the Hanshin Tigers sportsworld. This book demonstrates the usefulness of analyzing professional sports through the frame of the sportsworld concept and applies that concept to appreciate the distinctiveness of the Hanshin Tigers sportsworld and what it demonstrates about several key themes of modern Japan.

It is crucial, however, to recognize that this Hanshin sportsworld was not timeless, and the more I explored the history of the Tigers and of baseball in Japan, the more I came to appreciate how "timely," how historically specific, was the shape of that world to the 1990s and early 2000s. What I lay out in chapters 2–7 had both a past and a future, and that is the subject of the final three chapters.

Baseball's origins in Japan date back to the 1870s, and by the 1890s it was a popular sport among adolescent boys at elite preparatory schools. Baseball was propelled into the national consciousness by a series of games played by the most prestigious of those schools, First Higher School in Tokyo, against a team of Americans from the port of Yokohama. The boys' surprising success against the experienced American adults at a moment of patriotic fervor and a revival of a samurai warrior ethic as a national template popularized the boys, this sport, and the samurai imagery as a Japanese style of playing baseball. This is where chapter 8 begins. The game spread rapidly through a national public education system, promoted by newspapers and urban transport companies competing ruthlessly for customers and subscribers and seeking profits and publicity rather than political correctness. Baseball, even its schoolboy origins, was not just education but edutainment. It was an ungainly hybrid of moral pedagogy and profitable entertainment. Schoolboy teams and college players were held up as paragons of virtue but also publicized as celebrities of mass entertainment. Baseball, this chapter demonstrates, played a central role in the new metropolitan modernity of early twentieth-century Japan, and this provided a complex foundation for the professional sport that was Japan's central entertainment in the post–World War II decades.

The first professional league was organized in 1936 by newspaper and railroad companies eager to extend the commercial possibilities of the sport beyond the amateur horizons. The Hanshin Tigers were a charter member of the seven- and soon eight-team league. There was significant reorganization and expansion after the extended disruptions of the war, but professional baseball emerged in the 1950s as Japan's central sport, driven by several innovations: new stadiums with lighting for night games and two powerful new media, daily sports newspapers and television. The Hanshin Tigers world that I entered in the late 1990s was directly shaped by those decades. Chapter 9 looks forward to the late 1990s by situating the Tigers within the developing structures of professional baseball. It also looks backward from the late 1990s to the historiography of the Tigers throughout the preceding decades. A colorful literature has developed on Tiger history, and my interest is in the ways in which it has been written; in particular, books, articles, and newspaper series tend strongly to move between the two rhetorical poles of the "Fierce Tigers" and the "No-Good Tigers." Finally, the chapter connects the Hanshin sportsworld to changes in Japanese society more broadly, especially the two formative developments that I introduced earlier. The first was the corporate structures and ideologies of corporatism that became so potent in securing the dominance and prestige of major companies and public ministries. The second was the distorted pattern of regional development and the idiom of regional identity in decades marked by increasing Tokyo centrism. Both of these became central themes in the Hanshin Tigers sportsworld, a topic developed in chapter 9.

HAVE WE REACHED THE END OF AN ERA?

I do not propose that all ethnographies should wait a decade after fieldwork before publication; if they did so, dissertations would never be written, tenure would be jeopardized, and the long investments that most of us in this slow social science make to reach and communicate our understandings would grind to a halt! Indeed, I started writing about the Hanshin Tigers and Japanese baseball while I was in the midst of the fieldwork, and I continued afterward with many articles and chapters. But this book comes much later, and in writing it, I realized how valuable it has been to return to this sportsworld a decade later. This book turns what had been for me an ethnographic present into an ethnographic past. This is the subject of the final chapter, which addresses the question of whether the sportsworld of the Hanshin Tigers presented in the previous chapters is no more. My conclusion is that it has changed fundamentally, and the chapter identifies the major factors that have brought an end to that era.

It turns out that the main period of my fieldwork, from 1996 to 2003, was critically important in the Hanshin Tigers baseball world, although this was serendipitous and I did not realize it at the time. In retrospect, these years were the end of an extended era that began in the early 1970s, when the Tigers simultaneously became the heart and soul of Kansai pro baseball even as they entered an extended period of frustration and failure. This ended in the early 2000s, when two powerful managers were brought in from the outside, the longtime owner Kuma retired, and the Tigers finally won a Central League championship for only the second time in thirty-nine years. There were other consequential changes at the end of the first decade that I discuss in the concluding chapter, but it is important to note that the "ethnographic present" for this analysis is the end of the 1990s and the very beginning of this new century.

The intensity of the fieldwork experience can lead anthropologists to exaggerate their extended moment in the field as a time of portentous change, and they may be tempted to write their ethnographies, looking backward, as efforts to capture the condition of a world that is just passing or, looking forward, as the moment when a new structure is emerging. Either because I knew so little of the professional baseball world when I started or because my fieldwork extended over five seasons, I didn't think of the Hanshin Tigers in either way. Rather, only gradually have I come to appreciate the historical boundaries of that world and the Tigers' special significance. In part this understanding arose as I explored earlier periods of Tigers history, through interviews and reading. In part it was because, although I have published a fair number of articles and chapters on my research, it is only now that I am writing this book and can place those years in the context of more than a decade of subsequent Tigers baseball.

Much happened in that period, beginning with the Tigers winning the Central League championship in 2002 under a new manager, brought in from the outside. The team won the league championship again in 2004, and although it has yet to win a third, it has come very close. More important, it has shed its image of perennial loser; it is not a regular winner, but it is a regularly competitive team. Ironically, this has generated palpable disappointment and even a growing lack of interest from longtime fans and commentators, who seem unable to adjust to what they had hoped would happen for so long.

Other changes have been equally significant. The Kansai economy continues to be in the doldrums, but the team has been reconfigured by two seemingly contradictory developments. On the one hand, in 2002 the club began a much more aggressive marketing program for Hanshin goods and team events and put up the money for some high-profile, expensive player acquisitions. Then its parent company, Hanshin Electric Railroad Company, was suddenly bought out in 2006 by Hankyū Holdings, the umbrella company of Hanshin's historic rival, the Hankyū Railroad Company, and the regional professional baseball scene was also revised by the 2005 merger of the two Pacific League teams, the Orix BlueWave and the Kintetsu Buffaloes, now known as the Orix Buffaloes (Orikkusu Bafarōzu).

The fan club organization has lost most of its autonomy, and Kōshien Stadium has undergone extensive renovation, noticeably altering the game experience. The sports dailies and television broadcasting continue, but digital media and satellite broadcasts are cutting extensively into print media sales, television viewership, and stadium attendance. The profitability and popularity of professional baseball is constantly being squeezed by the growing attractions of J.League soccer and MLB baseball.

In short, major changes in the Tigers baseball world—and in Japanese professional baseball more generally—occurred after my fieldwork, and the silver lining in the delay in turning to this book project has been a retrospective appreciation for what has changed and what remains the same, the subject of the final chapter.

CHAPTER 2

The Rhythms of Tigers Baseball

Stadiums and Seasons

Stadiums, games, and seasons form the basic space-time grid for baseball and other professional team sports, and the Hanshin Tigers world was no exception. Kōshien Stadium, lying just beyond the western edge of Osaka in Nishinomiya City, was the physical "home," the institutional locus, the temporal center, and the emotional core of this world. Tigers games at Kōshien, season after season, were what playing for, reporting on, and cheering for Hanshin were all about.

At the same time, there was far more to the spatial and temporal rhythms of Hanshin than the season schedule of games at Kōshien. The Tigers played only half of their games at home at Kōshien; the other half were played away at opponents' stadiums. The Tigers had several pre-season training camps elsewhere in Japan and a practice facility and dormitory near Kōshien for the two-thirds of the player roster on the farm team. The Tigers sportsworld also included the club offices, the parent company headquarters, the sports bureaus at newspaper companies around the region, Tigers fan bars around the country, and television sets broadcasting Tigers games and news into households throughout the region. Time was as variegated as space. A single game might be nine innings played over about three hours, but within it were many microrhythms (pitches, at-bats, late innings, etc.), and beyond it, a game was but a single unit in series, seasons, careers, and many other cyclical and linear time frames.

The time-space dimensions of Tigers baseball were not just a matter of complexity but also of consequence. There was a front stage, as well as many back stages. Preparation and practice were much more time-consuming than performances—and beyond the performance on the field were other kinds of performances, in offices, press conferences, bleachers, and bars. There were rivalries built from twelve competing "home" fields. Baseball is a sport that articulates three temporal rhythms in a matrix of fixities and flows. It is composed of oscillating intervals such as the stop-and-go at-bats, the back and forth of being in the field and then at-bat, and the top of the inning and the bottom of the inning. It is also composed of repetitive cycles: one pitch follows another, one at-bat finishes, another begins; one game is over, a new game begins; and seasons follow seasons. Baseball time is also linear: games finish and add to the team's accumulating record and to players' statistics; the season wears on; careers unfold as players come in as rookies, become starters, then veterans, then ex-players, and occasionally coaches and commentators; staff and media move up office hierarchies; and so forth.

These multiple places and temporalities were crucial to the suspense and the drama that bound the Hanshin world. They created both the statistics and the stories that drove players, reporters, and fans and that formed the "soap opera" quality of the world. This combination of narratives and numbers sustained suspense over hours, days, and years, while mitigating the inevitable losses. This was an essential quality for a team and a world like Hanshin, because it allowed for a continuing sense of possibility, however improbable. In this chapter I begin at the center, game day at Kōshien, then characterize the multiple times and places of Tigers baseball that have been key elements in the melodramas of this sportsworld.

KŌSHIEN STADIUM

Sports are played and watched in a vast range of spaces, artificial and natural, dedicated and borrowed—backyards, school yards, playgrounds, urban streets, and mountain slopes—but the enclosed stadium is the preeminent "theater of sport." It is both a quintessentially modern monument to mass leisure and entertainment and an enduring echo of the spectacular sports of the ancient world: the stadium at Olympus, the Colosseum in Rome, the royal ball courts of Mesoamerica.

More than many other public spaces of our cities and towns, the lifeless physical structures of sports stadiums regularly become animated spatial-temporal communities. A stadium at game time can attract tens of thousands of people, many of whom come regularly, a few continuously for years and years. It provides entertainment, food, shelter, clothing, law enforcement, and ongoing social relations. Deep and diverse emotions are invested not only in the experiences of watching a team but also in the place where the spectating occurs. Romance, domestic quarrels, parent-child bonding, friendships, work, weddings, and fights all take place in stadiums. It is a place of leisure and a place of labor, where many come to relax by watching the work of a few. And this is especially true in baseball stadiums, because the much greater frequency of baseball games over all other professional sports routinizes these social activities and embeds them in the stadium space to a much deeper degree.

Over the past two decades, there have been four main stadiums in metropolitan Kansai where one could regularly see professional baseball. The Orix BlueWave played in the aptly named Green Stadium, a spacious, suburban ballpark west of downtown Kobe. Up to the late 1990s, the Kintetsu Buffaloes were playing the last of their games in their cramped and dilapidated Fujiidera Stadium, set in the midst of a grimy town along the Kintetsu commuter line running southeast out of Osaka. In 1997 the team moved into the brand-new Osaka Dome, a city-center extravaganza ringed with shopping and entertainment arcades. On the western edge of Osaka on the Hanshin line to Kobe was Kōshien Stadium (or more precisely, to give it its full name, Hanshin Kōshien Kyūjo), the most famous of them all.

When I arrived in 1996, Kōshien was little changed by the seven decades of use since its opening in 1924. Additional seating had been added along the first and third baselines in 1929 to accommodate the school tournament throngs. But otherwise its ivy-covered brick walls, the still natural grass outfield, the open wooden press box behind home plate, and the dingy locker rooms all sustained an aura of timelessness and kept vivid the memories of past contests, amateur and professional. A stadium that had been ultramodern in the 1920s had become shabbily nostalgic by the 1990s.

GAME DAY AT KŌSHIEN STADIUM

Game day at Kōshien and the other ballparks shared a common rhythm, opening slowly and leisurely, quickening to the faster pace of the contest itself, and ending frenetically as the game wrapped up and everyone hastened to leave. For several decades almost all Japanese professional games have been played in the evenings, beginning between 6:00 and 6:30 p.m., depending on the stadium. Kōshien's starting time was 6:00 p.m., but the stadium leisurely came to life long before the first pitch was thrown. The night security guards opened several service gates at 7:00 a.m. for the first of the cleaning crews, groundskeepers, and concession food deliveries, and throughout the morning the empty stands and hallways echoed with the hollow noises of cleanup. The team coaches began to arrive around midmorning, often for an 11:00 a.m. planning meeting, and a trainer or two would begin to set up the training room. The front office staff were at work in their offices underneath the outfield bleachers by midmorning, and the print beat reporters were also early to their pressroom, which was adjacent to these club offices.

The Tigers players themselves drifted in from late morning onward, by car and taxi from their homes or apartments. The visiting team arrived by bus from its hotel shortly after noon. One of the important features of Kōshien and all of the older stadiums in Japan was the cramped locker rooms and limited team spaces, for the Tigers as well as the visiting opponents. Modern American stadiums and some recent Japanese ballparks have spacious locker rooms, comfortable lounges, exercise facilities, wide-screen televisions, and other amenities that encourage players to hang out and hang around. A player arriving at Kōshien made his way through the players' entrance (which also was for officials and the credentialed media), up some stairs to a narrow hallway on the second floor that passed a warren of tiny offices and a small player cafeteria, to a locker room that would seem puny to many high school teams. Twenty-five players were crowded into about two hundred square meters. The lockers were open stalls of wire and metal. There was little room for spreading out, and certainly none for lounging and card playing. Ironically, then, the one segment of the stadium's daily population for whom it offered the least social space was the players themselves.

Baseball at Kōshien was a game of three to four hours' duration in the evening, but the pregame preparations took even longer, stretching throughout the afternoon with their own distinctive rhythms and social patterns. Starting around midday, players visited the trainers for ailments, massages, and taping; worked out in the small weight room; and grabbed lunch at the small team cafeteria. They gathered in the early afternoon for a team meeting with the manager and coaches, and then they broke into more specialized meetings. The pitchers and catchers,

FIGURE 5. Hanshin Tigers pregame warm-ups, Kōshien Stadium, July 1999. Photograph by author.

the infielders, and the outfielders met with their respective coaches and the scorers to watch video, hear reports about the opponents' recent tendencies, and go over a game plan.

The players and staff then took the field for warm-up calisthenics, fielding drills, and batting practice (see figure 5). The two teams rotated practice time on the field itself, with Hanshin taking it from 2:00 to 4:00 p.m. and the visiting team coming out afterward, from 4:00 to 5:30 p.m. In the Central League, pregame field practice was limited to two hours, but players also utilized several long, dirt-floor rooms under the infield bleachers that were equipped with batting cages and pitching alleys. Hanshin coaches often had additional player meetings after their field time.

The afternoon hours were also important as the time when the media were allowed onto the margins of the infield and into the dugouts for extended schmoozing—with one another and with the teams. The beat reporters drifted out of the club pressroom and were joined by more senior columnists and photographers from their papers and the radio and television technicians and broadcasters. Depending on the day's contest, more than fifty or sixty media members might be hovering around the edges of the warm-ups, engaging one another and coaching staffs and players in casual banter and more serious conversation to begin their news-gathering jobs. The manager and head coach usually stood resolutely behind the batting cages, and more senior journalists and commentators approached them for some conversation. Brief interviews were conducted to get footage for early evening news programs, gossip was exchanged, rumors floated, and opinions were debated. The Tigers' media relations staff was in constant motion, both arranging access to and protecting players and coaches from the incessant media requests.

The stadium gates opened to spectators at 4:00 p.m., although on Yomiuri game days they might open as early as 2:00 p.m. Many people with unreserved seating arrived early to secure a place, but they then suffered the scorching afternoon sun, which baked the outfield bleachers of the south-facing stadium. Others came to get a closer pregame view of their favorite players.[1]

At many levels, then, the afternoon served to build the mood and anticipation, to set in motion the pressures and possibilities that the game itself would reveal, and to bring into engagement the actors who would collectively "play" the game. Lots of little pregames were played in the afternoon. For instance, for any one contest, each team was allowed a roster of twenty-five players, the same as in MLB. However, MLB rosters change infrequently (due to injuries and trades), whereas NPB rosters could be manipulated more often by moving players up and down between the first and second teams. Only in the late afternoon were the roster and the starting lineup posted in the downstairs corridor. At precisely 5:10 p.m., as warm-ups concluded, the grounds crew prepared the field, and the players were back in their locker rooms changing into their game uniforms; the two managers exchanged their starting lineups behind home plate. In the Central League, the starting pitchers were not announced until that moment (the Pacific League required previous-day designation). The coaching staff said it liked to make small lineup changes as a tactic of gamesmanship to keep opponents off balance.

As the game's start approached, the stadium came to a more formal order. Spectators were still streaming in (coming from offices and factories, some didn't arrive until much later), but the Tigers fan clubs were in full regalia in the outfield, the media had been ousted from the dugouts and were in their press box and broadcast booths, the concessions were doing a lively business, and the starting players were announced over the public address (PA) system. They took the field as the fan clubs beat out their welcoming chants. At precisely 6:00 p.m., the first batter stepped into the batter's box, and the home plate umpire called "play ball" (in English). For the next three hours or so, the focus of attention was the baseball diamond.[2]

The game of baseball has a simple and regular formal cadence—three outs per team, inning after inning, repeated nine times—that is belied by multiple plotlines, irregular and overlapping rhythms, and sudden shifts in momentum and pressure. But the experience of a Tigers game was shaped as much by the deafening noise of the spectators in the stands as by the unpredictable suspense of the course of play on the field. I detail the activities and organization of the Tigers fan clubs in chapter 6. Here, though, it must be noted that one of the subtler tensions during the games and throughout the ballpark was that between the staff of the stadium and the baseball club and these fan clubs to control the rhythm of the game and the behavior of the spectators.

At the opening, for example, the scoreboard showed an animated and musical introduction to the Tigers players, but the fan clubs would break in with their own song chants. The club had a mascot pair, Lucky and To-Lucky, whose acrobatics on the field were often ignored by the fan clubs. During the game, the stadium cameras would pan the crowds and show spectators on the scoreboard screen, but they deliberately avoided shots of the organized fan clubs' cheerleaders.

In both US and Japanese baseball, the seventh inning is a special temporal moment. In American ballparks, the "seventh-inning stretch" is a chance for the fans to collectively stand up and stretch. It is a musical interlude as well; the stadium organ often encourages spectators to sing along to "Take Me Out to the Ball Game," although after September 11, 2001, some stadiums switched to "God Bless America."

At Kōshien, the focus was more on the home team. This was the moment when the game entered its final innings and the fans needed to encourage the team to make a final push if behind—or if ahead, to muster enough energy to retain the lead. It was the "lucky seventh"; the break was at mid-inning as the Tigers came to bat, and the suspense tightened. At Kōshien, the tens of thousands of spectators blew up long "jet balloons" (although their shape sparked an alternate slang label, "condom balloons"), which they held while singing the Tigers anthem and then released into the air (see figure 6). Tens of thousands of brightly colored balloons exploding into the stadium night were like fireworks, adding to the festival-like atmosphere and offering a final collective push to player efforts (and requiring more than a few minutes for the grounds crew to clean off the field before play could resume).

FIGURE 6. Hanshin spectators releasing the "condom" balloons in the seventh inning break, Kōshien Stadium. Photograph by author.

The overwhelming soundscape of the stadium was indeed these fans and their intricate, choreographed cheering (interspersed with individual barbed jeering), but as in a tropical rain forest, there was much more for the attentive ear. The players were chattering to one another while the manager and coaches yelled directions. The umpires were making their calls with booming voices and grandiloquent gestures. The press box media were tapping away on their laptops while the radio and television broadcasters were bantering in their booths. Behind the backstop, team scorers were quietly filling in charts to record the action, while "007" advance scouts of upcoming opponents were writing memos and whispering furtively with one another. The food and drink vendors (*uriko*) hustled about the aisles shouting their wares.

Most of the vendors who sold goods in the stands were high school and college students, hired despite a formal ban on high school students working by local boards of education. There was much turnover, and they were paid on commission, with predictable competition for choicer assignments of what and where to sell. Beer of course was most profitable; a stadium officer claimed that upward of thirty thousand cups of beer were sold at a popular game (in 350 ml and 500 ml sizes, for about

US$4 and US$6, respectively). The vendors carried the beer through the stands in backpack kegs and dispensed it into large cups. Other vendors sold wine (also from kegs) and whiskey.

And the concession aromas! The smells of food and drink that greeted everyone entering the stadium remind us of how multisensory any baseball stadium experience is. It is not just the sounds of the game—the shouts of the players, the calls of the umpire, the crack of the ball against the wooden bat—but also the buzz of the crowds, the music and voice of the PA system, the smells of frying oil and stale beer, and the shouts of the vendors. All these densely textured olfactory, tactile, and auditory signals identify and familiarize the place and draw in the visitors.

Kōshien was just such a sensory world, and for many spectators the atmosphere evoked a downtown carnival spirit. The concession stands looked like festival booths, the concessionaires' uniforms were reminiscent of the 1950s and 1960s, and many of the food items on sale were traditional Osaka favorites, like *takoyaki* (balls of octopus fried in batter) and *okonomi-yaki* (a grilled pancake with various ingredients). All of this fed a local nostalgia and festival atmosphere for the spectators, themselves noisy and garishly festooned with Tigers apparel and gear.

Food, beverages, and Tigers paraphernalia created the commensality of the spectating experience, and stadium sales were crucial to the profits of Hanshin. During my fieldwork years, the stadium featured around 110 food and drink concession stands and several sit-down restaurants and coffee shops that were licensed by the Hanshin Stadium Company to private operators. A smaller number of stands sold Tigers clothing, other apparel, souvenirs, and cheering items like clackers and balloons.

The best-known Kōshien stadium food was its (rather blandly flavored) curry rice, of which about four thousand meals were sold on a well-attended night (and two thousand or so take-home packets of the curry base were sold at about US$2.50 each).[3] Kōshien was also known for its grilled squid (*ikayaki*) and chicken parts (*yakitori*), both of which were prepared and served on wood skewers. Despite foreign assumptions and cartoon drawings, sushi was not particularly popular. Noodle dishes and other rice bowl dishes sold far more, along with nuts, crackers, and dried fish, common accompaniments to beer.[4]

As the game was concluding, the reporters rushed from the press box down to ground level, and immediately after the last pitch the managers retired to rooms behind their respective dugouts for interviews. At the same time, if the Tigers had been victorious, there was a fixed routine on the field. First, a "hero interview" with the designated star of the game was conducted over the PA system by a reporter on the field. Then the two mascots came out to lead some cheers, and then the private fan associations took over, first going through the lineup calls, then singing the Tigers anthem (sometimes more than once), perhaps adding the hitting marches of the stars of the game, and ending with the triple "Banzai!" Meanwhile, reporters were trying to grab players for a quick quote as they walked up to their team rooms.

The game day wrapped up quickly and frenetically in the late evening. The cleaning crews immediately moved into the stands as the spectators streamed out the exits, packing the Hanshin trains and buses to get home. The players departed almost as quickly; the visiting team didn't pause but boarded a bus for its hotel and disappeared. Hanshin players might be grabbed briefly by coaches for a few words or might require the attention of the trainers, but they too showered and dressed quickly. Among the last workers there were the reporters, hunched over their laptops and filing their game summaries and sidebar stories in the dim light of the open press box, surrounded by the cavernous emptiness of the stadium at night.

THE ANNUAL ROUND OF TIGERS BASEBALL

Time, too, moves in cyclical and linear fashion at many different levels. This game day routine is repeated over and over each year, "at home" in Kōshien and when the Tigers are "the visiting team" at stadiums around the country.

In 2000, for example, the Hanshin Tigers played a regular season of 135 games, from opening day on April 1 through a final game on a very chilly late October night. This schedule, the same as that of the other eleven teams, was a very long season. Indeed, the only longer season among all team sports in the world is that of Major League Baseball, which runs over the same months but packed 162 games into its 2000 regular schedule and a postseason of three championship play-off series. By contrast, the National Basketball Association had a regular season of 82 games and the Women's National Basketball Association teams played 32 games; the National Hockey League 2000 season consisted of 82 contests, while the National Football League teams played 16 regular-season contests. In Japan, J.League soccer teams played 30 regular games that year in a two-stage season.

Baseball's full playing season is even longer, because its regular season is preceded by a two-month "preseason" of training and exhibition games; for some teams it continues into a "postseason" of play-offs for the sport's championship. When Hanshin won its league championship in 2003 and went to a seven-game Japan Series, it played a total of 165 games from late February to late October (and a comparable MLB team would play upward of 200 games).

This extraordinarily long season has consequences for all concerned: players, teams, and fans. It means, for example, that the ratio of practice to games is quite different from, say, professional football, whose games occur once a week, allowing six days for rest and preparation in between, or professional basketball, which may have three or at most four games per week at the height of its shorter season. The almost daily contests of baseball not only abbreviate physical recovery and tactical preparation, but also demand that teams and individuals not dwell psychologically on daily losses and victories.

Although Japanese pro teams play about twenty fewer games a year than their American counterparts, baseball in Japan is even more of a year-round business. In the United States there is a long winter break (for players, staff, press, and most fans) from late October to mid-February, during which most sports fans turn their attention to professional and collegiate versions of football, basketball, and ice hockey. There are some off-season instructional and winter leagues in Florida, but they do not attract public attention. In contrast, Japanese teams keep practicing through November, and the sport remains very much on the front pages of the sports dailies and at the top of sports broadcasts. To many Americans, this has become another convenient stereotypical national difference. We assure ourselves that we have a healthy seasonality and thus diversity in our sporting life, while the Japanese remain fixated year-round on the same sport, with a grim monotony. This is evidence that we "play" baseball while they "work" baseball.

To be sure, the prominence of baseball in Japanese sporting life is undeniable, but whether it bespeaks a unique national doggedness is another matter. It is more accurate to think of the sporting life in Japan as being closer to that of Italy, Brazil, Argentina, and other countries whose sports consciousness revolves around the single sport of soccer, or perhaps Cuba or the Dominican Republic, where baseball monopolizes national attention (following the US major leagues in the spring and summer and the local island leagues in the winter). This, more broadly, reveals a basic difference between national sportsworlds. Most are unicentric, in which a panoply of seasonal and small-audience sports revolves around a single dominant national sport. A much smaller number of countries, prominently the United States, have multicentric national sportsworlds, in which several "major" sports occupy the center, surrounded by even more specialty sports.

Baseball does not monopolize Japan's sports consciousness, but it has long been the basic metronome of the Japanese sportsworld. The bimonthly sumo tournaments and the spring and summer Kōshien high school tournaments punctuate the sports year; J.League professional soccer directly challenges the baseball calendar; and World Cup soccer, the Asia Games, and the summer and winter Olympics are other periodic coordinates. There is also constant though much less publicized action in the Big Three gambling sports of horse racing, powerboat racing, and bicycle racing and in pro wrestling and pro boxing. These sports generate huge revenues and spectatorships, but as in the United States, they have never gained a metropolitan respectability. Above all of them is baseball, which for half a century has commanded the center spotlight year-round, giving it unrivaled exposure and status but demanding that it keep itself constantly newsworthy.

Part of this newsworthiness is drawn from its distinctive seasonal rhythm; an annual round is just that: constant change within a comfortably repeating frame. Major League Baseball too has always seen itself as seasonal: organic and cyclical. It simmers over the winter (in the "hot stove league"); it buds in the early spring (as the "snow birds" flock to the Florida training camps to see the players begin to flex their muscles); it blossoms in the later spring, gaining energy and stature throughout the long, hot summer ("the boys of summer" was Roger Angell's felicitous phrase); and it culminates in the feverish pennant races of the autumn and finally in the "fall classic," the presumptuously named World Series between the two best North American teams. The Japanese season roughly mirrors the US rhythms, albeit with some distinctive features and of course a lot more constant public attention. Let us follow the basic contours of the Tigers' annual round as they appeared to me over the six years of this project.

January: Preseason "Individual Training"

As does the rest of corporate Japan, both the parent company and the Tigers front office conclude the weeklong New Year holiday break with brief, formal office-opening ceremonies a few days into January. Then on January 6 there is a ceremonial gathering of the top officials of the three (now two) Kansai-area baseball clubs. A Kintetsu Buffaloes executive complained to me that the event is always a bit galling because after the three club presidents join for news photos, the media quickly surround the Hanshin president and manager for quotes and prognostications, ignoring the other two clubs standing off to the side. From the start of the year, the region focuses on the Tigers.

The players' contracts with their clubs begin legally on February 1, but in January they are expected to embark on what is in name and in fact independent training (*jishu tore*) in various domestic and foreign locations. Some return to their hometowns to train in familiar facilities, some find warmer resorts (Kyushu, Okinawa, and Guam being most popular), and some remain in Kansai and work out daily at the Tigers' farm team facility. In 2000 Shinjō and Funaki Satoshi went to Florida to work out at the Detroit Tigers rehab camp. A few players couldn't resist the limelight and sought arrangements that drew the attention of the Kansai sports media, which were always eager for their own Tigers news. In 1997, for example, then rookie Imaoka Makoto, who was to wear uniform number 7, started his training at 7:07 a.m. on January 7 to a phalanx of cameras. Several days later, the flamboyant Kameyama, whose clashes with his manager Fujita I had witnessed the year before and who never appeared in a regular season game that year, vowed to make 1997 his "make-or-break" year. He announced that he would hold his personal workouts with a female pro wrestling stable run by the Yoshimoto Entertainment Group (*Nikkan Sports*, January 10, 1997, page 1).

Meanwhile, local fans are drawn to both their television sets and their shrines and temples. January is something of a silly season for local television networks, which compete to attract the more popular Tigers veterans and the new faces of the rookies to talk shows, game shows, and variety shows. Shinjō, Wada Yutaka, and other Tigers stars cavorting in goofy skits and engaging in light banter are greeted with much ambivalence by the more serious fans (Okamoto 1996:47–48). These appearances confirm players' celebrity status, although a local viewer/fan with whom I was watching one of these shows wondered out loud, "Maybe if they were a little more serious, the team would do better!"

Early January is time for prayers as well as play. One of the year's most important rituals is the first ceremony for the folk god Ebisu, or "Ebessan" as he is known locally. Ebisu, one of the Seven Gods of Good Fortune, is believed to have "landed at Nishinomiya after being cast adrift by his parents Izanagi and Izanami" (Reader and Tanabe

1998:157). The Nishinomiya Ebisu Shrine is the most popular Ebisu shrine in Kansai. With his fishing pole in one hand and a sea bream in the other, Ebisu has long been a symbol of business prosperity. "Bring in your [old] bamboo grass for business prosperity!" is the temple's call to the region's store owners and businesses to come to the temples and receive new *sasa* grass. The shopkeepers and residents who flock by the tens of thousands to the Ebisu shrines on the tenth of January are also offering fervent prayers for the Hanshin Tigers' success in the coming season, knowing full well that their local economy is greatly affected by the team's performance.

For the front office and coaching staff, much of the month's work is devoted to final logistical arrangements for the spring training camps and negotiations for team marketing and broadcasting. The team often coins a new motivational slogan for the year; for example, in January 1997 then manager Yoshida Yoshio announced the team's official slogan to be "Hustle! Hustle! Hustle!" He told me he got the idea from one of the new foreigners that year, Phil Hiatt. It's actually more clever than it sounds, because *hustle* is Romanized in Japanese as a homonym for the Japanese verb *hassuru* (to arise), and the triple repetition is a lucky number (as Yoshida put it, *hassuru san renpatsu*).

There was still usually troublesome previous-year business left over as well, especially a few player contracts that remained to be concluded. These were the contentious ones in which players held out over several sessions for higher salaries, and as they stretched into the New Year, they garnered unwelcome press coverage. For example, in the 2004–2005 off-season the pitcher Igawa Kei demanded to be posted to MLB; by mid-January, the story consumed the front pages of the sports dailies. He finally agreed to stay with Hanshin in late January after obtaining what was a healthy raise for him but a costly one for the front office.

The coaching staff would begin meeting again at midmonth, and one of their tasks was to classify the players tentatively as "first team," "second team," and "injured squad," which offered the players a first glance of their relative standing. The first staff meeting was also in midmonth, and there was a final coaches' meeting at the end to ratify the assignments (after they had leaked to and been discussed in the press).

An item that often attracted public interest was the assignment of uniform numbers to the new foreign players (the new regular rookies had been assigned numbers when they were signed in the fall). Hanshin generally let the players select their numbers from those available in order of date of contract signing (it was somewhat difficult to find an open number!). In 2000, of all the numbers through 70, only 42, 49, 61, 62, and 69 were open for the four new Americans. Tony Tarrasco chose 42, Greg Hansell took 49, and Roberto Ramirez selected 62. Howard Battle had long had a number that ended in 9, but he didn't want 69, so he was allowed to take 99. All the new players wanted to avoid the bad luck of 61 and 69, which had been the numbers of Darrell May and Mike Blowers, the two foreign players released in 1999 after many difficulties (*Nikkan Sports*, January 20, 2000, page 1).

Toward the end of the month, many of the players headed for the training camp location and worked out together under the team's players union. They did their own packing, but the club's equipment manager would arrange transport for their gear (each Hanshin player carried twenty to twenty-five bats, four or five gloves, four or five uniforms and workout suits, and various personal items). The club officers and the owner paid a visit to Hirota Shrine in Nishinomiya to ask for the team's health and success before departing for camp. In 1998 the new manager, Nomura Katsuya, never at a loss for a sound bite, stood before the shrine altar, clapped his hands twice in Shinto style, and imprecated the shrine's god rather caustically:

"You think it is OK for your powers to work slowly, don't you. Well, even a god must wake up. You've been sleeping thirteen years, huh. Wake up!"

Alas, the Hirota god would sleep through that season, too.

February: Spring Training Camp

February was official spring training month in Japan, and all team camps opened on the first of the month. For over four decades, the Tigers held their training camp at Aki, a small town of five thousand people on the narrow south coast of the island of Shikoku, about an hour by car east of Kōchi. To the west, the town had carved a baseball complex out of the mountainside, so there were three tiers of diamonds. The main field was above, well maintained, with small concrete stands, covered dugouts, and a glassed-in room behind the plate. Below that was a subfield with two practice diamonds and some pitching bull pens; the lowest level was a prefab hut that grandly announced itself as Tiger Town, next to Aki Dome, an indoor field that the team also used for practice.

The beginning of camp was a welter of emotions for the players: excitement, relief, anxiety, anticipation. Could those who did well last season continue their success? Would those who had been disappointing revive their fortunes? Was a year older a year better or a year slower? (Wada captured these hopes and anxieties well in his diary for the 2003 season.) As one would expect, the sports dailies filled their February issues with camp reports and early prognoses, as much about individual players as about teams. The papers' feature writers and guest columnists circulated throughout the twelve camps for on-site reports.

The tardy arrival of the foreign players, usually a few days or even a week or so after camp opened, was a boon to media stories. Throughout the month, though, Hanshin's camp remained something of a circus; Hanshin Group officials, corporate guests, and a huge media contingent were coming and going each day. One year the club media affairs staff handed out color-coded hats: blue billed for the press, yellow billed for special guests, white billed for ex-Hanshin players, blue for themselves, black with a purple and gold logo for scouts and other noncoaching staff, and black with an "HT" logo for coaches.

Media treatment in February was extensive and quite positive. The sports papers' front pages were generally filled with laudatory stories about the Tigers, which the reporters said they enjoyed filing because it was a sharp break from the general tone of Hanshin coverage during the regular season. "Bright" (*akarui*) was the common adjective describing the camp's mood. Part of the cheerful theme was simply the nature of spring training everywhere, and this was part of the sport's rhythm. It was the season of renewal, when hopes ran high, before competition showed how the team would really fare, and when much of the focus was inward: on individuals getting back in shape, on who would make the first team, on competitions for positions, and so forth.

The camp days were long. The daily schedule set by manager Fujita in 1996 varied little under the next four managers over the next ten years: wake-up and first exercises at 7:30; practice from 10:00 to 5:00, with a one-hour lunch break; and after-dinner practice and meetings from 7:30 to 9:00 p.m. At the same time, each manager sought to impose his own tone on the team and convey his own image to the public. Fujita, for instance, installed a strict regime with compulsory evening practices, a dress and haircut code, and restrictions on off-day activities. The next year, Yoshida relaxed these rules and made evening practices optional. In 2000 and 2001, Nomura insisted on playing what the press dubbed "BBM" music (for Beethoven-Brahms-Mozart) over the PA system during practices, on the rather strange theory that the classical music would stir up alpha brain waves to activate the right side of the players' brains.

Coaches commonly talked blandly about organizing their routines to test and train the three elements of "body, spirit, and technique" (*taishingi*), but the actual organization of the month was more detailed and graduated. The Hanshin camp month was divided into three-day units called *kūru* (from the French *cours* or "course," the same term the Japanese use for the conventional thirteen-week run of a television serial). A rest day followed each practice unit. After a first week of conditioning and light throwing, the third "course" introduced more direct competition among players in the form of game practices, "sheet batting," and intrasquad scrimmages (called *kōhaku-sen*). Wada (2003) wrote in his diary that it was at this point players started focusing on their chances of making the first team, of being in the opening-day lineup, and so forth. That is, the locus of competition in spring training gradually shifted from the individual himself (determining the shape he was in and whether he could push himself beyond his previous levels) to more direct competition among players, as they tested themselves against their teammates under the critical eyes of the coaching staff and media.

Spring training was also the time for what was to outsiders the most infamous drill in Japanese baseball, the thousand-hit fungo (*senpon nokku*). It was something of a marathon endurance test for a player, who had to field one thousand ground balls hit to him one after another; it was exhausting and shameful for those who could not last the full drill. In fact, I never saw or heard of the full thousand-ball test being done in those years. At the Hanshin camp, what was called *zen'in nokku* was held on the last day of each course. For this, all the players were organized in groups of four to five and positioned in six areas around the main ground. For each station, balls were hit straight on for three minutes, then to the left for two minutes, and then to the right for two minutes. In a group of five, with about 16 balls hit per minute at infield stations, each player would handle about 22 balls during each seven-minute drill, or perhaps 150 balls in total (the outfield pace was less). The coaches used megaphones to bark orders and criticism. It was tiring, and perhaps major leaguers in the United States would object, but it did not seem beyond normal endurance, and it reminded me of tough football preseason workouts. Here and with other teams, it had become the signature routine of the camp, a media and fan fixation and a kind of ritual hazing.

The month was demanding for everyone. If anything, the coaching staff maintained an even longer daily schedule than the players, and the trainer staff was constantly busy from early in the morning to late at night: taping and wrapping early in the morning, standing by the fields all day to monitor injuries and attend to accidents, and then back in the hotel suite that they had turned into a trainers' suite, giving massages and other treatments until and even beyond midnight. And the media were constantly swarming around, searching for stories and photos.

March: The Exhibition Season

American players who went to Japan regularly complained that the Japanese training camp days were much longer and more strenuous than those of MLB camps, but this was due largely to their different purposes. In the United States, spring training includes both the initial camp conditioning and practices and also the exhibition season games—and teams treat both as a way to get into shape. Major League Baseball camps open in mid-February for pitchers and catchers and even later for other players; their exhibition games begin soon, within two weeks or so. Japanese players, by contrast, spend a full month in camp, and they then return to their home ground for a second "preseason" of exhibition games, which they treat as more meaningful than do US players.

The Tigers broke camp with a ceremony on the last day of the month and returned to Osaka for a month of exhibition games (while continuing daily practices). Although the game scores did not count much, March was a month of intensifying competition within the team among individual players. Much of this was orchestrated by the coaching staff, who ran side-by-side drills, manipulated lineups, offered assessments, and announced projections to prod and cajole players—not just the rookies but also anxious veterans, players coming off injuries and showing up out of shape, and players coming to the club from off-season trades. By opening day, a first team of twenty-eight players had to be created from the total roster of sixty-five to seventy. Who would be named to the first team, and within that, to the starting lineup, became one of the motifs in this month of rebirth and optimistic possibilities of success.

Hanshin and other clubs did take the exhibition season more seriously than MLB clubs, but it would be too simple to explain that as yet another instance of how the Japanese take everything too seriously. There was a more particular context. After spring training camps in the United States, major league team rosters are set and most players are assigned to minor league teams. In Japan, though, the coaching staff was still calculating the assignments between the first team and the farm team throughout March, so there was an obvious need to treat the exhibition season more seriously. Most Japanese players could not afford to lose focus.

By mid-March and the final preseason games, most teams were finished with experimenting and began to devote more time to the expected starting lineup and regular pitching staff. The players had been competing with each other for ten weeks—from individual training in January through camp in February into the March exhibition season—and there was still much anxiety about who would be favored by the staff.

April: The Season Opener and the "Starting Dash"

This month also began with an official club prayer for victory (*hisshō shigan*) at the Nishinomiya Shrine. Every year the corporate owner, the club president, all front office employees, and all first team players appeared formally to supplicate Ebessan. The only exceptions to mandatory attendance were the team trainers. For a number of years, their presence was felt to be bad luck, a fear that their own "business" (caring for player injuries) would prosper! In 1996 manager Fujita overruled this superstition and included them for the competing value of total team spirit. Now they are usually included.

In the evening of the shrine day, Hanshin usually held a formal "encouragement banquet" for the club at a downtown hotel. It opened with formal greetings from the owner, the club president, and the manager, and ended with everyone singing the Tigers anthem. In 1999, for example, the media made much of owner Kuma's public order that the team at least win its opening three-game series against the Giants, to which the new manager, Nomura, responded with two promises: that Hanshin would avoid finishing last and that the team would remain in the pennant race into August. They did not seem very bold promises at the time, but even they proved unattainable.

During the brief break before the start of the regular season, the daily sports papers and the television networks ran specials on their season forecasts. With spring training and exhibition games as a basis, they assessed each team and predicted the order of finish. The Tigers generally fared poorly in these previews, which injected the first signs of realism after a spring of favorable coverage.

Opening day was generally on the first Friday or Saturday of April. The three teams that opened at home won that right by finishing the previous season in A-Class (i.e., in first, second, and third place); the visiting teams were the leagues' lower three finishers (B-Class). This first game was the curtain-opening contest (*kaimakusen*), and all the teams aimed for an opening dash (*kaimaku dasshū*), a quick jump to the head of the pack. There was a sense in which strategy, statistics, and superstition combined to put a premium on getting a head start: the first hit, the first out, the first base runner on, a first pitch strike, and the first run of a game. It was about momentum, which in sports is a constant struggle to get something good going and keep it going.

The formal calendrics of the Japanese professional baseball season were an intricate grid of weeks, cards, and cycles (see figure 7). The regular season was divided into twenty-seven six-day weeks (*setsu*), numbered one to twenty-seven. Each setsu ran from Tuesday through Sunday from the beginning of April to the end of September and consisted of two "cards"—that is, two three-game series, on Tuesday, Wednesday, and Thursday and on Friday, Saturday, and Sunday. Teams usually traveled on Mondays and on Friday mornings. The third temporal unit, the cycle, was the set of cards against each of the other five teams. In a 135-game season, a team played one cycle against each of the other league teams; each cycle was 27 games in nine three-game cards. Games that were rained out or that ended in a tie were usually made up in early October.

Several other aspects of the schedule are important. With the introduction of stadium lighting in the 1950s, professional baseball became a sport of evening contests. Very occasionally, there would be afternoon games on Saturday or Sunday, but roughly 95 percent of all contests were played in the evening.[5] Games began at 6:00 or 6:30 p.m., and network television often did not begin until 7:00 p.m., on the assumption that most of the anticipated audience would not get away from work and to a television set until then. That is, it was a game that was packaged for evening spectating, at the stadium or on television, for working men.

This preponderance of evening games spawned complaints and some lawsuits by neighborhoods surrounding the stadiums, which were disrupted by spectator noise and the bright lights. Evening games that extended into extra innings also risked running beyond when the public transportation that most spectators relied on to get home was available. Both of these factors (and not some putative "Japanese" lack of competitive spirit) were what compelled the leagues to restrict game lengths, which produced an occasional tie.

	Sun	Mon	Tues	Wed	Thurs	Fri	Sat
July		1	2 6:00 CD	3 6:00 CD	4 6:00 CD	5	6 YG
	7 YG	8	9 6:00 YBS	10 6:00 YBS	11 6:00 YBS	12 CD	13 CD
	14 CD	15	16 6:00 HC	17 6:00 HC	18 6:00 HC	19 CD	20
	21	22	23	24	25	26 6:00 YG	27 6:00 YG
	28 6:00 YG	29	30 6:00 YS	31 6:00 YS			
August					1 6:00 YS	2 6:00 YBS	3 6:00 YBS
	4 6:00 YBS	5	6 YG	7 YG	8 YG	9 YBS	10 YBS
	11 YBS	12	13 HC	14 HC	15 HC	16 CD	17 CD
	18 CD	19	20 YS	21 YS	22 YS	23 6:00 HC	24 6:00 HC
	25 6:00 HC	26	27 6:00 CD	28 6:00 CD	29 6:00 CD	30 YS	31 YS
September	1 (YS)	2	3 HC	4 (HC)	5 (HC)	6 (CD)	7 6:00 CD
	8 6:00 (CD)	9	10 6:00 YG	11 6:00 (YG)	12 6:00 (YG)	13 (YBS)	14 YBS
	15 2:00 YBS	16 CD	17 (CD)	18 (CD)	19	20 6:00 (HC)	21 2:00 HC
	22 2:00 (HC)	23 6:00 YS	24 6:00 (YS)	25 6:00 (YS)	26	27	28 YG
	29 YG	30					
Oct.			1 6:00 YBS	2 6:00 (YBS)	3 6:00 (YBS)	4	5

	Sun	Mon	Tues	Wed	Thurs	Fri	Sat
April		1	2	3	4	5 YG	6 YG
	7 YG	8	9 CD	10 CD	11 CD	12 6:00 HC	13 2:00 HC
	14 2:00 HC	15	16 6:00 YS	17 6:00 YS	18 6:00 YS	19 6:00 YG	20 6:00 YG
	21 6:00 YG	22	23 YBS	24 YBS	25 YBS	26	27 YS
	28 YS	29 YBS	30 YBS				
May				1 6:00 YBS	2	3 HC	4 HC
	5 HC	6 2:00 CD	7 6:00 CD	8 6:00 CD	9	10 6:00 YG	11 6:00 YG
	12 6:00 YG	13	14 CD	15 CD	16 CD	17 6:00 HC	18 6:00 HC
	19 2:00 HC	20	21 YG	22 YG	23 YG	24 6:00 YS	25 2:00 YS
	26 2:00 YS	27	28 6:00 YBS	29 6:00 YBS	30 6:00 YBS	31 YS	
June							1 YS
	2 YS	3	4 6:00 CD	5 6:00 CD	6 6:00 CD	7	8 YBS
	9 YBS	10	11 HC	12 HC	13 HC	14 6:00 YG	15 6:00 YG
	16 6:00 YG	17	18 6:00 YS	19 6:00 YS	20 6:00 YS	21 HC	22 HC
	23 HC	24	25 YBS	26 YBS	27 YBS	28 YS	29 YS
	30 YS						

FIGURE 7. The 1996 regular season schedule for the Hanshin Tigers. Based on Hanshin Taigāsu (1996:122).

May: The Teams Shake Out

After the anticipation and excitement of the starting dash, the second month was often seen as a time of settling down and shaking out. May opened with Japan's Golden Week, formed by two extended holiday weekends. Invariably, the week featured a Hanshin-Yomiuri three-game card, intended to solidify a television audience for the season. May was also the month when the various foreign players first came under serious scrutiny. The coaches and the press usually assumed that the opening month was their honeymoon; some of the foreign players struggled to adjust to new patterns of play, while others had especially good starts because the pitchers had not yet figured out their weaknesses. In either case, routines settled in during this month, and strengths and weaknesses became apparent.

In the 1990s and early 2000s, Hanshin's continued poor performances left its fans impatient, and often the first signs of their frustration and anger emerged by midmonth. In 1996, for instance, *Nikkan Sports* ran a May series under the title, "What do you think you're doing? Hanshin at a Standstill" (the original headline was in Osaka dialect: *Nan de yanen: Teishin Hanshin*). At the game against Yakult on May 26, several fan clubs stopped playing their trumpets during the marches, and on May 28 there was an organized fan boycott of a game at Kōshien (which the Tigers went on to win, 7–4, against Yokohama). Then on June 1, after a Hanshin loss to Yakult, a group of fans surrounded the hotel in Chiba where the team was staying, carrying signs demanding manager Fujita's resignation. They surrounded the starting players Yabu Keiichi and Hirazuka Katsuhiro when they left by taxi from the hotel. "How dare you go out casually to dinner after such an embarrassing loss!" the crowd demanded. They also accosted another player (Yamazaki Kazuharu) at the elevator in the lobby.

June: Last-Chance Changes

If May was a month of assessment, June was a month of action, or rather reaction and redress—a last chance to make some major personnel changes. In that same year, 1996, speculation that manager Fujita would be removed began early in June in the press and among some front office staff, and ten days later Hanshin released its two slumping foreign players (Glenn Davis and Scott Coolbaugh). It immediately signed two replacements to half-season contracts, Kevin Maas (for

¥30,000,000) and Craig Worthington (for ¥40,000,000). The sports dailies ran a slew of articles about Maas and Worthington upon their arrival, dubbing Worthington the "wily schemer" (*wazashi*) and Maas the "big cannon" (*daihō*). Fans greeted them at the airport with large signs proclaiming, "Tigers' savior: Maas #32" (*Tora no kyūsaisha Maasu 32*) and "Blood of Fiery Indians: Craig #28" (*Moeru Indian no chi Kuraigu 28*).

June was also when injuries began to take their toll on any predictable lineups, testing the manager and prodding the front office to look for last-minute trades. Players injured in the preseason were coming back from the disabled list, but others were coming down with game injuries or chronic problems. In early 1998, for instance, Hanshin faced a series of devastating pitcher injuries. Three of its starting pitchers and two of its relievers went down with injuries), and two new American lefties (Doug Creek and Darrell May) were still tuning up on the farm team. Manager Yoshida tried using a couple of rookies as starting pitchers, but they failed miserably. He pleaded with the club president, Miyoshi Kazuhiko, to make a trade or cash purchase, but it was already too late for much help. Hitting was no better, and by May 28 of that year Yoshida had already tried twenty-eight different starting lineups in an unsuccessful effort to find a winning formula.

June was also the month of the Hanshin club's annual meeting, and a key decision of that meeting was about the round of personnel moves of club executives and directors that officially took place on July 1.

July: The Tipping Point

As in MLB, midseason in Japan was marked by a break for all-star games, with teams from the two leagues being formed of players selected by position through public voting. In the United States, the all-star game was a single event; in Japan, it was a series of three games, which opened up a longer, full-week break in the regular schedule. At this point in the season, clubs, the media, and spectators were all trying to discern the long-term trends of the season in the fortunes of the teams and the trajectories of the players. It is both an advantage and a disadvantage of baseball's long season and daily competition that individual games can and must be put behind the team quickly; routine and balance are sought amid the constant imponderables of the sport, although such studied equanimity can become numbing to the players and boring to the spectators.

Nonetheless, July was the month when individual games began to assume statistical and psychological importance. Clubs needed to hold fan interest, and teams needed to sustain player performance, both especially challenging for Hanshin, given that most of the people in its sportsworld expected that whatever early success it had shown, it would surely wilt with the summer heat. As figure 8 shows, the relative standings in this midseason month were generally predictive; if anything, the second half of the season tended to exaggerate the differences in the teams that had emerged to that point.

Acknowledging the need to sustain player commitment, media attention, and fan interest, the Japanese leagues had several metrics of competition for remaining in play, and midseason was when they came to the fore. Rising above or falling below a .500 winning percentage was the most common, and the sports media used the accounting metaphor of "savings" (*chōkin*) for team records above .500 and "debt" (*shakkin*) for records in deficit. In most years, getting out of debt and avoiding falling hopelessly in debt became a motivational focus for Hanshin in July. And unlike MLB league standings, which presented how far each team was from the first-place team, NPB standings measured how far teams were behind not relative to the top team but rather in the number of games (*geemu-sa*) behind the team just above them. This was another way of keeping competitive interest even among the weaker teams, highlighting a more realistic measure of advancement.

August: The Tigers' "Road of Death"

As Nomura revealed in his preseason banquet promise, all clubs aimed to remain competitive at least through August and to sustain media interest and stadium attendance through this vacation month of good weather. Nonetheless, by early in the month teams were sorted into those who were still in the pennant race and those who had fallen out of contention. Integral to the baseball season's rhythm was the growing separation of team moods. In August and often through September, pennant "races" in the two leagues were created, fanned, and followed until, one by one, teams dropped out (whereupon they would create secondary goals and rivalries, such as to move up into A-Class, to avoid the cellar, or to win their season series with X team).

For Hanshin, though, the hot and humid days of August brought a special burden, because for nearly three weeks Kōshien Stadium was the

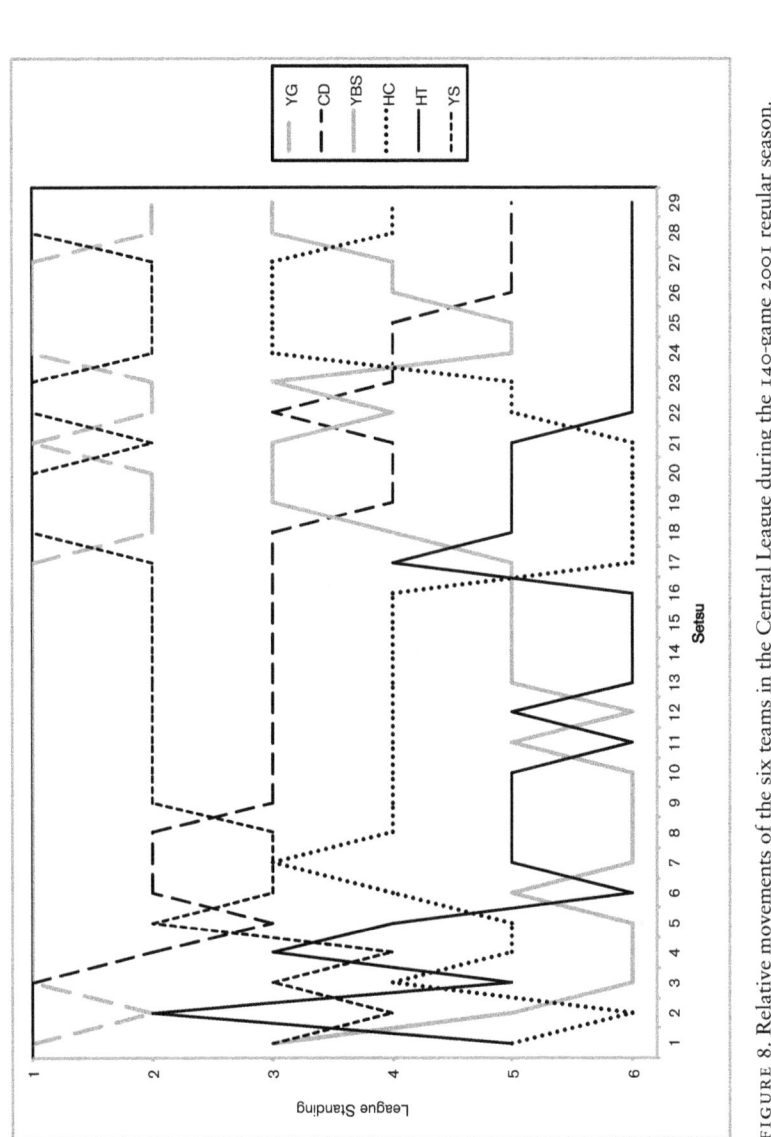

FIGURE 8. Relative movements of the six teams in the Central League during the 140-game 2001 regular season. Hanshin was in contention for the first 20 games but fell off the pace quickly and finished 22 games below .500. Calculated from data at www.japanesebaseball.com, accessed October 13, 2014.

venue for the national summer high school tournament. This sent the Tigers out on the longest road trip in the NPB schedule. It was known as the "road of misfortune" (*ma no rōdo*) or even the "death road" (*shi no rōdo*), and indeed, the team performed badly year after year in this stretch. Fans and the media (and the team) anticipated it with dread and chronicled the team's daily misfortunes. The players literally did not come back home during long stretches; a club official complained to me about the toll that took on their spirits, being away from family and friends and their usual leisure spots, being cooped up with teammates, coaches, and "them" ("*koitsu*," nodding to some reporters nearby). He and others believed that the well-known prospects of the April and August road trips scared off potential draftees to the team (although I have no evidence of this).

September: Pennant Races and Cellar Struggles

A seasonal autumn rain (*shūrin*) made mid-September to early October an unpredictable mix of scheduled games, rained-out games, and makeup games (using the *yobihi*, the days specifically set aside for makeups, especially for teams like Hanshin, whose home stadium was open air). At this point, the three-day cards went by the boards, and teams were playing out of sync; the season end was uneven, and the rhythm of the main part of the season was disrupted. The league season certainly lacked a strong sense of closure, and NPB's small scale posed a serious problem for sustaining interest and revenue. That is, in MLB, with six separate divisions (both the American and National Leagues are subdivided into three regional divisions), there is a much higher chance of at least several divisional races going to the wire, pleasing clubs, media, and fans. In NPB's September, in contrast, what now constituted rhythm and focus were the pennant races for the two league championships, if indeed a single team had not already opened up a wide lead.

An unusual—and complicated—idiom of the pennant race in Japan was "V-Magic," which was basically the number of games that a team must win to finish in first place with the title; it became prominent in a lot of sports writing and broadcasting as the season drew to a close. Oddly, though, the actual calculations were not understood by most fans and players. V-Magic was about a team controlling its own destiny; that is, it was the point in the schedule when a team, by winning all of its remaining games, would take the championship no matter what any other team did. Although I could not find anyone in the baseball world who made the allusion explicit, the spirit behind V-Magic refers to a distinction in Buddhist theology between enlightenment or salvation through self-help (*jiriki*) and through the mercy of others (*tariki*).

If V-Magic is the key phrase for following the final moves of the leading teams, staying in A-Class (the top three teams in the six-team leagues) and avoiding B-Class (the bottom three teams) became the goal for the teams in the middle of the pack. By September in most years, even this was elusive for Hanshin, and instead it had to pursue two other goals to salvage some consolation for the off-season: avoiding the last-place cellar or winning the annual series against a particular rival. Thus, even when the Tigers finished far out of first, they could pride themselves if they beat the Giants in their overall series.

Yet another tactical and rhetorical response to falling well behind the other teams in the league (and trying to retain fan interest and player motivation) was to declare a policy of foundation building (*dodai-zukuri*), that is, to give up on the present season and start focusing on the following season. This led to moving promising young players up from the farm team, releasing current players, and making much of the upcoming player draft. All of these actions characterized most autumns at Hanshin. For all the years I followed the team, invariably the manager would start talking to the media about building a foundation for the next season, and the club would publicize the series of coach and scout conferences held in September and October to draw up priority lists of players to be drafted. Club officials were dispatched to the United States to try to identify a few new American players to sign. The sports dailies would start to identity the players in danger (the phrase they used was "player in delicate position" or *bimyō na senshu*). These were the players on the lookout for the daily visits of the senior front office executive, who was the designated grim reaper, delivering the official release notice (the term for this, *senryoku-hazure*, literally meant being "removed from the firepower"). In the late 1990s this messenger was Nishiyama Kazuyoshi, and when I was at the farm team complex in late September, I noticed the players were always looking for signs of "that car" in the Naruohama parking lot, especially on the days following the front office personnel meetings (which they learned of from the sports dailies). The nervous players would drop into the trainers' room because they knew that the trainers generally had accurate inside information.

October: Struggling to the Finish

Not surprisingly, for many years through the early 2000s, October was a grim month for Hanshin. Indeed, it was a month of stark contrasts across the whole baseball world, between those few teams still fighting it out in pennant races, attracting attention and attendance, and the rest of the teams, which were trying to squeeze out a bit more stadium revenue, make some final assessments about their current players, and look ahead to improving prospects for the next season. The manager and coaches often gave the final month a positive spin by framing it with the foundation-building language, and veterans and other vulnerable players remained on guard about a visit from the grim reaper. Even Kōshien was a bit emptier for the final weeks' games (including the backlog of makeup games). These last games seldom had much bearing on the overall standings, but they nonetheless could be important for teams trying to fight their way into A-Class top three teams or at least avoid the ignominy of a last-place finish (usually Hanshin's challenge). They were also crucial to those players in pursuit of individual records or a few improved statistics that would help their contract renewal. Players on the farm team roster hoped for a call-up to showcase themselves on the first team.

Meanwhile, Down on the "Farm"

While the main team was competing throughout the season, the farm team followed a much less publicized routine of long training sessions and a short season of competition. Over at Naruohama, the other two-thirds of the Hanshin roster practiced daily from the beginning of March, when the entire club returned from spring training. The Naruohama field was built with the same dimensions as Kōshien (absent the surrounding stands); it was adjacent to the team dormitory and a covered facility with pitching allies, batting cages, and weight rooms. The farm team had its own staff: the second-team manager, nine or ten coaches, several trainers, and other support workers. The Tigers front office frequently used the farm team manager position to test a promising candidate for promotion to main team manager.

The farm team system in Japan began in the 1950s, when club rosters were much smaller in number. Throughout the decades it functioned as a kind of junior varsity: a transition for younger players from school baseball to the routines of the professional level, a place for rehabilitating injured players, and even a holding pen for players who could not be squeezed into the limited main team roster. To provide game experience for the farm players, the farm teams of the twelve NPB clubs were organized into two leagues, the Eastern and Western Leagues, which played an eighty-game regular season from late April to September, concluding in a short championship at the end of the month.[6]

The unvarying routine for most players I talked with was necessary monotony and an anxious waiting game. Their schedule was more diurnal than the major team's, beginning earlier in the morning with a break for lunch and concluding late in the afternoon. Except on game days, there were drills from 10:00 to 12:00, followed by lunch, a five-inning practice scrimmage, and more individual training drills until about 4:00 or 5:00. These practice games were conducted with surprising seriousness. Club staff operated the outfield scoreboard, used the PA system to announce lineups, and kept careful records of strike counts and pitches from an air-conditioned room behind the plate. The umpires were often first-team players down for injury recovery, and the only liveliness was often the antics of the plate umpire, some of whom took to their task with comic gesticulations. Tiger Town was set among high-rise housing estates, and there was a small daily crowd of spectators—mostly young kids, retired men, and truckers and taxi drivers on breaks.

After the game, players drifted into the rather simple dining room, with a buffet-style offering of noodles, salads, sandwiches, some fruit, a coffee machine, and a juice bar. On a number of occasions, Furuzawa Kenji, the pitching coach, complained about the diets of young players, who grew up with a "convenience store" mentality of just eating what they felt like, paying little attention to nutrition. They resisted a healthier fixed menu at the dorm and for training lunches, and he was a vocal critic of their lack of physical strength. The club hired a nutritionist in the late 1990s, who tried to improve the menus, but she became discouraged by the lack of interest and quit. Most afternoons were filled with more drills from 1:30 to 3:00 or so, and many players worked out afterward in the weight room or batting cages.

Some players expressed to me a sense of isolation; the location was distant from commercial districts, the dorm and practice field were side by side, and practices were day-in, day-out. Tiger Den was only a couple of miles away from Kōshien, but few of the farm team players ever went to the night games. I always felt an odd juxtaposition of proximity and distance between the two teams and the two venues.

After their Western League season ended in late September, the farm team did enjoy a slight break in the practice routine by returning to

Shikoku for two weeks of practice and a short autumn league season (the so-called Kuroshio League).

November and December: Rebuilding the Team

The three months from November to the opening of the next season's training camp were considered the off-season, but NPB remained the center of national sports interest even then. Occasionally Hanshin news might be displaced on the daily front page of the Kansai sports newspapers by a big horse race, a marathon, a sumo match, or another event, but pro baseball news remained on the second, third, and fourth pages of the papers, and Hanshin developments continued to lead television sports news broadcasts.

The team held a fall camp for two weeks in November, usually at Kōshien, which was the first time that some of the young players had an opportunity to use that field after a long year working out at Tiger Den and Aki. The formal playing year concluded with a fan appreciation day in late November at Kōshien, which could attract tens of thousands for an afternoon of speeches, awards, and a scrimmage.

Primarily, though, the final two months of the calendar year were focused on personnel matters. The draft of amateur players took place in early November, and there was plenty of lead-up coverage on the potential top drafts and Hanshin's "listing up" of its scouts' favorites. Afterward the focus shifted to the choreography of signings (e.g., ceremonial calls on a draftee's school coach and a series of photo-op visits by the draftee to Kōshien). Hanshin held tryouts of players released from other clubs in search of overlooked talent and pursued star players who had gained free agency and were moveable, both of which activities were fodder for the media. Front office staff were also busy during these months trying to negotiate trades with other clubs and scouring the American market for foreign recruits who might prove to be that elusive success story. All NPB players were under annual contract for ten months, from February 1 through November 30, and thus a major activity for six weeks from late November was the negotiation and signing of each of the sixty or so players to new contracts.

All of this was common among the twelve NPB clubs, and I take up the details of these annual personnel issues in the next chapter, but it is important to note here the critical difference between NPB and MLB. In the United States, as soon as (or even before) the final World Series broadcast in late October, media focus and fan attention turn quickly to football, basketball, and hockey. In Japan, by contrast, at least through the early 2000s, there was no rival sports season to compete with NPB even in its off-season. Thus, even minor personnel moves drew coverage and fascination. And this was especially true for Hanshin. Given its woeful record, the region remained fixated each year on whether this was the off-season when the club could finally solve its problems. Each manager turnover, every tryout, each potential free agent, each front office staff assignment, and every trade rumor and contract negotiation drew scrutiny and assessment. The Kansai spotlight remained on the team and the club right into the new year, when once again the players took off for their "individual training," and the annual baseball round began anew.

BEYOND KŌSHIEN: THE WIDER WORLD OF HANSHIN BASEBALL

Game day at Kōshien was the center of the Hanshin Tigers world, but every game at Kōshien was also taking place in newsrooms, in hundreds of bars and restaurants across the region, in front of television sets in tens of thousands of homes, and in other venues where producing and following the game was taking place. Only about half of the 134 regular season games were played at Kōshien, so the team played a dozen times each season at the five other Central League stadiums (where it was the visiting team).[7] Each stadium had its own field dimensions, atmosphere, spaces, and spectators. Each trip was a routine of travel (by train or airplane), hotels (the same hotels over the year), and downtime.

The stadiums on game days hardly exhausted the places of the Hanshin world. A fuller cartography included, for the players and staff, the club's practice facility and farm team field at Tiger Den; the spring training camps in Okinawa, Kyushu, and Shikoku; and the fall practice camps. The front office staff was found below the bleachers in a warren of offices that looked like those of any small company. The sports desks of the newspapers, the television broadcast studios, the dedicated Tigers fan bars, the headquarters of the parent company, and many other places were sites of consumption, production, and participation. Every evening the beat reporter, sitting in the press box, quickly typed up his game summary, connected his laptop, and transmitted it to his editor, who revised the text and passed it to the graphics department to mock up with photos and charts for the next issue, which was printed in another part of town for delivery to kiosks around the city, where the papers were bought by commuters within hours, to be read (and displayed) in trains and subways throughout the region. This was but one line of connection among the multiple lineaments and synapses by which narrative, sentiment, and commentary were continuously created, circulated, and experienced.

SENSORY WORLDS AND TIMELINES: BUILDING FAMILIARITY AND MITIGATING FAILURE

The sights, sounds, and smells of Kōshien Stadium; the spatial distribution of Tigers activities; and the game days, the seasonal rounds, and the player careers of the Hanshin Tigers demonstrate that this sportsworld was richly multisensory, geographically complex, and densely polyrhythmic. These places, senses, and rhythms were absolutely critical to constructing Tigers baseball as a profound and distinctive experience because they created associations, affinities, and connections among the many different types of people who were thus drawn together in and as this sportsworld.

Senses are associational, and professional baseball is about building affiliation, identity, and intimacy for players and spectators alike. Walking into Kōshien day after day and seeing, smelling, and touching the black-red dirt of the infield and the tightly mowed carpet of outfield grass, the grimy plastic seats, and concrete corridors under the stadium—these and many other elements marked the stadium as a distinctive place, enhancing the pleasure and suspense of what was to come by evoking the memories of the past. Even for those not physically present—listening by radio and watching by television—the crowd noise (carefully engineered with stadium microphones), the announcers' voices, and the omni-optical camera eye bred a sensual familiarity that was hard to escape once one was drawn in. Kōshien was the spatial pivot from which radiated the sensual triggers, the working and watching routines, that conjoined so many otherwise disparate people throughout the region. For players, preseason camps and postseason training sites were Kōshien's before and after, and the home and away rhythms of the seasonal competition brought them out and back. The stories filed and the editors' daily instructions connected the beat reporters at Kōshien to their newspaper offices and printing plants. And the broadcast transmissions and daily newspapers were the connective tissue between the action at Kōshien and the tens of thousands of followers around the region, sitting in bars, trains, and living rooms that became the satellite sites of the stadium.

Hanshin baseball's temporality worked differently from its spatiality. The diurnal tempo of a single game and the seasonality of a full annual year that we have transited here were only two dimensions of baseball's time reckoning and time consciousness, which were also characterized by an intricate conjunction of the linear and cyclical. Games began with the first inning and moved through middle innings to late innings and even extra innings until they reached resolution, but a new game started all over again the next day. Seasons ran through an almost organic life cycle but then began again the following year in a Buddhist-like reincarnation. Players had at-bats that had resolution (out or safe, and then the next batter), but the same player returned to the plate again several innings later for another at-bat. A player's records cumulated over time to delineate a career, sometimes stretching over many years, sometimes ending in early failure or a sudden, career-ending injury. Even broader timelines were the histories of Hanshin, its rival teams, and the sport itself, in professional form since 1936, and from its introduction to Japan, since the 1870s.

This interplay of linear progression and endless repetition was made more intricate by the embeddedness of shorter cycles within larger cycles. A series of pitches to a single batter was his at-bats; a series of at-bats up to three outs was a team's half-inning; both teams' at-bats were an inning, one of nine within a game; a game was one of three games in a series against a particular team; these series recurred over the year to constitute the league's regular season; and so forth.

Like time patterns everywhere, this one seldom rose to the level of explicit awareness. Baseball's time consciousness is really, I suppose, its "subconsciousness." But this patterning imprinted itself on everyone connected with the game, and I want to emphasize here what I believe to have been its primary effects of sustaining suspense and mitigating failure because "losing" was such a dominant theme in the Hanshin Tigers world during my research and in the two decades before.

At one level, the problem is generic; one of the central issues of modern sports is dealing with perpetual failure. Against the athletes' will to win, the fans' demand to win, and the broad imperative of professional sports that "winning is the only thing," almost everyone loses in the end that final championship trophy, again and again. Only one of the twelve teams emerged as champion each year in Japanese professional baseball; the other eleven lost. How to sustain the illusion of hoped-for success amid the realities of almost always coming up short haunts the structures of sports and drives the proliferation of timelines.

In NPB, as elsewhere, there were manifold individual titles (from game hero to player of the month to midseason all-star selection to season leader in any of multiple categories to a Most Valuable Player award to career records) that offered momentary and multiple forms of recognition for individual players, regardless of team outcomes. Likewise for teams, league competition was structured in a way that offered a number of measures by which teams and their players and supporters could remain in play. Rising above and falling below a .500 winning percentage, measuring games behind or ahead, finishing in A- or B-Class, avoiding the cellar, winning a season series against a particular rival—these were but some of the measures that constantly displaced one another in reaching for one goal but shifting to another when the first became out of reach. And there was the next game, and the next month, and the next season to anticipate even while a team was failing in this game, this month, and this season. The manifold times of baseball kept everyone in the game, building suspense while deflecting frustration—a perpetual delay of final gratification that we find also in soap operas and other experiences of interlocking, overlapping, endlessly repeating narratives. Perhaps this is why a longtime sports reporter for the *Washington Post*, Tom Boswell, titled a 1983 essay "How Life Imitates the World Series."

This is generally true, but it was particularly powerful for Hanshin because of the special qualities of the stadium and the manifold links across workplaces and leisure spaces throughout the Kansai region. It is to those places and the people who work there that I turn in the following chapters.

CHAPTER 3

On the Field

Players, from Rookies to Veterans

We watch professional athletes with mixed emotions. Awe, pleasure, respect, envy, and resentment are among our feelings about their immense talents and achievements, their high salaries, their good fortune to be paid for "playing a game," their high public profile, and the occasional pride and more frequent disappointment they cause those of us who invest part of ourselves in caring about their performance.

In this book I am trying to persuade readers to see Hanshin Tigers baseball as a sportsworld featuring a large cast of characters, including even readers of this book, who together create and sustain this ongoing lifeworld. Yet I am not going to deny the obvious, which is that there is a center to that baseball world: the contests on the field between the foul lines by two teams of nine players. The anthropologist Ian Condry (2006) centered his study of hip-hop in 1990s Japan on the *genba*, the clubs and other places where hip-hop was actually performed by rappers and dancers (he was adapting a term that originally referred to a construction site). In a sense, the field at Kōshien is the Tigers' *genba*, and in this chapter I focus on these players, their characteristics, and their careers. In the following chapter I turn to the managers and coaches who train, direct, discipline, and judge the players (and who themselves, almost without exception, are ex-players). Together they are the genba performers (the 1996 players and coaches are shown in figure 9).

FIGURE 9. Team photo of the 1996 Hanshin Tigers players and coaching staff. "Fresh. Fight. For the Team." was the motto selected by manager Fujita for that season. Credit: Hanshin Tigers Baseball Club.

Of course it is ambiguous to call them "players."[1] Sports are play, to be sure; they are competitive games, and we often engage in them, or watch them, for recreation and leisure. At the same time, doing sports intensely—at any level—is hard work, mentally demanding and physically taxing (that is why we say we're "working out"). Professional athletes are by definition engaged not just in hard work but also in paid labor. The eighteen-year-old drafted by Hanshin out of high school or the twenty-one-year-old drafted out of college has already been through ten or more years of playing school baseball, often year-round with few breaks, and he has survived a ruthless winnowing to reach the professional level. What he then finds is that the training and winnowing are hardly over.

The life career of a professional athlete is Hobbesian—nasty, brutish, and short—which is to say, ruthlessly competitive, highly unpredictable, and decidedly brief. This is certainly true for baseball players in Japan, despite preconceptions that Japanese professional athletes are like Japanese salarymen working for Japanese organizations, securely enmeshed in a dense nexus of long-term loyalty and mutual commitment. This image is false. As with other aspects of the sport, the contractual status of players and the course of their careers are broadly similar to their MLB counterparts, in part because professional sports is everywhere a risky career and in part because NPB has borrowed many features of the MLB model.

Still, players in Japan have distinctive conditions of work, and in this chapter I outline the principal characteristics and career paths of those who played for the Tigers, especially in the late 1990s and early 2000s. In both Japan and the United States, teams can have a maximum of twenty-five men on their playing roster for each game. Beyond that, however, are some important distinctions. Each of the thirty MLB clubs may have a total roster of forty players "reserved" under contract. For the Tigers and the other NPB clubs, their maximum roster size is seventy players. On opening day of 1996, for example, the Hanshin Tigers had a roster of sixty-five players; its 2003 opening day roster was sixty-eight. This was true throughout the NPB clubs. All twelve team rosters fell within a narrow range of sixty-five to sixty-nine players each, and this range had held steady for over a decade.[2]

This is only the surface of an elaborate system of quota categories, eligibility requirements, contracts, drafts, bonus limits, and other personnel distinctions—arcane, mind-numbing detail to most of us, but career determining to the players and teams. The organizational consequences are crucial for all of us in appreciating what it is like to be a player.

One such consequence follows from the handling of the backup players. Major League Baseball maintains a wider gap between the major league team and its several minor league affiliate teams. In recent years, MLB teams have had from three to six minor league team affiliates. The affiliates are independently owned, organizationally distinct, and often geographically distant, and they are arrayed in a hierarchy of descending skill level from AAA down to single A.[3]

To populate this minor league system, MLB teams draft a large number of amateur players each year, from high school graduates, to university players, to youths from other countries. In 2001, for example, the Boston Red Sox drafted forty-seven players, all of whom were distributed across the lower levels of its affiliated minor league teams. The top picks might be given a sizable signing bonus, but most were given a token bonus and sent off into a grueling minor league life of minimal salaries, long bus rides, cheap hotels, and unrelenting competition. Very few of them ever made it to the MLB training camp, let alone to the major league game experience. These youngsters may have felt excited and honored to be drafted by the Red Sox, but they could never mistake that experience for becoming part of the team.

The situation in Japan is quite different. Far fewer rookies are drafted; Hanshin drafted a mere five players in 2001, about average for recent years. To be sure, the five rookies went to the farm, the second team, and none played in a regular Tigers contest the next season. But all five became part of the Hanshin sixty-eight-player roster and, structurally and psychologically, part of the Hanshin Tigers team. They practiced, played, and if unmarried, lived only a couple of miles from Kōshien Stadium at the Tiger Den facility.

The point is that the Hanshin Tigers were a much larger team than the Boston Red Sox, with a much wider spread of baseball abilities, playing experience, and seniority, from untested eighteen-year-olds just off their high school teams to Hall of Fame caliber veterans. The manager and coaches of the farm team worked under the first team manager and reported daily; they practiced at Tiger Den (and sometimes after the regular season at Kōshien itself), following routines laid out by the first team staff. Players moved back and forth between the two levels frequently, and there were many days when someone played a farm team game in the early afternoon and was then called up for the evening game at Kōshien. In many respects, a Japanese NPB team like Hanshin was more like an American National Football League (NFL) professional team than its MLB baseball counterpart.[4]

Because the Tigers were such a large organization, we might imagine them to have been an indistinguishable mass of players, more compliant, less individual—in short, a more corporate model than the smaller teams of MLB, for whom free agency and salary escalation have provoked ever more mobility and less team solidarity. Even the facial expressions and postures in the Hanshin team photo (see figure 9) were uniform!

"Lifetime employment" is no doubt the most familiar phrase associated with Japanese working conditions, celebrated and criticized by Japanese and foreigners alike. We now better appreciate how inadequately the notion of lifetime employment described the wider Japanese economy of the twentieth century; its rhetorical force greatly exceeded its actual reach.[5] But it is still frequently assumed that one of the ways that Japanese baseball is so, well, "Japanese" is because it too offers this cozy cocoon of security, to the detriment of the sport's fundamentally competitive nature.

We would not be entirely wrong in thinking this, or rather, our image would accord with some official views of Japanese teams and players. There is indeed more routinization of Hanshin players' lives and certainly less mobility and room for maneuver, but overwhelmingly, their careers too are short, unstable, and unpredictable. They bear little relation to those of the prototypical office workers who follow them. Consider the career longevity of the 731 Hanshin players who were registered on the first team in the decades between 1937 and 1997. These included 228 pitchers and 503 players in fielding positions (that is, non-pitchers). Of the pitchers, fully 25 percent had but a single season career; 56 percent had careers of five years or fewer. A mere 7 percent of all pitchers over those sixty years lasted ten years or more. Fielding players did not fare much better. Of the 503 such players, 19 percent (98) had one year or less registration on the first team; 51 percent had careers of five years or fewer, and only 8 percent remained on the first team for ten years or more.[6]

Most players I talked to and read about expressed a deep-seated anxiety about the unpredictability of their work conditions and the vagaries of recognition. Rarely were success and adulation so constant or failure so unrelenting that players could avoid mood swings between euphoria and humiliation, intensity and boredom, and pride and bitterness. The pitcher Nakagomi Jin talked to me about his anxiety when I first met him in 1997 and then in later years. At that point, the then twenty-seven-year-old had already had three operations on his elbow (including surgery by the famous Dr. Frank Jobe in the United States) and had been on and off the roster with recurring injuries. He was meticulous in conditioning, took ten daily vitamin supplements, and only drank green tea and mineral water. He said he was constantly nervous about his elbow, believing on the one hand that he had to throw every day to keep it in shape, but on the other hand fearing that such a routine would hasten its eventual breakdown.[7]

These intense and contradictory feelings were heightened by a feature of every professional athlete's work that we often overlook, which is its openness to unrelenting public scrutiny by teammates, coaching staff, media, and spectators. There are no other company employees who work every day in front of up to fifty-five thousand spectators intent on following their every move. What other job is measured by some twenty separate performance statistics that are recorded and published daily in newspapers with circulations in the millions and followed and debated endlessly by the spectators?

This was especially true for Hanshin ballplayers. Playing for the Tigers was both the second best and second worst job in Japanese professional baseball. Performing before the most vocal fans in baseball's most storied stadium, they basked in attention and adulation exceeded only by that shown the Yomiuri players at Tokyo Dome. Adulation, though, was fickle, while attention was constant. Hanshin players who were inspired by the cheers shouted through the fans' megaphones sometimes had to dodge the megaphones themselves, thrown onto the field in disgust after yet another disheartening loss. The single most frequent reason the players gave me for why so few of their wives and children ever came to watch them play was their anxiety about being crudely booed and jeered.[8]

RECRUITMENT

Look again at the Tigers team photograph (figure 9). The sixty-five players began the season with an average career to date of 5.6 years, ranging from four rookies to the veteran pitcher Kubo, who was then entering his twentieth season, and outfielder Ishimine Kazuhiko, who was beginning his eighteenth. Neither Kubo nor Ishimine would play much that season, and none of the four rookies made it into the main team games. Second from the right in the first row was Yagi Hiroshi, a thirty-one-year-old ten-year veteran and starting first baseman, but he was the exception. Most of the players had first team tenures of fewer than five years.

Like arcane statistics of performance and the details of baseball history, the nuances of contracts are absorbing to diehard fans and boring to most others, but clearly they are the formal underpinnings of player life, and we must be familiar with at least their basics. Most fundamentally, we must recognize that NPB players are not full company employees (*shain*), continuing members of a corporation. Rather, in the tax code and labor laws they are independent contractors (*jigyōsha*), and to the club they are just that. Like members of the coaching staff and even some in the front office, they must negotiate and sign annual contracts. The club does not deduct income tax for its players, nor does it include them in company pension or medical plans (although they are covered for job-related injuries). Players file income taxes as self-employed individuals.[9]

On the other hand, the twelve NPB clubs retain exclusive rights to their players under contract, who are "reserved" for them. In a sense, contract conditions are the reverse of those of employees of most large companies in Japan, including those from the parent Hanshin Railroad Corporation. Such companies have continuing obligations to their regular employees, who themselves are under no legal long-term obligations to the company. Significantly, then, the Japanese baseball world is an upside-down version of the large corporate model of lifetime employment. It is a contractual world in which the contractors remain at a significant disadvantage.

Since the mid-1960s, there have been three ways by which the twelve NPB clubs have recruited their players. They have signed them as "rookies" upon graduation from high school or from college or from one of the industrial leagues of amateur company teams; they have obtained current professional players traded or released from other NPB teams; and they have recruited foreign players from abroad. For instance, on opening day of 2003, there were 805 players under contract to the twelve clubs. Of these, 748 were "regular contract" players in that they had been recruited in Japan under league draft, trade, and release rules; all of them had had to sign the same uniform player contract, whose only difference was the annual salary figure.[10] These 805 were almost entirely Japanese nationals, although it is a category of recruitment and not ethnicity, and it actually includes the rare noncitizen who has graduated from a Japanese high school or university.[11] The other 57 were "foreign" players (*gaikokjin senshu*), and they were subject to modified contract regulations. Hanshin began that season with sixty-eight players, sixty-three under regular contracts and five foreign players. Let us first consider the regular players and then turn to the foreign players.

Entry into a professional baseball career is highly restricted.[12] About four thousand high schools in Japan have interscholastic baseball teams, and each team has between twenty and eighty members. There are fifty or so universities with varsity baseball clubs and even more companies that sponsor industrial league teams. Thus, there are about ten thousand baseball players eligible each year. In the November 2004 draft, eighty-two players were selected, of whom only a few would actually enjoy multiyear first-team careers. In short, entry into professional baseball is much more selective than admission to Japan's most competitive university, the University of Tokyo, and its most competitive national bureaucracies and corporations. This is a feature of baseball work that many people use to construct analogies to other work situations.

Each team has a group of scouts and a network of contacts across the several worlds of amateur baseball (high school, university, industrial leagues, and foreign leagues) to identify, assess, and woo talent (Abe 2009). There has always been debate in the baseball world about the relative advantages of signing young teenagers just out of high school or more seasoned amateurs after a college career, and this was a main point of disagreement among the Hanshin scouts I talked with over the years. For NPB as a whole, the age distribution of the seventy-four rookies drafted and signed to their first contracts in 1999, a typical year, shows a fairly equal distribution. The twenty-nine eighteen-year-olds were all graduating high school seniors. Almost all of the twenty-two-year-olds were graduating college students, while most of the others were coming from the leagues of primarily corporate-sponsored teams that play abbreviated schedules, with one major national tournament.[13]

Perhaps the single accomplishment of a young player that most burnishes his reputation is appearing in the national high school baseball tournament at Kōshien, especially on a team that advances far into the tournament. Kōshien experience is always listed on a player's résumé for the rest of his career.

STARTING A CAREER

The economic interests of those who own professional sports teams in a league format pull them in contradictory directions. On the one hand, they want their own team to win all of the time—good for profits, up to a point—but they also want and need a competitive balance across the league's teams to generate the constant suspense that attracts an interested, paying spectator base (and media contracts) for the league more broadly. Team owners compete for the best talent, which tends to drive up salary costs and encourage predatory strikes on other owners' players, but they also frequently agree not to compete by creating and enforcing allocations of binding rights on players that limit contract costs and restrict such predatory practices (the "reserve clauses" in athletes' contracts).

The common response to these contradictory owner anxieties has been a regulated, annual draft of players, now a contentious feature of both US and Japanese baseball. The procedural details can be arcane, but its most important feature is the order of drafting new talent. If a draft is essential to maintaining competitive balance, it must allow the weakest teams the first opportunities to select the most promising rookies.

Japanese baseball authorities instituted a player draft in 1965, hoping to contain what owners saw as escalating salary competition and flagging fan interest in uncompetitive leagues. Over the decades, the draft has proved more effective in containing club costs than in promoting league competitive balance (Tachibanaki 2016:49–72). Almost immediately, the draft's leveling effects were blunted by the stronger owners, especially Yomiuri's Shōriki Matsutarō, who insisted that the draft order be decided by lottery. This began in 1967, and the twelve managers pulling cards from a bowl proved to be a photogenic media event, but it did little to help the weaker teams.

In 1978, procedures were changed so that clubs had to publish their lists of preferred draftees in advance; lotteries for signing rights were then held only in cases where more than one club chose a player. This was roundly criticized by the public for eliminating player preferences, but it was also attacked by the two strongest teams, Yomiuri and Seibu, who felt the lottery interfered with their efforts to attract the best talent. Indeed, owners of both teams continued to lobby for the abolition of the draft system altogether, in favor of what they called a "free market."

These pressures led to further changes in 1993 that remained in place until 2005, under which players from university or industrial league teams who were drafted in the first or second position designated the team or teams they were willing to sign with. Their preferences were matched against club preferences, and if a player was chosen by more than one club whom he had agreed to negotiate with, a lottery was used to determine allocation of draft rights. A further change in 1994 instituted a contract cap that limited the maximum initial contract to ¥100,000,000 (roughly US$1 million at the time), with an additional signing bonus of ¥50,000,000.

The changes produced a curious result: there have been no multiple designations. It is fair to assume that it would be in any player's self-interest to designate several clubs whom he would be willing to negotiate with and play for, but in fact that has never happened since 1994. Instead, the system has produced feverish and controversial maneuvering by the clubs during the summer and fall before the draft to secure an exclusive commitment from their top two draft picks. That would seem to suppress competitive offers, but they undermined this by seeking these advance, exclusive designations with illegal under-the-table payments to the players above the official signing and salary ceilings that they had publicly agreed to. Especially for top prospects, this was a lot of money, and the sports papers loved to dig into these cases and specu-late. In Yomiuri's push to secure the top rookie, Takahashi, in the 1997 winter draft, for instance, the sports papers widely reported he was paid more than ¥200,000,000 (roughly US$2 million). A member of the Hanshin front office told me that the figure was probably half that, but he was puzzled by how so much money could be conveyed, even if it was distributed as quasi-legal consultant fees to people around the player acting as his baseball guardians (kōken'in).

Pointing to a number of such notorious incidents, some have argued that the one constant of the draft system in its four decades has been the success of the Yomiuri club in using it or evading it to secure the best players. This may be an exaggeration, but Hanshin and other clubs have certainly developed a Yomiuri complex in their own draft deci-sion-making, constantly measuring their interest in particular players against the likelihood that they will have to compete with Yomiuri. In late June 1998, for instance, Hanshin scouts and player development staff held their first meetings of the season to prepare for the fall draft. They had drawn up and discussed a list of 110 prospects and agreed on three graduating university players as their top picks (the scouts had labeled them "special A rank"). Much of the meeting, though, con-cerned the Giants' interest in these players and what Yomiuri was doing to attract them. In the end, Hanshin chose none of them (and Yomiuri obtained two of them).[14]

Recruiting is a high-profile activity, and Hanshin's lack of success has been a constant source of media criticism and front office anxiety. Every September, Hanshin announced (or leaked) its top picks among that year's available pool. The sports press used the phrase "issuing a love call" because this began a process of wooing the players to designate Hanshin. The problem was that Hanshin was often burned by setting its sights on the best prospects, only to have Yomiuri swoop in and per-suade them to sign with that team. This had been the case with Taka-hashi, noted above; as soon as Hanshin's interest leaked, the Giants put the rush on him. Beyond bruising the club ego, this also complicated Hanshin's switching its attention to another prospect and persuading him to join it.

ADJUSTING TO THE PROFESSIONAL LIFE

From the young player's perspective, the professional life requires immediate, severe adjustments, and all of the players I spoke with over the years were quick to admit that they had underestimated just how wide was the gap between the two levels and how difficult they found it to adapt to the demands of the professional life. They had assumed the contrary, that it would be an easy transition from one level to the next of the same game. Most of them were coming from school teams that had tough routines, a demanding manager, and nearly year-round practice, where they were feted by their schools as heroes. They had been courted by the Tigers, given a big bonus, and featured in the national press.

As soon as the ink on the contract dried, though, they went from being the stars of the team and center of attention to being lowly rookies, relegated to the edges of publicity and often riding the bench rather than starting the game. Instead of one manager, they were under the daily supervision of a phalanx of coaches. What had been dressed up as team spirit was now just hard work. They faced a far longer season of games and a far more noisome press.

Interestingly, their coaches pointed out another adjustment that none of the players themselves articulated in speaking with me. High school and university baseball is played tournament-style rather than league-style. In a tournament, you must win every game to advance; lose, and you go home. The league format that is used by almost every professional team sport puts all teams through an equal schedule of games over a season. The team with the best record wins the league title. As a consequence, even the team with the best season record loses a lot; the league champions in NPB over time only average winning six of every ten games. For schoolboy players, each loss is devastating; a professional has to shake it off overnight and move on quickly. Developing this professional consciousness (*puro ishiki* was the phrase used over and over) was the single most difficult adjustment, most coaches and veterans insisted. It had strategic as well as attitudinal dimensions. Surviving a tournament, including the ultimate schoolboy dream of winning the national Kōshien tournament, is, ironically, more a matter of not losing than of winning (*makenai ishiki* was the term frequently used); defensive, risk-adverse strategies are seen as more rewarding. A professional must be much more aggressive about winning precisely because losing is so common; risk calculations are quite different. There was no way I (or the coaches for that matter) could get inside the heads of the many players I watched and talked to, but professional consciousness was the crucial idiom by which they were judged by those who controlled their career fates.

PLAYER LIFE

> People assume that just because you're on a team, you're tight with every-body. But this isn't the Foreign Legion. First of all, any football team is really two teams plastered together—the offense and defense. And then the players are divided by age and race and status—you know, what position you play and how good you are—and when you take all that into consideration, a guy's lucky if he ever has more than a handful of really close friends. In a way, this season is always kind of a battle to see if the one thing that holds the team together—trying to win football games—can outlast all the factors that are pulling in the opposite direction. (Rashad 1982:43–44)

Ahmad Rashad, writing as his NFL football career came to an end, expressed a commonplace of professional sports. Although it can be phrased even more cynically ("25 players, 25 taxi cabs" is a popular and pointed phrase in major league stories), the more serious point is that any elite sports team needs both internal competition and internal cohesiveness at all times. The Hanshin Tigers team did seem to be wracked with dissension at several points in the years of my fieldwork, but that condition was less interesting and less important to me than the constant reality that the sixty-five members of the team roster were always sixty-five very different sets of talents, dispositions, and career points.

It continually surprised me how little many players knew about the lives of their teammates or how little the coaches and manager knew of their players' circumstances. Daily life in the locker room and on the field was a jarring juxtaposition of intimacy and estrangement. There was a lot of joking around (at least before games and in the locker room and trainers' room). Everyone had a nickname, and there were no hon-orifics like "–san" used among players. They addressed the manager as "*kantoku*" and his senior assistant coach as "head" (for *heddo kōchi*), but other coaches had nicknames.[15] There would be occasional golf out-ings (both organized formally by the club for charities and held infor-mally by groups of players) and sometimes some mahjong or karaoke sessions. However, based on my interviews and observation, there was much less after-hours or out-of-season socializing among players than I expected to find.

This was less a matter of animosity—players seldom expressed hard feelings against teammates—and more that time and space did not encourage it. During the season, players arrived in the early afternoon for the evening game and immediately began warm-ups, meetings, and sessions with the trainers. The game finished late in the evening, and most just wanted to go home and get to bed. Even if there was time to relax at the ballpark, there was no space for it. Major League Baseball clubhouses are often spacious, with sofas, card tables, lounge areas, weight rooms, and so forth, and the facilities, well, facilitate relaxed sociality. The Tigers had a tiny locker room, not a "clubhouse," and it was grimmer than any high school gym that I recall from my youth. Players' lockers had wire baskets and hooks on which to hang a change of clothes; there was little room to linger. Down the hall was a room where pregame meals were available, but this too was a functional space, with Formica tables and chairs (and a fairly sparse menu of sandwiches, noodles, milk, juice, tea, etc.). The trainers' room was the largest of all the backstage spaces and the scene of most casual conversation. It put the trainers in the middle of player life, and I always found them to be the most knowledgeable and most understanding about the players' lives.

BACHELORHOOD, MARRIAGE, AND FAMILY

Hanshin rookies got big signing bonuses—far more than the salaries of their front office bosses or most of their fans. We often focus on the effects of that sudden shower of riches on a youngster, but another challenge of professional sports life, especially for Hanshin players, was adjusting to the local media and starting a life in Kansai under the intense fan spotlight. Finding housing, driving a car, starting a family, and other everyday actions that most of us do in anonymity could be subject to intentional or unintentional publicity. Osaka is a city of alluring nightlife and great restaurants, drunk driving laws are extremely strict in Japan, and media companies have large networks of sources and freelance photographers. All of this made the front office and coaching staffs nervous about players' free-time activities and kept most of the players circumspect in their dealings with the local public.

Almost all of the younger players on the roster were unmarried, and Hanshin, like other clubs, maintained a club dormitory on the grounds of Tiger Den, its practice facility and farm team headquarters. The facility was the same as apartment buildings that most major corporations maintained for their young bachelor employees. It had two floors of single-person efficiency apartments with some common room facilities. It was clean and functional, subsidized and supervised (the dorm head during my fieldwork was an avuncular former Tigers player). In some years, the club required unmarried rookies to stay in the dormitory.

Some players I talked to were happy with the convenience, given the demands of their profession; others chafed under the company paternalism and were frustrated by the dorm's location on the edge of the city, which required an expensive taxi ride for shopping and going out.

The 1990s and early 2000s was a period when the national population had stopped growing, the age of first marriage was rising rapidly, and there was growing official panic about falling fertility rates. Interestingly, professional baseball players, despite the constant travel and uncertain career prospects, got married earlier and with somewhat higher frequency than their peers nationally (of course the sports dailies reported on whatever player dating, romance, and marriage information they could dig up). Still, the players' family lives largely remained off-limits, by mutual agreement. I never once saw a spouse or children of a Japanese player at the stadium (although I was told they sometimes came, and the club would provide seating for them behind the backstop). Nor did the spouses engage in any charity work, although players were sometimes dispatched to events and schools. As with most workplaces in Japan, there was a rather rigid barrier between their Hanshin jobs and their private lives, unstated but widely accepted. The most common reasons given by the players themselves were that the evening games were too late for their young children and that they did not want to expose their families to the jeering of the crowd. I was never able to interview the wives, so I do not know their perspective.

FOREIGN PLAYERS: SPECIAL TREATMENT AND THE SAVIOR-SCAPEGOAT CYCLE

The use of foreign players (and a couple of managers) is a distinctive feature of NPB baseball, and a few of them have made noteworthy contributions. The rules governing the numbers and deployment of non-Japanese players have changed somewhat over the decades from 1951 to the present. Since 1996 there have been no limits on the number of non-Japanese players a club can sign to its seventy-man roster, but it can only put four of them on its twenty-five-man playing roster at any given time (from 1996 to 1998, the limit was three). Overwhelmingly, foreign players have been drawn from the United States. As the 2000 season began, for example, the twelve clubs had a total of 63 non-Japanese players among the 798 total players under contract. Thirty-six were from the United States, five were from the Dominican Republic, four each came from Brazil, Puerto Rico, and Venezuela; three each were from South Korea and Taiwan; and one each came from Australia, Canada, China, and Panama.[16] Many of the Americans were younger players in the upper levels of the minor leagues who were worried that they had no path to promotion to a major league team and thought that the higher salaries in Japan and the opportunity to play at a major-league level would be a springboard to an MLB contract. Others were players from major league teams who had been released or who were otherwise at the end of their careers. In both cases, the Japanese clubs generally offered salaries and bonuses far beyond their current salaries.

In the eight seasons between 1996 and 2003, the Hanshin Tigers signed thirty-six foreigners to its roster; each season it went through between four (in 1996) and eight players (in 2000) per season. The phrase "went through" is appropriate because their tenures were remarkably brief; twenty-eight of them lasted one season or less. Only eight (25 percent) were signed to a second season, and only one lasted into a third season (Greg Hansell, who pitched from 2000 to 2002).[17] Turnover has continued at this rate up to the 2017 season, although there have been several recent success stories.[18]

The players' experiences with the club ranged from quite rocky to mutually rewarding. The most controversial case during my fieldwork years was that of Mike Greenwell, who had a sometimes standout twelve-year career with the Boston Red Sox from 1985 to 1996. At the urging of the Hanshin club president, he was signed to what most people felt to be a mind-boggling $3 million contract in December 1996, but problems began immediately. He showed up at training camp a few days late, hurt his back, and returned to the States shortly thereafter. He returned in late April, played listlessly in a few games, and broke a bone in his foot when he fouled off a pitch. After a seven-game career with Hanshin, Greenwell announced his retirement in an infamous press conference in early May that was heavily covered by the sports media, embarrassing the Hanshin front office (see figure 10). He offered to return 40 percent of his contract money, which still represented a huge loss (of money and PR) to Hanshin. In the end, he walked away with $1.8 million for the seven games.

It was understandable that the foreign players (especially the Americans) attracted inordinate attention from the Western press and from foreign commentators on the Japanese game, who tended to put these players' opinions and experiences at the center of their accounts.[19] However, it was highly misleading to do so. Their stories were interesting (and actually quite varied), but they need to be threaded into a far richer narrative fabric that was the Hanshin soap opera.

FIGURE 10. Front-page article announcing Mike Greenwell's sudden departure. *Nikkan Sports*, Osaka edition, May 15, 1997, 1. Courtesy of Nikkan Sports Newspaper.

When I interviewed Japanese players and front office staff and asked them their views of the presence, the value, and the problems of foreign players, the two phrases they most often used were *special treatment* (*tokubetsu-atsukai*) and *savior* (*kyūsaisha*). The foreign players in these years were treated by Hanshin (and most other clubs) as in all ways distinct from regular players. Their contracts were individually drafted and did not have to conform to the uniform player contract of regular players; they were paid salaries that were significantly higher than regular players with comparable records and experience; they could follow many of their own training routines and did not have to conform to many of the team practice schedules or policies; during the February preseason training camp in Kochi they were put up in a luxury golf resort hotel, while the first team and farm team rosters were housed in separate, less luxurious accommodations; they were assigned permanent interpreters; the club leased luxury housing for them and their families in a condominium complex in Kobe owned by the Procter & Gamble Corporation; on road trips, they traveled on the express train by first-class Green Car while the rest of the team went regular class on the same train; and they were often housed in separate hotels while on the road.[20]

This set of benefits and policies and the foreign players' contributions to the team raised many frictions and concerns, and it has always been quite difficult for me to assess their motivations and impact. Club officials insisted that such special treatment was necessary to attract the players they wanted and to accommodate their special needs. I actually did not interact very directly and intensively with the foreign players during my years of fieldwork, beyond an occasional interview. I did observe closely their interactions with the press, coaches, and other players and their participation in practice and warm-ups. Many of them were grateful for the accommodations that the club made to ease their adjustment to a new team, to different baseball routines, and to Japanese society more generally. Some of them tried hard to fit in with their teammates and to follow the guidance of the coaches and manager. I was surprised that most of the Japanese players I talked with expressed no strong resentment toward most of the special treatment, even the very high salaries and exemption from some of the training and workout demands. Most of them shrugged it off as necessary. For some of them, this inequality was mitigated by the opportunity to watch these foreign players closely for how they practiced and played the game; some of the Japanese teammates were curious about and remarkably attentive to details of their bodies; how they handled equipment; and their warm-up schedules, weight lifting and stretching routines, diet, and baseball techniques. Like ordinary Japanese fans, the Japanese players watched MLB baseball games on television, but to have American teammates and be able to observe them so continuously and closely was apparently some compensation for the bubble in which these foreigners were kept.

The other term most frequently used in reference to the foreign players was *savior* (with its somewhat irreverent connotation of Christ as the son of God sent to the human world to save us). Fans would sometimes show up at the airport to greet an arriving newly signed American with signs welcoming "our new savior." In fact, very few of the three dozen foreign players had any impact at all during those years, and many ended their brief terms in mutual frustration and recrimination, offering yet another stock melodrama played out on the front pages of the sports dailies.

Savior was only half of the stereotype. What was enacted, over and over, was actually a savior-scapegoat cycle, by which the inflated initial expectations quickly proved unrealistic, the foreign players struggled as the team also slid in the standings, and they were eventually released with loud public criticism of their laziness, selfishness, and lack of fighting spirit. Watching this play out several times—blaming the foreign player as the scapegoat for the team's failings—I was reminded of an old Japanese folk curing practice called "rubbing dolls" (*nade-ningyō*). These were paper cutouts of human figures to whom were transferred, by rubbing and incantation, the ailments of a sick patient, who was finally cured when the paper figure was burned.

We must not fall too quickly for the common stereotype of the foreign player as inevitably the undeserving victim (from the player's point of view, and that of much of the US press) or selfish malcontent (a common Japanese daily sports paper image). The treatment of the foreign players during those years is an example of the difficulties of accountability, especially under conditions of team weakness, where there is as much pressure to identify causes of the weakness as there is effort to avoid being labeled the cause. Who was responsible for the Mike Greenwell fiasco or for Darrell May's difficulties? How much of it was poor scouting by the club, fundamental deficiencies in the players' declining baseball skills, bad attitude and character flaws, incompetent coaching, unbridgeable cultural differences, poor luck (the fluke injury)—or some unknowable combination of these factors? The separate categorization and special treatment of the foreign players made them a favorite target for blame, but the debates in the clubhouse, in the press, and among fans are endless.

RETIREMENT AND LIFE AFTER PLAYING

Where did Hanshin players go at the end of their generally short careers, given their narrow range of skills and a Japanese labor market in which prestige jobs were in "real" corporate sites largely closed to lateral, midcareer entry?[21] Many expressed a strong desire to stay in baseball in some capacity, even those with minimal accomplishments as players, sometimes because of a love of the sport, sometimes because they could not imagine any options. "Nokoritai!" (I want to be left behind!) was a phrase I heard from a dozen or so players in talking with them about their post-playing days, meaning that they hoped to somehow impress the club of their resolve and talent for some position in the Hanshin organization or any of the other eleven clubs.

Retiring players in the United States with major or minor league experience have one large field of opportunity: coaching the sport at youth, high school, or college levels. From the 1960s through the early 2000s, this was not possible in Japan. Because of a controversy in 1962, the amateur baseball organizations banned anyone with professional experience (as player, coach, or umpire) from moving back to any level of amateur baseball.[22]

There were three principal paths for Hanshin and other NPB players. The biggest names would be signed by one of the media companies as commentators or analysts for the sports dailies, television, or radio broadcasts (or some combination of assignments, depending on their talents). The contracts were for one year, and the usual remuneration was ¥20,000,000 (about US$165,000 in the late 1990s and early 2000s), which was roughly the annual salary of a Hanshin coach. Some of these ex-players would remain in media, but most aimed to be hired into the coaching ranks after a few years as a commentator. A very few of them would eventually rise to one of the twelve positions as manager, but once again they were entering a very tight field of competition.

A few other Hanshin players whose records were unimpressive but who had conveyed a proper attitude were retained by the club as bull pen pitchers, scouts, clubhouse secretaries, and so forth. In their interviews with me they made clear that this desire and the paucity of such positions put subtle pressure on these players to remain uncomplaining and hardworking throughout their careers.

Most, however, were simply let go to make their way in a labor market rather indifferent to their experience. In this regard, the clubs were not much different than their parent companies. Hanshin Dentetsu, like most corporations, offered plush second-career sinecures to a few top executives upon their reaching retirement age and arranged less attractive positions for some retirees at lower ranks. However, the Japanese corporate phrase *shūshin koyō* ("lifetime employment" in direct translation) more precisely means full career employment, and most employees were lucky to receive a single-payment severance sum when retirement day arrived.

Consider an example from the autumn of 1996, when twelve players were released from the roster, including the only two American players (who themselves had been brought in at midseason to replace the two foreigners who were fired at that time). Of the dozen, the two retiring stars, Nakanishi Kiyo'oki (a thirteen-year veteran pitcher) and Ishimine (an eighteen-year outfielder), signed as commentators with national media companies. Nakanishi worked for Asahi Broadcasting and the *Nikkan Sports* newspaper and in 2004 was brought back as a pitching coach. Ishimine was hired by Mainichi Broadcasting, and in 2005 he became a batting coach for another club, the Chūnichi Dragons. Shimao Yasuhito was hired to do commentary for Mainichi Broadcasting but got into acting a year later. Three other retiring players with significant Hanshin roster time were kept on in subsidiary coaching and batting practice pitcher roles, while four others left baseball for jobs at a construction company, an insurance company, a small restaurant, and an unspecified family business.[23]

A popular monthly magazine produced a special issue in 2012 that tried to trace the post-baseball careers of all 424 Hanshin players who had retired, been released, or otherwise left the team between 1980 and 2012, which averaged out to about 13 players per year (Bessatsu Takarajima Editorial Division 2012). Even using the tables in that issue, biographical data are too incomplete for me to generate reliable statistics, but the 1996 cohort does seem fairly representative of other recent years. It appears that a significant number of ex-players went into bar and restaurant businesses, working for Kansai-area establishments or opening their own places in Kansai or in their hometowns (see Bessatsu Takarajima Editorial Division:233–238 for profiles of six ex-players who did that).[24]

Finally, Hanshin, like most other clubs, had an active "OB-kai," or old boys association, which is in effect an alumni association for ex-players who had been on the official club roster. The OB members were provided free access at Kōshien and could enter through the stadium's work entrance by displaying their OB badges. There was a designated OB room just inside the entrance, and whenever I stopped by during games there were always a few ex-players passing the time and watching the game on the room's television. Nonetheless, this superficial sociality was of little importance, and very few ex-players availed themselves of the privilege. More significantly, the formal OB association had long served as a platform for the endemic factionalism that drove internal club politics.

NEGOTIATING CONTRACTS AND MOVING AROUND

At the start of almost every game I observed at Kōshien, a tall, gray-haired fellow in a Hanshin Tigers warm-up jacket would move toward a seat in the lowest left corner of the press box, pausing to exchange quiet greetings with reporters and others. Just as the game began, he would open his notebook and start recording the action. This was Ishida Hirozō, a former Hanshin player who had joined the front office in 1981 and from the 1980s to his retirement in 2002 was in charge of player "assessment" (*satei tantō*). His main responsibility was to handle all annual player contract negotiations; to do that, he would observe every game during the season, taking notes on player performance that he would match up with the official statistics at the end of the season.

Negotiations with players over their contract renewals began in late November according to a schedule that was made public to draw media attention and generate stories in the early winter postseason. Ishida started with the younger players and the easy cases, scheduling three or four meetings a day. He held them in a room in the club offices under the outfield bleachers. The player would enter and sit down in front of Ishida, who would review an assessment of the player's season, referring to various statistics and noting high and low points. He would then hand the player a single sheet of paper that had the club's salary offer for the next season. It was actually the one page from the Uniform Player's Contract that varied from player to player; the rest of the contract was not subject to customization. The player could accept the figure and sign; most players, especially the younger ones, signed quickly (*ippatsu* was the term). Some players resisted, either countering with a specific higher figure, indicating specific disagreements with the assessment or general unhappiness with the offer, or simply saying that they would return for a subsequent meeting, before which time they hoped the club would rethink its calculations.[25]

These were consequential meetings, because salaries could go up and down significantly. There was no ceiling on raises, but by the late 1990s the NPB Players Association had negotiated with the owners to establish a floor for reductions that was still sizable. For players with salaries under ¥100,000,000, the largest permissible reduction was 25 percent;

for those with salaries ¥100,000,000 and above, the reduction could be as great as 30 percent.

Although Ishida himself tried to maintain a very low profile in the press, these annual salary meetings were featured news throughout December in the sports dailies. The print and broadcast media hung around in the pressroom and at the back gates to the stadium to film and interview the players as they were going in and out. The papers carried daily reports, and any controversies received front-page focus. Charts of the meetings and the offers and counteroffers provided details. Interest built by the first week of December, when Ishida began meeting with the higher profile players. The favorite media stories were about the holdouts (*horyū senshu*), the players who argued back against the data, reasoning, and salary offer that Ishida presented them with, even if it was a raise. Tsuboi Tomochika had a spectacular rookie season in 1998, but at his November 26 meeting, when Ishida presented him with a huge raise from his 1998 salary of $100,000 to an offer of $285,000, Tsuboi responded, "Thank you very much. It's close to what I thought." Ishida said, "So we have a deal?" But Tsuboi demurred, saying, "Today, I just came to listen to what you have to say. That was my plan all along. I will be back again to talk." At least that was what he told the waiting press, which gleefully reported the exchange. (He signed for that figure in the next meeting, when Ishida wouldn't budge.)

Tsuboi's teammate Yamamura Hiroki followed shortly, hoping that his elevation to the main team would force the team to raise him to the ¥10,000,000 level (from ¥7,400,000). When Ishida offered him ¥9,200,000, Yamamura said nothing and proceeded to sit mute for forty minutes, never responding to anything Ishida said. Ishida kept trying to show him various statistical measures of his performance, but Yamamura left without saying a word.

As many as 40 percent of the players insisted on a second meeting, and perhaps 15 percent went on to a third round. In each of those years, there were three or four players who dragged out the negotiations into January over four meetings. Sometimes Ishida and the club made concessions and engaged in some bargaining, but by early to mid-January, virtually all players had signed.

This series of salary meetings, sometimes perfunctory, sometimes fiery, held during the slowest off-season month, were but a sideshow to the baseball itself. However, as mini-dramas of assessment and assent, I found them significant because they exposed many of the anxieties of the players and the club and encapsulated what I found to be the main features of the Hanshin Tigers world.

Satei is the general term for assessment, used here and elsewhere for ways of measuring performance and determining appropriate compensation. It was obviously crucial to the club to establish metrics for assessment that were transparent, objective, and widely accepted as fair. To that end, the front office created Ishida's full-time position as assessment coordinator, and it maintained exhaustive records of dozens of categories of player actions for every game that he and others processed and analyzed to create grounds for salary decisions and to present to players for their consent. To evaluate pitchers, Ishida told me, he began with such basic statistics as the number of innings pitched and the earned run average (ERA), with no distinction between starting and relief pitchers, but to such obvious metrics, he applied some fifty categories of assessment that added and subtracted points.[26]

The very density of data about individual performances cannot obscure how impossible it was to reach objectively defensible judgments about what individual players were worth and why. There may be fifty different measures, but how is one to determine and justify how to weigh measures against one another? What does "run prevention" really mean, and is it 20 percent or 75 percent more (or less) important than walk totals? Is it really to the pitcher's credit that a runner does not score? These and countless other points have been endlessly debated in clubhouses and front offices in every baseball stadium in every country that plays baseball, with no consensus. If anything, the uncertainties and divided opinions only produce more data and more measures year after year.[27]

The lesson I drew from the Hanshin world was not that such data were spurious for player assessment or for in-game decisions (another area where such quantitative analysis is applied). Rather, all of these quantitative measures were fundamentally irreconcilable. Everyone in baseball, from players to trainers to managers to owners, attends closely to a matrix of metrics. For their separate motivations, they all want these data and need them to make judgments about individual action and accountability in a team sport for which it is impossible to parse individual contributions to such a fine degree. There is an inherent contradiction in the conditions of a sport that is played with such a large group of specialist players and with such game frequency that it generates so much quantifiable data, but at the same time, that very complexity of team play undermines any attempt to isolate those individual contributions.

These anxieties about assessment hang over any professional team sport, and in this Hanshin was hardly distinct. However, there were several aspects of the December contract negotiations at Kōshien that were distinctive. Although the club, including Ishida, was reticent to offer details of the meetings, it did not prevent players from meeting with the media about them; it did not publish official salary figures, but it never denied the "estimated" figures that were published in the press. I recognized that the negotiations, along with the draft, player trades, postseason signings, and preseason training, were all useful to keep focus on the club and to sustain the multiple story lines that took the fans (and the club itself) from one season into the next year.

Moreover, assessment was fascinating to many fans because it was so central to their own working lives. The very term, satei, was the word that ruled their own job assessments and assignments. How to generate appropriate measures of accomplishment, who was to apply them, and with what consequences—these were topics that had strong affinities to their own situations. And the 1990s was a difficult decade in the Japanese economy; serial recessions shook the fortunes of even the major corporations; and "restructuring" (risutora), used to describe corporate reorganization, meant not only downsizing work-forces but also reneging on previous employment guarantees and understandings. This especially impinged on the Kansai region, because the subsidiary companies and subcontractor levels of the economy that so characterized Kansai firm structure felt the restructuring first and foremost. New university graduates faced what the press dubbed an "ice age" of reduced job openings, and midcareer workers were laid off suddenly and in large numbers with dismal prospects of finding comparable work. There was much talk of personal responsibility and performance-based pay replacing seniority-based pay. Many conversations I had about Hanshin player contracts and salaries turned eventually to analogies (and differences) with what was going on elsewhere in the economy.

It was not only difficult for the players, the club, the media, and the fans to agree on just salaries, but it was also impossible to obtain agreement about more collective equity across the sixty or more players, each with a different trajectory and set of metrics. However, one cumulative figure was clear: Yomiuri, year after year, was able to outspend Hanshin in player salaries by a wide margin, usually by two to three times. This was well publicized and often bemoaned by everyone in Kansai as an annual handicap with which Hanshin had to begin each season.

PLAYING FOR A TEAM AND WORKING FOR A CLUB

As Japan's preeminent sport for a century, baseball had demonstration effects as well as entertainment value. For late twentieth-century Japan, the "corporatization" of certain values—for instance, that effort loomed larger than talent and that there were reciprocal benefits of individual sacrifice for group success—found resonance within professional baseball among the front office, parent company, media, and fans. No one that I spoke with ever considered there to be a simple and direct connection between the $800,000 annual salary of a star shortstop and his own, say, $80,000 take-home pay as a section chief. The standards of practice of assessment, remuneration, organizational routines, company expectations, relations with superiors and peers, and more were seldom equivalent, but they were commensurate, and in this (and in the possibilities of knowing so much more about this for Hanshin than for other teams) lay much of the fascination.

However, playing baseball is an exceptional profession, and there are at least five qualities of professional baseball in Japan, and especially in the Hanshin sportsworld within Kansai, that make it difficult to use in valorizing corporate structures. First, as we have seen with Hanshin players, baseball was their "profession," but it was often a short and insecure career. They may have had longer careers than the female clerical-technical staff (OLs) of Japanese companies, but very few of them lasted beyond their early thirties. In 1998 the average age of the sixty-nine Tigers players was twenty-seven, and there were only four who were age thirty-five or older. Nor was employment in the same workplace (i.e., team) as permanent as in major corporations. In 1998, eleven of the sixty-nine Hanshin players were traded or otherwise signed from other Japanese teams, and with new foreign players and rookies, fully twenty-one of the sixty-nine were on the roster for the first time as the season started. That is a 30 percent personnel turnover.

Second, the job performances of players were far more publicly visible and precisely measured than almost all other jobs. Hanshin baseball raised workplace surveillance to a level that other corporate executives could scarcely imagine. There were no other company employees who worked every day in front of fifty-five thousand spectators watching their every move; there were no other company employees about whose performance some twenty separate statistical indicators were calibrated and recorded and then published daily in newspapers with circulations in the millions, where they were followed and debated endlessly by reader-fans.

A third distinctive feature was that hierarchies in the Hanshin sports organization were unstable because talent and seniority were rarely congruent. The sixty-nine Hanshin players on that 1999 team ranged in age from nineteen to thirty-six, in years of professional experience from zero to fourteen, in salary from $40,000 to $1.5 million a year, and in their performance by a similarly enormous variance. However, age, experience, pay, and performance record did not correlate positively. In fact, they often varied quite independently of one another; the older players were not always the higher paid, the higher-paid players did not always perform better, and so forth.

Even pay controverted the Japanese corporate model of steady upward increments. Given the careful measurement of performance, we have seen how salaries were adjusted annually at contract time—in such a public fashion. Of the fifty-five salary offers for returning players in 1998, fewer than half (for twenty-five players) were raises, ranging from 5 to 250 percent. Eighteen players were forced to accept salary reductions (of 5 to 40 percent), and another twelve signed at the same amount as the previous year. Furthermore, the risk of injury created unpredictability for the organization's human resource planning. In 1998 the Tigers pitching staff was decimated by unexpected injuries in the early season that left it floundering in the cellar and left several of the pitchers with career-ending conditions.

A fourth difference between the Hanshin players' workplace and the other workplaces in the sportsworld and around Kansai was that baseball's requisite skills were highly positional and artisanal. This worked against corporate authority and contrasted with a Japanese corporate preference for hiring a generalist workforce. There were pitchers, catchers, infielders, and outfielders, each with bundles of specialty skills. And each of these positions was even more finely graded into an extreme version of Durkheim's modernist organic division of labor. Among pitchers, for instance, there were important differences between and distinct uses of right-handers and left-handers; starters, long relievers, short relievers, and closers; power pitchers and finesse pitchers; and others. All infielders required some common skills of catching and throwing, but first basemen, second basemen, third basemen, and shortstops were so distinct that rarely could the same player master more than one of these jobs.

It is true that these baseball skills must be honed through constant repetition, and certain fundamentals are liable to collective practice and supervision. However, excellence, generally the prerequisite for long-term survival in a short-term profession, demanded that an individual player constantly test conventional styles. Players were engaged in a highly competitive search for an edge in and with these skills, and such rivalries could seriously disrupt team play and collective interests.

Those in formal control, the managers and coaches, were often ill equipped to teach such specialty skills. A younger pitcher, for instance, was usually better off seeking to learn a new pitch from an older pitcher who himself had used it. This could create tense dynamics characteristic of many artisanal-apprentice settings, including the reluctance to fully share specialist knowledge and the need to "steal" the master's secrets. It certainly disrupted the normal lines of pedagogical authority in a corporate-style organization.

A final challenge when using baseball to demonstrate and consolidate corporate authority is what we might term the embarrassing propensity toward failure, at least the failure to win. The odds against winning consistently in a team sport like baseball are high. In every contest, obviously, half the players are winners, but over the season, only one team will emerge as champion; the other eleven teams will all end the season in defeat. This specter of losing in such frequent, highly visible, and easily quantifiable fashion puts a constant strain on team morale, company image, and corporate authority claims. There are ways of deflecting attention, but it is one more reminder of how hard the powerful must work to remain dominant. This was especially true for Hanshin, where both exposure and defeat were constant in the quality of life.

CHAPTER 4

In the Dugout

Manager and Coaches

Look again at the 1996 Tigers team photo (figure 9 in chapter 3) and you will see, sitting front and center, the manager (kantoku), Fujita Taira, surrounded by his large coaching staff.[1] At first glance, it is an impressive array of hierarchy and authority relations: the domain lord flanked by his lieutenants and sitting at the center of his players/troops. Indeed, Yoshida had been a Hall of Fame shortstop in his long career as a Hanshin player, from 1953 to 1969, and one of his nicknames was Ushi-wakamaru, the childhood name of a famous twelfth-century warrior general, Minamoto no Yoshitsune. The samurai moniker hinted at a metaphorically military quality to the team leadership in a contest that took place on the playing field against a rival team led by its own domain lord/manager.

There is more than meets the eye in this photograph. Absent in the picture but powerfully present in the background were two higher levels of command. These were the front office of Hanshin club officials and above them, the parent company, the Hanshin Electric Railway Corporation, whose officials from the CEO down took an active interest in the affairs of the club. Every club in NPB was a complex chain of command, running upward from the team's field staff to the club front office to the parent company, and these next two chapters analyze this three-tiered corporate hierarchy. This chapter focuses on the manager and his coaches—those in uniforms who orchestrated the players and the game from the dugout. Chapter 5 pairs an account of the front office with that of the parent company, the two white-collar workplaces. The line from parent company to club front office to the team was indeed a hierarchy of authority, but the relationships between the "suits" of the company and club and the "uniforms" of the team turned out to be much more intricate.

The Hanshin Tigers have been notorious for decades for manager turnover. In the eight years between 1996 and 2003, Hanshin went through four managers (a fifth was named late in 2003 for the next season). Their average tenure, two years, was just short of the historical mean. In the sixty-seven years between 1950 and 2017, there were twenty-five managerial changes involving twenty-two men.[2] Eighteen of these managers were ex-Hanshin Tigers players, usually with long careers, notable records, and popular reputations. Two of those without a Hanshin pedigree, Nomura and Hoshino Sen'ichi, served in the early 2000s, and I discuss them later. Two others were early anomalies in this overwhelming preference for Hanshin experience.[3]

This chapter uses brief profiles of the four managers of the 1996–2003 period to emphasize three themes about this position in the Hanshin Tigers sportsworld. Despite the popular image of the team manager as the "field general" commanding his players/troops, the Hanshin manager actually had to fill three quite distinct roles. To be sure, he managed the team and directed game strategy, but he also served as a public face of the Hanshin brand, and he functioned as a midlevel executive in a corporate hierarchy that extended from the subsidiary firm that was the team, through the front office, up to the CEO suite of the parent company. Baseball acumen, popularity, and corporate deference coexisted uneasily and presented all of the managers with difficult challenges.

Exacerbating this trio of expectations, which applied to all NPB managers, was the endemic inbred mentality of Hanshin, which continually looked to its own for its managers. Whatever the benefits of this mutual familiarity, the cost was decades of factional infighting among rival ex-players and their supporters, and that is a second theme here. The composite demands of being a manager and Hanshin's infighting raise a third issue, just what these managers could and should have done. The manager was the one person in uniform on the field who could not swing a bat or run the bases. He managed but did not actually play. For what was he responsible? For how much of a team's success and failure should he be held accountable? This is a perennial debate in professional team sports. That it has never been satisfactorily resolved has not protected managers from being first on the firing line. There are uncanny parallels between players' performance and their staged salary negotiations and managers' responsibility and their much more public hiring and firing rituals. The fundamental indeterminacy of managerial accountability added to the melodramatic and moral qualities of these rituals.

EIGHT YEARS, FIVE MANAGERS

During my eight years of active fieldwork, I saw five managers come and go. As I have noted before, these changes corresponded to one of the worst stretches of league finishes in Hanshin history—five last-place finishes, one next-to-last finish, and one fourth-place finish——before the team rose to take the league title in 2003. This dismal record only heightened the pressure on and the vulnerability of the team manager.[4]

Fujita Taira (July 1995 to September 1996)

Fujita had been drafted out of high school in 1966 and played for Hanshin for eighteen years. When he retired in 1984, just before the 1985 championship season, he was quickly hired as a commentator for Asahi Broadcasting. After ten years in the baseball media, he was brought back to Hanshin in 1995 as farm team manager. The manager at the time, Nakamura, had been a teammate of Fujita, and Nakamura was coming under much criticism from the front office about Hanshin's dismal record. The team was headed for its third last-place finish in five years under Nakamura.

Nakamura was known in the sports press as an "office worker manager" (*sararīman kantoku*) for his uncomplaining deference to front office directives, and the club president at the time, Miyoshi, was interested in Fujita because he thought Fujita would show more initiative and bring more real baseball experience and judgment to the role. Nakamura was persuaded to take a leave of absence midway through the 1995 season, and Fujita became acting manager (which did not stop the Tigers' slide into another last-place finish). He was formally elevated to manager before the 1996 season and was immediately caught up in controversies and tensions. Although his years as a commentator had given him a broader analytical perspective on the game than he had in his playing years, he began with no coaching or managing experience beyond those months in 1995.

Fujita had a hot temper (this is why he was nicknamed the "devil manager" or *oni kantoku*), and the sports papers began to uncover and play up player dissatisfactions. They wrote that the team had little respect for Fujita and that the players had taken to calling his head coach Shibata Takeshi "manager" because the latter seemed to make most of the managerial decisions during the games. Early in the season, Fujita sent several veteran players down to the farm team (which probably had to do with long-simmering factional struggles between Fujita and other OBs). He quickly soured on the two US players and dumped them without consulting the front office. He replaced them with two others, whom he quickly came to criticize in the press.

As the season wore on and the Tigers slid into the cellar, management lost patience, leading to the public drama I recounted in the first chapter about the marathon meeting Fujita had with the owner Kuma, Miyoshi, and seven other officials from the parent company and club on September 13.[5] Miyoshi asked for Fujita's resignation, which was the common form of severance, by which the manager took ritual responsibility for the team failure. Fujita, however, refused. He insisted that the team's woes were the fault of the club and parent company, not him, and tried to force the club to fire him. The meeting started at 5 o'clock in the afternoon, and Miyoshi assumed it would be a brief exchange, in time to make an announcement for the evening news deadlines. At 2:30 the next morning, Fujita was still agitated and resisting; with the reporters waiting outside, Miyoshi adjourned the meeting. The next day, September 14, Fujita finally relented and tendered a curt, formal resignation, leaving with a memorable quote for the papers: "Miyoshi is a fool" (*Miyoshi wa aho ya*)![6]

The drama surrounding Fujita played out over months, in fact throughout the entire season. It was a staple of sports papers (as shown in figure 2 in chapter 1), evening sports television news, and stadium fan talk, and it occasioned a wide range of opinion and commentary. However, it was, and remains, impossible to separate events from their varying interpretations; to give credence to some of the accounts; and most of all to determine who was to blame for specific incidents, the general slide in the team's performance, and the growing frictions that seemed to isolate Fujita and lead to his dismissal.

But that is not the point. Whether he had been "right" to punish Kameyama and Shinjō (see chapter 1), whether Shibata had "really" taken over game control, and whether Miyoshi really wanted Fujita to assume decision-making but then had second thoughts and backed away from his previous guarantees, the public trafficking in these stories and the kinds of stories they were are more telling than the relative truth value of any of the perspectives or versions. They were revealing and instructive of lines of authority; the expected forms of comportment; the particular fault lines of infighting; and the ways that several baseball workplaces, the media, and the surrounding readerships and spectatorships were drawn together.

Yoshida Yoshio (December 1996 to October 1999)

After Fujita's forced resignation, the five sports papers spent two months detailing the club's inner turmoil in selecting a new manager. It was widely presumed that the club would be picking from among four or five prominent ex-Hanshin players. As discussions between the club and company continued, it became clear that the sports papers were not only reporting but also subtly advancing the candidacies of one or another of these ex-players, often those who were signed as commentators to their own papers or affiliated broadcasting companies.

After two months, the parent company settled on Yoshida Yoshio, bringing him back for an unprecedented third term as manager. Yoshida's story was a popular one among Kansai baseball fans. He had been born in 1931 in rural poverty north of the city of Kyoto and raised by his mother and older brother. He played baseball in the village and at school, and his prowess got him into a prestigious private university in Kyoto. He was drafted by Hanshin during his freshman year in 1953 and immediately became its starting shortstop. He remained in that role for a standout career of seventeen years, retiring in 1969 and eventually being elected to the Baseball Hall of Fame. After his playing days, he followed a friend's advice and spent part of each year for five years studying MLB baseball in the United States. He was appointed Hanshin manager in 1975, but the team didn't finish above the middle of the standings in his three years. He was brought back for a second term as manager in 1985, and this time, in a miracle season that stands as the high point of any Hanshin history, he led the Tigers to their very first and still only Japan Series title (see figure 11).

That would seem to make his selection in 1996 easy to justify, but there were other complicating circumstances. Yoshida's success in 1985 was not unalloyed. Some club and media people complained that he had simply been lucky in 1985 in having a strong team in a year with weak rivals; as proof, they noted that the Hanshin team had fallen back

FIGURE 11. Hanshin players tossing manager Yoshida in the air while celebrating their 1985 Japan Series championship. Credit: Yomiuri Newspaper Company.

into mediocrity the very next year, and in 1987 registered its worst finish in team history. Yoshida went back to media commentary; in 1989 he went to Pairs to begin what became a six-year stint leading the French national baseball team, residing in Paris for half of each year and trying to promote baseball in a country that had little experience and enthusiasm for the sport. This took him away from Hanshin and Japanese baseball, and some wondered if that, as well as his age, made him an effective choice in 1996. Yoshida himself wasn't particularly drawn to a third chance. But club president Miyoshi supported him, and the parent company's CEO personally implored him to take up the challenge of re-creating a 1985-like recovery.

That was not to be. The club had promised it would try to build up the player ranks, but its campaign to sign Kiyohara Kazuhiro, one of the reigning stars of the era, failed (he chose the Giants instead), and then the front office suffered the public indignity of the Mike Greenwell fiasco (see chapter 3). The team languished all season, finishing fifth out of sixth, and then in 1999 once again fell to the cellar. There were no especially explosive controversies during this period, but there was continual griping from some players and front office staff. The sports media's tone was critical and dismissive, and there were occasional outbursts from the fans (thrown megaphones, jeering, surrounding the team bus, etc.).

Nomura Katsuya (October 1999 to December 2001)

As the 1999 season drew to a close, it was obvious that neither the club nor Yoshida wanted him to continue, and the sports press started gearing up for another campaign among the same cohort of ex-Hanshin players. The familiar narrative was disrupted when Kuma personally intervened again to woo one of the most highly regarded baseball managers of his generation, Nomura Katsuya. Nomura was even more celebrated than Yoshida. He had had a similar hardscrabble Kansai childhood. He had played his way onto another Osaka team, the Nankai Hawks, as an unsalaried trainee and had risen to become probably the greatest catcher in Japan's history. He had already been a manager for the Hawks and for the Yakult Swallows for a total of seventeen years. His Swallows teams won the Pacific League title four times in the 1990s and went on to win the Japan Series in three of those years. Although he had had no connections to Hanshin, it was not only Nomura's success and his eminence but also his lifelong, caustically expressed dislike of the Yomiuri Giants that excited Kuma and won over any Hanshin doubters.[7]

Nomura had a well-developed sense of public relations and immediately charmed Kansai media and fans. He took up residence in a penthouse suite in the just-opened five-star Ritz-Carlton Hotel. Upon becoming manager, he immediately started issuing a phrase a day (which the press published as the "Analects of Nomura" or Nomura *goroku*), and he deftly held court with reporters before and after games, propounding his particular brand of baseball. I witnessed many of his before-game sessions, and he struck me as profound and pompous in equal measure, part baseball sage and part self-help guru, lacing his gruff but charming commentaries with precise data and vague philosophy of life maxims.

In breaking the lineage of Hanshin-pedigreed managers, he was endowed with the savior qualities of the foreign player-mercenary. Given the high (and what most staff said privately were unattainable) expectations of him, his public relations style was masterful (and apparently deliberate). He fed the insatiable media, hogged the spotlight, and

FIGURE 12. Front page article covering the expanding product endorsements of the recently appointed Hanshin manager, Nomura Katsuya. *Nikkan Sports*, Osaka edition, January 20, 1999, 1. Courtesy of Nikkan Sports Newspaper.

drew attention away from the players so that they could escape the daily scrutiny.

Nomura was also an economic boon to the depressed Kansai economy, not just in direct revenues to Hanshin, but in several dozen product endorsements that were quickly arranged (see figure 12). A bevy of wealthy Kansai businessmen formed a Nomura supporters' club, and rival department stores embarked on multiple sales campaigns to draw on his popularity. The most ostentatious example of the commercial fever was the commissioning of 50-gram 24-carat-gold statues of Nomura that were put on sale for ¥1 million (about US$8,400).

Alas, the team did not improve. Nomura lasted three seasons, and Hanshin finished in the cellar every year. Thus, in the six years between 1995 and 2001, the team finished in last place five times and next to last once. Futility and frustration continued, but it was not Nomura's record as manager that ended his Hanshin tenure. Rather, it was another major controversy, played out in the media (and the courts) over several years, regarding massive financial fraud by his wife, Sachiyo. Nomura Sachiyo ran the family business operations, which had become extensive, and by 2000 rumors were circulating that she was under investigation for tax evasion. Details dripped out regularly, and while it appeared to most analysts that her husband had little or no knowledge of what she had done, when she was finally arrested in the fall of 2001, she was indicted on multiple counts of tax evasion and business fraud on the order of $8 to $10 million. Kuma, who had hoped to sign Nomura to a fourth year despite the team's record, bowed to the inevitable and accepted Nomura's resignation.

Hoshino Sen'ichi (December 2001 to November 2003)

Once again Kuma put himself in charge of the manager search, and once again he made an appeal to yet another outsider candidate, Hoshino Sen'ichi. Hoshino too had been a Hall of Fame player; he had been a long-serving, successful manager of one of Hanshin's toughest Central League rival teams, the Chūnichi Dragons, and if anything, he was even more stridently "anti-Giants" than Nomura. His hatred dated back to 1968, when the Giants promised him he would be their number one draft pick but then selected someone else. He went on to a Hall of Fame career as a pitcher for the Dragons, based in Nagoya, Japan's fourth largest city, a team that felt trapped and lost between the Tokyo-Osaka rivalry but seemed to direct most of its animosity toward Tokyo (perhaps because the Dragons had usually outperformed Hanshin easily in the decades since the 1970s). Hoshino was famously hotheaded and always rose to the occasion of pitching against the Giants. If anything, his selection as manager was greeted by the front office, press, and fans even more warmly than the appointment of Nomura.

It was really under Hoshino that Hanshin began to pull itself out of its decades-long doldrums. In his first season, he managed to guide the team to a fourth-place finish and then, with Kuma's authority to override the front office, he used the off-season to pare the roster and sign two major stars, the outfielder Kanemoto Tomoaki and the pitcher Irabu Hideki. After beginning his career in the Pacific League, Irabu was one of the first Japanese players to jump to MLB, signing with the New York Yankees for the 1997 season. His tenure in MLB was controversial and his record mediocre, but Hoshino was able to use him very effectively in 2003. Kanemoto had been the leading hitter for Hiroshima Carp for eleven years and made an even bigger impact for Hanshin in 2003, Hoshino's second season, when he took the Tigers to the league championship. (I return to this turning point in chapter 10.) Hoshino was very sick for much of the 2003 season, a condition that the normally quick to expose sports press deliberately underplayed, and as the season ended, he announced that he was unable to return in 2004.[8]

Okada Akinobu (November 2003 to October 2008)

With Hoshino's departure, Hanshin turned again to one of its own, Okada Akinobu. On October 28, 2003, in the bittersweet aftermath of winning a league championship but losing the Japan Series, the Hanshin club held a news conference to announce the "transfer of authority" (using the political term *seiken kōkan*) from Hoshino to Okada. The two stood amicably in front of a gold screen, another symbol of ceremony and authority (see figure 13). No wonder everyone is beaming with self-satisfaction in the photograph; *Nikkan Sports* senior writer Terao Hirokazu noted in his interviews with Kuma (Terao 2004) that such a photograph had not been taken in fourteen years, going back to the Murayama-to-Nakamura transfer in 1989.

In picking Okada, the club returned to its preference for its own. Okada had played for Hanshin from 1980 to 1993 (and thus had that crucial pedigree of 1985). He had been traded to the Orix BlueWave for the final two years of his career, and after staying on with Orix as a coach, he returned to Hanshin in 1998 and served as a very successful farm team manager and coach until his selection as Hoshino's successor. He had a disappointing initial season after Hoshino's 2003 league championship, but he led the team to a second league championship in 2005, although Hanshin was beaten by the Chiba Lotte Marines in four

FIGURE 13. Front-page article depicting the new manager, Okada Akinobu (right), shaking hands with Hoshino Sen'ichi (left), who had just resigned because of illness. Hanshin owner Kuma Shunjirō is at center. *Nikkan Sports*, Osaka edition, October 29, 2003, 1. Courtesy of Nikkan Sports Newspaper.

games in the Japan Series. Still, his managerial tenure was marked by much less public dissent. He remained manager for another three years, taking the team to two second-place and one third-place finish. That is, Hanshin was an A-Class team, and one of the most common sayings of those years was that it had finally returned to being the "regularly winning team" (*jōshō kyūdan*) that it had been fifty years before. Okada's tenure coincided with a number of other fundamental changes in club and parent company organization, and indeed with significant changes in the larger baseball world (I return to these in chapter 10).

THE THREE HATS OF A MANAGER: FIELD GENERAL, NAME BRAND, AND DEPARTMENT HEAD

The dominant image of the Japanese manager is that of a feudal domain lord, enjoying a secure tenure and absolute authority, often unwarranted by his personal leadership abilities but secured through the small, clubby networks of ex-players through which he scrambles. This is reinforced by television coverage of games, which constantly intercut the action on the field with close-up shots of the rival kantoku, standing resolutely on the front step or sitting impassively in the first seat of the dugout, intensely following the plays, appearing to bark orders or give a strategy sign. He is featured in pregame and postgame media interviews.

Even the cursory profiles of Hanshin's four managers in the 1996–2003 period demonstrate that this image of strength, stability, and security masks a far more diverse reality. It is indeed the case that managers in Japan have long been drawn from the small pool of famous ex-players, often valuable to the club as the faces of the team (as television and print media reinforce daily). Yet with a few notable exceptions, their tenures have been short; career loyalty to a single team has been the exception (except with Hanshin); their authority is usually hemmed in by player egos below and corporate intrusions from above; and their personalities and managing styles have varied widely over the seven decades of the professional sport. They have been often admired, sometimes feared, but seldom envied and frequently embattled.

One root of the dilemma is that, in baseball as in all sports, there is no direct correlation between success as a player and competence as a manager. It is even argued by baseball people in both Japan and the United States that ex-players of modest accomplishments and shorter careers will make more effective managers (and as a corollary, because this is much more the MLB pattern than the NPB pattern, that managers in America are generally more competent and "professional" than their Japanese counterparts). The usual explanations are that often the most successful players may have worked hard, but because of their superior talents they haven't had to reflect as much on what it takes to succeed as have the struggling players; they have been the center of attention and therefore have not had the need or opportunity to study the wide range of positions and talents that any team requires; and as star players they simply haven't spent as much time on the bench watching the games and watching the manager direct the games. No doubt there is some truth to these assertions, although structural differences of the professional game in the two countries are also critical. In particular, the extensive tiers of minor league teams in the United States allow not only for player development but also for training and assessing coaches and managers. In NPB, there is but a single preparatory level, that of farm team manager.

Every game day, the manager had as full a schedule as an upper management executive, with the added pressures of public appearances. His principal responsibilities were the following:

- He held multiple pregame meetings with coaches and trainers and front office staff.
- He had to stand behind the backstop during afternoon warm-ups, be seen, and be available to coaches and senior media.
- He had to give pregame and postgame interviews to print and usually broadcast media (and frequently special one-on-one interviews).
- He had to be visible and vigilant throughout the game, standing on the dugout steps in the gaze of the television camera.
- He had to make occasional strategic decisions during the game, such as directing the pitcher to throw a particular pitch, ordering a defensive shift or a steal attempt, and changing pitchers.

The manager's strategic interventions fell far short of controlling the game or even orchestrating his team's play. His coaches were therefore necessary intermediaries with players. They were lieutenants in a military idiom, but in a corporate idiom, the head coach functioned as the assistant department head (*fuku-buchō*), and the coaches were the various section chiefs (*kakarichō*).[9]

Equally critical but less obvious were the limits on the manager's role in preparation and in human resource management. All of the managers discussed here supervised daily practices, decided game lineups, and controlled playing time and the movement of players between the major league team and the farm team. On the other hand, all of them had very limited input into the composition of the team roster itself; on trades, signings, and drafts; on player salary negotiations; and on other matters that were largely decided by the front office. Season by season, each of them had to work with the team he was given, and his success was dependent on those personnel, on the actual performances of the players themselves, and on the highly unpredictable fortunes of injury. During the September 1996 commotion in which Fujita was fired, the *Nikkan Sports* columnist Enoki Takeshi used a culinary analogy. Fujita, Enoki wrote, felt that if there weren't good ingredients, even the best cook couldn't prepare a quality meal (*Nikkan Sports*, September 4, 1996, page 2). The front office view, on the contrary, was that an excellent cook should be able to prepare a feast even with mediocre ingredients!

In these respects, the Hanshin manager's position was as exposed and vulnerable as the foreign players': highly visible, set apart, with oversized expectations, and serving as an obvious target as a kind of designated sacrifice when the season's fortunes turned sour. In one respect, however, the manager's position was the inverse of the foreign mercenary's. Among all the NPB clubs, Hanshin stood out for the management's strong preference to hire managers from among the club's former players. The Japanese term for this is *haenuki* (homegrown). In rice agriculture, the connotation is favorable (an indigenous species), but with Hanshin, it stood for hidebound and parochial. As we will see, this preference has created intense factionalism in the Hanshin world among networks of ex-players and media that support one or another managerial candidate and work to amplify the manager controversies and shorten managerial tenure.

The club and company ownership had another preference as well, and that was for university-educated managers. Almost all Hanshin team managers over the decades have been players who moved from high school to university before being drafted into the professional ranks. Not all were graduates; Yoshida, for example, was drafted onto Hanshin before he could graduate from Ritsumeikan in Kyoto. The front office explanation for this preference was not that such managers could present a better public image, but that they would be taken more seriously by the front office and company executives they had to deal with. One deleterious effect of this preference, however, was that the manager could be further drawn into the university alumni factions that were found among the offices. It is to these higher levels and their workplaces that we now turn.

CHAPTER 5

In the Offices

Front Office and Parent Corporation

INTRODUCTION

The Hanshin farm team usually played its games at midday, and after each game, the farm team manager telephoned or visited the main team manager to report on how his team and certain individual players had done. Similarly, the main team manager met daily with the club president to discuss the main team's circumstances. Finally, every Monday morning, the club president traveled by company car from the stadium front offices to the Hanshin Group headquarters office near Osaka's Umeda Station to report formally about the entire ball club to the chairman of the Hanshin Group, who was the designated owner of the club, which was one of thirty subsidiary companies within Hanshin Group. The media always followed the club president to his meeting and awaited a press conference or at least an announcement afterward. Mondays were rarely game days and thus were in need of some news filler.

This ritualized reporting up a chain of command to the very top represented the complicated mix of detachment and direct concern that bound the day-to-day fortunes of the ball team to the prestige of an entire corporate group. It was indicative of a widely recognized corporatization of Japanese professional baseball. Large transport and newspaper companies founded the seven teams of the first league in 1936, and this has remained the pattern of ownership for seventy years, by which the companies operate their clubs as subsidiary companies. The generic language of the Japanese business world, in which a "main company" or "parent company" has beneath it a family of "child companies," is used in the baseball world as well.

As a consequence, most teams have been named after their corporate owners, not the cities they play in. The Yakult Swallows, for instance, play their home games in Tokyo but were named after the Yakult beverage company that owns the team. The Hanshin Tigers of course were named for the parent company and not the city of Nishinomiya in which their stadium is located. Indeed, as of 1997, eleven of the twelve NPB teams were known by the corporate owner's name. American reporters and commentators have frequently criticized this practice as evidence that the Japanese don't really understand the true locality-based spirit of baseball.[1]

On closer examination, this turns out to be too simple a dismissal of NPB naming practices, which have shifted considerably over the eighty years since its one-league origins in 1936. The Tigers were first named the Osaka Tigers by Hanshin; the company had to change that to simply "Hanshin" (in Japanese characters) in 1940 when the government mandated eliminating English words from baseball (i.e., "Tigers"). Starting in 1946, the company reverted to Osaka Tigers, which remained the name until 1961, when the team became the Hanshin Tigers. Other clubs, including the Yomiuri Tokyo Giants, have experienced similar shifts over time. The trend in the last decade has been toward place-names, sometimes in combination with company names. The Hanshin Tigers have retained that name, but as we will see in chapter 9, Hanshin is more than the company's name. The five interurban railroad companies that competed in Osaka and Kansai throughout the twentieth century gave their names to the broad business and residential corridors that formed along their lines. To Kansai residents, Hanshin (and Hankyū, Kintetsu, etc.) are place-resonant names as well as company names.

Nonetheless, corporate ownership has generally been held to be a distinctive feature of NPB that distinguishes it from its American counterpart, which has largely been operated by wealthy individual businessmen, and it is argued by many to be the source of many of NPB's problems (Ikei 1991; Kitaya 1992; Kobayashi 2002). These Japanese corporations, it is said, have been content to run the clubs at a deficit, as public relations loss leaders, and they have not been driven by profit motive to produce winners at any cost. Baseball, to them, is a promotional expense;

from the early days, for example, tickets to Giants games have been distributed by Yomiuri newspaper deliverymen as thank-you gifts to their subscribers. This lack of true competitive spirit, the stereotype runs, is reinforced by the parent companies' constant meddling in club and team affairs, dispatching baseball-ignorant executives to the "child" club and preventing any true baseball expertise prevailing in club operations. Some commentators then explain this by an innate groupiness of Japanese society or by the sway that the corporate-organizational frame has held in the contemporary period.

All of this can lead to a rather glib notion that Japanese athletes are grim "men at work," whereas we Americans are the spirited "boys of summer." We "play ball" in the United States, but the Japanese "do baseball." As *The Economist* of London put it: "To Americans, baseball is all about enjoyment and sudden surprises; of spectacular hits, dexterous fielding and cheeky running between the bases. . . . To the Japanese, *yakyū* (field ball) is seen to this day as a martial art to be practised remorselessly to perfection and then grimly executed with the sole purpose of crushing one's opponent" (*Economist* 1996:104). *The Economist* has hardly been alone in disparaging the Japanese "workaholic" sportsmen, whose relentless effort, self-sacrifice, and exacting discipline turn even play into work, while presenting the image of American professional athletes, fun-loving "playboys," retaining a truly ludic sporting spirit.

Like many characterizations of the Japanese version, such an image draws our attention away from some of the subtler and more interesting commonalities and differences. Certainly when observing the sport domestically, most US baseball analysts and fans readily recognize the sport as a business, and a very big business at that. The "boys of summer" was Roger Kahn's famous characterization of the Brooklyn Dodgers (1972), but "men at work" was the title of George Will's equally compelling 1990 book of baseball essays. The umpire may shout "play ball!," but the owners and players are always thinking "pay ball." The long history of court cases and player union strikes in MLB contradicts such cozy stereotyping.

In both the United States and Japan, baseball is and has always been a business (that's why we call it a professional sport). And it is simplistic to contrast individual entrepreneurs like Connie Mack and George Steinbrenner with faceless corporations like Yomiuri and Seibu. In fact, the world of Japanese baseball has always been shaped by strong executives within the companies acting imperiously and autocratically, such as the Giants' Shōriki and his successor Watanabe Tsuneo, Seibu's Tsu-

tsumi Yoshiaki, and Hanshin's CEO, Kuma Shunjirō. Nor have MLB clubs been entirely free from corporate ownership and intrusive management.[2] Clearly, like the playing field, the executive level features a constant struggle between team and company imperatives and individual talent and ambition.

Thus, both Japanese and American ballplayers are "ball-workers," but I think that there is an important difference in how baseball is seen as a business in the two countries, and that is what I highlight in this chapter. When academics and journalists (and fans) analyze the business of baseball in the United States, they usually look at the economics of the sport. They focus on such issues as team ownership, television broadcast contracts, stadium finance deals, free agency, salary caps, and contract clauses. They are less inclined than Japanese spectators and commentators to consider baseball teams as workplaces and baseball clubs as work organizations. In contrast, many Japanese understandings of baseball as a professional sport are built around a clearer recognition that baseball teams are workplaces, and that they are constructed socially of work relations and ideologically of work authority claims. In that sense, Japanese ballplayers are literally "men at work" and not just working men.

For over four decades, from the mid-1960s to the early 2000s, the two sports teams in all of Japan that garnered the most public attention and following were the Yomiuri Giants and the Hanshin Tigers. Their organizational differences were as sharp as the rivalry between them, reflecting two realities. The spotlight on Yomiuri was national, while the Hanshin spotlight, of the same wattage, was regional. The Yomiuri parent company was a powerful megacorporation in its own right, profiting from but hardly dependent upon its team. In contrast, for the Hanshin parent company, the subsidiary club was a never-ending drain on corporate nerves, yet the Tigers were the single corporate asset most vital to the company's survival. Were it not for the Tigers, it is hard to imagine that Hanshin would have survived as long as it did as a corporation. The club has simultaneously been a public relations bonanza and nightmare. With Yomiuri, the dog wagged the tail; with Hanshin, the tail wagged the dog.

THE FRONT OFFICE: WHERE THE UNIFORMS MEET THE SUITS

The manager ran the team of players, but the team itself was folded within the Hanshin Tigers club (kyūdan), which was headed by a president (*shachō*) and operated the team through a large staff. The club was more commonly called the furonto, or front, from the MLB term front office.

Front office, though, was a double misnomer in the case of Hanshin. First, it was the players, not the club staff, who were front and center in the public eye; they had far greater prestige and made far better salaries, and the front office tried hard to remain behind the scenes. Moreover, the front office itself was backstage. At Kōshien, the front office was literally hidden under the right-field bleachers in a long suite of bland offices on the second floor of the stadium. The drab furnishings, linoleum flooring, and grey-metal desks—many pushed together in groups with the work section name posted above them—were indistinguishable from business offices throughout Japan. At times when I was sitting in the bleachers I asked my fellow spectators where they thought the front office was, and many had no idea they were actually sitting on top of it!

Front office employees would sometimes complain to me that their jobs were even harder than those of the players. Like subsidiary companies everywhere, they were caught between and at the mercy of the heavy demands and constant intrusions of the parent company, on the one hand, and the performance of the players over which the front office had only limited control (and even less success) on the other. Baseball was once a six-month job, for the staff as well as for the players. It remained seasonal in the popular imagination, but it was a grinding year-round job now, and if anything, the office staff had less personal time and space than the players.

By the 1980s, Hanshin had grown into one of the largest front offices in NPB, with a staff of more than seventy men and women. Its organizational chart for the late 1990s and early 2000s divided it into four rather generically named divisions (see figure 14). We can best appreciate the corporate nature of its organization by looking briefly at the composition and duties of each division and its constituent departments and groups.

The General Affairs Division handled the financial matters of the club—both budgets and accounts. It had the final say over all initiatives (salary budgets, trades, new facilities, etc.) because it could extend or withhold the money. It was also the division most closely tied to the parent company, because its senior members were largely midlevel managers with financial backgrounds in the parent company, dispatched for multiyear assignments to the club (*shukkō* was the Japanese term, again, common in the business world). Two of the division's three

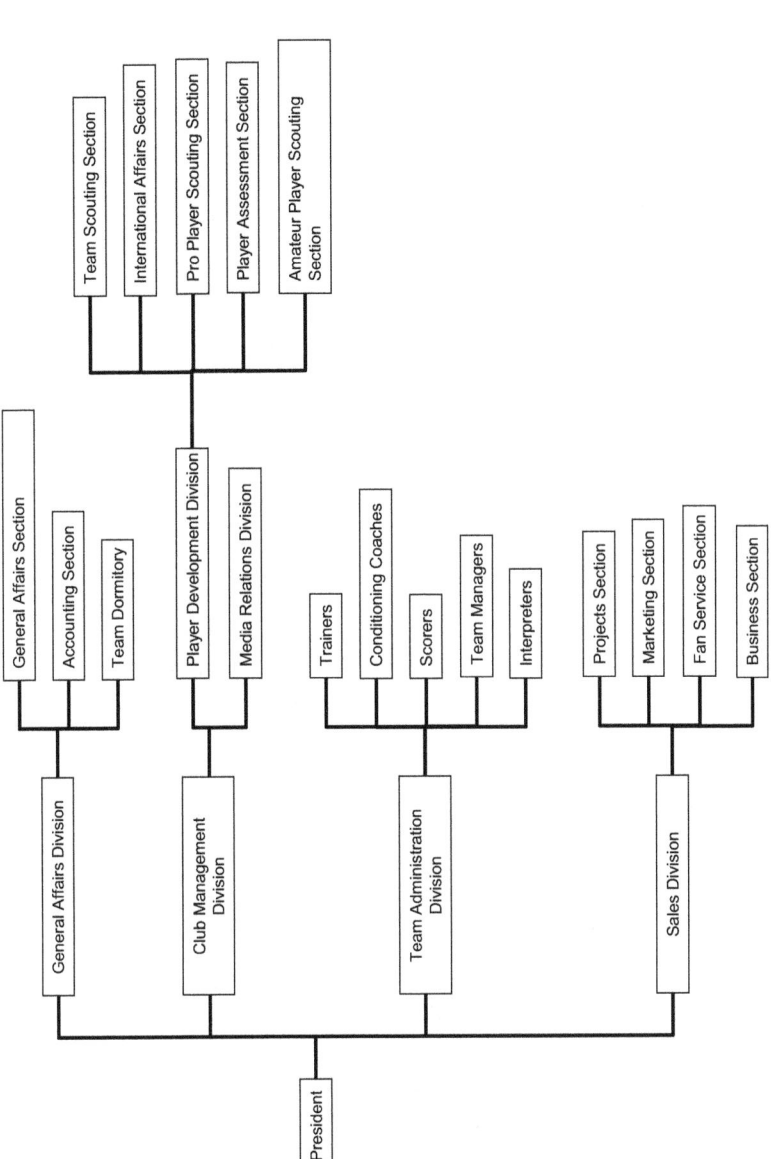

FIGURE 14. Organizational chart of the Hanshin Tigers front office, 1999. Based on author interviews with front office staff.

sections, General Affairs and Accounting, did most of the work; the former controlled all financial planning and had greater prestige.

The Sales Division divided its jurisdiction into four sections. The Business Section handled the general paperwork of the division; the most critical task of the Projects Section was to sell the team's television broadcast rights and branding rights and to manage all commercial ventures of the team, the players, and the manager. Executives dispatched from the parent company ran both of these sections. The two or three employees of the Fan Service Section were charged with promotional duties such as arranging pregame ceremonies, charity events like golf tournaments, and the annual Fan Appreciation Day. This section was also the liaison with the many clubs and support associations formed around individual players (from their hometown or school), and they hired and supervised the two mascots and the "cheer girls." The Marketing Section produced the glossy monthly fan magazine and managed the club's home page, which offered animated play-by-play coverage of games and other services. Probably its most difficult responsibility was to work with the stadium ticket office in handling the block ticket sales to the private fan associations.

The other two front office divisions had larger staffs and more directly managed the team itself. The less powerful of the two, the Team Administration Division, brought together the various logistical support staff for baseball operations. These included the managers (the equivalent of "traveling secretaries" in MLB parlance), the equipment men, the trainers and physical conditioning staff, the scorers, and one or two interpreters for foreign players. Most of these staff members did not have desks in the front office itself but worked in rooms closer to the team. As befit their intermediary status, they wore Hanshin-logo athletic wear, neither the white shirts and ties of the rest of the front office nor the real uniforms of the players.

Two of these team administrative categories deserve special note. In recent years, Hanshin had maintained a staff of five trainers. The chief trainer had been with the club for over twenty years and had studied in the United States with sports medicine specialists there. The trainers provided daily treatment for chronic and acute injury assessment and therapy (e.g., massages, steam and whirlpool baths) and preparation for games (bandaging and wrapping, etc.). The chief trainer was present in the dugout during all games to provide immediate care and assessment. The trainers worked both with the coaching staff and with a cohort of specialist doctors that the club had on retainer.

Throughout my years of fieldwork, I heard continuing debate within the club, among the players, and between the trainers themselves about the deficiencies of NPB trainer expertise and certification and overreliance on older methods. I certainly lack any qualification for judging these concerns, but I did quickly appreciate just how critical and how sensitive was the intermediary role the trainers occupied. As I sat in the trainers' room at Kōshien and at Tiger Den for many days, it was evident that, together, the trainers had more collective knowledge about the players and their psychological and physical condition than anyone else in the Hanshin Tigers sportsworld. Chronic and acute injuries were a condition of life for every player, but the tensions between denial and acknowledgment, between understanding and misunderstanding the nature of the injuries, were managed quite differently. Players wanted to disguise injuries from the coaching staff (and often each other and even themselves), but they also needed treatment. They depended on the trainers for attention and discretion. On the other hand, the coaching staff needed accurate assessments of player conditions for game management and relied on the trainers for discrete and privileged intelligence. The trainers were caught in the middle and repeatedly had to weigh the interests of the players against the interests of the team and the club.

The other staff category within the administrative division of particular interest was the scorers. The title is misleading because their actual responsibility was intensive, detailed data gathering. There were upward of eight to ten scorers during my years of fieldwork, and they were all are ex-Hanshin players, usually with limited careers but found to have good observational and analytical talents. At least two scorers sat in one of the small observation rooms behind home plate and kept detailed records throughout each game, charting every pitch, the course of each ball, the defensive setups on every play, and so forth (Miyake 2012, 2013; see examples at https://professional.wwkelly.net/ht). Their records, together with the video taken by other scorers, were the primary data for analysis and planning by the coaching staff. Other scorers traveled to do advance scouting of the team's next two opponents, collecting similar data.

The size of the scorer contingent and the details of their data gathering fed the prolonged game preparations supervised by the coaching staff, resulting in frequent meetings and strategy sessions with groups of players almost every day throughout the season. There were some on the team, and certainly among foreign sports commentators, who felt the number of meetings and sessions was excessive, especially when the entire season was played against the same five teams. However, several coaches and scouts explained the need for these meetings to me as arising from the larger numbers of roster players who needed basic training in fundamentals and strategies (and, I would add, the larger number of coaches who need something to do).

The fourth division of the front office, the Club Management Division, was the most powerful in the club and the core of most criticism and controversy. On the formal chart, it was divided into two departments (oddly, also termed divisions or *bu*, although they were subordinate on the chart). The Media Relations Division worked primarily with the press clubs of regular beat reporters and photographers, managing the daily volume of interview requests from other media and trying to put the right spin on stories. The club had had someone to handle press relations since the 1950s, but it was only in 1988 that it created a formal media relations staff. This was in the aftermath of the controversial firing of manager Yoshida, and the club realized what little control it had over the release of information. By the mid-1990s there were five members in the division. Below the department head were a full-time press officer delegated to the kantoku, two people who handled team media events and general press relations (interview and photo permissions, broadcast conditions, etc.), and another press officer who dealt directly with the players (e.g., getting them into the events and interviews). Club staff would occasionally muse with me about Hanshin buying a newspaper as Yomiuri and Chūnichi had done, so it would have at least one outlet it could control, but I never heard of any serious efforts to do this. Instead the media relations staff constantly enunciated (and as far as I could tell, practiced) a principle of even-handedness (*byōdō gensoku* was the term they used) with the various media groups.

However, the core of the Club Management Division was the Player Development Division. The name referred specifically to team development, and it was essentially the personnel department for recruiting and evaluating players. Its staff was subdivided into five areas of responsibility, formally designated as "sections" in the chart.

- The Team Scouting Section was really just one person, a baseball veteran, whose job was to provide overview assessments of team strengths and weaknesses for both Hanshin and the other eleven teams. He often delegated his administrative assistant to prepare the press book and other materials for the media.

- The several individuals in the International Affairs Section were charged with scouting and recruiting foreign players, primarily from the United States and the Caribbean. Given the club's lack of success in identifying effective foreign talent, these individuals often drew sharp criticism from both within and outside the club.

- The Pro Player Scouting Section handled player issues within the NPB ranks. Its primary duty was to scout for trades and free agents among the other eleven teams.

- The Player Assessment Section (consisting of Mr. Ishida and his assistant) did ongoing evaluations of all Hanshin players, primarily for contract negotiations at the end of each season.

- The Amateur Player Scouting Section was responsible for assessment and drafting from the amateur baseball worlds of high school, college, and the industrial leagues.

Such was the hierarchy of posts and distribution of responsibilities within the front office. Its large size was unusual, but the division of work and the taxonomy of posts were not much different from other NPB front offices or even many other moderately sized retail businesses. And beyond the organizational chart, many of the daily business routines were also generic to Japanese corporate life: the steady stream of conferences within and across units, the flow of decision-making upward rather than laterally, and the bookkeeping and budgetary procedures that followed parent company conventions. In form and activity, the Hanshin front office was a corporatized workplace—bureaucratic, hierarchical, and procedural—intermediate between the parent company above and the team below. As we will see, however, it was also a combustible mixture of employee types, caught in the middle between an often poorly performing team and an anxious and intrusive parent company.

KUMA SHUNJIRŌ: OWNER OF THE HANSHIN TIGERS BASEBALL CLUB

At the highest level of the parent company is an anomaly. Foreign observers frequently contrast the wealthy individuals (or families) who own and operate most MLB clubs with the large corporations that own all twelve NPB teams, usually as subsidiary companies. They generally do this to highlight the sometimes knowledgeable and committed, sometimes flamboyant and wasteful, entrepreneurial characters who run the US clubs with the faceless and distant corporations who manage Japanese clubs. This plays well to US-Japan stereotypes of individualism versus collectivism, but it ignores the fact that individuals—their talents, authority, egos, and personalities—loom large even in the upper echelons of Japanese baseball governance.

The Hanshin sportsworld is an apt case. In contrast to the steady flow of players and the frequent turnover in managers, the Hanshin club had a single, continuous "owner" for two decades, from 1984 through 2004. This was Kuma Shunjirō, who for most of those two decades was the president and then chairman of the board of the Hanshin Electric Railway Corporation (Hanshin Dentetsu). He assumed his positions as president and owner in the winter of 1984 as the result of company turmoil, and he was thus fortunate to preside over the team's magnificent 1985 Japan Series championship season. Kuma was a lightning rod for criticism for the next seventeen years of Hanshin "stagnation" and finally resigned in 2004, caught up in a scandal about under-the-table payments to a prospective draft player (he is shown standing in the center of figure 13 in chapter 4).

I placed the word *owner* in quotes above because it is an official title (*ōnā*). All twelve of the NPB clubs were legally owned by corporations, but for the purposes of league governance, a single individual within the corporation was designated as owner and represented the corporation on the NPB executive Owners' Council.[3] This was far more than ceremonial. In most cases, the designated owner was the company president (CEO or shachō). Occasionally it was the company chairman of the board (the *kaichō*, a more exalted position, usually filled by a former CEO); more rarely, it was delegated to a very senior executive just below the president. The NPB Owners' Council wielded enormous power, ceding little to the commissioner and the league presidents. This group of privileged individuals represented their corporate interests, but the distance from American professional leagues, where wealthy owners have similar oversight and judicial powers, was not as great as many commentaries claim. Over the years before and during my fieldwork, Kuma and the Giants' owner, Watanabe, were the two most powerful and newsworthy members of the Owners' Council.

Kuma was born in Kobe in 1921 but went to high school in Kochi in Shikoku (hence Hanshin's commitment to its spring training camp in that Shikoku prefecture). He entered the prestigious law faculty of the

(Imperial) University of Tokyo during the Pacific War years; his class was graduated early to enter officer training, and he joined a naval unit just at the end of the war. He joined Hanshin in 1946 and rose through the ranks for thirty-five years before assuming the CEO position. Most of his career was spent in finance and accounting. He had little operational experience and no connections to the baseball club subsidiary.

Kuma was certainly a favorite target of criticism—even derision and anger—from the sports media and Kansai fans. By his own admission, he knew little about the baseball club when he was designated its owner in 1984, but he had the good fortune to assume that role in time for Hanshin's only Japan Series championship in his first year. To some in the media he remained ignorant of baseball affairs but constantly intruded upon matters big and small, especially managerial changes, front office affairs, and selection of foreign players. Critics charged that he was secretive and arrogant in these executive decisions (see, e.g., Rokusaisha henshūbu 1997). Others characterized him as tirelessly concerned about the poor fortunes of the club but judicious in trying to balance the resource needs of the team against other significant financial commitments of the group. In Kansai business circles, Kuma was much respected for remaining very conservative during the mid-1980s bubble economy, when most of the other companies in transportation, leisure, retail, and transport undertook highly speculative investments and projects. The national and regional economy's slowdown in the early 1990s caused widespread damage to this sector; Hanshin was one of the very few companies that escaped unscathed. Kuma was also known for his attention to and skill in handling company labor negotiations, and Hanshin Dentetsu had a reputation for rather smooth management-labor relations. As CEO and then chairman of the board, he primarily emphasized the group's master plan to develop the Nishi-Umeda area to the west of Umeda Station as a large corporate business-retail complex.

It was impossible for me to assess the merits of the charges and the broader chorus of criticisms. I never had a direct conversation with Mr. Kuma. By the late 1990s, he rarely came to the stadium, and he was very elusive in public. The media were required to submit questions to his office in writing, and he (or most likely his staff) answered via fax. Indeed, all of the top parent company executives avoided direct contact with the sports press—and with this visiting anthropologist. My only substantive evidence of his own perspective was a very long speech he delivered about Hanshin in January 1993 (Kuma 1994) and an extended interview with Terao Hirokazu, a senior *Nikkan* sportswriter, that he gave after his retirement and that appeared as a seven-part series in *Nik-kan Sports* (Terao 2004). Throughout the years, the more private and elusive Kuma became, the more public and strident were the voices in the Tigers sportsworld that blamed him for team failures and club dysfunctions (see, e.g., Rokusaisha henshūbu 1999). Whether he was the real villain or a quiet steward of Hanshin's interests and image is impossible to determine, but he played a continuous and central part in the ongoing stories about the company.

HANSHIN ELECTRIC RAILWAY CORPORATION: THE PARENT COMPANY

Kuma was the designated owner of the Hanshin baseball club, but structurally of course, the club was a subsidiary company of the Hanshin Electric Railway. The parent corporation still operated its original railway line, but its subsidiaries included a wider range of businesses, primarily in transportation (buses, taxis, and freight), retail (a department store), and leisure (baseball, an amusement park, golf ranges). Collectively, it styled itself as the Hanshin Group, but its architecture was more that of a patriarchal family, in which the many subsidiary "child companies" operated below the "parent" corporation.

Hanshin Dentetsu, the parent, was itself organized along familiar corporate lines. The highest authority was vested in the chairman of the board, who often ascended to this position after serving as company president, the chief operating officer. There were three or four company vice presidents and a board of company directors (from twenty to twenty-five).[4] Each subsidiary company also had a board of directors, and this enabled the interlocking directorates that are prominent social bonds in Japanese corporate networks and that greatly affected Hanshin club operations. Many of the parent company directors were sprinkled among the boards of the various child companies. Three of the Hanshin club's seven directors were appointments from the parent company. A clear measure of the Tigers' importance to its parent company was that unlike in any of the other thirty Hanshin subsidiaries, those three were the chairman, the president, and the principal managing director of the parent company.

Two of the aspects of corporate philosophy at Hanshin Dentetsu that had consequences for the ball club were its strong identity as a transportation company and its internal education credential hierarchy. The common view of Hanshin throughout its sportsworld was that the

Tigers were the most prominent feature of the Hanshin Group as well as its most important source of profit and prestige. Parent company executives and some commentators (important examples are Okada [2003], Ōtani [2003], and Tamaki [1991]) emphasized the opposite: that the Tigers were a valuable asset, but fundamentally Hanshin's core was as a transportation company, committed to a conservative business strategy that valued public safety and service. I thought that sounded like predictable corporate babble when I heard it, but it does explain the excessive caution that lay behind executive decisions about the team. I found it very telling in September and October 2003—as the Tigers finally rose above serial last-place finishes to take the league championship and as all of Kansai seemed to be caught up in Tigers fever—that the one place I did not see a single sign of the Tigers was in the lobby of the parent company headquarters. If I hadn't walked from Umeda Station through a maze of Hanshin sales billboards and Tigers-mania posters on storefronts and walkways, I would not have known that this was the company that was responsible for this regional celebration.

ARE THE TIGERS A LOSS LEADER, A PROFIT CENTER, OR A CAREER KILLER?

Like the other companies that own ball clubs, Hanshin always used its baseball team for internal company morale, public relations, and generally to "image-up" the Hanshin name. It may be that treating baseball as a loss leader denied clubs like Hanshin the expertise and resources necessary to compete effectively. But this has always struck me as somewhat illogical. Wouldn't a winning team be an attractive image for a corporation? It certainly was profitable for the Yomiuri Giants for many decades, for Seibu in the 1980s, for Yakult in the 1990s, and more recently for Rakuten. Part of the difficulty in determining the profitability of baseball for the owning corporations is the same problem that plagues economic analyses of American professional sports: the lack of transparency in club and league finances.

The Tigers may be a poor choice for resolving this debate, because some have argued that the Hanshin Dentetsu was unusually small among the baseball-owning corporations and depended heavily on the club's revenues and the team's brand. Hanshin baseball, as I put it previously, was the tail that wagged the Hanshin dog.

It is difficult to calculate the profitability of Hanshin baseball and how crucial its profits (or losses) were to the parent company. Like everything else about the Hanshin sportsworld, company and baseball club finances attracted scholarly as well as journalistic interest, but we still lack definitive analyses. The Tigers club was a stock company, but its stock ownership was not public, and therefore it was difficult to track its finances. The Hanshin Group did not disclose how it assigned income and charges among its constituent companies. In the case of the ball club, income largely came from stadium ticket revenue, broadcasting rights, and direct marketing and licensing of trademark goods. However, the stadium ticket revenue was divided between the club and Kōshien Stadium, which comes under the parent company's operations division, *jigyōbu*, and neither the proportion nor the rationale was publicly disclosed.

Given that most of the direct and indirect revenues were retained by Hanshin companies, club profitability was probably less critical than total Hanshin Group profits earned by operating the club. It was essential that the Tigers play at Kōshien Stadium and that Kōshien attract people who rode the Hanshin railroad, buses, and taxis to get to and from the stadium. The Tigers themselves and the stadium in which they played were highly valuable images, the most well-known and well-loved of all Hanshin assets. Sometimes those assets were quite financially lucrative, such as when the Tigers won the 1985 Japan Series and the 2003 and 2005 league championships. It is estimated that their 1985 championship may have increased Hanshin corporate revenues by as much as US$400 million (Kunisada 2002:60-62; Tamaki 1991:36–60).

The centrality of the Tigers to the economic viability of the parent company led me initially to think that the club would be a highly desirable assignment for elite-course managers. I soon learned that the opposite was the case from people inside and outside the organization. The Tigers were the quite public face of the company—but more so for their many troubles than for their successes. Many young fast-track management types wanted to stay away from such unwelcome limelight. They joined the company hoping to develop careers in the main transportation, marketing, and land development projects of the corporate group, and they expected that that would be their work. One group of Hanshin critics cited the case of a young fast-track manager who was posted to the Tigers but whose father objected so strenuously to friends in the company that the personnel department withdrew the assignment (Rokusaisha henshūbu 1996).

Reporters and even several employees told me that consequently, many who did go to the club were drawn from more problematic head-quarter types, including what in Japanese business parlance were "window watchers." A couple of journalists also alleged, more controversially, that some of the dispatched staff were drawn from among certain "transport" specialists (*un'yō*) in the company's project department and from those who served as personal assistants to high executives (*hisho*, or "secretaries," in Japanese corporate parlance). The former were in charge of rail line development and improvements, and this could lead to some shady behavior. Tamaki Michio pointed out to me that unlike a bus company, which can reroute itself around trouble, a train line must run as straight a route as possible; its stations and along-line development prospects are fixed and limited. If someone doesn't want to sell, the company needs to find ways of persuading them to do so. And if someone wants to cause trouble at a station or along a line, the company cannot just reroute its cars. Accidents happen with taxi operations; sometimes accidents and injuries are even staged for insurance claims. Such pressures are also part of department store construction plans or running the stockholders' annual meeting (and heading off the notorious *sōkaiya*, the individuals who buy a few shares of stock and show up at the meetings to try to make trouble and ask embarrassing questions). That is, the project types and the personal assistants are needed to do whatever the bosses don't want to be seen doing, and this leads to suspicions about connections with organized crime, the various yakuza groups that are present throughout the Kansai region.

These claims also were impossible for me to assess; they were of interest and relevance because they provided yet more story lines about company operations. It seemed to me that there were two other germane aspects of Hanshin Dentetsu and Kuma in particular. The first was the company's insistence that it operated—and had to operate—in the public interest as a transportation service. There was a long-standing and shared conservatism inherent in the private railroad companies of metropolitan Japan, which keenly felt themselves to be private companies with public responsibilities. They proudly projected self-images as private railroads that were competitive and profit making, in contrast to the national railroads and municipal transport agencies. At the same time, they felt they wore the mantle of corporations charged with the special public responsibility of transporting residents. They emphasized safety, efficiency, and cautious management as integral to their company images, and I came to think that Hanshin took that sense of mission seriously.

In addition, Kuma himself was well known and respected within the company and in Kansai business circles for remaining very conservative during the 1980s bubble economy, when most of the other companies in transportation, leisure, retail, and transport were getting into very speculative dealings. The Kansai economy suffered enormously in the 1990s in the aftermath of this ill-advised corporate behavior, but the Hanshin Group made it through with very little damage to its bottom line. Kuma was also known for his attention to and skill in handling company labor negotiations, and business reporters told me that Hanshin's reputation for smooth management-labor relations was accurate. Finally, as president and then board chairman, Kuma gave top priority and massive company funding to the master plan to develop the Nishi-Umeda area to the west of Umeda Station as a large corporate business-retail complex. In cooperation with other corporate groups, Osaka Garden City (recalling the popular prewar term for perimeter garden zones) did in fact come to fruition despite the continuing slump. The point is that there may be some basis to Kuma's defense that however popular the Tigers might be in the region and for the Hanshin image, corporate attention and financial resources have always been more limited than what the media and fans thought was necessary and deserved. The Hanshin Group was often criticized for its underinvestment in and its unimaginative marketing of the team.

At the same time, a persistent theme in Hanshin baseball was the continual interference of the parent company in club affairs.[5] What may seem on the surface to have been bickering between players, or between the manager and the front office, was often precipitated by the parent company lurking behind the scenes. I often heard complaints from front office and parent company staff about a pressing need for structural reform; I think they were open with me because they knew that their comments would not be made public, as opposed to occasions when they spoke to the press (in order to ensure that something would become public). To their credit, these individuals' complaints were often accompanied by suggestions about what should be done.

Sometimes they were motivated to take constructive action. Toward the end of the very trying 1999 season, as another last-place finish loomed, a longtime front office staff member drew up a memorandum to present to the club president, Miyoshi, identifying what he and others saw as key sources of Hanshin's problems. He was reluctant to give me a copy, but he did let me read it in his presence and discuss it with him. It seemed to me to be an astute identification of personnel weaknesses and concrete solutions: broadening the data-gathering duties of the scorers; giving the front office a larger role in educating younger players about how to handle their careers (coaches, he insisted, could handle their baseball education, but most of the young players were naive and immature about most life issues); upgrading scouting operations; better recruiting of interpreters and other staff; and rationalizing the system of pay and hours. He pointed out that the younger front office employees were working very long hours on a pay scale that was stacked against them. "There is just no relation between effort, talent, and remuneration," he argued. I told him that it sounded like he was really saying that the front office needed a real personnel department to do what such departments ideally do in major corporations: handle employee selection, training, and long-term career formation. He agreed; the club had a section called "Business," but it consisted of one employee.

Although the baseball clubs have always been operated by business companies, the corporatization of the clubs themselves was more recent and came from particular circumstances in the late 1960s and early 1970s. Staff numbers, sections, and responsibilities proliferated steadily, although not always logically, over several decades. They were corporate organizations, but they were seldom model corporate organizations, and the complications were fascinating to fans and frustrating to those who sought to manage and profit from sponsoring the sport.

THE SUITS VERSUS THE UNIFORMS: WORKPLACE POLITICS BEHIND THE ORGANIZATIONAL CHART

It is hardly surprising to find that social relations in a bureaucracy are only loosely channeled by its formal structure. There is always an informal mapping of social relations and power that is often much different from the lines of authority inscribed on the organizational chart. In the case of Hanshin, office politics were arcane. On the one hand, they followed the fault lines that separated the three levels: parent corporation, front office, and team leadership. At the same time, there were tensions within each of these levels that created alliances across them. For instance, there were factions that included people in the parent company, the front office, and the team leadership, such as the line of support that ran from Kuma to Miyoshi to Yoshida to Ichieda, his head coach in 1997. There were also factions drawn from university alumni (the Kobe University and Waseda University factions were particularly large).

Only indirectly expressed in the formal organizational charts of team, club, and parent company was an even wider chasm that has been an enduring source of friction since the 1970s, the expansion of the front office, and the growth of the Hanshin Group. This was the gap between what I would call the "suits" and the "uniforms," which is to say, between the ninety-member business-suited front office (and its superiors in the parent company) and the one-hundred-member uniformed team (players and coaches). Salary negotiations, scouting, trade and draft strategies, practice schedules, travel arrangements, foreign player recruitment, media relations policy, marketing—in countless issues, the suits and the uniforms fought over who should make decisions and on what basis. Who should have the final say in any of these matters, those in uniforms with baseball credentials or those in business suits with educational credentials? Physical ability and baseball smarts were seldom congruent with business experience and school credentials, and for all of these issues, it was hard to allocate responsibility and expertise between field and front. Because every decision about a salary offer, a trade, or a draft was both a "baseball" decision and a "business" decision, second-guessing and recriminations were endless.

This rift was aggravated by inversions of salary and public recognition. The players, who would be the ordinary employees (*hira shain*) in a regular office hierarchy, and the manager were obviously accorded far more public attention and were paid far more in salary than their "superiors" in the front office (and even in the parent company). At the same time, the front office itself was fraught with distinctions that crosscut the organizational chart of divisions and departments. Most important, the front office actually included four types of employees:

- Some were permanent employees of the parent company, dispatched on assignment to the club for periods of two to five years, often in key budget and financial supervisory positions.
- Others were permanent employees of the ball club subsidiary. Some were ex-players who moved into positions in the front office after retirement, although others had no player experience.
- Some were employees of the ball club who served on annual contracts (including some clerical workers, equipment managers, and junior trainers).
- Some were seasonal employees of the ball club, hired for fan service and other in-season jobs.

The effect of these multiple statuses was to produce (or rather reproduce) within the front office the broader antagonisms between parent company and subsidiary and between authority claims to business sense and baseball smarts.

It was perhaps another manifestation of such conservatism that an unstated but strict education credential hierarchy guided Hanshin personnel moves. An executive of Hanshin Dentetsu who had served in several subsidiaries, including the ball club, described to me the company's strong preference for graduates of the top-ranked national universities (especially the University of Tokyo and Kyoto University), followed by the most prestigious private universities (Waseda, Keiō, and Dōshisha), then second-tier national universities, local public universities (e.g., Osaka Prefectural University), and finally most private universities (like Kobe University and Kansai University). Even graduates of Dōshisha, Waseda, and Keiō, he insisted, found it difficult to rise above the rank of department head.

The importance of ranked university credentials clearly conditioned management feelings about its baseball players and those in the front office, whom they found to be educationally inferior. Even club employees talked of parent company employees as being a cut above themselves (*hitotsu ue ni iru hitotachi*). Hanshin was a corporate hierarchy of distance, detachment, and even occasional disdain. The owner, parent company executives, and even upper-level club officials were not visible to the stadium audience, the players, or even front office staff. There was no owner's box at Kōshien as there is at many American ballparks, where it may be very prominently visible down by the home team dugout or at least a skybox. At Kōshien, company executives watched the game from a small ground-floor room behind home plate, invisible to the stadium audience (in my few times in that room, I found it offered a poor view of the game, with few of the sights and sounds of the stadium). During his twenty years as owner, Kuma very rarely attended a game, avoided interactions with fans, refused interviews with the media, and appeared with players only at occasional formal ceremonies.

This first struck me as curious because Japanese companies often claim that barriers between their executives and ordinary employees aren't as pronounced and impenetrable as in the United States. In many manufacturing companies, for instance, everyone wears the same uniform, and management personnel circulate among workers. Baseball clubs did not operate in this fashion, and I realized that this was because they were subsidiaries; they were not part of the same workplace.

CHAPTER 6

In the Stands

Fans, Followers, and Fair-Weather Spectators

"Whew! The season's over! We got through another year
without incident! I can't tell you what a relief it is. I feel like
a huge burden's been lifted from my shoulders!"

—Comment by Fujita Kenji, executive officer of one of the outfield
fan clubs, on leaving Kōshien Stadium at the close of the final home
game of the 1997 season (field notes, September 30, 1997)

"You're all just trash!" (*Omaera wa gomi ya*).

—Comment made in 1996 by a stadium official to officers of the
Private Alliance of Hanshin Tiger Fan Clubs (as told to me on two
separate occasions by Alliance officers in 1997)

The people of Osaka and the Kansai region followed and supported the
Hanshin Tigers in at least four ways: by coming out to the stadium for
the games, by listening to them on the radio, by watching them on television, and by reading about them in the sports press. Some ardent fans
I knew attended every home game at Kōshien but seldom watched the
Tigers on television even when they were playing away games; others
didn't have time to go to the stadium or even watch them on television
but read the sports papers every morning for results and analysis. Generally, however, Kansai people freely combined their media of engagement, for instance by going to the stadium occasionally and regularly
watching televised games and reading the daily press.

There were other ways of being a part of the Tigers sports world:
belonging to one of the many fan clubs that populated the stadium,
watching the games in Tigers-themed sports bars, talking with friends
about Tigers games and issues, participating in online chat rooms or

social media, following Tigers-based manga, collecting Tigers paraphernalia, and so forth. And people varied widely in their intensity and commitment, from deeply passionate fans to merely occasional spectators. Across the region, there were large numbers of what we might call passive supporters who did not follow the actual baseball team at all but still felt some subjective affiliation to the idea of Hanshin. "Nan to naku, Hanshin" is how someone once expressed it to me.

The fans across Kansai whom I met and talked with over the years explained several different bases of their attachment to the Tigers. For some, it was familiarity and access; Hanshin was the team always featured in the press, whose games were always on television, and about whom they knew the most. Others said they were socialized to Hanshin fandom because it was the team their parents or significant others had supported. Some expressed territorial loyalty to neighborhood, city, or region and felt Hanshin was the team that represented and "fought for" their territory (more about that later). Still others were less drawn to the team and more interested because they found the Kōshien stadium experience so intense and so much fun.

This chapter explores these many modes of belonging in the Tigers world and the sensory experiences, technologies, and people that enable these attachments. In a general sense, we find this variation across these qualities in all mass sports spectatorship and certainly in baseball in the Unites States and the Caribbean as well as in NPB (see, e.g., three fine-grained ethnographic studies of baseball fans: Carter [2008], Magazine [2007], and Swyers [2010]). Nonetheless, there were two distinctive features—two points of emphasis—of Hanshin Tigers fandom that struck me repeatedly during my fieldwork. The first was the importance of creating and sustaining a raucous, festival-like atmosphere at Kōshien. The way the games were played and watched was as much a measure of fan satisfaction as the game results themselves, and the tens of thousands who attended every evening felt entitled and responsible to build this atmosphere. Cynics may be right (and fans would occasionally agree with me on this point) that they were just trying to compensate for the pain of frequent losses, but I argue that there was more to it than this.

Equally distinctive was the depth of engagement by Kansai residents (and others beyond, especially in Tokyo) with the rich and extended context of Tigers games—the continuing, intertwined narratives of the players, coaches, front office, parent company, player OB, and others— as colorfully and not always accurately portrayed in the daily sports

FIGURE 15. Fans in the bleachers and the yellow-jacketed cheerleaders of the Private Alliance of Fan Clubs, 1997. Courtesy of Nikkan Sports Newspaper.

papers and television news. As I have argued in preceding chapters, these were narratives as much about work relationships as about base-ball performance. What intrigues me is that both of these qualities of the Hanshin world—creating a stadium atmosphere that was lively, sensory, and social and relishing a complex, ongoing club narrative—share a melodramatic tone. Festival, soap opera, and melodrama—these are key to understanding the Hanshin world of the 1990s and early 2000s.

We begin at the ballpark itself, which we already know to be the geographical center of the Tigers world. Each night the actions of the nine players and the course of the game were set by the two contesting managers as they determined the batting order, called pitcher signals, and made lineup changes. However, there was another individual in the stadium who controlled a far larger contingent, the fifty-five thousand spectators at a fully packed game. This was Moritani Kazuo, who was seventy-five when I first met him in 1996. At every home game, he sat in the far right corner of the right-field bleachers. Moritani had already been the chairman of the Private Alliance of Hanshin Tiger Fan Clubs for twelve years, and at precisely 6:00 in the evening, he would stand up, raise his arm, and shout "Let's go!" (*Ikee!*). His command rippled through a hierarchy of alliance officers to the cheerleaders stationed throughout the bleachers (see figure 15). A deafening chant arose, and from that moment, Moritani and his lieutenants controlled the stadium soundscape for the entire game.

In those years, approaching Kōshien Stadium from the train station, one encountered the main ticket windows, where one could pay ¥2,500–3,500 (roughly US$25–$35) to buy a seat in one of the several infield sections. Walking all the way around the outside of the stadium to a smaller shed in the rear, one could spend ¥1,400 (roughly $14) for a ticket to the unreserved outfield bleachers and take a rear entrance to a very different part of the stadium.

This was the territory of the Hanshin Tigers fan clubs, whose members filled the right-field stands and spilled over into the left-field bleachers and into the right-side infield "Alps" section. Tigers paraphernalia and motifs were everywhere. It was a throbbing sea of yellow and black face paint; Tigers happi coats; and Tigers uniform shirts, jerseys, and headbands. It seemed as if everyone was wearing a Hanshin baseball cap and beating together a pair of miniature plastic baseball bats to accompany their lusty chants: "Kattobase Yamada!" "Kattobase Hiyama!" "Kattobase Wada!" Kattobase was the all-purpose cheer: "Let it rip, Yamada!" "Let it rip, Hiyama!" "Let it rip, Wada!"

What should we make of such colorful, frenetic fan behavior? Japanese baseball fans, like the players, the managers, and the owners, have been subject to the same characterological gaze by American journalists and baseball tourists to Japan. The casual visitors find them entrancing and enjoyable, while the baseball purists are appalled that their nonstop antics prevent any "proper" enjoyment of the game. What they share is a tendency to attribute this behavior to some ingrained Japanese need to melt into the group and follow it mindlessly, even to such maniacal ends. But if you sit long enough and watch and listen and ask, a much more complex account of Kōshien fandom emerges.

IT'S NOT ALL "KATTOBASE!": THE CHOREOGRAPHY OF CHEERING

I admit that my initial impression in the Kōshien bleacher sections was that this constant cheering was not only excruciatingly loud but also exceedingly monotonous. All they seemed to be chanting, over and over, to a thumping percussive beat, was "Kattobase! Ya-ma-da" ("Let it rip! Yamada"), "Kattobase! Hi-ya-ma," "Kattobase! Ma-ko-to," or whichever player was at bat. Yet there turned out to be more to Kōshien cheering than what first assaulted my ears. Closer listening allowed me to discern small differences in the lyrics and the beat.

Each starting player and each regular substitute had his own "hitting march," and the most fundamental cheering, then, was singing a version of the hitting march of whoever was up to bat with a "kattobase" refrain. The hitting march cheer began when the batter stepped into the box and continued until his at-bat was finished, no matter how many pitches or foul balls it took. If he reached base safely, either by hitting or being walked, he was rewarded with another quick chant. If Hiyama Shinjirō, for example, singled in a run, he would be greeted with "taimurii, taimurii Hi-ya-ma" ("timely" being a fabricated term for a clutch hit).[1]

The chants were accompanied by a noisy choreography of trumpets, bugles, whistles, Japanese *taiko* drums, Western bass drums, flags, and banners. Each had a distinct location and an orchestrated role. The taiko drummers were below in the first row of bleacher seats, while the trumpeters and bass drummers played in the upper seats; huge flags were waved from the upper tier skillfully and precariously just above the heads of those seated below; and player banners were tied along the walkway between the lower and upper seating tiers. The right to display and wave the banners, one per player, was held by individual fan clubs.

Larger cheering routines sustained the pace of the game (figure 16 shows hand signals used by cheerleaders to communicate with each other). For example, there were pregame chants and opening player name calls. When an opposing pitcher was removed from the game, he was serenaded with a rendition of "Auld Lang Syne"; in the middle of the lucky seventh inning, when the Tigers came to bat, a spirited mass singing of the Tigers fight song concluded with the release of tens of thousands of balloons (tagged "condom balloons" for their distinctive shape); and at the end of victories, everyone stood to sing a cycle of the hitting marches, followed by the Tigers anthem, *Rokkō oroshi*, with a banzai cheer.

This was a variegated choreography, not a monotonous drone (as one sometimes experiences at professional soccer games in Europe). The fan club cheering was a structured flow, from batter to batter, through the innings, over the stretch of the game. True, the lyrics were not inspired; they combined the exaggerated heroics of a praise song with the polite imperatives of an encouraging command. I do not want to exaggerate the inventiveness or sophistication of this structured flow. It was not like following Bach's Goldberg Variations or the Paul Taylor

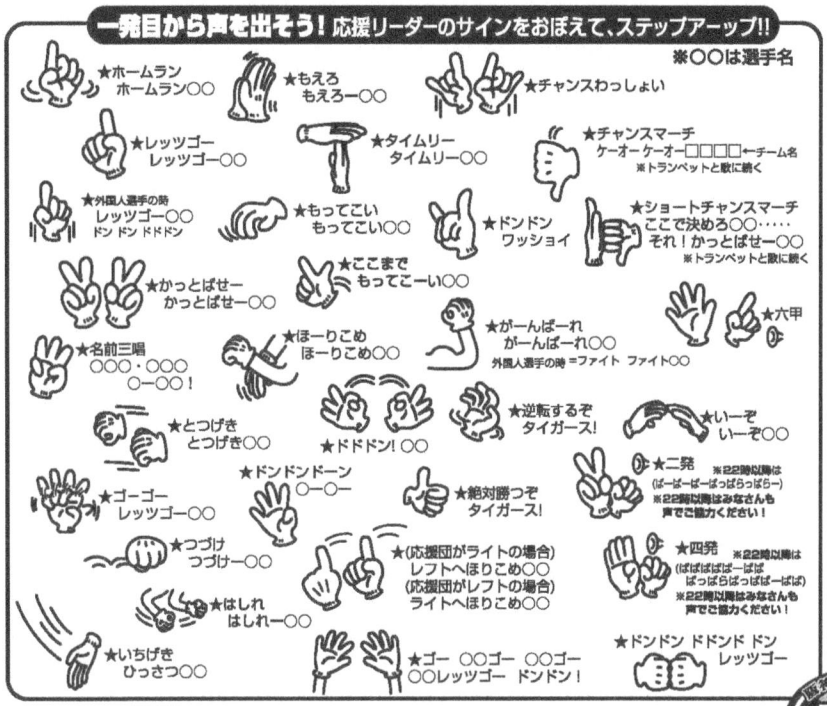

FIGURE 16. Flyer distributed to spectators at Kōshien Stadium in 2003, explaining hand signals used by Private Alliance cheerleaders to communicate with each other and to call for certain spectator cheers.

Dance Company. But it does miss the intent and the effect of the outfield cheering to dismiss it as mindless, repetitive droning.

This constant, collective chanting was a way of claiming an active role in the game. Sitting in bleachers that were a distant 250–300 feet from the main action at home plate, it was nearly impossible to follow the subtleties of pitching, to judge the close umpire calls, to hear the dugout chatter, or otherwise to share in the intensity of the game as those in the infield seats could. With their cheering, the outfield fans participated as "mood makers." More precisely, they became mood "remakers," because this particular cheering pattern assertively layered the normally punctuated rhythms of the game on the field with the continuous rhythms of vocal chants and body sways. They converted (or perhaps diverted) the game from interval to flow. This participatory intervention was a key dimension of their role and identity as fans.

Indeed, there may have been an even deeper structure to cheering. The sport sociologist Takahashi Hidesato studied the rhythmic pattern of Hanshin Tigers and Hiroshima Carp cheers and concluded that they shared a "three-seven" beat that was reminiscent of agricultural song cycles from the medieval centuries (Takahashi 1994). These songs were appeals to the gods of fertility and harvests, and he contrasted them rhythmically to the two-beat patterns of other chants and songs that were messages *from* the gods to the human world.[2] He concluded that, symbolically at least, the fan club cheering was *for* the players but directed *to* divine agents. They were actively supplicating on behalf of the team the goddess of victory (*shōri no megami*, the deity of outcomes being coded feminine in Japanese sports cosmology).

I found little support for Takahashi's hypothesis when I asked fans and others in the stadium audience to whom they were cheering when they urged Hiyama to "let it rip." Not surprisingly, they all found my question rather silly; of course they were directing their support to Hiyama. At the same time, though, the goddess of victory is a folk belief of wide salience, and it is not entirely fanciful that chanting patterns should bear symbolic association, however unrecognized, with such rhythms.

THEY HAVEN'T BEEN SITTING THERE FOREVER: A BRIEF ORGANIZATIONAL HISTORY OF THE PRIVATE ALLIANCE OF HANSHIN TIGER FAN CLUBS

Another impression one might easily have had while sitting in the Kōshien bleachers was of anonymous uniformity. Wasn't everyone just following in unison the few yellow-jacketed, white-gloved leaders down in front? This impression also turned out to mask an elaborate social structuring of the fans that had deep historical resonance and sprang from fairly recent local circumstances.

Cultural historians might recognize affinities with handclapping clubs (*teuchi renjū*) of urban commoners in the seventeenth and eighteenth centuries who organized around particular kabuki theater actors and sumo wrestlers. Exhibiting their loyalties with color-coded scarves and seat cushions, these claques were celebrated for their precisely timed shouts and complex handclapping routines whenever their actors or wrestlers appeared. They were also castigated for their often violent encounters with rival clubs in the theaters, in the temple grounds on sumo days, or in the streets.

Baseball cheerleading origins, however, are as foreign as the sport itself. When the Waseda University and Keio University baseball clubs toured the United States in the early twentieth century, they were so impressed by American collegiate cheering (especially in football) that they made extensive notes of the patterns and instruments, which they then introduced back home. Cheerleading became its own club activity, a flamboyant and disciplined display of school spirit that remains prominent today at the high school and university levels.

As we will see in more detail in chapter 8, the teams of the first professional league, which started in 1936, were sponsored and owned by major corporations. They faced a skeptical public, anxious that playing for pay would sully the amateur ideal that it associated with school baseball. To allay these suspicions, the teams adopted a number of features of school baseball, including organized supporter groups (*kōenkai*). These began as employee groups who were given free tickets and encouraged to lend their voices to the company team with flags, megaphones, and cheer songs (although records of the early decades indicate that most spectators were not part of these groups).

The contemporary structure of Kōshien fan clubs had more recent roots in the mid-1970s, after a decade in which professional baseball's appeal greatly broadened to a national audience of viewers and readers. The 1960s had been a decade of national pride, double-digit economic growth, the spread of television, and other factors that accelerated and "massified" metropolitan consumption. Baseball was particularly stimulated by the proliferation of sports dailies, the popularity of several series of baseball comic books, and especially the Yomiuri Giants' nine-year run as Japan Series champions from 1965 to -1973 (earning them the sobriquet the V-9 Giants). Television, and Yomiuri's ownership of a national network, made the Giants organization and its success emblematic of corporate nationalism and economic resurgence (Kelly 1998a). Polls identified its star third baseman, Nagashima Shigeo, as the most popular public figure in Japan.

However, the stadiums themselves, especially the outfield bleachers frequented by the working class, remained rowdy places, not quite fit for prime-time television. Individual spectators and informal clubs of ordinary fans shared the bleachers with bookies and gangsters. Betting during the games was still common, and at least some spectators' attention—and anger—focused on whether their team was making or not making the betting spread. Inebriation and fights were common, often between rival gambling groups. It was not uncommon to see spectators jump out onto the field to accost umpires and players. The veteran Asahi sports reporter and analyst Kishimoto Chiaki commented to me a number of times during fieldwork on how "gentlemanly" professional baseball fans had become, compared with his early days of playing and reporting in the 1950s and 1960s. He recounted stories of how the home team's fans would go over to fight with the visitor's fans, and they were merciless to players they didn't like, standing on the dugout after the game and pouring beer on them, throwing rocks and other objects out onto the field, and lighting fires from newspapers in the stands.

It was television, Kishimoto and others argued, that brought an end to this behavior, because networks, clubs, and ordinary fans themselves realized that such violence would make for disastrous television images (e.g., field notes June 7, 1997). I interviewed a number of people, in their seventies and eighties by the late 1990s, who were involved in initial efforts from 1974 onward to create some regular cooperation among the ordinary fan groups at Kōshien. In effect, theirs was an effort to take back the stands from rowdies and gamblers, widen the base of spectators, and alter the participatory spirit.

This gentling of spectator behavior can be related to larger societal trends in law and order. The early postwar period was marked, of course, by considerable turbulence. Labor union strife in the 1950s; massive demonstrations against the US-Japan Security Treaty renewal in 1960; anti-Vietnam protests and the large-scale student unrest of the 1960s; and consumer movements, youth motorcycle gangs, and the Narita airport agitations in the 1970s were among the public expressions of constant social discontent. I do not believe—and have found no one who has argued—that there were direct connections between these movements and the (quite apolitical) sports rowdiness of the era. At the same time, the rowdiness was one more anxiety for corporate and official Japan, which tried hard to contain and erase collective dissent. What was remarkable at Kōshien was that it was the ordinary spectators themselves, acting independently of the stadium officials and the ball club, who redirected the energy and attention of the crowd.

One of the bleacher denizens at the time who led the efforts to create a spectator fan organization was none other than Moritani Kazuo, an elderly gentleman in the late 1990s who sat in the corner of the bleachers and whose command "Let's go!" (Ikee!) initiated the pregame chants. Moritani was a Waseda University graduate and lifelong Hanshin follower. With his wife, he ran a small bar, Ta'ichi, that was near a Hanshin train station about a ten-minute ride from the stadium. The bar, with just one long counter, was a gathering spot and information center for local Hanshin fans. Mrs. Moritani ran the bar during all of the season's home games when her husband was at the ballpark.

In 1973 Mr. Moritani and several others started to build up what they came to call the Private Alliance of Hanshin Tiger Fan Clubs (Hanshin Taigāsu shisetsu ōendan). Their plan was to create an umbrella organization that would bring together the dozens of small fan clubs scattered throughout the stadium so that their collective cohesion could bring an end to the fighting that constantly erupted and that gave Kōshien what Moritani called such a "scandalous" (fushōji) reputation. They initially met with little success because many fans didn't want to give up their own style of cheering. In February 1975, the Fierce Tiger Club, the Young Tiger Club, and two groups merged into what they optimistically called the Private Alliance, but they only totaled 120 members. It was not until 1980 that a large enough number of clubs had merged to give the organization a presence in the left-field bleachers. In that year, they legally constituted an association with eleven-clause club regulations and twenty-eight clause rules of conduct.[3]

A major obstacle to their efforts to organize was that all outfield and Alps seats were unreserved. Club members had to line up with everyone else for every game. Often club members and nonmembers were mixed together, and that precipitated squabbling and fighting, fueled by drinking. Organized crime group members (yakuza) were still present as constant troublemakers. They simply displaced ticket holders from choice spots, including the seats at the walkways and railings for hanging banners.

The major impetus in Alliance growth was the Tigers' championship year of 1985, the only time in team history that it has captured the Japan Series. The region was engulfed in Tigers pride, demand for tickets was far beyond capacity, and the exuberance of the spectators greatly concerned stadium officials as the season progressed. This convinced them to create large blocks of season ticket seats in the right outfield and to give the association some advance preference for seats. This in turn made fan club membership and Alliance participation attractive to both individuals and clubs.

By the late 1990s, the Private Alliance had grown into an elaborate association. Its constituent Tigers fan clubs stretched from Hokkaido to Okinawa, with over ten thousand members in four branches and forty clubs. It had more than one hundred officers in parallel administrative and stadium hierarchies; administrative officers handled alliance organizational matters, and stadium officers orchestrated the cheering at the stadium itself. Moritani's title was General Head of Stadium Affairs, and as the title suggests, he had overall authority for everything that happened at the stadium. His chain of command ran from his two vice-heads to a club head (with five vice-heads) and then to a chief of cheer-leaders (who had eleven vice-chiefs), who supervised, trained, and eval-uated the sixty-six leaders who actually led the stands in cheers. There were separate officers and instrumentalists for the trumpet and drum brigades. Club membership was surprisingly diverse in age, class, and gender, but the club and association leadership was overwhelmingly male. Even at the lowest levels, there were only two women among the sixty-six cheerleaders.

The Private Alliance, complex as it was, did not exhaust the orga-nizational map of the right-field stands. There were still fan clubs that remained outside this alliance, twenty-four of which joined together in 1989 as a second association, the Middle Tiger Clubs Association (Chūtora rengōkai). Its relationship with the Private Alliance was generally cordial, and Moritani and several others sat on the advisory board of the Middle Association. Beyond the two alliances were what Moritani estimated to be about two hundred fan clubs throughout the country that were unaffiliated, although they usually cooperated with the two main alliances.

All of this created a well-defined social ecology and procedural order. Cheerleading initiative was accorded the Private Alliance officers, the so-called yellow-jacket squad (ki-jāji kumi) because of their yellow and black uniform waist jackets, who occupied the seats across the bottom rows. Its officers served two-year terms, and there was constant move-ment up, down, and across the organizational charts. The Alliance offi-cers licensed all cheerleaders and instrumentalists, who were required to meet for practice before each game in the grounds of the temple adja-cent to Kōshien. Composing the "hitting songs" was also a Private Alli-ance prerogative. They were usually drafted by several of its musical consultants, who were music professors at local universities, and vetted and approved at the several levels of meetings that were held through-out the year: of the general membership, of all leaders, and of the top officials.

Clubs in the Middle Association occupied many of the seats along the walkway between the lower and upper tiers and certain left-field bleachers and Alps sections. They and some Private Alliance clubs con-trolled the support banners for all regular players and the large club flags that were waved from the upper tier. The flag-waving and all other elements of cheering comportment were decided in meetings between the two associations and stadium officials. For example, until 1992 or so, clubs waved their flags throughout much of the games; this not only obstructed the view of many of the spectators, but also meant that individual clubs couldn't stand out. Negotiations then restricted flag-waving to the at-bats of specific players and certain other moments in the game.

Thus, in looking around the right-field bleachers, one must be aware that there was a rather complicated, two-decade-long history of organizing that had created the complex social structuring of this time and space. It is ironic that while they were often criticized for a perceived rowdiness, the clubs were organized precisely to bring some order and decorum to the outfield stands. Its own charter announced that the purpose of the Private Alliance was "to love the Hanshin Tigers and to support the team in a decorous and orderly fashion." Like vigilante groups in many places,, this self-policing was politically ambiguous. It was an initiative to stake out and regulate a zone within the private corporate space of the most famous stadium in all of Japan. And yet the Private Alliance members were agents of regulation, shaping the spectators' experience toward a proper metropolitan sensibility.

IT'S NOT ALL CHEERING: THE SOCIALITY OF ŌENDAN

A third feature of the bleacher cheering that was not immediately obvious was that it was not nonstop chanting, but rather a pulsating rhythm of alternating frenzy and calm. That is, a cardinal tenet of Kōshien cheering was that you cheered when your team was at bat, but not when your opponents were at-bat and the Tigers were in the field. There were hitting marches but no fielding marches. A good defensive play was applauded, and groans and jeers greeted an opposing team's home run. But when the visiting team was at-bat, the cheering initiative shifted to the (much fewer) visiting team fans, who were seated in the left-field stands.

So what did go on when the Tigers were on the field? Drinking and eating, of course. Almost all games were nighters, beginning at Kōshien at 6:00 p.m. Most people came right from work, so this is where they ate dinner. There was also some preparation for the next Tigers at-bats. However, mostly what went on was schmoozing. Half the game—the top half of each inning—was spent talking, sharing news, chatting up fellow club members, visiting with other fan clubs, flirting, gossiping, and pushing deals. For many of the denizens of the bleachers—especially those from the small business sector—fan clubs and baseball games were substitute activities for the hostess clubs and quasi-obligatory drinking that filled the watery evening zone between workplace and home for their bosses and others with corporate expense accounts. It was the layering of another, quieter flow over the interval action on the field.

Consider the Roving Tigers Club (Namitora-kai), a rather typical club belonging to the Middle Association. The Roving Tigers Club had about two hundred dues-paying members in the late 1990s and early 2000s. Most were in its headquarters Kobe club, but it had five branches in Kyoto, Okayama, Nagoya, Tokyo, and Toyama. These were all places where the Tigers played a couple of times in the season, so the branches allowed for reciprocal hospitality and guaranteed seats. At Kōshien, the club purchased a ten-seat block of season tickets in addition to the seats purchased by individual members. Club officers occupied the seats and railings along a section of the middle walkway. The club was honored with cheering responsibility for two players, Hiyama and Yamada Katsuhiko, and it featured two trumpet players and a drummer. From a walkway perch, one of the experienced members waved the large club flag precariously low over the heads of spectators seated below during the Hiyama and Yamada hitting marches.

The club's executive officer in those years was fifty-year-old Fujita Kenji, who was president of a small Kobe port company that supplied repair parts to ocean ships. Several of his ten employees came to the games at his expense, and everyone piled into his minivan for the one-hour drive from the company offices to the stadium. Before entering, they stocked up on food and drinks at their favorite local shops to carry in for their evening dinner and refreshment. Fujita paid for all of the purchases, about ¥10,000 per game, out of his own pocket.

Among the club members were a number of Fujita's business associates, from the airfreight and trucking companies he used and from other ship parts companies. Like many other fan clubs, the Roving Tigers Club was a venue for maintaining business ties. This was especially so for the medium and small businesses that made up the bulk of the Kansai economy, but large workplaces were also in evidence. Adjacent to the Roving Tigers was a block of seats for the Love the Tigers Club from the labor union of the Central Osaka Post Office, and to the side was group seating for the Tiger-Crazy Alliance, a club from giant Mitsubishi Heavy Industry and Mitsubishi Electric, as well as another block for the Strong Tiger Guys from Nittō Electric.

Some of the small businessmen and corporate managers told me the fan clubs offered an alternative to business socializing that was at once easier and more burdensome than expense-account entertainment in bars. The baseball season and times of each game set a predictable framework to such obligations that limited both drinking and expenses. At the same time, there were considerable costs of this club fandom on the efficiency of small companies like Mr. Fujita's. To arrive at the ballpark on time required him to close the office around 5:00 p.m., in order to drive to Kōshien and then stock up on supplies; afterward, he and the other Kobe members got home around midnight, making it difficult, they acknowledged, to arrive at work the next morning in peak condition. This occurred only (!) sixty-five nights a year, and he claimed they worked until seven on nongame nights to make up for lost time, but year after year, that is a lot of travel and drinking. And there was pressure: both the sense of obligation out of which some employees participated and the very heavy responsibility that Fujita himself frequently expressed for ensuring, game after game, a safe and enjoyable experience for members and those around him. No wonder he was so visibly relieved at the end of the final game of the season, when I went with him and other officers for a long celebratory night of drinking in the Osaka bar district, at an establishment managed by a Roving Tigers club member. When he exclaimed that it was a season "without incident" in this chapter's opening quote, he was referring to his fan club fortunes, not those of the ball team.

However, not all Roving Tigers members were business acquaintances. Also participating were a young woman in her twenties who worked as a Yamaha electric organ teacher, a fellow in his thirties who worked for a janitorial service, a Japan Railroads train conductor, some Osaka college kids (who played the club's two trumpets and bass drum), and others. What they had in common was that they all showed up, and were expected to show up, regularly. If they missed thirty games or so in a season (Fujita had no specific cutoff point), they would be dropped from the rolls—and from the access to the club's reserved seating, trips to away games, and the several social events and club assemblies held throughout the year away from Kōshien.

Workplace groups tended to be the core of most Tigers fan clubs, but there were also clubs based on neighborhoods and other kinds of social networks. There were, for example, the Tiger Ladies Club, about thirty-two middle-aged women, and the Fierce Tiger Club of the Civil Engineering Department of Kyoto University. The association network fostered social ties among the clubs as well. Adjacent to the Roving Tigers Club was a club whose members are predominantly *tekiya*, itinerant stall operators and hucksters at markets and carnivals around the country (and often thought to have yakuza connections or at least protection). Given its members' peripatetic schedules, the club was often shorthanded, and Fujita and his group would help in hoisting their banners and flag. Fujita was also generous in providing beer and food to younger adult members of adjacent clubs because, he said, they just didn't have the pocket money. During a game one evening in late 1997, a club director took two of his members, a father and son, around the bleachers to introduce them to officers of various other clubs so they could distribute invitations to the son's upcoming wedding reception. More substantially, following the devastating 1995 Kobe earthquake, the Private Alliance and constituent clubs provided much logistical and financial assistance to those many clubs and members who had suffered (often enormous) losses.

It may not be immediately obvious that schmoozing is a necessary form of baseball fan conduct. However, it is a means of resolving the stadiumgoer's dilemma. People went to Kōshien to root for the Tigers, to get passionate and worked up; every game was an emotional roller-coaster of excitement and despair. The same people went to Kōshien to relax, to kick back from all the demands and frustrations of the workday. There is no evidence that the alternating pattern of cheering hard during the team's at-bats and then sitting down, opening a beer, and chatting quietly for the next half-inning was developed with these goals in mind, but for the Kōshien fans, it offered a neat way of combining coordinated high-energy emotional release and quieter, routinized sociability. Together these activities formed what Lawrence Grossberg (1992) called the "affective sensibility" of the fans' space-time, whose rhythms were both distinct from and intimately attuned to the field of play.

NEITHER UCHI NOR SOTO: WHOSE SIDE WERE THE FAN CLUBS ON?

Fans are by definition *fanatics*—maniacs (*mania* in Japanized English)—and mania is a schizoid condition. It expresses itself, on the one hand, in abiding devotion to an object of loyalty, even the most hapless of teams. A Tigers fan is "Tiger-crazy" (*tora-kichi*), having the same depth of feeling with which English football fans are "supporters" and Italian fans compose *la fede calcistica*, the football faithful.

At the same time, and in apparent contradiction, Tigers fans were ever vigilant for any slip or mistake by the objects of their adulation, quick to criticize in response to any expectations not met. Tigers players, managers, and club officers were all vulnerable to sudden swings in fan support. At several moments in games during those seasons of dismal performance, the fan club alliances even boycotted the team by refusing to cheer.

The audiences at Kōshien were famous for their jeers (*yaji*), and even in the midst of the fan club cheering, one could hear them. The heckling took many forms, from boorish catcalls ("Yoshida, you idiot!" or "Get the bum out of here!") to more witty satirical barbs, phrased in Osaka dialect and thrown out with timing and pitch that recalled audience interjections (*kakekoe*) from kabuki aficionados during kabuki plays.[4] In fact, a group styling itself the Crazy-About-the-Tigers Heckling Research Group published a collection of jeers heard during the 1994 season at the stadium. Like an annotated poetry volume, each jeer was identified by date and moment, given in original dialect, with explanations of the circumstances and meaning.[5]

Fandom in sports, like other fandoms, is a peculiar combination of attachment and fickleness, of long-suffering patience and a demand for instant gratification. Just whose side the fans are on is never entirely clear, or at least it is never stable. We must remember that the fans in the right-field stands of Kōshien were not only solidly organized but also resolutely independent of the Hanshin ball club; that is why the alliance titled itself a "private" (*shisetsu*) association. This was not the case with the fan organizations of other clubs. The Yomiuri Giants, among others, tightly controlled the association of Giants fan clubs, and in 1989 a number of the fan organizations of Pacific League teams, embarrassed by the rowdy image of Hanshin and other fans, were brought together as an Association of Pacific League Fan Clubs that was recognized and supervised by the league office.

At Kōshien, by contrast, the years witnessed continuous, mutual antagonism among the fan clubs, stadium officials, and Tigers club. To be sure, there were some obvious converging interests. The fan clubs sought and benefited from certain concessions by the stadium company, especially in converting the six thousand right-field seats to a season-ticket basis, to which fan club members were given special access. In return, the fan clubs provided the intangible but essential color and background for stadium ambience and television and radio broadcasts.

Nonetheless, that colorful, noisy presence was a mixed boon to the Hanshin club, and fan club practices did not always reinforce the stadium company's and the club's own marketing efforts to attract and appeal to audiences. The official promotion days, team mascots, and scoreboard-led cheers were greeted only lukewarmly by the fan clubs. In a real sense, the outfield sections were a separate territory, largely self-disciplined by the fan club alliance with only limited oversight by stadium guards. As I have mentioned, fan club alliance leaders and stadium officials held periodic meetings to negotiate rules for banners, seating, flag-waving, drinking, and concessions. The baseball club, for its part, refused to get involved in any way with the fan clubs. When I made my initial introductions to the Hanshin front office in 1996, for example, I expressed an interest in contacting the fan club officials. The media relations staff curtly informed me that the club had no relationship with the fan organizations, and I would have to approach them on my own. An even less-guarded front office opinion is quoted at this chapter's outset.

The matter of beer coolers illustrated this tension. They were not allowed in the stadium, and yet at every game, packed with cans of beer and sake (and cans are not allowed either, their usefulness as projectiles having been demonstrated on more than one occasion), fan club members carried cooler after cooler through the turnstiles and right past the stadium guards. The coolers were left openly on the walkways to quench the thirst and lubricate the hospitality of the fan club officers and their guests. As long as the association officials could control their members' drinking behavior, the stadium company tacitly conceded them the right to have coolers. It even sent around a senior supervisor at the end of every game to bow and offer words of thanks to the head of each and every fan club "for their cooperation" that evening.

The fan clubs were also skeptical, even hostile, toward the media. Radio and television, especially, needed and encouraged the Kōshien fans to be animated participants in the drama they were presenting. The cameras would pan the stadium crowds, and microphones were fixed in multiple locations to pick up the cheers, groans, and catcalls. The organized fan clubs always offered the most desirable camera shots, and the clubs took some pride in the show they provided. At the same time, many members felt misused and misrepresented by those broadcasts, especially when they associated the clubs with the zanier and sometimes violent behavior of fans who were not even members. An article in the Private Alliance regulations required members to channel all media requests through association officers, who even objected to pictures being taken of them and their clubs in the stands without their permission.

Given these tensions, the potential for fan violence was never far below the surface, although it was hard to gauge its extent. On the one hand, sitting in the right-field bleachers at more than fifty games over three seasons, I only saw three fights break out among fans, and club officers quickly broke them up. The general level of fighting and posturing was well below an average Sunday afternoon NFL crowd. Nonetheless, even the occasional incidents made team and stadium officials and fan club officers anxious. On June 1, 1996, for example, during my first year of observation, a slump in May angered Hanshin supporters, about fifty of whom surrounded the hotel in Chiba where the team was staying for an away game. They accosted several players leaving the hotel to go to dinner and surrounded another player in a threatening manner in the hotel elevator. Then in August, a drunken fan club member beat up a stadium guard outside the ticket entrance after another loss. Throughout the disappointing season, fans repeatedly jeered manager Fujita and the front office. In May 1998, a scoreless game with Yokohama was interrupted in the eighth inning by Hanshin fans who pelted the outfield with trash and bottles; after the game, five fans jumped the fence and ran around the outfield trying to stir up the spectators. Two days later, angry Hanshin fans threw their megaphones at the team bus as it left the stadium. This prompted the stadium to add fifty extra guards to the normal complement of two hundred for the next series against the Yomiuri Giants, always the most tension packed. There were no further incidents (two of the three games were rained out) but with the Tigers already settled in last place, the sports dailies began railing against what they labeled Tigers fan "hooligan behavior."

Moments of fan exuberance could also be tense. Returning to Umeda Station from a game at Kōshien against the Yakult Swallows on a sweltering August night in 1997, I was riding in a packed Hanshin train car into which, at the last moment, spilled a spirited fan club of young males. They drew wary looks from the other passengers, as they demanded their fellow riders join them in singing; they soon had most passengers entertained and involved in a nonstop series of chants for the twenty-minute ride. They began with the songs for each Hanshin player and then shifted to insult chants against Yakult. Then they announced, "Because the wave is banned at Kōshien, let's do it here," and they got most of the passengers in the car to bob up and down three or four times in a back-to-front wave, before launching into another series of insult chants against archrival the Yomiuri Giants; they attacked the players, Giants manager Nagashima, the Yomiuri sports paper ("only good as toilet paper"), and the Yomiuri television network ("idiot-TV"). They then sang some insult verses directed at Hanshin's next opponent, the Yokohama BayStars, by which time the train was pulling into the station to their pulsating chant of "Umeda, Umeda, Umeda." The group poured out of the car, rushed down the platform, and reassembled in the main foyer for a final round of songs before disbanding. Station personnel and fan club officers who happened to be riding the train looked on with a skeptical bemusement, ready to intervene if necessary.

These and many other incidents sustained a wary standoff among the fan clubs, the rest of the stadium audience, the Kōshien stadium company, and the Tigers baseball club. The fan clubs did not officially condone violence or even rude displays against the team or its opponents; indeed, they actively patrolled the bleachers and monitored their members. Most of the serious reported incidents did not involve association members. Nonetheless, members could be quite vocal in their dissatisfaction with the team and its performance and expressed this with pointed gestures and demeanor. In short, the fan clubs were neither insiders nor outsiders (as expressed in Japanese, neither *uchi* nor *soto*). Like fans everywhere (and like some anthropologists?), they were participants and observers in an ambivalent zone, more passionate and partisan than ordinary spectators, but quick to assert their independence from the team itself.

The association's efforts did not entirely rid the bleachers of criminal elements, and there has always been a minor undercurrent of violence and petty crime among the fans. The special access that constituent clubs have to block sales of tickets attracted several yakuza groups, which could profit from resales, although the team's generally dismal record over the years kept that from being a lucrative opportunity. The team's success in 2003 and beyond did seem to attract yakuza interest, leading to several serious incidents and a major shift in Kōshien fan club organization, which I discuss in the final chapter.

BEYOND THE FAN CLUBS

These denizens of the right-field bleachers were the epicenter of Tigers fandom, but its members extended throughout the stadium and spread out to the far corners of the Kansai region and beyond, much as the Red Sox Nation is a sports country whose capital is Fenway Park in Boston and whose citizens populate the entire New England region. Of course as the epicenter, the bleacher clubs were distinctive. Even at Kōshien, the larger numbers of spectators in the infield sections followed the fan club cheers, but they were never as noisy or as organized. And of course those who came to the stadium were only a small percentage of those who regularly followed baseball. Many self-described fans seldom got to the ballpark; instead, they kept up with their favorites through nightly television or radio broadcasts and by reading a daily sports paper, often as they commuted by public transportation to and from their work. There has been much theorization about how media (especially television and sports papers) interject themselves between the action and the audience, packaging the former as spectacle and creating the latter as indirect spectators (e.g., Whannel 1992). Television in particular is accused of dissolving local team identification and encouraging sports spectators to "shop around" for favorite teams (Alt 1983). Fandom, it is argued, has been largely eroded by such near-total mediation.

I doubt that, but certainly the husband who sprawled in the family room of his south Osaka apartment every evening at 7:30 p.m. after work with a cold beer taking in the Tigers game on television, or the company man packed in a crowded commuter train who avidly read about the previous night's Tigers contest in his favorite sports daily on his way to work, were having a different fan experience from Fujita's club members who showed up at Kōshien every night (see figure 17).[6] This is not because the stadium experience offered an intimacy, immediacy, and spontaneity unmatched by the televisual and print media, but rather because these qualities were transmuted by these media. Sports on television create some of the same "quasi-intimacy" that Andrew Painter (1996) has argued for Japanese daytime variety shows; indeed, baseball televiewers peer right over the shoulder of the pitcher, are given multiple camera angles on and replays of the action, and are privy to the authoritative commentary of announcers who speak directly to them. And the vivid color graphics; exploding font shapes and sizes; and multiple stories, stats boxes, and sidebars by which sports dailies

FIGURE 17. A Tiger fan anxiously watches the evening televised game, his megaphone in one hand, a can of beer in the other. Front cover of Ōtani (2003). Courtesy of Shinchōsha.

dramatically reported Tigers games made the experience more akin to reading a *manga* comic than a news story.

FAN CLUBS, FESTIVAL FEVER, AND SECOND-CITY PRIDE

Baseball is like church—many attend but few understand.

—Wes Westrum, San Francisco Giants catcher and manager
(quoted in Hye 2004:6)

The baseball stadium as church—the metaphor may be even more apt than Wes Westrum realized. Like going to church, going to the stadium is a multisensory experience that can be appreciated on several levels. Some go to church for the hymns, some for the sermon, some for the prayers; some go to be seen and others for the socializing afterward. Is religion's core the public communal rituals or the personal meditative introspection? Is religion a matter of simple faith or detailed spiritual knowledge? Does religion require regular attendance at the sacred sites (churches, temples, mosques), or can the irregulars and nonattendees remain faithful through other acts of devotion?

All of these questions are familiar dilemmas when transposed irreverently to the realm of sports. A Tigers-Giants game at Kōshien commonly filled the stadium's fifty-five thousand seats, and several million fans would be watching on television and listening by radio in their homes, bars, and other locations throughout the country. Many other people in Kansai seldom, if ever, watched or listened to Tigers broadcasts, but they still expressed (or feigned) an interest in how the Tigers were doing when they found themselves in such conversations. And of course there were Kansai residents who supported one of the other two area teams (although they were a small slice of the population) or even a team from outside Kansai.[7] Other residents had no interest in the Tigers, in baseball, or in sports. Clearly, the range of interest and passion varied enormously, from the truly "Tiger-crazy" (tora-kichi) to the occasional fair-weather spectator to the decidedly unconcerned.

The Hanshin Tigers sportsworld embraced all of them, and the key mechanism was the ōendan. There were, in effect, two media streams in the Hanshin sportsworld: the media proper and the fan club associations. The latter were just as critical a connective tissue as the former between the game on the field and the public and private spaces across Kansai, populated by the spectrum of the committed and uncommitted, the passionate and indifferent. The fan clubs served this role not only by their presence but also by how they demonstrated their presence.

The noun *matsuri* and the verb *moriagaru* were frequently used by people at the stadium (and commentators on Tigers fans) to characterize the mood and the manner of stadium spectatorship. A matsuri is a festival, fundamental to Japanese religious life and local social organization. It is usually associated with shrines and temples, especially with their annual festivals to entertain, supplicate, and celebrate the tutelary deity. Much like a saint's day celebration in Catholic towns and neighborhoods, it is a time of processions, feasting, prayers, and a fair amount of partying. The processions can be massive, raucous parades in which the deity is enshrined in a palanquin that is shouldered and carried through the streets of the village or neighborhood. The mood swings widely (and wildly) from the solemn to the boisterous, always almost bursting through the choreography with which everyone is familiar. The aim is to generate emotional participation, to build up and get into the spirit (in both senses of the word) of the moment. Moriagaru is the verb for creating and sustaining this festival mood.

The parallels to a game at Kōshien are obvious, and I think they are deeper than just a humorous cartoon analogy. As in a shrine festival, there was a mixing of the sporting sacred and the stadium social, and there was the doubled attention of the fans to the action on the field and to the schmoozing with fellow spectators. The chants, the uniforms, the gestures, the collective participation—these and more were infused with a matsuri-making frame of meaning familiar to everyone. The fan club cheerleaders, drummers, and trumpeters played a crucial role, as do the people at festivals who bear the palanquin on its rounds through the streets and create the momentum and often the music and dance. Fan club cheerleaders were not cheering for the rest of the audience; on the contrary, they orchestrated and demanded the full participation of all.

And the matsuri mood was sustained in spite of disappointment. Kōshien audiences were seldom sullen and silent. They could be restless and irreverent, with their jeering, but they always showed up in large numbers and continued to come out to the ballpark even in the final month of a dismal season. They took it upon themselves to build up to (moriagaru) a festival mood—collectively—and their attitude was that even if the team disappointed them on the field, they would not disappoint the team in the stands. Perhaps more precisely, they were playing not only to the team but also to the larger entity that was the Hanshin Tigers.[8]

A final element crucial to diffusing the Kōshien stadium experience throughout the wider region was that it was heavily inflected with Kansai expressive culture. The happi coat styling of the cheerleaders and vendors, the food itself, the banners, the cheering patterns, the dialect-heavy jeers that rained down—everything was colored in the aesthetics of an Osaka performative culture that had deep roots and distinctive features (Inoue 2006; Ōtani 2003; Stocker 2002; Sugimoto 2006; Tada 1988).

Assertively organized and resolutely autonomous associations for fan clubs developed in the 1970s and 1980s, motivated initially by local fans trying to take back the stadium from the intimidating rowdies, area gangsters, and bettors who disrupted the stadium experience, especially in the bleachers. They were abetted in their efforts by television media's preference for a colorful and exuberant but disciplined spectatorship to enhance game broadcasting. Unselfconsciously, they incorporated key elements of Kansai expressive culture into their cheering and comportment. Their independence was unnerving for the Hanshin company that owned the club, the team, and the stadium, but it grudgingly ceded much of the stadium space and crowd discipline and game time to the alliance. By the 1990s, the Hanshin stadium and front office did try to supply its own mechanisms for orchestrating the crowd, with its stadium announcer, mascots, cheer girl squad, and the scoreboard itself. But the fan clubs were dismissive of these corporate efforts, and the rest of the stadium followed the lead of the fan clubs, not the mascots and cheer girls.

This autonomy was critical for asserting initiative, identity, participation, and involvement—that is, for claiming a place in the Hanshin Tigers sportsworld. It was also the essential element in diffusing the stadium experience throughout the wider Kansai fan base. There is a Japanese normative affective state of *ittaikan*, a feeling of oneness.[9] Sitting at home, or at a night watchman's desk, or somewhere else across the city watching or listening to the evening's game—beyond the announcer's account of the game details and beyond his commentator sidekick's analysis, the third auditory channel of the fans tied the distant viewers not to the action on the field but to their fellow fans in the stands. Hanshin was not unique in this connectivity, but the qualities of the stadium and its audience, grounded in the historical conditions of the Hanshin club and the widely shared features of Osaka expressive culture, gave distinctive depth and form to the role of fans in this sportsworld.

At the outset of this chapter, I noted the distinctive importance of oppositional identity to sports fans, given the nature of the contests they follow. The team rivalries and local identity are fostered by the home and away structure of games and the permanent location of teams in stadiums. Team support and local identity can be mutually affirming. Kōshien spectators might become Tigers fans because they were Ōsakans and the team was invested with Osaka pride, but as they became Tigers fans they might become more ardently and reflectively Ōsakans. Similarly, some people joined a fan club because they had prior ties to its members, but the club experience could create and sustain bonds among members as well.

Consequential also was the enormous emotional charge given the Tigers for symbolically bearing the pride and determination of the Kansai region in its intense rivalry with the formidable concentrations of the Kantō capital. The other two area teams both were doing much better than the Tigers over those years, but because they played in the Pacific League, they did not confront the Yomiuri Giants thirteen times a season as the Tigers did. As I detail in chapter 9, one of the key trends of Japanese state making beginning in the 1960s was the dramatic shift in the Kantō-Kansai balance of power, especially Osaka's loss of economic parity with Tokyo and its subordination in the Tokyo centrism of the present political economy. In a circulation of rhetoric, local media commentators and ordinary fans alike were quick to recite a litany of contrast pairs (Tokyo vs. Osaka; national bureaucrats vs. local businesspeople; national imperviousness vs. regional pride; powerful, big corporations vs. vulnerable, small business) that came to be symbolically condensed in the Giants-Tigers rivalry.

This helps us to understand, too, the local resolution of the universal sports challenge of coping with losing: for half of each game's participants and their followers, for all but a single team in any league in every season. What does it mean to invest so much of one's identity in a frequently "losing" cause? This is another element of special relevance to the Hanshin case because the team has been consistently and woefully unsuccessful over the past five decades (while the Giants have been the opposite). Hanshin's baseball success came in pro baseball's early years, in the 1930s and 1940s, when Osaka itself was roughly equal to Tokyo. In the postwar decades, as Osaka's power ebbed, so did the fortunes of the Tigers. Many fans felt an inevitability—and an injustice—in the declining success of the Tigers. This did not incline them toward passive resignation but rather toward a certain arch cynicism about the Giants' (i.e., Tokyo's) domination, which could veer menacingly toward the Hanshin company when it was suspected of failing to fight with proper resolve and resources, despite the odds. Again, the distinctive and defended autonomy of the Tigers fan club associations was derived from this freighted sensibility.

CHAPTER 7

In the Press Box

Sports Dailies and Mainstream Media

If a sports fan's fondest (and most far-fetched) fantasy is to be an elite athlete himself, then in second place would be to become a sportswriter or broadcaster. What could be more fun than associating daily with the players and managers, seeing the action up close, and communicating games and the life of the sport to others? What the fan forgets in this reverie are the professional demands on sportswriters: the daily drudgery, the frenetic pace, the hierarchies of status, and the murky ethics that characterize all sports media.

These characteristics were certainly found in the diverse media that covered the Hanshin Tigers: print journalism; radio, television, and internet broadcasting; and even anime and manga treatments. If anything, several structural features of the Hanshin sportsworld intensified the pressures and dilemmas of reporting and commentating for these media, and this chapter explores the work and backgrounds of the reporters, broadcasters, commentators, and others who figured so centrally in the construction of this sportsworld. To call them *sports media* is misleading if it merely connotes the passive transmission of Hanshin baseball to its viewers, readers, and listeners. What they did was far broader, which was to constitute certain actions as "Hanshin baseball" through their powers of representation. They made Hanshin baseball meaningful.

The media did this in remarkably varied ways. There were newspaper reporters, radio announcers, and television broadcasters and photographers, of course, but stadium public address announcers, camera operators, sports editors, cartoonists, poets, novelists, filmmakers, and others were instrumental in shaping Hanshin baseball. Each medium had what Raymond Williams (1977:128–135) would call a distinct "structure of feeling" in constructing its objects of description and its techniques for creating and sustaining audiences. Of course the audiences—spectators, viewers, listeners, and readers—overlapped. But even for the same person, watching a game at the stadium, following it on the television set in the corner of a crowded bar, listening to a radio broadcast through earphones on a late-night commuter train, and reading an account in the sports paper during the next morning's coffee break created unique aural, visual, and tactile experiences. It was the same game but very different game experiences. The fact that many fans mixed and matched these encounters with the Tigers only amplified the power of the media to construct and not just report Tigers baseball.

One might suppose that of all the media, television was most important because many more people in Kansai followed the Hanshin Tigers games on television than came out to the stadium, and television broadcast rights were as important to club profits as were stadium revenues. However, I argue in this chapter that it was not television but the daily sports newspapers that were the central medium of the Hanshin sportsworld. They provided blanket coverage of Hanshin happenings with detailed baseball analytics, compelling presentation, and tabloid sensationalism.

Just as Kōshien Stadium was the geographical epicenter of a Hanshin sportsworld that stretched far and wide, and just as the main team players were the central actors in an athletic contest that required a large and diverse supporting cast, so too were the sports dailies at the vortex of a medium that engaged multiple forms of meaning making and storytelling. While suggesting how and why the sports dailies assumed that central place, this chapter also tries to show the common work of reporting across the media and to contrast the sports dailies, in particular, with the practices of radio and television broadcasting, the other major modes.

As I show in the following sections, each of these three media had a distinct sensibility of presentation and communication. The daily sports newspapers were a concatenation of stories, graphics, and statistics. They covered every game and everything in between, on and off the field. They combined the florid rhetoric of tabloids, the graphic richness of manga, and the data acumen of statistical compendia. Television brought viewers closer to the game action and individual movements than anyone in the stadium itself, including the players and managers. Close-ups, multiple camera angles, and replays created a deep space-time intimacy. Radio, in contrast, relied on a single stream, the auditory, to convey action that was in fact intensely visual, but for that very reason, a listener's imagination was constantly in play; the voice of a gifted radio announcer could stimulate and sustain the close engagement and virtual presence of an entire listening audience.

THE TIGERS BEAT

The press box at Kōshien Stadium was just that—a box—containing a dozen tiers of simple wood desktops with old metal folding chairs, rising up from the regular seats behind home plate and separated from the spectators only by low wood framing (see figure 18). Other stadiums, such as Orix's Green Stadium, had glass-enclosed, air-conditioned, and well-appointed pressrooms, usually high above home plate, but Kōshien's press box remained essentially unchanged from seven decades before. The media members were open to the elements and exposed to the spectators, in the thick of the sense-scape that was a Kōshien baseball game. It was enveloping and exciting, but this very assault on the senses was also a distraction to their work. I sat there on many a July and August evening with sweat dripping onto my notebook—and then two months later, blowing into my hands to keep them warm enough to write on chilly October evenings! The reporters got little relief when they retreated down some metal steps behind the box to the tiny space that was their common press clubroom, without air-conditioning, with crude tables, filled with cigarette smoke, and packed with bodies.[1]

The media workday was as long as that of the players, beginning well before the game. The first television and radio broadcast staff and the newspaper beat reporters arrived at Kōshien before noon, catching some players and coaches as they showed up at the stadium and stopping by the press room at the Hanshin front offices below the bleachers (which was not much better appointed than their own room below the press box). By the early afternoon, the press photographers, the television cameramen, and the commentators and feature writers from the sports dailies started to drift in. By the time the home team took the practice field at 2:00 p.m., the evening television commentators had arrived, and the assembled media representatives—more than fifty for an average contest, and even more for a big game—were standing around the field and lounging on the dugout benches.

Their work practices were quite diverse. Some produced stories and photos for evening editions of sports papers; some shot interview seg-

FIGURE 18. The press box in the stands behind home plate at Kōshien Stadium, 1999. Photograph by author.

ments for afternoon and early evening broadcasts; and some did the live radio and television broadcasts of the game. Some wrote game reports, commentaries, data, graphics, and photos for late evening editions of sports dailies; others had to write text and shoot video summaries of the game for the late night television sports digests shows; and still others were charged with writing fuller versions of game stories; doing post-game interviews; and acquiring data, graphics, and photos for the next morning's newspapers. All of this proceeded under intense competition, necessary cooperation, and even occasional collusion. I was constantly reminded that the media are indeed plural: the roles and demands of a national newspaper beat reporter, a sports daily feature writer, a radio game broadcaster, a sideline photographer, a television broadcast "color commentator," and a front-page layout editor back at the newspaper office are as different as their common aim is the same.

Two qualities set almost all of the media apart from everyone else at Kōshien—the teams, the club, and the spectators. First, for the media, the ideal game was orderly (with no surprises), fast (to meet their tight deadlines), close (for a catching lead), and consequential (so the editor would give them more space). The desk editor for the *Asahi Newspaper* sports page apportioned the three teams' game reports using a rough formula of eighty manuscript lines, fifty lines, and thirty lines.[2] He would stay in touch with his three beat reporters as the games progressed and decide on their story quotas based on how the games compared to one another. For the sports papers, there was no competition among the coverage; Hanshin always got the front page and most of the other coverage. Thus, as the game at Kōshien proceeded the senior feature writer and the head beat reporter checked with the rest of the contingent to decide on the day's promising stories, dividing up tasks as the game wore on.

By the middle innings, one of the commentators would dash off a report to meet his 8:00 deadline for the 11:00 p.m. edition. The other reporters would have their laptops going as well, drafting tentative leads and early developments and trying out story lines with one another. Many of them kept their own pitch-by-pitch scoring books, and some even painstakingly copied out the box scores from the previous day's games around the league so they could have a complete record of every Central League game during the season. This struck me as unnecessarily time-consuming (because the official score sheets were available as soon as the game ended), but the reporters insisted that the act of scoring was a useful mnemonic routine for generating a story and figuring out an analytical angle.

The press's worst fear was an extra-inning game, which quickly pushed everyone against the deadline wall. I happened to be sitting in the press box at a couple of games when the Tigers came to bat in the bottom of the ninth inning with the score tied. The suspense was as palpable in the press box as in the dugout and the stands. A walk-off winning hit would end the game and impress an editor to give the reporters extra space. More often than not, the Tigers didn't score, and the groans and sarcastic comments among the media were audible because they now had to wait out the extended game.

The Kansai sports media covered a huge number of teams at all levels in many sports across the region, but of all the assignments, the Hanshin beat was the most coveted and the most demanding. To the Kansai media, the Hanshin Tigers were a godsend. If the Tigers were the tail that wagged the parent corporate body, then the media may well have been the trainer who kept the Tigers on a leash. The fortunes and misfortunes of the club profited the entire regional media. Even here, though, the boon was bittersweet. Tigers beat reporters spent far more time in those years detailing the agony of defeat than celebrating the thrill of victory, but most of them, when prompted, said that they would much prefer reporting a league championship than tracking yet another managerial firing. Those who had been long enough in their careers to remember waxed nostalgic about the championship year of 1985.

Two of the notable features of the Hanshin media were the press club organization and the heavy use of ex-players as commentators and analyst. It is a common feature of the Japanese media to have organized press clubs composed of all reporters assigned to cover particular government ministries, industry sectors, local police districts, and so forth. The United States has something similar, the White House Correspondents' Club, but such clubs are much rarer here. Press clubs in Japan function to credential members of the media and, critics argue, can be liable to self-censorship and pack journalism. Such clubs function in Japan for major sports as well, and they are divided by geographical region rather than individual sports. In the late 1990s, the register of the Kansai Sports Reporters Club listed over one hundred organizational members, including local stringers for media from other parts of Japan.[3]

Press club leadership rotated among the newspapers, and the club at Kōshien negotiated with the Hanshin Media Relations Department to assign desk space and enforce some protocols of newsgathering. The current president generally had the prerogative of leading the daily interviews with the team manager. There was a separate club for sports photographers and cameramen. Members of both had to wear a club lapel badge when they were working; the badge allowed them entrance at the stadium's Kankeisha-iriguchi along with players and club staff.

Another consequential feature of the media in the Hanshin sportsworld was reliance on ex-players as commentators and analysts for the print press and television. This was baseball's version of the revolving door. As noted in chapter 3, retiring professional players could not return to the amateur ranks to take coaching or managerial positions. The better-known players who aimed for the very limited coaching or managing positions in NPB needed to stay involved in the game, remain visible, and hone their knowledge of the sport while waiting for those few opportunities. To do that, they would usually sign exclusive contracts with one of the media groups for a mix of assignments, from short written game analyses for the sports dailies to appearances as color commentators on radio and television game broadcasts and television sports news programs. The newspapers and broadcasting networks maintained a stable of such analysts (*kaisetsusha*) and commentators (*hyōronka*) and relied on their knowledge and connections for access to and insight on players, managers, and front office.

From my observations in the press box over the years and conversations with about a dozen of these talking (and writing) heads, I found that they worked closely with their paper's reporting staff. During the games, a reporter would turn to one of his paper's analysts with questions about the finer points of the game and rely on him to arrange a particular interview with the club media relations staff. In return, the reporter or a feature writer would usually ghostwrite the commentator's short column for the next edition.

The number of these ex-player media analysts was substantial. The 1999 Shukan Bēsubōru Yearbook profiled some 20 of the leading commentators, and the 2015 Player Guide had a more complete listing of 142 individuals (Ino 2015:223–227). In the late 1990s, two senior journalists for a major media company told me that the company paid its most prominent commentators annual retainers of about $100,000 per year for written commentaries and television spots during the year, and this was corroborated by the estimates published in the 1999 guide.

REPORTING THE TIGERS IN THE SPORTS DAILIES

Baseball and the modern newspaper have been intertwined in Japan since the beginnings of both. As the next chapter details, Tokyo region newspapers reported the early contests of Japanese schoolboy teams and Americans in Yokohama during the 1890s; *Asahi* and *Mainichi*, the first two national newspapers, began rival national middle school baseball tournaments in the mid-1910s; and in the 1930s the third national paper, *Yomiuri*, sponsored exhibition tours of American professional players and organized Japan's first professional league.

These three general national dailies still have some of the largest circulation in the world, and they are still powerful in sports promotion and reporting. (To the constant chagrin of *Asahi* and *Mainichi*, the Tokyo-centric *Yomiuri* has the largest circulation even in Kansai.) However, their sports coverage was surprisingly thin during the years of my fieldwork and is still so today. An average twenty-four-page morning edition of *Asahi* carried only two or three pages of sports news. Game reports were brief, box scores were cursory, and other statistics and graphics were rare. Sports columns and feature stories were scarce by American and European standards.

For that reason, the sports department at the three national papers was not a desirable rotation for many reporters (just as the Hanshin front office was avoided by many ambitious employees in the Hanshin parent company). These newspaper companies actually gave two kinds of entrance tests: a generalist exam for most aspiring reporters and editors and specialist tests for others, including sports. They often recruited the sports specialists from graduating seniors who had been active in university sports clubs. The half dozen or so selected each year by the paper would be assigned to one of the headquarters sports departments for a year and then be sent for several years to a regional desk, before returning to a major sports department. Most reporters I knew in the sports departments were specialist employees who would always be on that track (but I found them to be uniformly very bright and hardworking). The few who were on the generalist track looked forward to moving quickly to other assignments.

This did not mean that the Japanese baseball fan eschewed newspapers for another medium. I have already indicated that these national dailies long ago gave way to another press, the daily "sports papers." Their circulation totals were less than the national dailies but still in the millions, and at about $1.25 per issue during the years of my fieldwork, they were priced about the same as the national dailies. However, there was one crucial difference between the daily sports papers and the national newspapers that was consequential in the Hanshin sportsworld. The sports dailies depended heavily on spot sales in subway, train, and street kiosks and in convenience stores, while the national newspapers relied almost entirely on home subscriptions (see figure 19). The sports dailies had to compete side by side, front page to front page, every day, morning and night, for buyers. The national newspapers also wanted to keep and expand their home subscriber bases, but they did this through subscription promotions, delivery service claims, and periodic gifts to subscribers, including free baseball game tickets. The sports dailies had only their front pages to catch the eye of commuters, and they did that with dramatic headlines and intense graphic art. Individual stories were relatively short, and the papers were designed to be consumed on the ride to work or at breaks during the workday. Evening editions attempted to grab the same workers on the home commute, although most circulation was of the morning editions.

The mode of distribution and presentation of newspapers created the most powerful media effect in the Hanshin sportsworld. To ride a morning commuter train in the Osaka-Kobe area in those years was to encounter a bright sea of such papers, and anyone could read the headlines over the shoulder of whoever had bought a copy. It was hard to avoid seeing the papers, and most of the riders would be arriving at work at least aware of the game results and the basic emotional mood in the Tigers world. Even those who didn't commute to work but who might be opening their small shops or doing housework at home were drawn into this media space because the sports dailies had tie-ins with a number of the popular morning television variety shows (*waidoshō*).

FIGURE 19. "Fountains" of competing sports dailies gushing up in front of a train platform kiosk, Umeda Station, Osaka, 1999. Courtesy of Nikkan Sports Newspaper.

These shows presented their sports news by taping the front pages of several of the sports dailies to the wall behind the announcer, who would literally go over the papers' main stories, one by one, as the camera panned the pages. Through these daily routines, sports dailies' representations and imagery of the Tigers diffused broadly throughout the region, even among those who did not care much or follow what was on the inside pages.

There were five national sports dailies, four of which dated from the late 1940s, although their big jump in circulation and notoriety happened in the 1960s. All five had regional headquarters in major metropolitan areas, each of which produced separate editions. All of them were affiliated with major media groups. The sports papers evolved over six decades, not just in function and significance but also in form. By the 1960s they had seized the leadership in sports reporting; although television sports news became influential, the sports dailies presented statistics and stories in far greater detail. They also gave detailed coverage to popular gambling sports, especially the three key race sports of horse racing, velodrome bike racing, and short-course powerboat racing. They later added television listings, entertainment world gossip, soft-porn stories, and political scandal coverage to their back pages in an effort to package themselves as the only paper that a commuter needed to read.

Of course, as the name suggests, these papers covered all sports, although Hanshin Tigers overwhelmingly dominated the front pages, total coverage, and staff assignments of all Kansai editions.[4] Even in the off-season, the front page was usually given over to the Tigers. Notice that figure 12 (in chapter 4) was the front page of *Nikkan Sports* for January 20, 1999, even before the start of preseason camps and in the midst of the Tokyo New Year's national sumo tournament. The new manager, Nomura, and his endorsements led the coverage, and the sumo tournament was only reported on the middle pages. During the season, the highlights of the previous day's Tigers game filled the entire front page, as several examples in this book show. The next two pages fleshed out the game with more stories and columns. Other NPB games, including those of the other two Kansai teams, were relegated to the fourth or fifth pages, which also included updates on Japanese players who had moved to MLB.

The middle pages of the paper had brief news items about other sports before moving on to more thorough coverage of two sectors of quasi-sport: "battle" combat sports (pro wrestling, boxing, and mixed martial arts) and "race" sports (primarily results and next-day handicapping of all local venues for Japan's three main gambling sports). For much of the year, there was also a fishing page, identifying conditions at all local shores and seas, reporting on big catches and new tackle, and so forth. The pages toward the end of the paper were devoted to other news and features of a more general tabloid nature, including pachinko, entertainment world gossip, political world scandals, and other stories of a salacious or sensationalist nature.

New printing presses in the 1980s allowed wider color page production, so the dailies developed full-color back-page spreads to match those of the front page. They often used this space for the most prominent nonbaseball sports event or news of the previous day, such as a major horse race or a Japanese athlete's performance in an international marathon or golf or tennis tournament. By the early 2000s, however, the dailies began giving space to J.League soccer and the Japan national soccer team—not only game reports but also backstories on team selections, training, coaching, and player profiles, which some reporters said was a bid to attract younger readers. I address this in the final chapter.

The most striking difference between the sports dailies and the national dailies was the front page. The front page of the sports papers was almost always conceived as a whole to present a single lead story (thus, the front-page layout editor was credited at the bottom of the page). Consider, for example, the March 14, 1999 issue of *Nikkan Sports* (figure 20), which devoted its front page to Hanshin star Shinjō's home run during an exhibition game against the Yakult Swallows after spring training camp (yes, the same Shinjō who had been so publicly disciplined in 1996 by then manager Fujita). It is an excellent example of the layout of intensive coverage: an eye-catching array of colors and font sizes and shapes, mixing text, tables, and photos. Four different headlines run up against one another; the juxtaposition of photos of Shinjō hitting the home run and the aftermath of congratulations converts an exciting time interval into adjacent space. The experienced reader will immediately apprehend an even deeper embedded time on this flat space because the simple box score of the game drops over the left shoulder of the catcher; as the eye moves down through the nine innings, it can begin to recapture three hours of action (filled out in the full box score on the second page). The eyes are not only drawn along the four coordinates of the page but are also led into the page and then out and off the page. Vision is directed in, to focus on the box score and the small font text, which wraps around the bottom third of the page, combining two separate reports of the game with a commentary (in the bottom right-hand corner, set off in green) by a former star player now on the *Nikkan* staff. At the same time, the reader's eyes are drawn off the page, following the upward and outward gaze of Shinjō and the catcher as they watch the ball he has just hit disappear into the sky (while the yellow arrow representing Hanshin's sixteen hits and sixteen runs points diagonally to a fracturing "ya" character, for Yakult). That day and every day, the layout editor (one is tempted to say artist) created, perceptually, a vivid four-dimensional visual experience.[5]

The dailies' front pages always reminded me of manga comic art, and the parallels are not coincidental. Sports dailies are not comics, but from the late 1970s through the early 1980s, they drew key inspiration from elements of comic design and layout and from comic narrative strategies. This was true both for the infrequent celebratory reports of victory and for treatments of continuing narratives of team slumps, star player woes, and managerial difficulties and replacements. Always, the straightforward rectangular geometry of the conventional news page was ignored for a multicolored pastiche of short stories and sidebars in square and circular and even more irregular frames, announced by huge headlines and decorated with overlays and underlays of graphics and

FIGURE 20. Front-page article featuring Shinjō's bases-loaded home run during an exhibition game victory. *Nikkan Sports*, Osaka edition, March 14, 1998, 1. Courtesy of Nikkan Sports Newspaper.

photos. The reader was drawn to the entire page, which portrayed and conveyed the incident as a riveting picture story.

Most of the sports papers were independent corporations but affiliated with larger newspaper and broadcasting corporations. Nikkan Sports, for instance, was part of the Asahi Newspaper group and had several hundred employees in five main offices in Sapporo, Tokyo, Nagoya, Osaka, and Fukuoka.[6] The Kansai sports dailies were generally organized into six divisions. Taking again the case of Osaka Nikkan Sports, three of these were newsgathering units and three were editorial and production units:

- the Sports Department (*undōbu*), in which Hanshin coverage was most important;
- the Race Sports Department, which covered the gambling sports;
- the Society Department (*shakaibu*), which covered everything else;
- the Editorial Department (*henseibu*);
- the Layout and Production Department (*seiribu*); and
- the Business Operations Department (*eigyōbu*), which handled sales, advertising, and circulation.

Reporters and editors of both national and sports dailies insisted that there was much competition for jobs at the sports papers. Like the national dailies, they only recruited from university graduates, often those with sports club experience, and had a rigorous selection process. The same reporters claim there was little turnover.

For instance, Hamaguchi, a new employee at Nikkan, had come from a business family in downtown Osaka and had gone to community college in Tacoma, Washington. He wanted to stay on to finish at the University of Washington, but it was too expensive, so he returned to Japan and was admitted to Dōshisha University, where he majored in business. Graduating in his midtwenties, he applied to various sports papers because they were one of the few places that would consider someone of his age. Even so, Supo-Nichi turned him down for that reason, but Nikkan hired him as one of thirteen new employees in 1993. Ten of his cohort were sent to the Layout and Production Department, and the other three, including Hamaguchi, went to the Business Department. It was several years before they were assigned to actual reporting.

Like the front office, the media corps at the stadium was almost exclusively male. Television game broadcasts sometimes used a female guest commentator as a third voice, and broadcast networks often had a regular female interviewer to conduct pregame interviews and coanchor sports news programs, but in my years at Kōshien, I only encountered a single female beat reporter. Ueyama Noei was in her late twenties and early thirties during my research. She was born in south Osaka and graduated from a small private university in 1992 with a major in

Spanish literature. That was the year of the Barcelona Olympics, and she was hired by an Osaka evening tabloid newspaper to report from the Olympics, a real break for a new recruit. On her return, she was made its beat reporter for the two other Kansai baseball teams, Kintetsu and Orix. After a year or so, she felt there was little opportunity for advancement, so she quit and went to live in Guatemala. When she returned some months later, she covered the 1995 summer high school tournament at Kōshien as a freelancer for one of the national sports dailies. The editor liked her ability to draw out the players and the student supporters. Unusually, the paper made her a regular employee and designated her one of its Hanshin beat reporters. She remained on the Hanshin beat for five years, until 2000, when she moved to the paper's new Electronic Media Section.

What the sports dailies brought to Hanshin newsgathering was a constant presence of large numbers of relatively experienced reporters and commentators. The beat reporters tended to be young, but even they often had five to ten years' experience of daily newsgathering and writing about Hanshin and other clubs; the papers' stables of older commentators were themselves former players, so the overall depth of knowledge was quite deep. Moreover, the need to fill three or four pages for several editions every day made the gathering and writing intensive. A *Nikkan Sports* contingent for each Tigers game usually consisted of three beat reporters, the most senior of whom was known as the cap, *kyappu*; one or two feature writers, who would file their own stories and also ghostwrite the contributions of the one to three commentators; several support staff, including a female clerical worker who used a computer with a special screen to produce the detailed box score that appeared in the paper; and two or three photographers, who were positioned in the special camera press sections beyond both dugouts and also roamed the stadium.

The sports media were constantly talking to one another, to players and coaches, and to any members of the club staff they could persuade to open up. The huge gap in resources between the national papers and the sports dailies was evident, however. While the cadre of reporters for *Nikkan Sports* was scouring the field and stadium for stories throughout the day and evening, the single Hanshin reporter for *Asahi Newspaper*, who was often in and around the stadium for the same long day and evening, was phoning his editor in midgame to find out if he could file a two-hundred-word story on the game or whether there was just space for a fifty-word summary.

THE SPORTS DAILIES AS TABLOID, MANGA, AND DATA

As Kōshien Stadium was the geographical center of the Hanshin world and game time was the temporal center, the players stood for the club and company, and the Kōshien fan associations stood for spectators, so the daily sports papers were the media center of the Hanshin sportsworld. And they were a controversial center. I often heard reporters and editors from the sports departments of the "respectable" national papers and television networks bemoaning the tabloid sensationalism and loose journalistic standards of the sports dailies. However, we must keep in mind the media structures in Japan. In the United States, especially during the long decades of print newspaper dominance, the sports news section was integral to every large metropolitan daily (and papers like the *New York Times* and *Washington Post*, with national distribution). They competed with one another (and with television and radio) in their sports coverage. The Japanese press evolved differently after World War II. Every one of these respectable national papers had a television broadcasting company, a radio network, and a sports paper. In a sense, the sports dailies were the real sports pages of the national press. An American sports fan turns to the sports section of his or her daily paper, but a Japanese fan finds little substance there and must go to the sports dailies instead.

To be sure, the language of the sports dailies was a skillful blend of hyperbole, speculation, and innuendo. Headlines and front-page text were full of exaggerated language; a couple of losses became "stagnation" and an unexpected press release became an "unprecedented pronouncement." The occasional media stakeout at a source's house was known by the anachronistic military term "night raid and dawn attack" (*yōchi asagake*). CEO Kuma himself was an occasional target for his reticence; reporters would wait all night to shout questions in the early morning as he or his wife stepped outside to get the newspaper.

Frequently accused of inadequate confirmation (*kakunin*) of their stories and claims, the reporters did signal the speculative nature of their claims with phrasing like "according to a source involved in this" (*kankeisha no hanashi ni yoru to*) and "it became clear that a fact like X" (*X-teki jijutsu ga akiraka ni naru*), in which *like* is the key word to denote an event, development, or decision similar to something more factually based. They skillfully inserted the preposition "toward" to hint at a possible but unconfirmed development or outcome, and they took advantage of Japanese syntax that can leave the subject actor unspecified. Thus, during the 1996 controversy about manager Fujita, *Nikkan* ran a headline, "toward firing front office executives," which avoided specifying just who might have been contemplating a move "toward" firing them but clearly implying that it was the owner, Kuma).

This colorful language was pleasingly framed in eye-catching graphics. As examples in this book demonstrate, by the 1980s the sports dailies had honed the art of multicolored, multilayered, multisized pictorials—especially front pages, which were a montage of photos, drawings, tables, and prose. Balls exploded off bats, the stands of spectators erupted, front office executives bowed deeply, players emoted. It was graphic, over-the-top melodrama, edition after edition.

Finally, one read the sports dailies not just for the latest plotlines and game summaries and not just for their manga-like visual pleasures, but also for data and real baseball analysis. The ranks of ex-player commentators were constantly providing information and analysis; with articles and sidebars, they were breaking down plays and pitches in excruciating detail (such as "so-and-so is working on a curve, but you can see he is overrotating his wrist," or "so-and-so has a poor bunting technique because he is not getting his chest weight directly over his bent hips"). The sports dailies also outstripped all other media with their compendious presentations of statistical data. Most illustrative of this was the development of the box score, a tabular summary of a game that was published the next day. Newspapers invented these in the late nineteenth century, and they are what every American baseball fan would turn to in the morning paper. However, the Japanese sports newspapers have elaborated the box score format far beyond the American standard, into an ingenious graphic device for narrating time-action in a compact space. Consider the example in figure 21, which is the box score of a game between the Tigers and the Hiroshima Carp on July 6, 2000, that appeared on page 2 in the next morning's edition of *Nikkan Sports*. This was a game in which thirty-five players (including nine pitchers) appeared in 90 at-bats and 330 pitches; it ended with an 11–6 victory by Hiroshima.

The box score is a dense graphic array of characters, numbers, and symbols. For the knowing reader, it conveys the story and statistics of a 3-hour, 48-minute game, packed into a rectangle that averages about 7 inches high by 3¼ inches wide. The top row sets the scene: date (July 6), place (Osaka Dome), starting time (6:00 p.m.), and attendance (34,000). The two teams are divided by a line score of the nine innings in the middle of the box. The Hiroshima Carp, the visitors, are above, and the

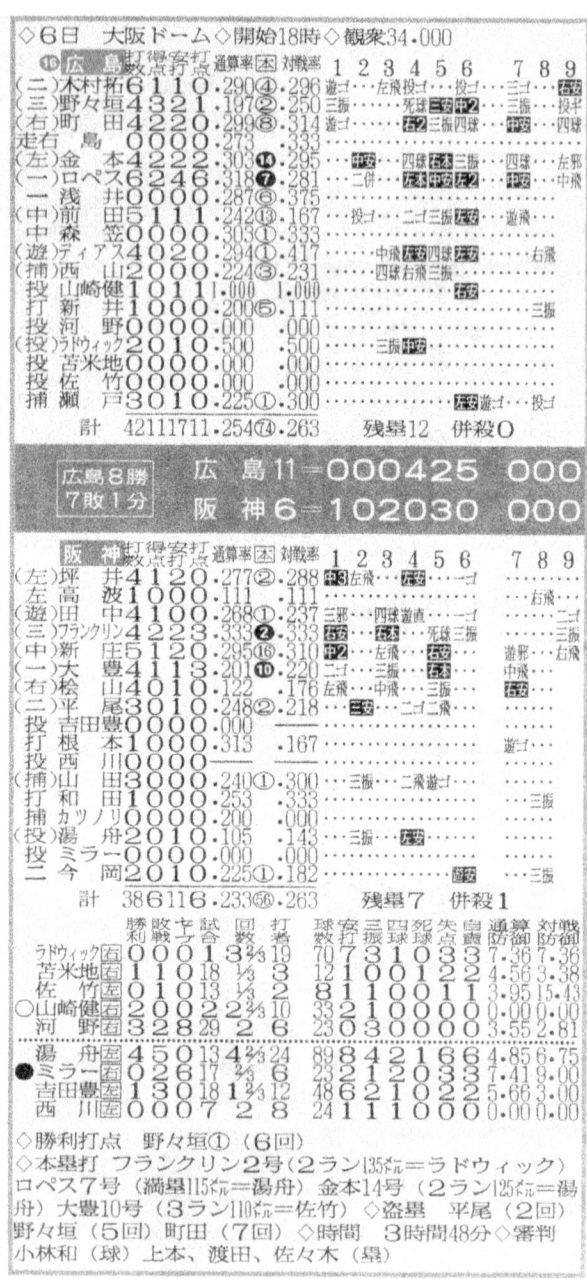

FIGURE 21. Box score of a game between the Hanshin Tigers and
Hiroshima Carp on July 6, 2000. Courtesy of Nikkan Sports
Newspaper.

Hanshin Tigers, the home team, are below. It is early July, halfway through the season, and the teams have already met sixteen times, counting tonight, with Hiroshima winning eight games (including this evening's), Hanshin seven, and one tie.

The players who appeared for the two teams are listed above and below the line score in their batting order. In each row, their fielding position is in parentheses, followed by their name and summary statistics for the game (at-bats, runs, hits, etc.) and three cumulative season statistics. The rows and columns in the right half of the box score then narrate the game itself, at-bat by at-bat. One reads down the first column ("1") from the first at-bat of the game, Kimura's appearance at the top of the first inning, to Kimura grounded out, the second batter struck out, and the third batter grounded out. Hanshin then came to bat, sending its first six batters to the plate and scoring the first run of the game on a triple, a single, and a double. By reading down and to the right, inning by inning the game is re-created.

The final set of statistics details the performance of the pitchers. Hiroshima used five pitchers, Hanshin, four. The bottom of the box score provides further game summary: the game-winning run batted in (RBI), the four home runs (including a grand-slam home run hit over the left-field fence in the fourth inning by the Hiroshima slugger Luis Lopez), stolen bases, the game length, and the umpire crew.

Sports dailies, then, were dynamic composites of tabloid journalism and graphic comics, continuing stories and multiple statistics, keeping Hanshin at the center of regional attention. They were essential to hardcore fans because they supplied them with constant information, speculation, and data, and unavoidable for those with only a casual interest in baseball because the dailies were in their faces every day as they passed kiosk after kiosk and rode the subways, trains, and buses to and from work.

NARRATING TO THE TIGERS ON THE RADIO

The first live radio broadcast of baseball was at Kōshien at the thirteenth national summer tournament in 1928, and it was immediately popular. Radio returned after World War II with the restart of school and professional baseball. Watanabe Kentarō (2003), for instance, recounted the nostalgia of the early postwar generation who grew up with the voice of the NHK radio announcer, Shimura Masayori, who would create a florid scene of sports drama from even the most routine plays. Television did not entirely replace radio, and walking around the backstreets of Osaka on a game evening, I could hear the strains of radio broadcasts from the small factories and stores. Taxi drivers, too, liked to listen to the games on their radios (this was before dashboard displays began bringing television into automobiles). However, several announcers told me, sometimes ruefully, that their flights of rhetorical fancy were much constrained by the copresence of televisuals and even by the transistor radios that fans brought to the ballpark, juxtaposing the radio commentary with what they were seeing with their own eyes.

The distinctive and difficult requirements of radio broadcasting were brought home to me on a September evening at Green Stadium during a game between Kansai rivals Kintetsu and Orix when I happened to sit down in a seat just outside the press box behind two men from ABC Radio (a station that was part of Asahi Broadcasting). In front of them was a wood model of a broadcast microphone, and I realized quickly that this was a training session. The younger fellow was practicing his play-by-play as the other—an established announcer—critiqued him. The novice had quite a powerful voice, but he was ignored by those around them. I, however, hung on every word as it became my own impromptu lesson in radio voicing.

I realized, for instance, from the apprentice's efforts and the teacher's critique, how much of good play-by-play announcing involved synchronizing the voice with the crowd noise, which listeners would always hear in the announcer's background. The announcer couldn't fall behind the crowd, fumbling for words or being too verbose, but he also could not get too far ahead of the crowd, anticipating action. He had to sustain a delicate timing. "Report with your eyes" the announcer mentor kept repeating: train your eyes to follow the unfolding play and let your voice transmit only what you are seeing, not what you have seen or think you will see.

Another of his instructions was to maintain the same sequence in reporting repetitive information (e.g., "one out, men on first and third, x batter up, third pitch") and to use a consistent verb tense. The cub announcer tended to shift between formal and informal past tense (sometimes "nagemashita" for "here's the pitch," followed by "utta!" for "he's hit it to").

At the same time, it was crucial to present this consistent syntax with a variable intonation, and I realized from the session how effective game announcers adjusted their voices along several dimensions, modulating a rising and falling intonation, their speed of talk, and the intensity of their enunciation. They used all three to start, build, and bring to conclusion a "play" that was unfolding, and they deployed them over the full course of the game as well to connect and highlight its critical moments. The announcer had to create suspense, which meant conveying both a sense of being in control and of understanding each moment, but he also had to communicate awe and surprise.

Like television broadcasting, baseball radio for the Tigers was typically handled by a three-person team: the play-by-play announcer, a regular "color" commentator, and a guest commentator who was well known to the audience, though not necessarily from the baseball world. Thus, the announcer was also challenged to meld his flow with that of his commentator partner, who offered a break in play-by-play and served as a partner (*aite*) to whom he had to be responsive—and the two of them had to bring the guest in at appropriate moments.

BROADCASTING THE TIGERS ON TELEVISION

Most sports spectating has been done via television for decades, and this was certainly true for Japanese baseball, including Hanshin. Media theorists are fond of reminding us that sports television is inherently illusory. While it appears to be directly and transparently "broadcasting" games as they occur in stadiums like Kōshien, in fact it is really transmitting a "media event" of its own creation (Yoshimi [1996, 2003] and others have developed this idea for Japan). Such a media event is composed of visuals and stories, both of which are "unreal" in the sense that the viewer/listener is in a position quite unlike that of any spectator at the stadium. Replays of key action, for instance, interrupt the suspenseful spontaneity of the event and provide television viewers doubled satisfaction. The narrative of the game, too, is continually enhanced by the statistical framework and continual commentary of the broadcasters.

This has led to some sharp debate about the nature of the television sports experience. To critics like Yoshimi (1996) and Nagai (1997), television viewers are fraudulent fans because they neither absorb nor contribute to the aura and ambience of the stadium; they are denied the direct physical experience of being there. This, however, unfairly discounts two features of the televised sports experience that were crucial to the larger world of Hanshin baseball. First, the television viewers' experience was not as removed from the stadium and dependent on the medium as we might presume. This is not so much because the stadium experience survived in the broadcast as the constant crowd noise and occasional crowd visuals, but more because the television viewer was a virtual stadium spectator with the closest view of the action. The central camera shot of all baseball games hovers voyeuristically over the shoulder of the pitcher and looks directly at the home plate trio of batter, catcher, and umpire. The television fan is even more privileged than the pitcher or any other player because he has eyes throughout the stadium—seven television camera Cyclops in the case of Kōshien games—that allow him or her to jump quickly from looking in to looking over at the niches, to looking from the infield stands, out from the backstop, and down from the outfield stands. Not only that; stop-action and slow-motion replays make time slow down and stop and run backward in this parallel, non-Euclidean world.

There is another reason for being skeptical of charges of fraud. While nothing could simulate the pulsating sonics and visceral excitement of a game at Kōshien, watching numerous games in bars and homes impressed upon me the capacity of television viewers to create social environments of Tigers game action that in fact distributed the experience across the cities and towns of the region. Their cheers and groans could not be heard at Kōshien, and their beer purchases did not fill the coffers of the stadium concessionaires, but like pop-up stores and restaurants, they created temporary spaces of Tigers fandom distributed across the region, reconvening every evening to generate and express (moriagaru) their enthusiasm and support.

It is worth noting the striking difference between television and radio announcing that is created by the presence or absence of visual accompaniment. The stadium game and the ears of the radio listener are tethered by the thin link of the announcer's voice, which bears the entire burden of narrating the action. Television play-by-play doesn't have to describe so much of the action, which the viewer sees intimately, and the volume, tone, and substance of television commentary thus vary considerably. This does not mean that the television announcer has "freer" license. Indeed, the television announcer is even more tightly bound by the screen because both the announcer and the viewers are watching the game together.

THE PUBLICITY CONUNDRUM
AND BROADCAST RIGHTS

The sports dailies, radio, and television broadcasting all have their distinct sensibilities and strategies, even if they work in the same time and space of the stadium game day. The political economy of the Hanshin media was similarly a mix of common conditions and diverse features. The most important constant was that Hanshin had no media companies within its group.

A crucial business difference between MLB and NPB was that in Japan there were no exclusive and comprehensive league contracts with television networks, except for the all-star games. All broadcasting rights for a game were held by the home team club. Thus, Tigers television was big business for regional networks and for the club itself, and the marketing of broadcasting rights for a club like Hanshin without an affiliated media company was its most lucrative profit opportunity. The Giants and the Chūnichi Dragons had exclusive season-long contracts with a single broadcasting network (within their respective groups); all others, including Hanshin, were not aligned with a television company and signed contracts with multiple broadcasters for blocks of games throughout the season.

There were four regular broadcasting companies in Kansai. Asahi Hōsō (ABC), Mainichi Hōsō (MBS), and Yomiuri Terebi were national companies within the three media groups, and each had a production and broadcasting division in Kansai; Kansai Terebi, as the name suggests, was regional only. There was also a major UHF satellite broadcast company in Kansai, Sun television, which was part of the Kobe Shimbun group. NHK had production divisions in both Osaka and Kobe, and by the early 2000s it was bidding for satellite broadcasts for some games.

To appease the full media and to maximize revenue, Hanshin spread its broadcast rights among the four regular stations and Sun TV through complex annual negotiations. All the stations wanted as many Giants games as possible, so Hanshin packaged groups of Giants games with games against less popular teams and put them out for bid. The result was that there were different broadcasting teams throughout the season.[7] Radio overlapped even more. Hanshin sold those broadcast rights very cheaply, and popular games would attract four different radio stations.

Here too we find evidence of the Tigers' overwhelming share of the regional audience. For the 2000 season, for instance, Sun TV contracted to broadcast seventy-seven Hanshin games, ten Orix BlueWave games, and only one Kintetsu Buffaloes contest (*Nikkan Sports*, March 21, 2000). In the late 1990s, the Hanshin media relations staff responsible for negotiating told me that each home game against the Giants was worth ¥80,000,000 (about $740,000), while games against most other teams could only be sold for ¥20,000,000. In the early 2000s, those rights increased to ¥100,000,000 (about $800,000) for Giants games, while an average game against a team like the Yokohama BayStars yielded only less than a third of that. At the same time, in the Pacific League, Orix and Kintetsu could only yield perhaps 10 percent of these revenues for the few games that interested the networks.

I should note here that a frequent complaint of foreign commentators (and some Japanese fans) was that many baseball games on regular Japanese networks were not broadcast in their entirety. A network like Asahi ABC would often join a game in progress at 7:00 p.m. (with most games starting at 6:00 p.m. or 6:30 p.m.) and end its transmission at 9:00 p.m., whether or not the game had concluded (it usually hadn't). This was further evidence, these commentators felt, of some Japanese inability to appreciate the true spirit of sports. Television staff I spoke with acknowledged that game broadcasts could be truncated, although they did not like to do that. Their reasoning was that a regional or national network had to serve a diverse audience (and secure a diverse stable of advertisers); there were demographic groups that relied on other programming in the 6:00–7:00 p.m. slot and in the "golden hour" of 9:00–10:00 p.m. Baseball fans, they said, could tune in to radio and, by the late 1990s, satellite stations for the beginnings and ends of games.

TELL AND SELL: ARE THE HANSHIN MEDIA COMPETITIVE, CRITICAL, OR COLLUSIVE?

Media have been a perfect match for modern spectator sports like baseball. Sports, leagues, teams, and athletes need media exposure and media revenues as much as print, broadcast, and digital media depend on sports as their largest content filler and for their greatest profits. The media's blending of journalism, entertainment, and advertising parallels and underscores sport's own multiple qualities of instruction, diversion, and marketing.

In Japan since at least the 1960s, professional baseball has become the standard-bearer of sports news, and its dominance has created both the need for and the value of publicizing everything all year—the many games and the long seasons, of course, but even that does not fill the annual news calendar, so reporting and commentary about training, contracts, player and coach movements, club developments, and more have become topics of media coverage and reader knowledge. Television, radio, and print media have formed the triad of professional baseball, and this chapter has drawn out some of the distinctive differences in the communicative and representational strategies and sensibilities of the three major media. Of them, in many ways and for several reasons, it was the Kansai sports dailies that drove coverage of the Tigers across the region, with their large omnipresent staffs, contingents of ex-players as commentators, garish in-your-face graphics, innovative statistics, and tabloid speculation. They were an unavoidable presence, highly visible on commuter trains; fronting newsstands, kiosks, and convenience store counters; and displayed on morning television shows.

Nonetheless, despite the fit between media and sports, the relationship of these media and the club in the Hanshin sportsworld was deeply contentious and contradictory. Media coverage was hardly equal across the twelve NPB teams. It was well-known that Yomiuri's control of sports teams, stadiums, and multiple media allowed it to manipulate its coverage of the Giants, not only by providing favored, inside information to its own outlets like Hōchi but by intimidating rival media by threatening their access to Giants' news. After the Giants, the Tigers were long the most scrutinized and publicized club. They were the centerpiece of Kansai regional sports. The simple fact of not owning any media left Hanshin with far less leverage with the media, and the club's small media relations staff was beleaguered and besieged in handling the volume of daily requests and trying to control the spin of stories.

The divided role of the media relations staff—sometimes minders, sometimes facilitators—was itself indicative of these contradictions. They tried simultaneously to protect and project the players and manager. There were in fact two axes of competition and collusion: between the Hanshin club and the Tigers media and among the media themselves.

The club and even the mainstream media complained frequently about the intrusiveness of the sports dailies and the irresponsibility of their reporting, all while both depended on those sports dailies. As I noted previously, confirmation (kakunin) was the key element in their frustration. The sports dailies didn't confirm, went the complaint. A reporter would be told something by someone, and instead of confirming it with other sources, he would immediately file a story that seemed to give it credence. Daily deadlines plus murderous competition and mass public encounters gave reporters little opportunity or motivation to do this; in addition, the organization tends to deny rather than confirm.

On the other hand, I could understand the practices of the sports dailies, working against daily deadlines and a club and company that tended to deny and deflect anyway. Hanshin's stonewalling pushed the reporters to keep pursuing everyone, pick up any dissident tones or alternative views, read tea-leaf pronouncements, and print provocative statements to see if they get a rise out of the club or players. That is, there was a constant give and take going on, which could lead to hard feelings but also mutual profits.

Collusion, or at least a self-imposed reserve, could arise from the intimacy of long-term encounters, hardly an uncommon dilemma in news reporting. One day I observed a veteran reporter with whom I had had regular conversations talking with the visiting team manager for half an hour during his team's warm-ups. When I asked him about their relationship, he said that they had known each other for thirty years; he claimed that the manager told him many things that he didn't talk about with the rest of the press because as a friend, the manager knows that he will be circumspect in what and how he writes. The same was true for a veteran reporter who had known manager Yoshida since high school days. Both reporters wrote some thoughtful and even critical pieces about these managers and their teams, but they admitted to always exercising some self-restraint.

The other axis of competition and collusion ran through the media themselves, and I was given contradictory views of this. The press club system operated in sports as in most news-gathering scenarios in Japan and fostered a certain conformity to its club procedures (e.g., the head of the press club was always the designated questioner of the manager in the postgame interview, and others had to pass him questions they wanted asked). At the same time, the five sports dailies were lavishing inordinate attention and resources on Hanshin reporting and were competing fiercely for readers and advertisers.

Did this produce pack journalism or hypercompetition? A veteran *Asahi* reporter and editor complained that the business departments of the sports papers were in fierce competition, but the reporters themselves generally cooperated with one another. The Hanshin sports press, he felt, all wrote the same stories and seldom worked to develop unusual angles. *Nikkan*'s senior baseball feature writer insisted, on the contrary, that there was a strong undercurrent of competition. The difference was location. At the ballpark, he said, everything was relaxed and cooperative, and the reporters were amicable with one another, were exposed to the same developments, and tended to do similar reporting. But before and after the ballpark, he claimed, they would all be out beating the bushes trying to contact players, seeking exclusive quotes, and identifying new stories. If, for instance, Shinjō hit a home run to win a game, everyone would run the same quote supplied by the media relations staff. But if someone had managed to ride with him in his taxi to the ballpark and he had mentioned that he was feeling like he was going to have a big hit, that would be added to give an edge to that paper's story.

Frictions with the club were much more evident with the sport dailies than other media, and there were subtle differences between the competition among the sports dailies to cover the Tigers and the competition among television and radio networks to broadcast the Tigers. The papers had guaranteed access through their press club memberships. The networks were jockeying each year for contracts to broadcast blocks of games, and it is possible that the club would show favoritism to those networks that were less critical in their game coverage than others. The front office and announcers themselves always responded in the negative to my questions about this possibility, and I have no evidence that this was an important factor on either side, but it does further illustrate the perpetual struggle within the Hanshin sportsworld to define and defend positions of commentary.

CONCLUSION

In the previous five chapters, I delineated the Hanshin Tigers as a sportsworld, and showed how it has been mutually constructed by players, coaches, corporate staff, the media, and the fans. It is a world with complex temporal rhythms and spatial coordinates, centered on the season of contests played on the Kōshien field but also manifested in times and places well beyond that diamond. I was led to this formulation by trying to understand why the Tigers were such an intense focus of attention in Kansai during the years of my research, as measured by their overwhelming dominance of media coverage, stadium attendance, and club revenues and by the widespread knowledge and passion for the team throughout Kansai. Why was this so? The same sport was being played by the Orix BlueWave at Green Stadium and by the Kintetsu Buffaloes at Fujiidera Stadium as at Kōshien, yet it was Tigers baseball that so dominated Kansai. This could hardly be explained by the success of the team or the resources at its command; it was mired in defeat year after year, and its constant playing and personnel difficulties were daily topics of media coverage and fan debate. The Orix BlueWave were far more successful, and the Kintetsu Buffalo had a far larger corporate parent with broader reach and deeper resources.

I have suggested that Hanshin baseball was heavily inflected with the workplace melodramas that engulfed the Tigers and with its role as a standard-bearer in Osaka's second-city rivalry with Tokyo. This requires further substantiation, and in the next two chapters I explore more of when, how, and why it was the Tigers, among Kansai teams, who came to embody these particular themes.

CHAPTER 8

Baseball as Education and Entertainment

Even after forty years, the title and the first edition cover image of Robert Whiting's 1977 book about Japanese baseball, *The Chrysanthemum and the Bat*, are among the most striking and influential in the literature on the sport in that country (see figure 22). His title was an ingenious evocation of Ruth Benedict's *The Chrysanthemum and the Sword* (1946), and the publisher's artist had the samurai swinging a bat-sword in front of a baseball diamond that replaced the chrysanthemum design.

Modern sports since their systematization in the nineteenth century have been justified in moralizing terms of (usually masculine-coded) character building. Baseball in Japan is no exception. To those outside Japanese baseball, a notion of samurai baseball may seem more parody than paradigm, but for a long time within this baseball world, to some foreigners and some Japanese alike, the notion has been taken rather seriously as an accurate image of the way the sport is played—or at least should be played—in Japan. The vocabulary of baseball in Japan is a complex patois of English-derived terms (e.g., *faasuto* or first means the first baseman position) and indigenous terms (the Japanese word *dageki* is used for batting), but for a century, the Sino-Japanese character compound yakyū rather than English-derived *bēsubōru* (baseball) has been the name of the sport. And when commentators and practitioners wax philosophical, they start talking about *yakyū-dō* or the Way of Baseball.

What do they mean by such a term, and where did it come from? There is a broad consensus about the code of conduct for the Way of

THE CHRYSANTHEMUM
AND THE BAT

BASEBALL SAMURAI STYLE

ROBERT WHITING

FIGURE 22. Cover of the first edition of *The Chrysanthemum and the Bat*, by Robert Whiting. Published by Dodd Mead and Company, 1977. Courtesy of Robert Whiting.

Baseball. First, the Way spiritualizes hard work and intense practice. It demands an abiding loyalty to the team and abject obedience to the manager and coaches. It is an obsession with form and a doggedly conservative, run-by-run playing strategy. Much importance is placed on maintaining one's pride, and tie games are valued for mutual face-saving. Finally, the Japanese Way of Baseball instills an intense and insular national pride, with strong prejudice at the professional level against foreign players, whom the clubs sign reluctantly to their rosters and then systematically denigrate.

Sports everywhere, and team sports especially, place a premium on intensity, loyalty, teamwork, self-sacrifice, and honor, but many observers believe that the Japanese Way of Baseball carries these values to extreme degrees. The bundling of these qualities as samurai virtues arose at a particular time and with a particular team. The time was the decade of the 1890s, a period of assertiveness against the extraterritorial powers that Western countries had enjoyed in Japan for thirty years and of incipient imperial nationalism after Japan's successful incursions into China in 1895. The team was the baseball club of the First Higher School (Dai-ichi kōtō gakkō) in Tokyo, the elite stepping-stone to Tokyo Imperial University, known by its Japanese abbreviation, Ichikō. This chapter begins by considering this early association of baseball in Japan with the loyal and self-sacrificing samurai as a powerful yet disputed template of character development.

In the first two decades of the twentieth century, baseball was not only nationalized with the patriotic overtones of samurai ethics but was also commercialized by metropolitan interests. Baseball was implicated in the spread of intra- and interurban railroads competing for line development and seeking to attract riders; in several newspapers marketing themselves as national general interest media and seeking subscribers and readers; and with urban stadium construction and national schoolboy tournaments that drew tens of thousands of paying spectators. Both the moralizing language and the commercial initiatives expanded throughout the 1920s and into the 1930s.

Hanshin was deeply involved in all of this. It was one of the first commuter train companies in Kansai in the first decade (1902), it paired with *Asahi* newspaper to start the first national middle school tournament in the second decade (1915), it built Kōshien as Asia's largest stadium in the third decade (1924), and it joined Yomiuri and others in organizing the first professional league in the fourth decade (1936).

The effect of all these developments was to fundamentally shape baseball not simply as a sporting embodiment of samurai spirit but as a far more complex and often uneasy hybrid of didactic moralism and mass entertainment. Over the forty years between the portentous 1896 game between Ichikō School and an American team and the 1936 founding of the first professional league, baseball became Japan's quintessential "edutainment," and this remains the sport's indelible quality.

RAILROAD YARDS AND SCHOOLYARDS

Baseball began in Japan as recreation, not moral training, and like so many other technology transfers and institutional adaptations in Japan after the 1868 Meiji Restoration (Westney 1987), the sport was introduced by Japanese returning from studying abroad and by Westerners employed in Japan. Baseball's beginnings in the 1870s have been traced to an American teacher, Horace Wilson, and a Japanese railroad engineer, Hiraoka Hiroshi. Wilson was an American instructor at an elite boys school that would shortly become one of the constituent schools of the new University of Tokyo, and he organized after-class baseball games with his students as early as 1872. Hiraoka was a railroad engineer who had apprenticed in the United States at the Boston railroad yards from 1871 to 1876 and returned home with baseball equipment (donated by Albert G. Spalding) and a rulebook. In 1880 Hiraoka organized fellow Tokyo railroad workers into Japan's first team, the Shimbashi Athletic Club, and a year later the club laid out Japan's first ballpark on railroad property in downtown Tokyo.

Baseball found more interest and support among the schoolboys than among the railroad workers, and it soon became closely tied to the emerging agenda of elite higher education, which was reorganized after the Meiji Restoration under the new nation-state. Western sports made their way into the curriculum of the new Meiji schools because education authorities believed them to be more effective in fostering group training than indigenous physical practices. They did not ignore Japanese martial arts, but educators generally viewed these as too individualized to promote teamwork and disciplined coordination (so much for stereotypes of group-bound Japanese!). Instead, they hoped that these new Western sports could be infused with the mental and spiritual aims of such martial arts. This followed from a wider ideological project. "Japanese spirit and Western techniques" (*wakon-yōsai*) was a much cited catchphrase of the time, which expressed official hopes that a modern Japan could be built by conjoining indigenous values and institutions and technologies selectively adapted from Euro-American forms. From the start, Western athletics were spiritualized and given pedagogic functions and curricular significance. A number of commentators and ministry bureaucrats came to see baseball, in particular, as an ideal combination of the display of individual talents and the need to coordinate those talents toward team objectives.

SAMURAI SCHOOLBOYS: "JAPANESE SPIRIT, WESTERN SPORT"

It was at the First Higher School (Ichikō) in Tokyo and several similar schools that the sport rose to prominence and prestige, as Donald Roden (1980a) observed in his elegant essay on Meiji baseball and its role in defining the ethos of elite education. From the 1880s, these so-called higher schools prepared a small number of elite teenaged boys for the single national university. Drawing on British models of public schools, headmasters at Ichikō and elsewhere stressed student self-responsibility in operating their dormitories and their daily school life. Student-run sports and other cultural activity clubs were deemed useful by adult educators not only as an outlet for youthful energy but also to build physical and spiritual character. By the early 1890s, baseball was one of many such club activities, along with cricket, fencing, and other sports. Initially, in fact, it was not the most popular or prestigious sport. Rowing, especially the interschool races on downtown Tokyo's Sumida River, drew more public attention and school prestige.

Rather unexpectedly, a single baseball game that took place on a May afternoon in 1896 catapulted these elite schoolboy baseball clubs to national attention and moved the sport into the ideological orbit of a modern incarnation of an older warrior ethos. The game took place on the grounds of the Yokohama Country and Athletic Club (YCAC), which was a garden park and cricket pitch for foreigners that overlooked Yokohama harbor on higher ground away from the downtown port. Surrounded by a bamboo fence and attractively landscaped, it was legally foreign property, more English than American, and certainly off-limits to ordinary Japanese.

It was there, on May 23, 1896, that the first formal baseball contest was held between the Ichikō team and a team of Americans resident in Yokohama. These traders, teachers, diplomats, and others had organized themselves as the Yokohama Amateur Club (YAC) to engage each other and visiting American seamen in the sport. For several years the Ichikō club had issued requests to the Americans for a chance to play; finally, through the efforts of W. B. Mason, an American teacher at Ichikō, the YAC accepted the challenge and agreed to have the school-boys come down to Yokohama. The YCAC, being primarily British, favored cricket, but a baseball field was laid out on the grounds. The Ichikō baseball club manager, Chūma Kanoe, an alumnus of the school and by then a Tokyo University student, came down to Yokohama the day before to negotiate the arrangements. Several days of rain threatened to continue as May 23 dawned, but by midday the sky had cleared enough to play.

The Ichikō boys set out with a small group of supporters from Shimbashi Station on the new Tokyo-Yokohama train line. Arriving at Yokohama Station, they walked from there up to the YCAC grounds. The game started at 3:00 p.m. with an American umpire; oddly, the visiting Ichikō team took the field first. It was a shaky start for the Ichikō pitcher,

Aoi Etsuo, who was probably using an American-made baseball for the first time. His catcher was wearing a mask modified from a kendō martial arts mask, and the entire team wore Japanese-style thick socks (*tabi*), not the baseball spikes that the Americans wore.

The game began poorly for the schoolboys. Aoi walked the first batter, gave up a hit to the second batter, and walked the third batter, thus loading the bases with no outs and quickly drawing snickers from the crowd of foreigners. The fourth batter smashed a drive off the outfield fence, bringing in two runs, and before the Americans were finally out, two more runs were scored.

Another surprise greeted Ichikō when it came to bat in the bottom of the first and discovered the entire US team had large leather gloves (only the Japanese pitcher and catcher had hand protection, in the form of light cloth gloves). The pitcher walked the first two batters but picked each one off first base before he could advance. With two outs, the next batters dug in, and Ichikō rallied for two runs. Coming to the mound in the second inning, Aoi was more poised and proceeded to strike out three American batters. His teammates' bats came alive in the bottom of the inning to score four times.

The momentum had decisively shifted. The US team did not score again, while Ichikō went on to pile up run after run. The student supporters became animated, and even a crowd of rickshaw drivers clustered around the outside of the fence to follow the game through its later innings. The final score was an astonishing 29–4, and the exuberant rickshaw drivers took the entire team back to the station at no charge. Before boarding the train, the players sent telegrams to their school principal and to other schools informing them of the victory. By the time they arrived back at Ichikō at the end of the day, the entire school greeted them at the gates and held a victory assembly on the school grounds, followed by a party.

News of the victory spread rapidly throughout the country, and congratulatory telegrams and letters poured in. In the meantime, the Americans quickly asked for a rematch, which was held less than two weeks later, on June 4, at the same Yokohama cricket ground. This time the press reports had generated enormous interest in the contest. The Yokohama city folk cheered the students as they walked from the station to the park and packed themselves around the boundary fences in order to catch a glimpse of the game.

For this second game, the YAC augmented its numbers with five sailors from visiting US ships, veteran players whose size and power posed something of a fearful presence to the schoolboys. From the start, though, Aoi pitched well, and the Ichikō batters continued to hit. A large contingent of students from Yokohama Commercial School formed a noisy cheering section for Ichikō, and when the game ended with another lopsided victory, 32–9, they erupted in banzai cheers. Afterward the team was hosted at the Commercial School and then walked back through the city streets full of cheering crowds to the station.

Yet a third match was held later that month, on June 27, this time at Ichikō. Chūma himself served as umpire, and again Ichikō pounded the American team, 22–6. By now, the newspapers were feting the team as national heroes.

Ichikō finally lost in the fourth game, which was held on American Independence Day, July 4, in Yokohama, by the close score of 14–12. The rivalry then resumed the following year; in total, from 1896 to 1904, Ichikō played thirteen games against the Yokohama Americans, winning eleven and losing only twice. The repeated victories reinforced the prominence of the baseball club among other sports clubs at Ichikō and the status of Ichikō in the world of elite education. As these students moved into the university, they brought the sport upward to found clubs there, and after graduation, as many moved into teaching careers, they promoted the sport downward across the national secondary school system.

The victories were startling, but several other factors lent them even more causal weight in sports and diplomatic history. For several years before these games, the Ichikō team had articulated a very self-conscious code of spiritualized sporting practice; it wasn't called samurai baseball, but it was called "spiritual baseball" (*seishin yakyū*), and it fetishized intense workouts, absolute commitment to the team, and victory for team and school at all costs. (In fact, interschool games were rare, so daily practice was much of what Ichikō baseball was all about.) Patriotic feelings were enflamed at a moment when Japan had launched its first modern aggression (the Sino-Japanese War of 1894–1895, which opened both Korea and Taiwan to Japanese occupation) and when the government was determined to renegotiate the unfavorable trade treaties that it had been forced to sign with the Western powers thirty years before. Ideologues for over a decade had been formulating resurrections of putative Japanese warrior codes as a nationalist ethics. To beat the Americans on such contested ground as the Yokohama foreigners' compound was freighted with significance, especially since the team had already stylized itself with many of these qualities in its code of spiritual baseball.

The political importance of this series and the more general associations of elite schoolboy baseball with a samurai code of conduct have been the focus of much scholarship and commentary about Meiji-era baseball.[1] At the same time, there are several reasons to be skeptical about painting all of Meiji-era baseball with such a broad brush. First of all, there was much deliberate fabrication in these notions of being a "samurai," not unlike the selective amnesia that modern Americans have in regard to cowboy types. The samurai images that Ichikō players compared themselves to bore about as much resemblance to warriors of the past as the Marlboro Man does to the original ranch hands of the 1870s and 1880s. To be sure, loyalty to the extremes of self-sacrifice, the cardinal virtue promulgated by samurai baseball, was central to the codes by which warriors lived in epochs past, but what is conveniently forgotten are the many forms that it could take and the other virtues ennobled in the warriors' codes, including an overweening self-pride, moral purity, and sheer opportunism.[2] It is also worth noting that a certain anxiety and defensiveness may have motivated the Ichikō club in making such a public display of its masochistic training. There was indeed a powerful wave of patriotic nationalism building, but there was also some popular resentment toward the elite and suspicions about how deserving the very small segment of youth that was being channeled toward this leadership was, a channel that ran directly through Ichikō. A political satirist of the era lampooned these elite youths with a drawing (see figure 23) of a pampered student with a sniveling nose and insincere double tongue, whose eyes, ears, and hairline displayed his dissolute hedonism. Allegiance to a Spartan code of physical discipline and ethical rigor, framed in an idiom of samurai heritage, was an obvious antidote to that public skepticism about their moral fiber.

Despite the attention given, then and now, to Ichikō, there were other approaches to baseball at the time, both in the styles of particular teams and in the pronouncements of commentators and educators. An instructive contrast to Ichikō was Waseda University, which came to supplant Ichikō a few years after the Ichikō series with the Yokohama Americans. By the turn of the twentieth century, several private higher schools had gained official designation as universities; of particular importance to baseball were Keio University and Waseda University, both located in Tokyo. Both of their baseball clubs defeated Ichikō in 1904, and this shifted public attention to the collegiate game. In 1903 Waseda players

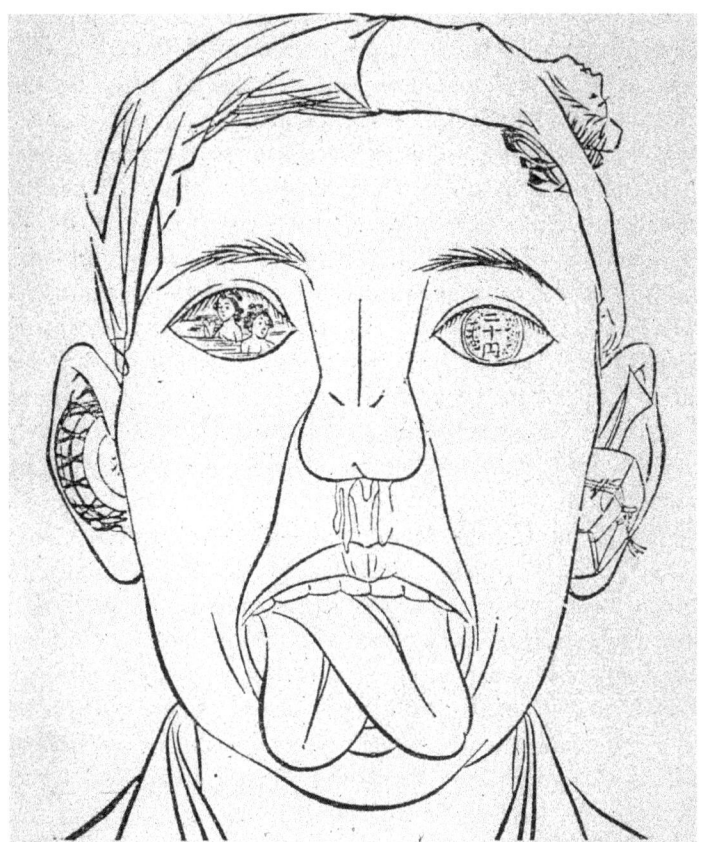

FIGURE 23. A satirical image, "Today's Elite Student," from *Osaka Manga Shimbun*, March 15, 1909. The artist criticized these elite youths as depraved by filling the eyes with images of bathing women and a coin, draping a half-dressed woman over his forehead, stuffing his ears with a party drum and gift box, and giving him a sniveling nose for obsequity and a double tongue for duplicity. From Osaka Manga Shimbun.

visited the Keiō club dormitory to propose a series of semiannual contests. Thus began the Waseda-Keiō Series (Sōkeisen), still the most famous rivalry in Japanese university baseball. It was a contentious rivalry, and in 1905 the series was suspended when the fan clubs of the two schools went on a postgame rampage through the main corridor of Ginza in downtown Tokyo.

The newspapers showered them with sharp criticism, and the special series did not resume for twenty years (although regular league play between the clubs did continue). Without their rivalry, both Waseda and Keio turned to US teams for competition, and international exhibition tours quickly became an important aspect of collegiate baseball. The Waseda team had already made the first playing tour to the United States in 1903, winning six of eighteen games. It went in the spirit of international exchange, not nationalist rivalry, and the club brought back a number of practices it had learned from the American collegiate teams, including new uniform styles, the use of gloves for all players, and bunting strategies. The Waseda team was also very impressed by the collegiate cheerleaders and raucous student fans they observed at American football games (they went during the fall football season), and upon their return they introduced drums, pennants, cheers, and other elements of organized fan club behavior. Strangely, then, we can trace the origins of Kōshien fan behavior back to early American undergraduates!

The faculty head of the Waseda baseball team and leader of the US tour was Professor Abe Isoo. Abe had converted to Christianity while a student at Dōshisha University in Kyoto, and he became an ardent socialist while studying at Hartford Theological Seminary in Connecticut. He returned to Japan and helped organize Japan's socialist party in 1901. He was appointed a professor at Waseda in 1903, where he continued his political activities while promoting both tennis and baseball at Waseda as character-building sports. He believed firmly that the basis of pacifism lay in nonviolence and that military conflicts between nations should be replaced by athletic competition, a view he traced to his readings of Tolstoy while a foreign student in the United States in the early 1890s (Ikari 1987:506–507). He firmly believed in the educational value of sports to shape virtuous behavior, but his ethical idiom was sharply divergent from that of the "samurai-ologists."

NEWSPAPER, RAILROADS, AND THE SPREAD OF BASEBALL IN THE 1910S

The observant reader will have noticed two other details of that game between the Japanese schoolboys and the American men in May 1896: the Ichikō team traveled by train to and from Tokyo, and newspapers (both the English-language press in Yokohama and the domestic press in Tokyo and elsewhere) were crucial in spreading news about the game. Over the next thirty years, trains and newspapers were to become central elements in a burgeoning metropolitan mass culture in Tokyo,

Osaka, and other urban centers, and sports and other leisure activities became profitable vehicles of their content and promotion. By the time that Kōshien Stadium opened on August 1, 1924, schoolboy baseball had become an uneasy mix of pedagogy and profit. This, as we will see, is because it was now embedded both in the changing educational system and in the leisure and information networks of metropolitan regions.

In 1905 a semiprofessional team from Hawaii toured Japan, and Waseda made four more trips to the United States over the next twenty years, as well as several visits to the Philippines. Keio and Meiji Universities also quickly took to touring. Waseda developed a particular rivalry with the University of Chicago, an athletic powerhouse during those years; the two schools met on their respective fields ten times between 1906 and 1936. Baseball teams—as well as track and swimming teams—from the University of Washington, Stanford University, and the University of California also made multiple visits to Japan.

Press criticism about the troubles during the Waseda-Keiō series persisted, broadening into larger concerns about baseball's popularity. The most famous expression of this was the "Dispute about the Evils of Baseball" (*Yakyū gaidoku ron)*, sparked by a three-week series of essays in the *Tōkyō Asahi* during August 1911 in which noted educators and officials took turns decrying various aspects of the sport and its deleterious effects on students and their schools (reprinted in Asahi Newspaper Editorial Department 1991:175–221). Notably shrill was the opening essay by Nitobe Inazō, which dismissed baseball as a "pickpocket's sport" in which "players try to swindle their opponents and steal bases." It was well suited to Americans, not Englishmen or Germans, he noted derisively, because "it is impossible for Americans to play a brave game like rugby, the national sport of the British, in which the players hang on to the ball even though their nose is being crushed and their skull dented" (Asahi Newspaper Editorial Department 1991:177; see also Kiku 1993). The rival *Tōkyō Nichinichi* responded with a two-week-long series in defense of baseball, and the *Yomiuri* newspaper joined in with a lecture series on the problems of baseball.

These newspaper debates did little to dampen the growing enthusiasm for baseball, and by the second decade of the twentieth century, the sport was further transformed in several respects. First, it lost its elite associations with the higher schools and universities as it spread downward in the national school system and out into youth and working-class amateur participation. Baseball was already part of the physical education curriculum at the middle school level, but now the middle schools began to organize ever-broader interscholastic competition. Baseball quickly became an emblem of school reputation in a still-unsettled hierarchy of middle schools and regional loyalty in an era of urban migration.[3]

A major impetus for this were the new national newspapers, which seized on a variety of sports as publicity vehicles of mass appeal. That is, the press of the late nineteenth century had been focused on political events and commentary, and the papers were often affiliated with political parties and movements (Huffman 1997). In the twentieth century several of them, in particular *Asahi* and *Mainichi* in Osaka, reorganized to become general-interest newspapers, recasting themselves as "mass media" rather than political newspapers and appealing to the new burgeoning metropolitan populations.

Ever more competitive for subscribers and markets by the 1910s, the papers vied to sponsor sports tournaments and individual athletes and to expand their sports coverage to report the very boom they were fanning. For example, *Jiji shimpō* organized the first Mt. Fuji Ascent Race in 1913, the same year that the *Osaka Mainichi* sponsored the First Japan Olympics Festival. The latter paper started the 10-Mile Ocean Swim in 1915, and the next year staged the Tri-City Track and Field Meet for teams from Osaka, Kyoto, and Kobe. *Asahi* responded with the First East-West Japan Track Tournament. By 1917, more papers had jumped in. *Yomiuri* sponsored the First Tokyo-Kyoto Team Relay Race (*ekiden*), to mark the fiftieth anniversary of the transfer of the capital from Kyoto to Tokyo. *Hōchi shimbun* organized the twenty-five-mile Tokyo-Yokohama Marathon, and the *Osaka Mainichi* countered with an Olympics festival. Track meets, marathons, swimming contests, ski meets, mountaineering ascents, and more—baseball was placed in a wide palate of new entertainments and recreations.

Together with the newspapers, the other major corporate interests critical for sports development were the private urban railroad companies that were starting up in Japan's growing cities. Developing a national railroad network had been a state priority from the early Meiji period, but local transport depended largely on private initiative (using electrical lines rather than steam locomotion), and metropolitan areas around the country experienced an electric train boom from the 1890s onward.

The Kansai conurbation was the competitive ground for five private rail companies vying to build passenger lines within and between Osaka,

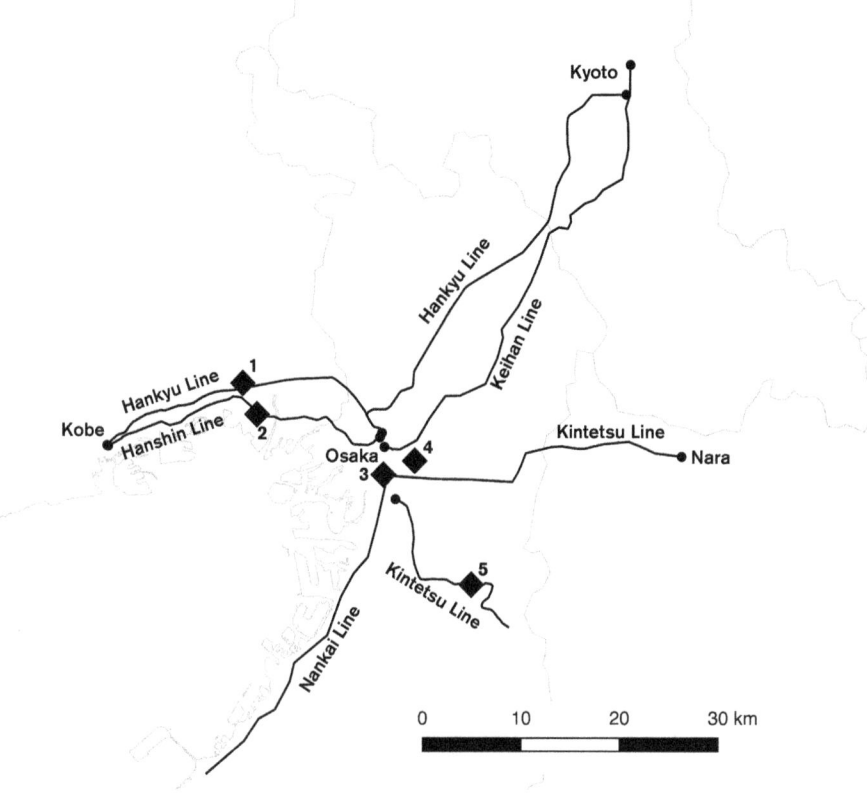

MAP 2. The main lines of the five private interurban railroad companies in the Kansai region in the 1920s. The black diamonds mark the locations of the five major baseball stadiums constructed from the 1920s to the 1940s. Based on Sugimoto (1989:42).

Kyoto, Kobe, and other emerging cities (Imao 2017; Uda et al. 1995). Building these early interurban train lines required considerable organizational effort, engineering skills, and financial resources. Much of the urban and suburban development in the early twentieth century was carried out by these companies, which had to buy land and use rights, lay networks of tracks and build stations in a competitive frenzy, create grids of electrification to run the trains, acquire rolling stock, and train engineer and repair staff. As map 2 illustrates, the trunk lines of the five companies radiated like spokes from central Osaka, connecting to Kobe to the west (Hanshin and Hankyū), Kyoto to the northeast (Hankyū and Keihan), Nara to the east (Kintetsu), and Kawachi and Wakayama to the south (Nankai). This profoundly shaped Kansai metropolitan development around competitive corridors and competing downtown terminals of development.

This transport geography was also to shape the companies themselves. They were competing for ridership, but to do that profitably, they had to provide destinations and services. They built department stores and other businesses at their main terminals in Osaka, Kobe, and Kyoto and promoted businesses at the stations along their lines. Having built grids of electrification, they sponsored residential developments along their lines, clustering around their line stations. And they vied to build leisure and recreation facilities as destination points to attract additional riders, residents, and businesses. In this manner, all five became integrated transport, commercial, leisure, and real estate companies. Safety—running trains and buses through crowded urban thoroughfares—was a prime ingredient of their relative reputations, so they fashioned themselves as quasi-public utilities, committed to service. At the same time, as private sector competitors, they were aggressively pushing commercial sales campaigns and promotions.

Hanshin was the second of the companies, founded under a different name in January 1898 by businesspeople in Kobe and Osaka to connect the two cities. In July 1899 the company took its present name, Hanshin Dentetsu, and in 1905 it completed terminals and tracks to inaugurate full service between the cities. Hanshin was notable for the fact that only 15 percent of its track ran on public roadways; the rest was on its own track, allowing for fast transport and large cars. However, Hanshin was soon to suffer a fatal setback at the hands of its most direct rival, Hankyū (Sakudō 1995). Hanshin had carved out its trunk line along the coast from Osaka to Kobe. Hankyū initially opened a line from Osaka into the northwest toward Takarazuka, which the Hankyū founder, Kobayashi Ichizō, developed as a resort and entertainment spot for city dwellers. In the 1910s, however, Kobayashi assembled enough land and resources to open a direct line from Osaka to Kobe. He ran it just inland of Hanshin's track on higher ground along the edge of the mountains, and like a maneuver in the Japanese game of gō, forever boxed in Hanshin and prevented its expansion. Hanshin never grew beyond its early lines, and its forty-five kilometers of track were by far the shortest of any of the competing lines, one-third the length of Hankyū. Kobayashi's maneuver created an enduring enmity between the two companies and also an emerging social class contrast, because the Hanshin line ran along the generally working-class and factory zones along the coast, while Hankyū ran through what developed as middle- and upper-class housing communities like Ashiya. Working-class, industrial Hanshin versus "high-collar" Hankyū was a socioeconomic contrast that was later expressed in the images of their two ball clubs.

This pattern of regional development through these competitive railroad companies had two more consequences that had a direct impact on the twentieth-century history of Kansai baseball. American commentators on Japanese professional baseball frequently disparage the naming of NPB teams for their corporate owners rather than locality names, the practice in MLB. This is a highly misleading contrast, especially in Kansai. The five railroads were not just company names but became names for the spatial corridors created by their rail lines; *ensen*, or along the tracks, and *kan*, or the space between, were common terms. They were derived from the companies, but more important, they divided the region into life zones of commercial activity and residential identity. Living and working (and relaxing) along the Hanshin ensen or with the Hanshin-kan was as or more powerful a marker of locality than Osaka, Nishinomiya, or Kobe (e.g., Hanshinkan modanizumu 1997; Miki 2003, 2010; Ogawa 1995; Shimoda 2006; Tada, Kawauchi, and Asahi 1993:ch. 3).

The second consequence of this pattern of competitive development was that all five companies quickly recognized that sports of all sorts were valuable for attracting riders and customers to parks, tennis courts, swimming pools, and other outdoor facilities; sporting events such as marathons and swimming contests; and other spectacles like circuses, fireworks, exhibitions, and theater. They built department stores, opened bus lines, and operated real estate offices, but they also put sports within a larger panorama of leisure and recreation as a centerpiece of their marketing promotions and "ensen" identity. Therefore, to the extent that commercialism and even commodification is part of sports professionalization, the stage for professional baseball was set well before the organization of the league in 1935. The professional baseball teams that four of the five companies eventually inaugurated and supported thus became expressions of these corridor identities as well as public relations vehicles for the companies.

It was in this context that school baseball attracted the attention and sponsorship of the new mass media and transport companies.[4] In the summer of 1915, the Asahi Newspaper Company sought to capitalize on school baseball's broadening popularity by inaugurating a new national middle school championship tournament at Toyonaka Stadium to the northwest of the Osaka city center, which the Hankyū railroad company had just built on its property as part of its efforts to attract riders and development. A description of the stadium, however, suggests that it was hardly fit for a national tournament. The field was also used for soccer, rugby, and track; the stands only seated four hundred people; and a single straw rope separated the field from the spectators. It was still in the midst of undeveloped land; there were woods in back of center field, where the teams waiting to play would take shelter from the hot sun (Kiku 1993).

Nonetheless, the initial tournament attracted teams from 72 of the nation's 321 middle schools. Ten won qualifying games to advance to the Toyonaka finals. The following year, participation more than doubled to 150 teams, of which 22 reached the finals tournament (Kiku 1993:60). The format of prefecture-based qualifying rounds, through which winners advance to a single-game knockout-style tournament held each August, quickly became the standard format, still followed today.

Asahi's publicity and baseball's popularity grew quickly, and for the third year (1917) it moved the venue to a site near the shoreline at the Naruo Sports Complex, which was operated by Hanshin. Naruo had originally been constructed as a horse-racing track, but horse race betting was prohibited in 1911, and horse-racing clubs like Naruo went into steep decline. In 1914 Hanshin Dentetsu arranged to lease the track and its surrounding land. As a former racetrack, Naruo had a large infield, in which Hanshin planned to build an eight-hundred-meter track, a tennis court complex, a swimming pool, and two baseball fields with spectator stands. This was attractive to Asahi; by holding two games simultaneously, it could run a faster tournament and save on player expenses, while charging separate admissions.

It remains something of a mystery why Hankyū president Kobayashi, who clearly recognized baseball's entertainment potential, allowed the tournament to pass to his archrival Hanshin, but the move was the start of cooperation between the Asahi Newspaper Company and Hanshin Dentetsu that has continued for over a century. Although the full facility plan was never completed, the baseball fields and their stands were home to the national tournament for the next seven years, from 1917 through 1923. As figure 24 illustrates, the tournaments became so popular that spectators were spilling onto the field.

FIGURE 24. An Asahi Newspaper photograph of crowds spilling onto the field during the National Middle School Baseball Tournament at Naruo Athletic Field, August 1918.

To promote the tournament further, the Asahi Newspaper Company pressed Hanshin to construct a larger and more permanent stadium. Hanshin agreed, and in 1922 it bought some land that had been created when a local river was straightened and improved. The land was both north and south of the main Hanshin line from Osaka to Kobe, and the master plan called for a railroad extension, a new station, housing developments to the north of the line, and a massive general sports recreation zone just to the south. A new stadium was to be surrounded with tennis courts, an enclosed swimming pool, parks, an aquarium, a track, and a sandy bathing beach. It was a risky investment for Hanshin, but the company felt pressed by its rivalry with the larger Hankyū company and thought its corporate public relations would benefit from supporting a sport that promoted a "healthy physique" (*kenzen na taikaku*) and "manly spirit" (*gōken na seishin*). By the 1920s, sports participation and spectatorship were a central part of the "mass culture" of the decade (Ikari 1987; Kiku 1993). The few Japanese Olympic medal winners became popular celebrities, and like Hitomi Kinue, the eight-hundred-meter silver medalist at the 1928 Amsterdam Olympics, they were often hired by the newspapers. Although Kōshien wasn't built for professional sports and sports fans, the architectural consultants were

FIGURE 25. An aerial photograph of Kōshien Stadium in 1931, taken by an Asahi Newspaper photographer. Comparing this to figure 1, it is remarkable how much the stadium in 2014 retained of its original shape and design. Note, however, that the centerfield wall in 1931 was not arc shaped but ran straight across from left field to right field. The "Alps" sections had been added to the right and left infield in 1929.

all active in baseball at the time and drew on study visits to professional baseball stadiums in the United States. They paid much attention to field conditions and seating layouts. The dirt field was well prepared, and the fifty rows of infield seating were covered with an iron roof (known as the "iron umbrella") to shield spectators from the brutal August sun. Ivy was planted on the outside walls, and in 1928 the outfield was seeded with grass. In 1929 a tall bank of concrete bleacher seats replaced the wood stands between the infield and outfield seats, and these became popular with the school supporters. The wave of white school uniforms rising up these bleachers inspired a journalist to tag them the "Alps," for the snowy peak of the Matterhorn. These all became trademarks of Kōshien. (See figure 25 for a photograph of the stadium in 1931.) The early to mid-1930s saw other small improvements: a public address system and new scoreboard in 1933 and an expansion of the outfield stands (they were known for a time as the Himalaya Stands).

The stadium formally opened on August 1, 1924, just in time for the opening of the tenth annual middle school tournament. Because 1924 was *kinoene* or *kōshi* year in the old East Asian astrological calendar, the stadium's name, Kōshien, was based on this. The "en" of Kōshien was also significant (Nagai 1997; Ōtani 2003). It had the meaning of green space, parks, and gardens, and it was a crucial third term in Kansai spatial development, along with *kan* and *ensen* (it was a different "en" than in ensen). Several of the key architects and planners in the metropolitan development boom in Kansai and Kanto in the 1920s were very influential in introducing English-style garden city planning into Japan. The concept mixed single-family housing with horticultural and science educational parks and recreational and cultural facilities (the "en") in areas on the metropolitan perimeter, connected to downtown of course by the railroad company that was promoting the garden city. On the east side of Osaka at the same time, Kintetsu Electric Railroad Company (still under its forerunner name, Osaka Tetsudō) completed Fujiidera Stadium in 1928 as part of a similar "cultural facilities" zone.

Significantly, with the opening of Kōshien, tournament spectators were charged admission for the first time. In the following March, the Mainichi newspaper moved its annual spring invitational tournament to Kōshien. In 1927 the 13th annual summer championship was the first to be broadcast over the new medium of radio. Despite fears that this would cut into spectatorship, broadcasting actually heightened stadium attendance. By 1928, 410 of the nation's 544 middle schools were represented (Kiku 1993:60, table 2-3). In 1929 the Alps stands were completed, and in 1931 an iron roof was extended over both sides of the Alps seats. Thus, the Kōshien fever that continues to grip Japan today was born of the corporatization of the news and transportation industries and was an essential ingredient of the mass-mediated "terminal" culture of Kantō and Kansai.

Beyond its sheer size, two other features that impressed the throngs were its flush toilets and its vendor food. Flush toilets were rare at the time, and they impressed and scared fans and players coming from all parts of the country. Of the food sold at the new stadium, the most popular was the combination that came to be known as Kōshien "coffee and curry rice." Curry rice was made at home, but it was time-consuming, and there was a boom in this menu at the stadium and in restaurants. During the middle school tournaments, more than fifteen thousand curry rice meals were sold.

In 1930 tennis courts were constructed surrounding the stadium, and two years later a swimming pool and an indoor track were built inside the stadium walls under the Alps stands. From the outset, Hanshin (often with Asahi and Mainichi cosponsorship) held soccer, American football, and rugby matches, equestrian events, and other sports (Tamaki 1989:44).

Kōshien's importance to the company increased over time. By 1935, its electricity supply business accounted for some 30–40 percent of Hanshin revenues, but in 1942 it suffered two shocks under the wartime system. Its electricity business was nationalized by the Kansai public electrical utility, and the large expanse of land it owned south of Kōshien was claimed under eminent domain for the Kawasaki Military Airport. The government kept the land after the war and used it for public housing complexes, which still blanket the neighborhood between the stadium and the sea. The cost of the war was considerable to Hanshin and only made Kōshien more important—to the point, many feel, that it became an excessively overprotective parent.

BASEBALL AS EDUTAINMENT IN THE 1920s AND 1930s

Many historians have described the 1920s as the decade in the United States when sports, movies, and other forms of entertainment and leisure became fully mass culture. In this decade attendance and attention spread broadly across the burgeoning metropolitan population, and sporting and cultural stars became national figures: Babe Ruth, Gene Tunney, Mary Pickford, Knute Rockne, Bobby Jones, and others. Metropolitan Japan—especially Kansai and Kantō—witnessed a similar effervescence of public life and cultural activity. Sports were comparatively less prominent in 1920s Japan than in the United States, but school and university baseball consolidated its position as the nation's central sport.

It was the central sport but also the celebrity sport, and if anything, throughout the 1920s and 1930s tensions became more evident in its doubled importance as a showcase of national virtue and a venue for corporate profit and mass entertainment. Baseball made the government as nervous as it made the spectators excited. In the wake of its spread to the new universities, the troubles in the Waseda-Keio series, and the 1910 debates in the newspapers, school baseball not only gained commercial sponsors, it also brought to the fore new ideologues. Perhaps the most important figure of the post-1910 era was Tobita Suishū, captain and later manager of the Waseda University team during these decades. Revered as the "god of baseball," he preached a spiritualization of baseball as athletic Bushidō that recast the elite aestheticism of the Ichikō spirit in an idiom more appropriate to an age of mass schooling. He demanded that his players demonstrate moral commitment through absolute loyalty to the manager and total devotion to the sport. Harkening back to Ichikō's motto, he called his training "death practice" (*shi no renshū*) and insisted on "perfect baseball," which meant total concentration and effort at the present moment: "A pitcher was expected to throw every pitch with all his might" (Ishii 1980:131, 146). He was in fact a successful coach, and in 1925 he finally avenged the early loss to the University of Chicago during a perfect 36–0 season. In 1925 he joined *Asahi* as a commentator and continued to propound a deeply conservative, "Japanese" vision of the sport (in the face of competing managerial philosophies).

Yet the same print media that gave a national platform to Tobita and other sports pedagogues also eagerly publicized numerous controversies about illegal recruiting, affairs with screen stars and café waitresses, and other scandals involving star student players, which were as captivating to readers and fans as Tobita's essays. In October 1928 the *Yomiuri Newspaper* reported a rampage through the Ginza district by Keio fans following the second game of the Keio-Waseda series; for the second year in a row, they had disrupted stores, invaded cafés, and scuffled with police. The *Jiji Shimpō Newspaper* revealed in May 1930 that professional ticket scalpers had cornered large blocks of Keio-Waseda series tickets, which they sold illegally at the games, demanding and receiving as much as ¥12 for ¥1 first-class tickets (Kelly 2000:109). These and many other accounts illustrated how much the hero status of star university players and the wide publicity that their play and exploits garnered in the press appealed to the newspaper magnates, who wished to prolong and capitalize more directly on that notoriety.

The making of student baseball players into popular media stars threatened the "spiritualism" that school baseball had cultivated, and the conservative and increasingly militaristic side of official interests was tempted to see this "degeneration" (*daraku*) and subversion as inevitable because baseball was fundamentally a Western sport. In this sense, Tobita's philosophy was an internal critique, aiming to reform and purify the sport without banning it altogether. He argued that sports generally must be emphasized in school curriculums to build the character necessary to combat the leftist tendencies of some "wayward" university students. This sports-as-character argument proved persuasive to many educational authorities, who were worried about growing student activism and hoped that sports properly framed would be effective in training and managing their youthful population. As Tobita wrote, in language familiar to sports pedagogues in the United States and England as well, it was necessary "to use athletics not only to regulate bodies but also to control minds and guide thought " (Tobita 1972:59). In 1924 the Ministry of Interior organized the National Games at Tokyo's Meiji Jingu Shrine, and in 1925, on the occasion of the forming of the Tokyo Big-Six College Baseball League, Home Minister Wakatsuki Reijirō published a series of articles in several newspapers inveighing against rowdy and degenerate trends in school baseball. This followed student protests against the military training that the government had introduced into the schools and other signs of student discontent. Indeed, through a series of directives and strong pressure on organizations like the National Middle School Principals Association, the Ministry of Education sought to harness all sports and physical education to official aims of inculcating body discipline and countering the feared "leftist" tendencies in the schools and universities.[5]

Perhaps it is a measure of government success that from the mid-1920s, major business corporations did begin to target sports club members for recruitment, and university students came to be see sports clubs as avenues toward such employment (Ikari 1987:525; Ozaki 1967). This was important, because by the late 1920s, employment prospects were quite difficult for university graduates. The popular film, *I Graduated from College, But ...* (*Daigaku wa deta keredo*) was released in September 1929, when only 38 percent of that year's law, economics, and humanities seniors would find jobs. By 1931 that rate had fallen to 30 percent. The growing unemployment, student agitation, and union unrest left companies and government quite anxious. Graduates who had been active on sports teams that were known for Spartan training and moderate thinking (*shisō onken*) were viewed as prime candidates for the limited job openings.

By the late 1920s, then, baseball effectively condensed and connected the emerging features of mass education and mass leisure. These in turn were largely shaped, respectively, by the state and by large media, transport, and retail businesses. The school and the stadium both stood at the intersection of the private and the public, where the individual child was drawn into state pedagogy and the individual adult into corporatized recreation. Schools and stadiums were both significantly inflected by class, place, and gender identities new to post-Meiji, prewar Japan.

With the formation in 1936 of a professional league by the ambitious founder of the upstart Yomiuri newspaper company, Shōriki Matsutarō, baseball in Japan was again transformed, but in ways that only intensified the sport's embeddedness in a web of school pride, national patriotism, and corporate profit.

PROFESSIONALIZING BASEBALL AND THE BIRTH OF THE HANSHIN TIGERS

Professional baseball in Japan usually traces its origins to the first league, which was organized in 1936, but the first professional team actually dated from 1920, when some Waseda baseball alumni organized a team called the Japan Athletic Society (Nihon undō kyōkai). They charged themselves, ironically, with the mission of cleaning up schoolboy baseball. One team member, Kataoka Masaru, wrote that their manager, Oshikawa-sensei, complained loudly that "today's student baseball makes light of serious study, a common failing of students, and assumes the conceit of stars, blowing the publicity horn of its school. We, however, must create a distinguished professional baseball and clean up student baseball" (Kiku 1993:133).

Kiku (1993) has observed that despite their self-appointed ambition, they could not attract a single star because fans could not accept the idea of commercialized, professional baseball. The team folded after four years for lack of spectators. The organizers then went to Kansai seeking investors. Hankyū's Kobayashi took them on; he changed the team's name to the Takarazuka Baseball Association (Takarazuka yakyū kyōkai), and from 1924 to 1929 it played exhibition games at the Takarazuka Athletic Field. But even the master impresario Kobayashi was unable to successfully promote professional baseball in the absence of regular, high-quality competition (which suggests that fans were not hostile to the idea of professional baseball but unimpressed with the level of play and indifferent to the team's identity; Kiku 1993:136–138).

The successful impetus for professional baseball came a few years later, not from Kansai but from Tokyo, from another aggressive entrepreneur, Shōriki. With a background in conservative politics and shady dealings, he was trying to bring his Tokyo-based newspaper, *Yomiuri*, into the national arena with the more established papers, *Asahi* and *Mainichi*. Exhibition visits by US teams were a regular promotion, but in 1929 Shōriki was persuaded by one of his editorial writers to bring over the very best all-stars, headlined by Babe Ruth, who was already a huge celebrity in Japan. Shōriki did not know much about baseball, but he was intrigued by the proposal and hired the head coach of Waseda to be his sports editor, with the particular job of getting Babe Ruth to come to Japan for such an exhibition tour. Initially, Ruth was unavailable, but the Yomiuri company was able to sponsor a tour of MLB all-stars in October 1931 that did include many of the other leading US players (including Lou Gehrig, Lefty O'Doul, Lefty Grove, and Mickey Cochrane). They played seventeen games in nine cities to huge, enthusiastic crowds, who did not mind the lopsided scores against industrial and amateur teams. The tour made a profit for Yomiuri, so Shōriki redoubled his efforts to persuade Babe Ruth, who finally agreed and, in the fall of 1934, headlined another MLB all-star group (with many of the same players from 1931). The party arrived on the steamship *Empress of Japan* on November 2, 1934, and played a sixteen-game series to wildly enthusiastic fans. (Fitts [2012] is a highly informative account of the tour and the circumstances surrounding it.) Ruth, then thirty-nine and at the end of his career, made a lasting impression on Japanese fans, with his home runs, antics, and way of charming the media and playing to the crowds. Again the Japanese crowds did not seem to mind that the American easily won all the games played against the Japanese side; the scores were so lopsided that they played a few games by mixing the Japanese and American players.[6] Ruth and the other Americans were polite but clearly unimpressed with the local baseball stadiums until they reached Osaka and entered Kōshien. Its grandeur—and the sixty-five thousand spectators who overflowed its capacity—were memorable.

Shōriki was already thinking of a professional league in Japan at the time of the second tour, and he conferred with Lefty O'Doul. Soon after the Americans went home, on December 26, Yomiuri founded Greater Japan Tokyo Baseball Club. Shōriki used his business contacts throughout the Japanese empire to round up more talent to augment the core all-star team players. Without much sanctioned competition in Japan, the team, which was named the Giants (Kyojin), was sent on a 110-game tour of the United States for over three months in 1935. Playing minor league and college teams, they won seventy-five of their games (against thirty-five losses and one tie), and day after day, the *Yomiuri* newspaper carried details of the games.

It was now clear to Shōriki and his associates that a professional team could not be viable on its own and required a number of teams playing in regular competitions across a number of venues. He was anxious to establish clubs in the three major metropolises of Tokyo, Osaka, and Nagoya, for tournaments that would rotate in the spring, summer, and fall among the three cities. Shōriki especially wanted to involve Hanshin in order to draw upon Kōshien Stadium, whose reputation was only further advanced in the aftermath of Babe Ruth's presence and the coverage of the games played there. It was apparently not difficult to persuade Hanshin (whose executives had already been considering something similar) and Hankyū. Over the winter months of 1935–1936, an association (the Nihon shokugyō yakyū renmei, or the Japan Professional Baseball Association) was formed by seven companies, who agreed to establish teams and begin playing one another under the seasonal tournament structure that Shōriki had envisioned. The association began with four newspaper companies and three railroad companies, distributed in Tokyo (three), Osaka (two), and Nagoya (two). The novelty of a professional league is revealed in the mixed nomenclature of team names; some had nicknames, some used the company name, and others used a city appellation.[7]

A contest was held among Hanshin employees to pick a name for their new team, and a number of them suggested the English moniker the "Tigers." Club histories are divided over whether in fact this was a direct inspiration from the Detroit Tigers (Osaka seeing itself as a manufacturing capital like Detroit). What is interesting is that the company named the team the Osaka Tigers (not the Hanshin Tigers, and despite Kōshien actually lying outside the official city limits!). It was not until 1961 that the team's name was finally changed to the Hanshin Tigers.

There were eighteen members of the 1936 Tigers, and the roster mixed well-known university graduates who were coaching or playing for amateur company teams with several middle school graduates who brought Kōshien tournament pedigrees. They were assigned uniform numbers in Japanese alphabetical order of their names. The highest paid were the manager Mori Shigeo and the Hawaiian American pitcher Wakabayashi Tadashi, who both received monthly salaries of ¥250 (at the time, a university graduate could expect to make a monthly salary of about ¥40).[8]

The Giants were still on tour in the United States in the spring of 1936, so the inaugural tournament began at the end of April at Kōshien with the other six teams. The Tigers started with a victory but ended up in third place with a 3–2 record. Their loss to Hankyū was particularly painful, and the manager and captain were called before the company executives for an explanation. The manager explained that he just didn't have the players to do better, but the corporate executives replied that they had spent a lot of money and expected results.

Then in May, tournaments were held in Nagoya and Takarazuka. The Tigers beat Hankyū in Nagoya and approached Takarazuka with confidence, only to be defeated again by their rivals. Once again, the manager and captain were called in for a scolding by executives, who found it intolerable to lose to their rival. Shortly thereafter, manager Mori was released, an early example of the impatience that would characterize Hanshin for decades.

One can detect an undercurrent of tension between the corporate interests of the railroad companies and the newspaper companies. As I noted previously, the railroads had fostered a pattern of metropolitan growth that elided identification with the train company and the corridor of living and commerce that grew up along it. Four of the five Kansai companies had built stadiums along their lines that were a home ground for their sports promotions. In contrast, the newspaper companies wanted broader, even national, support bases. Shōriki and others did not see the value in basing a team in a fixed stadium; as promotions for the papers, it was better to deploy them by moving them around in rented stadium venues. At the same time, the company's team would get favored coverage in the paper.

This tension remained unresolved in the early years of professional baseball, which used a seasonal tournament format and played at rotating venues, but which also began to record total victories in a proto-league play format beginning with its second season. By 1940, however, war's suppressive effects on leisure foreclosed any resolution of what kind of identity and structure professional baseball should have.

SAMURAI WITH BATS?

In the early 2000s, Samurai Blue was adopted as the nickname of the Japan national men's soccer team, and it proved to be a successful marketing and PR moniker. Inspired by that, in 2009 the national baseball team gave itself the nickname Samurai Japan, which became official in 2012 and is also used prominently and profitably. The image that adorned Whiting's 1977 book cover does seem to be alive and well.

As we have seen in this chapter, a samurai-inflected Way of Baseball has a historical basis in the 1890s, later amplified by a series of influential promoters like Tobita Suishū. It did breed an ethic that playing games like baseball inspired virtue, formed character, and developed manliness. In this way, baseball fit comfortably within one powerful ideological orthodoxy in the broader society. Invoking samurai imagery and its putative ethical coordinates to motivate and discipline has been widespread in the twentieth century, applied to soldiers and kamikaze pilots before World War II and to students and salarymen afterward, all of whom are urged to train themselves with physical, spiritual, and mental discipline to perform as warriors of the past did, with loyalty and superhuman effort.

Yet what this chapter has also shown is that this is only part of the story of baseball since the late nineteenth century. Schoolboy baseball and its ethos of self-sacrifice, team loyalty, obedience, and school pride appeared uneasily in the spotlight of a commercialized metropolitan mass culture that had been created by regional transit companies and national newspapers (Kelly 2000). From the first Waseda-Keio series in 1903 to the corporate sponsors lining up to support Samurai Japan and advertise themselves during the 2017 World Baseball Classic, baseball in all of its forms, school and professional, has always been an alluring popular and commercial spectacle.

If baseball is a complex and uncomfortable hybrid of education and entertainment, what does this imply for a "samurai way of baseball?" On its own, it is of limited importance in explaining the Hanshin sportsworld, either the experiences of those who work within it or those who maintain a close affiliation of support and identity over the years. In my experience over the years with Hanshin, the actual words *samurai*, *bushi* (warrior), and *Bushidō* were used very rarely in daily conversation or meetings in the baseball world. Hardly any of the players, coaches, staff, media, or spectators whom I interviewed thought the terms were particularly relevant. Nonetheless, when prompted, they were very quick to enumerate what they felt were sharp dichotomies between US and Japanese baseball, based on qualities of play that sounded very similar to those who propounded samurai baseball: American players were individualistic and Japanese players were team-driven; American hitters and pitchers were about power, while their Japanese counterparts were about finesse (power-ball versus small-ball); American players underpracticed and Japanese players overpracticed; and so forth. I found this a fascinating situational move (in a different conversation, they would use the same contrast pairs to distinguish among Japanese players!), evidence that there is still a raw sensitivity about national-level differences.

The crucial point here is that baseball in Japan cannot usefully be reduced to and explained as "Japanese" baseball. There are far too many other distinctions that create meaningful and moral difference: between amateur and professional levels, between teams of us and them, among players of divergent dispositions, and across generations of players and fans. These are the same multiple vectors of difference that make the motivations for playing and watching baseball in the United States equally mixed and even contradictory. But Whiting and others are correct that national-level differences, real and imagined, have played a larger role in Japanese baseball than in American baseball. This is because of the multiple occasions when baseball in Japan is represented as a domestic (and domesticated) version of the American original, because of twentieth-century 'Japan's broader challenge to define itself both within and apart from a Western-defined modernity, and because of the dominance that MLB still exerts as the world metropole of the sport.

Nonetheless, we must remain skeptical about three aspects of this samurai talk over the decades. First, as we have seen previously in the chapter, the ennobling of a samurai ethic by late nineteenth-century ideologues and educators was a deliberate fabrication. Proponents of a new Bushidō for modern Japan disagreed on its particulars, but their common focus promoted absolute and abiding loyalty as the prime samurai virtue. This was at best a selective culling from Japan's long and varied history of actual warriors and warrior conduct.

We must also remember that loyalty itself has been redefined over baseball's history to suit the times. The "original" baseball samurai were the boys at the most elite preparatory school in the new nation, the First Higher School of Tokyo, celebrated for their victories over resident American teams in the late 1890s. However, this was a proudly student-run school club, free of adult authority, and soon replaced by a new orthodoxy of an autocratic adult-manager for the college and middle school teams of the early twentieth century and for the early pro teams. This remains the high school model (in which often a single adult coach must direct fifty to seventy aspiring high school kids using his personal authority), but the professional ranks corporatized club operations in the 1960s and 1970s. Loyalty now is demanded for the impersonal authority of a large organization. If today's pro player is a samurai, his sword is more a briefcase than a bat!

Third, I must note—because most Japanese inside and outside the baseball world certainly do so—the difficulties of actually coaching and performing samurai baseball, especially at the professional level. For every legendary example of thousand-fungo drills, pitchers' overextending their innings, and absolute obedience to managerial whims, there are undercurrents and counterexamples of petulance, irreverence, and outright resistance to these practices and demands. As is often the case with moral injunctions, the frequency with which they are demanded is a clue to the difficulty of eliciting their acceptance. Thus, I want to avoid reducing the practices of a sport to its ideology. As in life, what people do in a sport is often at odds with what they say they are doing. It is in fact that gap between the saying and the doing that draws our fascination as spectators.

This is where the Hanshin Tigers, the subject of this book, offer an instructive and entertaining angle. A number of the team's outward features—the overt hierarchies of team, club, and company and its proud inbreeding—were those idealized as virtues of Japanese-style baseball. But such features long coexisted with factional infighting, inept management, and disgruntled players, on which the media lavished equal attention—as we have seen repeatedly. The game at the team's Kōshien Stadium was certainly not samurai baseball as farce, but it did expose samurai baseball as futility. And much of the allure of the Tigers for their long-suffering fans—especially the millions of Kansai residents through whose daily lives the team's fortunes and foibles percolated even when they were not paying attention—was in savoring the constant efforts while hand-wringing over inevitable failures to perform baseball as noble "samurai" sportsmen.

But the allure of the Tigers was more particular than this. The two themes that proved most constitutive of the Hanshin Tigers world did not emerge in the 1910s but in the 1960s, and that is what I turn to in the next chapter: the corporatization of baseball workplaces and the slide of Osaka and Kansai into second-city status as Tokyo and the Kanto region became the overwhelming center of Japanese society, politics, and economy in the latter decades of the twentieth century.

CHAPTER 9

Workplace Melodramas and Second-City Complex

I entered the Hanshin Tigers world in 1996 at a time when the team was floundering on the field, the front office was wracked with dissension, and the media were obsessed with reporting all of this on the daily front pages and in the evening television sports news leads, ignoring the sparkling success of Orix and the subtler turmoil in the Kintetsu organization. Initially I was reluctant to pay much attention to the Tigers' troubles. All sports teams go through hard times, even extended periods of poor performance, but such ephemeral conditions seemed more the domain of sports journalism than anthropological analysis. However, the Tigers' troubles and the media focus on them continued over the years of my fieldwork, and I came to realize that both had been a constant condition of the Tigers world for two decades before my study. This made me more curious about the nature of this malaise and the sources of the support and passion for the Tigers that nonetheless persisted throughout Kansai. What could this intensity of feeling in spite of perpetual loss tell me, not just about Tigers baseball, a rather narrow matter to anyone outside the boundaries of that world, but about Japanese baseball more broadly and the place of the sport in Japanese society? That is what I address in this penultimate chapter.

What I want to show in this chapter is that many of these characteristics of the Hanshin Tigers sportsworld have their origins in the decades from the 1950s to the 1980s, both within professional baseball and across the wider society. Much of what we now think of as long-standing features of professional baseball actually emerged gradually and unevenly throughout those years: large team rosters and front offices, corporatism in management and promotion, showcased managers, rigid distinctions between "regular" players and "foreign" players, the formal organizations of cheering clubs, reliance on television and sports dailies, and so forth.

Equally important is that these features resonated with wider transformations of postwar Japanese society, especially the consolidation of Tokyo as the national center; the celebration of a Japanese-style corporatism as a powerful business ideology; the formation of a societal mainstream and an official ethos of cultural nationalism; and the pervasive spread of powerful national media, especially television and the daily sports newspapers. Baseball was not merely a reflection of these societal changes; it contributed importantly to bringing them about.

These wider societal shifts were important motivations for Hanshin's changing place in Kansai, as it moved from being of local interest and support among the four teams in the region in the 1950s to attracting the most regional attention by the 1980s. The structural features of the Hanshin sportsworld discussed in the preceding chapters resonated and reinforced the capacity of Hanshin to condense for the Kansai region the two compelling themes of workplace melodrama and second-city complex.

REORGANIZING PROFESSIONAL BASEBALL IN THE 1950S

Baseball at all levels came under assault in the early 1940s in wartime Japan. Players were conscripted, the game itself was suspect by ultranationalists for its American associations, and the populace had little time or resources for leisure (Takashima 2012; Yamamuro 2010). The nascent professional league limped through an abbreviated season of thirty-five games in 1944 and then canceled its next season. Kōshien Stadium was requisitioned by the military, its famous iron roof torn apart for munitions material and its outfield converted to vegetable gardens.

Restarting baseball after the war was one matter about which the Japanese and the American Occupation authorities found ready agreement. Scarcely two months after the Japanese surrender, on November 23, 1945, a four-game exhibition series began in Tokyo, organized by leaders of the dormant professional league with those players they could muster and divided into East and West teams (Suzuki 1982). The American Occupation authorities were impressed that more than thirty thousand paying spectators flocked to the games (the contest in Kansai was played at Nishinomiya Stadium because Kōshien was under US military use). They were much more supportive of an "American" sport than the martial arts, which they banned, and middle schools and the newly expanded high schools were allowed to reopen their baseball clubs. They allowed the professional league to reconstitute itself the following spring; with minimal equipment and makeshift arrangements, it managed to complete a 105-game schedule. Going forward, however, Occupation authorities, possibly directed by General Douglas MacArthur himself, stipulated that the old professional association of a single league be reorganized as two parallel leagues, whose top finishers at the end of each season would meet in a national Japan Championship Series (mimicking the World Series and usually shortened to the Japan Series). To the Americans, this dual structure was more "democratic" than a single "authoritarian" league, and it was obviously based on the American League-National League binary of MLB.

The restart of professional baseball precipitated intense politicking around two heated issues that would be consequential for Hanshin. The first was how many clubs to allow into this new configuration. Even in the few years it had existed before the wartime hiatus, the professional game had gained acceptance, and a number of other major corporations hastened to organize teams and petition for entry, including movie production and food processing companies. The Mainichi Newspaper Company was especially eager to challenge Yomiuri's dominance.

The existing companies, especially Yomiuri, were reluctant to expand, but Mainichi's threat to start a rival league, along with American pressure, opened the way to planning for fifteen teams. Economic constraints on individual companies reduced this to twelve teams, and in the spring of 1950 the Central and Pacific Leagues, each with six teams, began play. Unlike MLB, which has expanded considerably over the last six decades, NPB has retained this two-league, twelve-team shape to the present day (although there have been changes of ownership and shifts in home bases).

The second contentious issue was how to align these teams in the two leagues. In Kansai, the Kintetsu and Nankai train companies jumped in to sponsor new teams along with Hanshin and Hankyū. This meant that four of the five major Kansai electrical train company teams, all strong business competitors, were now baseball competitors. Many believed that having them in the same league, along with Mainichi Newspaper Company (still centered in Osaka) and another train company, Nishitetsu, from the far western city of Fukuoka, would create the intense (and profitable) excitement of local rivalry and a Pacific League of western Japanese cities against a Central League that was largely made up of Tokyo-region teams.

To the anger of its fellow Kansai companies, however, Hanshin broke ranks. The ownership calculated that games against the Yomiuri Giants would be most profitable, so it was better to play the Giants twenty or more times during a regular Central League season than possibly meeting them in a final Japan Series. Hanshin turned its back on the other Kansai teams and opted into the Central League with Yomiuri, which had encouraged Hanshin's break. The other Kansai club owners were greatly angered by Hanshin's self-interested decision, and in revenge, they raided Hanshin's player roster. Mainichi, in particular, signed away six of Hanshin's best players, and the cost to the Tigers was immediate and long lasting. In the first year of the two-league system (1950), they finished in fourth place, a distant thirty games away from first. It would be thirteen years before Hanshin won a league championship.

Throughout the 1950s, the Kansai-centered Pacific League held its own against the Central League and the Giants, with the leagues splitting the ten Japan Series of that decade evenly. The Giants dominated the Central League, winning the league title eight of the ten years (and the Japan Series four of those years). Although the Tigers finished in either second or third place every year from 1951 to 1960, they were an afterthought in the region. The Nankai Hawks were the most powerful and most popular Kansai team, winning the Pacific League four times and beating the Giants in three consecutive Japan Series, 1956–1958. Osaka Stadium, the Hawks' home stadium in downtown Osaka, was smaller and shabbier than Kōshien, but it was the pulsating center of the Kansai baseball world throughout that decade (Nagai and Hashitsune 2003).

Japan's mass media recovered rather quickly as well, and sports, especially baseball and professional wrestling, became lucrative for their growth. Newsprint was a scarce commodity in the late 1940s, but in addition to manga comics and popular weeklies, both the *Asahi* and the *Mainichi* national newspapers found the resources to begin dedicated sports dailies (apparently the American Occupation officials authorized special rations of newsprint for these entertainment purposes). Professional baseball was front-page material from the start, but it shared space with professional wrestling and gambling sports, and several decades passed before it monopolized sports papers' attention.

The other mass media development of consequence was the appearance of television. Here too, it was Yomiuri's powerful owner, Shōriki, who quickly maneuvered to secure the first commercial broadcast license in 1952, even ahead of the government's own noncommercial NHK network. Shōriki aggressively built a television network (NTV) to match his radio network and filled it with professional wrestling, boxing, and baseball to build an appetite for what was still a rare and expensive technology. The new NHK network was left with the national high school baseball tournaments at Kōshien and the six annual two-week sumo tournaments, which effectively decommercialized those sports.[1]

For the first four or five years, television was watched in bars, beauty parlors, and coffee shops (much like air-conditioning, owners would purchase the expensive sets to draw customers) or in front of outdoor monitors that NTV set up in hundreds of public locations. It was actually professional wrestling that most attracted the nascent audiences. This was because the early cameras could focus effectively on the circumscribed wrestling ring and also because NTV and the promoters could orchestrate wrestling matches with strong nationalist overtones with visiting American wrestlers.[2]

Baseball's fortunes considerably brightened when stadiums were equipped with lights, and evening games began toward the end of the decade. Lighting came to Kōshien in 1956, and this was crucial in securing stadium and television audiences of the adult working population, who had been unable to watch day games during the week. Even in the midst of the consumer electrical appliance boom of the decade, manufacturers had particular success in lowering the cost of television, and by the early 1960s it was found in some three-quarters of the nation's households (Chun 2007; Partner 1999; Yoshimi 2005).

Throughout the late 1950s and into the 1960s, the Yomiuri Giants struggled against the western Japan teams of the Pacific League, but its parent corporation invested in the amusement park adjacent to the home stadium, Kōrakuen, and used the full force of its media (newspaper, radio, and television) to publicize the Giants' games and to showcase the team. The Giants' manager, Kawakami Tetsuharu, was building a team around two new stars, the university standout Nagashima Shigeo and the high school slugger Oh Sadaharu, and all of this was laying a foundation for the emergence of the Giants as Japan's team by the mid-1960s. What lay behind this was an intense Tokyo-centrism and a new corporate nationalism, both of which were to have profound consequences for Hanshin and Japanese baseball.

BASEBALL BECOMES TOKYO-CENTRIC IN THE 1960S

Hanshin broke out of its runner-up status twice in the early 1960s, taking the Central League title in 1962 and again in 1964. The latter year was especially dramatic and is much memorialized in Tigers history. At midseason, the Tigers were struggling at six and one-half games behind the first-place Taiyo Whales. Although they managed to narrow the lead, with seven games left in the season, they were still facing an almost impossible three-and-one-half-game deficit. With clutch pitching, especially by their American ace, Gene Bacque, they took three straight games from Taiyo, bringing the season down to a final game between the two. The game was tied into the eighth inning. With two batters down and the bases loaded, Taiyo's ace pitcher Inagawa Makoto threw a wild pitch past the catcher; however, the ball bounced off the concrete backstop, right back to the catcher, who fired it to Inagawa as he charged for home plate to nail the third-base runner. Against the odds, the Hanshin runner, Motoyashiki Kingo, timed his slide perfectly and narrowly beat the throw, setting up one of the most remarkable season finales (known as "the miracle comeback") in Japanese baseball.

The Tigers' opponent in the 1964 Japan Series was Nankai, the more popular Osaka team and the favorite going into the series (which is oddly still the only time in history that the Japan Series has been played between two Osaka teams). Both teams featured star American pitchers, Gene Bacque for Hanshin and Joe Stanka for Nankai (Connery 1962; Stanka and Stanka 1989). The series itself proved to be extremely tight, going the full seven games before Nankai, behind Stanka, won it. It was a series that riveted Kansai, but even so, it seldom made the top headlines of the sports newspapers, and the decisive seventh game, played on October 10 at Kōshien, only drew fifteen thousand fans.

What had pushed it off the national radar was that on that very day, October 10, was the Opening Ceremony for the 1964 Olympic Games in Tokyo. Knowing that the Olympics had galvanized the nation for months, NPB had compressed its season and moved up the Japan Series, but there was little it could do to avoid being thoroughly eclipsed. That it turned out to be an all-Osaka series added a symbolic insult to the region. More fundamentally, however, the international prestige and the massive infrastructure investments in transport, skyscrapers, sewers, and more that the Olympics brought to metropolitan Tokyo decisively accelerated a decline in Kansai's position that continues to the present day.

Among the many changes that happened in that Olympic year, perhaps most consequential was the opening of the first Shinkansen "bullet" train line between Tokyo and Osaka (extended in subsequent decades to the far reaches of the archipelago). That it ran between the two metropolises was the conventional phrasing, but in reality it critically enabled a substantially one-way flow of people, organizations, resources, and prestige from Osaka and Kansai (and Nagoya and elsewhere) to Tokyo.

The human geography of modern nations tends toward the unicentric or the multipolar. In some nations, like the United States, Canada, Brazil, Germany, and Australia, there are multiple, competing centers over which political, economic, and cultural powers are unevenly distributed (Washington, D.C., New York, Chicago, Los Angeles, etc.). In contrast, some national societies are shaped around a single center in which most of these forms of power are concentrated, such as France, Greece, Mexico, Spain, and Norway.

Japan was for several centuries the former type of nation. Edo and then Tokyo had been the political capital of Japan for three and one-half centuries, but Osaka was economically dominant; often larger in population; and more prominent in the development of metropolitan leisure, media, and entertainment (Hara 1998). The first two national newspapers, *Asahi* and *Mainichi*, were based in Osaka, and the city was the corporate headquarters and production and shipping base for many sectors of the economy. Although baseball got its start in Tokyo, and Tokyo's universities dominated collegiate play in the early twentieth century, the National Middle School Tournament and the many sports promotions by the Asahi and Mainichi newspaper companies shifted the locus of sports to Osaka by the 1910s. By the late 1920s, when the opening of Kōshien (and Fujiidera and other Kansai stadiums) was followed immediately by the construction of Kōrakuen Stadium and Meiji Jingū Stadium in Tokyo, there was a relative balance of spectator sports power and enthusiasm between the two metropolises. It was not until the 1960s that this balance was irrevocably upset, and Japan became decisively and irrevocably Tokyo-centric.

The national population continued to increase for two decades, but most of the robust growth was in Tokyo and its Kanto region, at the

expense of the other regions. In 1930 Osaka's share of national manufacturing was 30 percent, twice that of Tokyo (Hill and Fujita 1995:182).
As Edgington notes, Osaka enterprise numbers and employment both
began to fall in this decade. "In 1970, Osaka was responsible for 36.5%
of Japan's exports, 23.3% of its manufacturing output, and 15.2% of
its new factories. But by 1993, Osaka was generating only 4.3% of
national exports, 7.7% of manufacturing output, and 1% of new factories" (Edgington 2000:308–309). The Japanese government's National
Land Agency has a metric of "central management functions" by which
it compares metropolitan regions according to economic, political, and
sociocultural indexes (e.g., number of corporate executives, financial
institutions, tertiary educational institutions, government administra-
tors, etc.; see Hill and Fujita 1995:182–183). By all indexes, Tokyo out-
ranked Osaka by 1970, and this gap has widened dramatically since
then. All of Japan became "regional" to the concentrated national center in Tokyo, but Osaka and the Kansai region around it was particularly marked by its "second-city" status. The mutual effects of this
reshaping of national geography on professional baseball and of professional baseball's role in expressing this new geography were profound.

THE V-9 GIANTS RESHAPE PROFESSIONAL BASEBALL

The 1965 baseball season opened only months after the Tokyo Olympic
Games had occluded the all-Osaka Japan Series, and by a striking coincidence, the Yomiuri Giants set out on a streak still unsurpassed in Japanese baseball. They won the Central League title and the Japan Series
that year and every year for the next nine years. Dubbed the V-9 Giants
for this run from 1965 to 1973, in this period they forever became
"Japan's team" and fundamentally reshaped professional baseball.

They were of course not the V-9 Giants until they had won their run,
which ended in 1973, but year after year, throughout the 1960s and
into the early 1970s, their image of invincibility grew. There were several ingredients in their V-9 success, beginning with their pair of stars,
Nagashima Shigeo and Oh Sadaharu, two of the greatest hitters ever.
Nagashima had been drafted in 1957 as the most talked-about university player of the year; Oh was signed as the most-coveted high school
player the following year. It took them both several years to adjust, but
by the early 1960s, dubbed the "O-N Cannon," they were the power
duo that drove the Giants. Of the 1,192 games that the Giants played
during their V-9 years, only 60 were played without both players. In

those nine years, the two hit 651 home runs, with a combined average of 70 per year. Their combined RBIs totaled over 2,700, which was 300 per season or about 3 per game. One or the other or both were at the center of virtually every game for nine years—for the team, for the media, and for the spectators.

A second ingredient was Giants' manager Kawakami Tetsuharu, who had been known during his player years as the "god of hitting." As manager, Kawakami quickly became famous for a style of authoritarian leadership known as managed baseball (*kanri yakyū*). He demanded (or at least, appeared to demand) iron discipline, arduous practices, and stolid teamwork, and employed a conservative playing strategy. He also announced a no foreigner policy of using only Japanese players and early in his tenure dumped Wally Yonamine, a Japanese American from Hawaii', the first American brought into NPB after the war, and one of the greatest players of the 1950s with the Giants until Kawakami traded him in late 1959 (Fitts 2008). The aura and imagery of this team—the O-N Cannon, managed baseball, no foreigners, and so forth—was in effect a Yomiuri brand of samurai baseball, and it was purveyed and enforced by the full weight of the Yomiuri media empire: its national television and radio network that ensured that its games were broadcast to every household in the country, its national newspaper and sports daily, and its manga and other print venues. Yomiuri, although based in Tokyo and representing a single corporate group, nationalized itself in those years, in the double sense of building a truly national fan base and of communicating the Giants as the quintessential "Japan's team."

To some sports analysts, perennial winning undermines the nature (and profitability) of a sport itself, which needs a measure of competitive balance, the possibility of rotating winners, and the suspense of not really knowing the outcomes of games and seasons. But part of the explanation for the V-9 Giants' hold on Japan in those years was the opposite: that it provided the security of winning among a postwar population for whom security was still a precious ambition. The nation's total defeat in the war, the widespread destruction and dislocation, the uncertain recovery of the 1950s—all of this was still quite fresh. I recall living in the countryside in the 1970s, far from Tokyo, and watching the Giants on television with farm families. One of their frequent comments was that they enjoyed the Giants because it was comforting to know the likely outcome (*anshin shita* was the most common phase). To a generation raised in opposite circumstances, the Giants provided reassuring stability and success. By the late 1970s and into the 1980s, when the

Giants' fortunes were more uncertain, there were times in the evening when the Giants fell behind and the father of the household simply turned off the television and refused to watch further.

CORPORATE NATIONALISM, CULTURAL IDENTITY, AND SOCIETAL MAINSTREAM

The V-9 Giants totally dominated NPB and thoroughly reshaped the image of professional baseball. Their significance, however, was even more profound because, by coincidence, their preeminence overlapped with one of the most remarkable GNP growth decades in world economic history to that time. And this national economic growth was given a specific organizational and cultural-ethnic rationale. The Giants' image resonated powerfully with and served as testimony to a larger business image, sloganeered as "Japan, Inc." and "Japan-style management." The mid- to late 1960s was precisely the period when business-people and commentators revised the image of "the Japanese company system" from an inefficient, tradition-bound anachronism into a uniquely Japanese accomplishment and an effective, positive alternative to Western corporate forms. What Japanese and foreign commentators alike had disparaged as inefficient primordial rigidities were now spun as a potent and prescient "Confucian corporatism" that would be a new standard for late-capitalist organization. The key features of this form of economic organization seemed to contradict conventional Western capitalist logic, but it was touted as building strength through solidarity and collectivity with those same features:

- full-career employment (creating a sense of mutual enterprise fate)
- bottom-up entry for school leavers (not lateral midcareer shifts)
- hiring for general educational credentials (not specific skills)
- pay and promotion by seniority (these were age-grade societies)
- company-based unions (rather than skill-based trade unions)
- career development management, extensive in-service training, and provision of a panoply of social services by the company

The Giants epitomized how tempting a venue professional baseball was for publicly performing such corporate-style authority and exacting exemplary discipline. The Giants became and long remained a lightning rod for national prestige and patriotic pride.

And yet, behind that well-burnished image and the undeniable success of Giants baseball, it was not hard to discern undercurrents of contradiction, subordination, and sacrifice—within the Giants world and within NPB baseball more broadly, especially for the Pacific League and the Hanshin Tigers. Nagashima, Oh, and others who were important to the V-9 (such as Horiuchi Tsuneo) were indeed "lifetime employees," signed to the Giants for full careers, forever Giants like the Mitsubishi salaryman was forever a Mitsubishi man. A closer look at the roster, though, showed that was equally willing to go out and trade for any established star he could to keep the lineup in tune. Outfielder Harimoto Isao and Hall of Fame pitcher Kanemoto Masaichi were both lured at the peak of their careers to bolster the Giants. Kawakami was pragmatic and opportunistic—and quietly hypocritical. In an era when an ethnic homogeneity of "we Japanese" underwrote an official cultural nationalism, Kawakami's 100 percent Japanese guarantee fed jingoistic sentiment, but this disguised and demeaned the actual identities of the sport's stars, like Oh Sadaharu, born of a Taiwanese father and always a Taiwan citizen, and Harimoto and Kanemoto, both Korean-descent Japan residents, forced into a permanent second-class status. In these and other ways (superior performance on the playing field was sometimes enforced by brute intimidation of reporters, umpires, league officials, and sponsors), Japan's team was an unwitting reminder of the darker side of the national success story being written in those years (Kelly 1998a, 1998b).

Corporatization, as an organizational structure and as an organizational image, was broadly true of professional baseball clubs from the 1960s. From the beginning, they were sponsored by media and transport companies and were part of corporate programs, but the teams themselves were seasonal, and the support and administrative staff was minimal. The notion of a team promoted throughout the year and of an actual front office of permanent staff did not emerge until the 1960s. Player rosters and coaching staffs expanded, and a full-time club was created above and around the team, with regular club employees and owner-company employees rotated in on assignment. The club as subsidiary, as child company, was established, and this imposed a corporate organizational model on the club itself: a Japanese-style template of seniority, hierarchy, and procedures, with meeting protocols, accounting standards, and lines of decision making that regularized and familiarized the clubs to the business world and the fans themselves.[3]

More explicitly corporate procedures spread through NPB and the leagues as well. The commissioner remained subordinate to the owners through their council, but a universal player draft was instituted in 1965, and trade regulations and contract terms were regularized. It was only in the 1970s that NPB created a formal foreign player (*gaijin senshu*) category, contractually distinct from the regular players (*ippan senshu*). However, the effect of these changes was not to level the playing field among the clubs or to standardize their operations. Although the Giants demonstrate the success of such a reorganization of professional baseball, it came at considerable cost to the other eleven clubs, especially those in the Pacific League.

With the Giants' continued success, Pacific League popularity declined quickly. Without television exposure, viewership, stadium attendance, and sports dailies' attention dropped off. It was said that the last-place team in the Central League had higher revenues than the first-place team in the Pacific League. The Nishitetsu Lions, who shared Pacific League dominance with Nankai throughout the 1950s, were caught up in a notorious "Black Mist" incident of game fixing in 1969–1970 that decimated the team and tarnished the league. The team was sold four times in the 1970s and moved to Kanto. Later that decade, the owners of the two leading Kansai teams, Nankai and Hankyū, far more powerful railroad companies than Hanshin, sold off their teams as well. Nankai was moved to Fukuoka in western Japan after the Lions were moved from there, and the Hankyū Braves were sold to the Orient Leasing Company, which rebranded the Braves as the Orix BlueWave and moved them to the western outskirts of Kobe. I began my research in Kansai a decade and a half later, when the region had two Pacific League teams, Orix and Kintetsu, along with Hanshin.

The Kanto retail and transport giant Seibu bought the Lions in 1979 and began investing in the team, a new stadium on the outskirts of Tokyo, and innovative commercial strategies to attract new fans. These efforts were quickly successful; indeed, the team began an extraordinary domination of the league in 1982, and in the seventeen years between 1982 and 1998, Seibu won the league title thirteen times and was Japan Series champion eight times. Even this, though, could not restore the Pacific League and its teams to media attention and profitability; when I began my research in Kansai in 1996, even as Orix was challenging Seibu with its exciting star, Ichirō, its Green Stadium attendance was mediocre, its television broadcasts were minimal, and even Ichirō himself was largely ignored by the sports media.

Of all the teams, it was the Hanshin Tigers that were most affected by the changes in the 1960s: the Giants' ascendancy, the Tokyo centralization, and the prestige of the large corporate model. As Inoue (2001:87–94), Kikkawa (1997), and others have shown, the new Kansai television broadcasting companies in the 1950s and into the 1960s had focused almost exclusively on Pacific League teams and their games (e.g., Mainichi Hōsō, Asahi Hōsō, Kansai Terebi Hōsō, and, in the 1960s, Sun Terebi), but once Yomiuri began its V-9 run, all the networks started dropping those games and shifting to Hanshin's schedule. With the teams playing together in the Central League and meeting twenty-seven times a year, the series always gained the highest attendance, the highest broadcast rights, and the greatest television audience. This was equally true for the Kansai sports dailies.

Becoming Kansai's team was a mixed blessing for Hanshin, however, because the attention increasingly focused on the thematics of the second-city complex and the dynamics of work in the Hanshin world. The foibles and squabbles within the club, so publicly and melodramatically conveyed in the sports media and so difficult to diagnose given the nature of the sport, were especially unnerving to a municipal railroad company like Hanshin, which saw itself as having to meet demanding public standards of safety and efficiency in operating its transportation network. This led to the intrusive style of parent-company micromanagement of the club, which often had the unintended consequence of exacerbating the baseball weaknesses.

This national attention was in spite of—or rather, because of—the lopsided nature of the competitive balance and the contrasts in key features of the two worlds. The Hanshin parent company, for example, remained a small transport corporation, while Yomiuri was one of the largest media conglomerates in the world. Yomiuri thus carefully controlled the news about and image of the Giants, while Hanshin was at the mercy of a prying, independent Kansai media. Yomiuri sponsored the fan supporter associations and managed their behavior, while the Hanshin fan associations, the largest in Japan, were resolutely independent and often fiercely critical of the Hanshin club. Yomiuri always enjoyed the financial resources to sign anyone, while the Hanshin club lacked the funds and league influence to attract the best rookies and to bend the rules. For these and other factors, this Giants-Tigers rivalry evolved into a rivalry between "Japan's team" and "Kansai's team."

Thus, the rivalry that was played out thirteen or so times a season on the field of Kōshien (and an equal number of times in Tokyo) was not just a metonymic struggle of Tokyo versus Osaka as Japan's first city versus its second city (see figure 26). More broadly, it was the uneven

FIGURE 26. Front-page article about a melee between Hanshin Tigers and Yomiuri Giants players in a game that Hanshin won by coming from behind. *Nikkan Sports*, Osaka edition, August 3, 1998, 1. Courtesy of Nikkan Sports Newspaper.

struggle of the national center and the region whose position most reminded everyone of the reshaping of the Japanese political-economic landscape that was occurring over those decades. That Kōshien Stadium remained as it always had been, while Kōrakuen was replaced during the 1980s bubble economy with the Big Egg of Tokyo Dome, was a fitting architectural expression of that relationship.

LITANIES OF "FIERCE TIGERS" AND "NO-GOOD TIGERS" IN HANSHIN CLUB HISTORIES

Thus, from the late 1960s and especially from the early 1970s, continuing through the 1990s (when I began this study) and beyond, Hanshin was the main foil for Yomiuri, on the field and in narrative, and the bearer of Kansai's sporting hopes. This relationship was not only the basis for the elements of the Tigers world that I have laid out in earlier chapters, but it had an indelible impact on what we may call Hanshin historiography—that is, how the Hanshin club was described and written about in those decades. It was this club history that I had to learn in trying to appreciate the historical consciousness of those whom I was encountering in that sportsworld.

Baseball is in love with its own history, even compared with the narcissism of other sports like soccer and cricket. The sport itself is especially deep in storytelling possibilities. It luxuriates in story lines and characters. Doing and watching baseball demand narrative. Meaning creates suspense, and the unfolding action is only suspenseful when it is connected to the memories of previous plays and past events. As an interval sport with specialized positions, baseball is also especially liable to numbers and record keeping, and a dense statistical grid lies across the narrative lines to form a rich tapestry of nostalgia.

At the same time, there are multiple forms and layers of such historical consciousness. A few scholars of the sport and many more veteran media writers, ex-players, and longtime coaches and managers combine decades of direct experience with even longer horizons of memory and expertise. Yoshida Yoshio was one such individual: a key participant in five decades of Hanshin Tigers history as player, commentator, and manager, with a detailed recollection, season by season, of that world (and with at least four books of autobiography and commentary to his credit). Fans also, like Mr. Fujita, head of the Roving Tigers Club, had been going to games at Kōshien regularly (religiously, as we sometimes say in the United States) for thirty years and could recall details of games and players—a kind of Tigers griot of knowledge and memory.

Baseball literature is produced and consumed by these junkies. This is as true for Japan as for the United States. There are shelves full of league histories, team histories, player biographies, and manager studies. There are histories of owners, broadcasters, scouts, and fan clubs. Books have been written about single games and even a single sequence of pitches within a game. Most numerous in this Japan literature are books about the two most popular teams, the Yomiuri Giants and the Hanshin Tigers, and their players and managers. A recent online listing by an Osaka bookseller of books just about the Tigers ran to 286 titles!

But many others, especially the younger players and casual fans, had a much more shallow awareness of Hanshin Tigers history that lacked chronological detail and temporal coherence. Rather, for them the Tigers' past was a highlights/lowlights reel of noteworthy and notorious Hanshin moments. To them, history was less a well-formed, primary-sourced narrative and more of a frequently told and retold litany of famous games, star players, notable controversies, key victories, shocking defeats, and so forth.

I am far from having plowed through all or even most of the 286 Hanshin books, but reading a great many of them over the years has convinced me that of the two teams, accounts of Hanshin tend toward the greater extremes of hyperbole and melodrama. The two key terms in Hanshin history are *mōko* and *dame-tora*, the "Fierce Tigers" and the "No-Good Tigers": a stark, melodramatic, and moralizing binary.[4] Hanshin histories can be praise songs or lamentations, hitting the highlights or wallowing in the scandals, reaching for hagiography or leveling caustic criticism. There are those histories, especially the official volumes prepared for the baseball club (Hanshin Taigāsu 1991) or the parent company (Hanshin denki tetsudō 1985) and the commemorative volumes issued by newspapers (Nikkan Supōtsu 2015), that do follow a detailed, year-by-year, factual narrative. However, most other Hanshin histories and recollections, by former players, sports journalists, and academics, are organized around a common stock of well-known incidents—well-known precisely because they are circulated so often in such histories and in the daily reporting and fan conversations. These are stories constructed around the team's fortunes and misfortunes through a matrix of narrative and numbers: individual accomplishments, dramatic moments, and occasional team success amid prolonged disappointment. An image of team history emerges by which subsequent events are understood and evaluated but also by which history telling is filtered through a potent mix of presentism and nostalgia.

To demonstrate this, I focus here on ten club histories that have been particularly useful to me in the last twenty-five years.[5] The authors tend to come from the sports media: longtime reporters, editors, and broadcasters who are often synthesizing a career's worth of work within the Hanshin world; some are well-known cultural critics and freelance authors who write from a long-term fan's engagement. One is an editorial compilation by a team from Nikkan Sports (*Nikkan Sports Newspaper*, Western Japan, 2016), and one is a history written by Yoshida Yoshio, the former player, manager, and commentator. What interested me was how often the same events and moments from the early 1950s to the present were showcased. This is why I argue that the history that circulates within the Hanshin Tigers world is less an official and objective chronology and more a widely held and oft-repeated litany of certain individual and team highlights as well as controversies and struggles. Assessments of these moments can vary significantly—it is a litany recited in very partisan and perspectival fashion—but the events themselves form an orthodoxy. The following is not an exhaustive discussion, but is drawn and distilled from these ten histories, including principal points of Hanshin historical consciousness, which is largely a struggle between two versions of Hanshin Tigers history.

1. **The "dynamite batting order" of 1947.** Hanshin reconstituted itself quickly after the war, and in the second season of play, it soared to a league championship far ahead of second-place Chūnichi Dragons, powered by a lineup of hitters that the press labeled the "dynamite batting order." But it was dynamite on a short fuse, and most histories emphasize how short-lived was this moment of glory. Next season, Hanshin finished a distant third, seventeen games behind the league champ Nankai Hawks, which was to remain powerful for over a decade. Hanshin would not win another league championship for fourteen years, in 1962.

2. **The "abandoned game" of 1954.** A much-recounted early controversy was the Tigers' first "abandoned game" (*hōki shiai*), on July 25, 1954, against the Chūnichi Dragons. With the game tied in extra innings, Hanshin star player Fujimura Tomio came charging out of the dugout to dispute a call by the home plate umpire, Sugimura Shōichirō. Fujimura punched Sugimura in the stomach and was ejected. Hanshin fans began fighting with the stadium guards, and Hanshin held up play for sixty-seven minutes while Hanshin manager Matsuki continued arguing. When play finally began again, Fujimura, who claimed he had not heard his ejection announced over the stadium speaker, tried to come up to bat, which only reignited the uproar. The umpires eventually suspended the game and declared Chūnichi to be the winner, 9–0.

Again, the incident is also told as a case of soured relations with the parent company. Front office executive Tanaka Gi'ichi had reassured the team that the league penalties would be light, but in fact the league president responded harshly, fining and suspending the manager for five days and hitting Fujimura, the team's star player, with a ¥50,000 fine and a twenty-day suspension, which also ended his continuous appearance record at 1,014 games. The team's anger was directed not at the league but at its own parent company for acquiescing and not backing it up.

3. **Ostracizing manager Fujimura in 1956.** A frequent term in Hanshin histories is *oiesōdō* or infighting, an internal wrangling (e.g., Ōtani 2003:121–122). An early instance was in 1956. Players and the front office had been at loggerheads over replacing the manager at the end of the 1955 season. The parent company president, Noda Seizō, stepped in and appointed a totally inexperienced and unknown outsider, Kishi Ichirō, which only exacerbated tensions. Players openly criticized the latter, and by the end of the 1956 season, they were themselves divided into two factions that each followed one of their two stars, Fujimura and Kanada Masayasu. At least that was how the sports dailies reported it (even with diagrams of the factions), which further fueled suspicions among the players. Some of the hostility arose from their salaries, which were scaled to Fujimura's salary, the star with the highest salary; even if they had an outstanding season, their salaries were calculated downward from his salary. In early December, the club released both Fujimura and Kaneda, but the other players refused to attend the annual salary negotiations. The league president and even the Yomiuri Giants manager came to Osaka to try to mediate. Eventually Fujimura visited the parent company owner to apologize and express remorse, and Kaneda was brought back. Contracts were signed, and everyone acceded to a show of unity. This did not eliminate the undercurrents, and the factional squabbling continued throughout the 1957 season, enthusiastically reported by the sports papers. Club executive Tozawa Kazutaka later recollected that nothing positive came to the team from the incident; the only thing it did was sell newspapers. And that it did; spurred by this incident, the Kansai area sports papers grew quickly in sales and notoriety.

4. **The "emperor's game" against the Yomiuri Giants in 1959.** The Hanshin-Yomiuri rivalry was not yet ascendant, but when it emerged that the emperor wished to attend his first professional baseball game, the Giants' Shōriki immediately negotiated with the Imperial Household

Agency to ensure it would be a game at the Giants' Kōrakuen Stadium. The emperor and empress attended an evening game on June 25, 1959, against Hanshin. It was a closely fought contest; the lead changed four times, and the game was tied as the Giants came to bat in the bottom of the ninth inning. The scoreboard clock read 9:06, and the emperor was scheduled to leave the stadium at 9:15; everyone would be disappointed and embarrassed that he would not see the conclusion. The first batter was the new Giants star Nagashima Shigeo; facing Hanshin's own new star rookie, Murayama Minoru, at 9:12 Nagashima blasted a "sayonara" home run down the left field line to win the game.[6] Murayama went on to a Hall of Fame career, but he always insisted (and many Hanshin histories noted) that he thought Nagashima's hit was a foul ball and that the umpires may have deliberately ruled it fair in light of the circumstances. It certainly gave a dramatic quality to the emperor's game and brought publicity to NPB and the Giants, but it also fed a recurring story line over the decades of umpire favoritism to the Giants.

5. The 1964 Japan Series against Nankai Hawks. The Tigers had finally taken another league championship in 1962, but this fact is overshadowed in Tigers histories by their second title in 1964 because of the exciting manner in which they won the league on the last day and because it was a series against their crosstown rival, Nankai. As I noted previously, it is equally memorable in Hanshin historical consciousness for being overshadowed by the Tokyo Olympics and for being a prelude to the Giants' V-9 run of nine championships—and for Hanshin's even longer run as the Giants' primary foil.

6. President Tozawa's utterance of 1973. The year 1973 was pivotal because the Yomiuri Giants were aiming for their ninth straight league championship (Tamaki 1991:99–107). The Tigers and their fans were frustrated by serving as a perpetual runner-up to this historical record, and it was assumed that the team would make a special effort to break the streak. However, late in the season the sports papers reported that Hanshin parent company president Tozawa had opined that the best ending yet again would be for the Giants to win, with the Tigers fighting hard but finishing as a runner-up. His words have been recycled for decades by most commentators as evidence of Hanshin corporate greed and cowardice; a tight race would keep up attendance and a second-place finish would avoid the company having to raise player salaries in recognition of a championship.

Their scorn was not without alleged evidence. Hanshin led the league and could clinch the title with a win in either of the two final games, one against the Chūnichi Dragons and the other against the Giants. The Hanshin manager committed his ace pitcher Enatsu Yutaka to face the Dragons and take the title; however, Enatsu later claimed that he was called into the front office and assured by the club executive that "it would be alright to lose—and that's OK with the manager too" (Nakagawa 2016:258–300). Hanshin did lose the game in Nagoya but could still have taken the title by tying the Giants and denying them their V-9 in the final game. It was not to be. With the ace Enatsu unavailable, the Hanshin starter Ueda Jirō gave up two runs in the first inning and seven more runs later, collapsing 9–0. Tigers fans were outraged; they poured onto the field as the game ended, chasing the Giants players back into their dugout and preventing them from celebrating on the field.

7. The release of Tabuchi and the hiring of Don Blasingame as manager in 1978. Ozu Shōjirō became club president at the end the 1978 season, when Hanshin had its worst finish to date. Unlike his predecessors, whom most histories dismissed as pawns of the parent company, he was already the number three executive in the parent company. His reputation for ruthless power had made him known as "the sorcerer" and "the assassin" (and as some of the sports dailies rather tastelessly called him, Osuwarudo, after Lee Harvey Oswald!). To rebuild the team, he secretly traded away longtime star player Tabuchi Kōichi, news of which became public in a contentious after-midnight meeting that was covered fulsomely by the sports papers; he then pushed to hire Hanshin's first "foreigner" manager, the American Don Blasingame (known as "Blazer"), who had just quit as head coach of Hiroshima and returned to the United States. Tabuchi's trade paid off, but Blazer met fierce resistance in some quarters of the team and received little backup from the front office, so the new 1979 season brought continuous headlines of insinuations against the company and insubordination by many players, eventually leading to Blazer's dismissal. Another oiesōdō.

8. "The manager's a fool": Emoto's eruption in 1981. The managerial change improved neither the Tigers' on-field performance nor the off-field relations between players and the new manager and with the front office. The press gave particular emphasis to a remark that the star pitcher, Emoto Takenori, uttered in a growling Osaka dialect to reporters as he walked from the dugout to the dressing room after pitching a game in late August 1981: "The manager and coaches are utter fools! They don't know baseball. They're fools, fools, fools." For that he was dragged before the club executive, and during a three-hour confrontation, Emoto told him, "After that, I don't really want to play for the Tigers anymore. I'll take responsibility for what I said and leave the club." The sports dailies followed this through the end of the season, portraying what was tagged the "Emoto resignation drama" (Emoto taidan-geki), which in fact ended with his resignation being accepted by the club.

9. "Japan number 1!" Hanshin wins the 1985 Japan Series. After two decades, 1985 finally brought the team, the press, and the fans a season of joy and pride (see figure 11 in chapter 4), clinching the league title after a surprisingly easy run at the top throughout much of the season and then trouncing the Pacific League champion Seibu Lions to win the Japan Series. This was the team's first Japan Series (by comparison, the Giants by 1985 had already appeared in twenty-two Japan Series and won sixteen).

This championship remains the high point of most Hanshin histories, and many details of the season are lovingly incanted. There are still many replays on Kansai television of the famous san-renpatsu, three back-to-back-to-back home runs against the Giants in an early season game on April 17 by the Tigers' Randy Bass, Kakefu Masayuki, and Okada Akinobu. These three, plus Mayumi Akinobu, were the most formidable lineup in the league, drawing obvious parallels to the dynamite lineup of 1947. The aura of that single pinnacle of accomplishment had lasting effects on all who had been on the team and in the club. Randy Bass won the Central League Triple Crown that year and was named most valuable player for the regular season and the Japan Series; he has remained a hero to Hanshin fans since and has returned often for lucrative endorsements and appearances. Okada and Mayumi later served as Hanshin managers, and Yoshida, the 1985 manager, came back for a third time in the mid-1990s.

Histories of this championship are understandably celebratory, but many are not without undercurrents of debate and controversy. Commentators are divided on apportioning credit; for instance, the veteran Mainichi Newspaper journalist Tamaki was sharply critical of the manager Yoshida as ineffectual, carried only by his powerful lineup. Another sharp controversy fueled both the Yomiuri-Hanshin rivalry and discrimination against foreign players. By the end of the season, Randy Bass was on the verge of breaking Oh's record of fifty-five season home runs. Indeed, Bass had fifty-four home runs going into the final game against none other than the Giants, managed by Oh himself. He was deliberately and repeatedly walked and never given a chance to tie or break the record, and this cowardice by the Giants pitchers has dogged Oh and his reputation ever since.[7]

Nonetheless, the 1985 championship remains the highlight of the club's entire history, and it is still a source of pride and point of reference in all subsequent histories, critical and celebratory. Randy Bass remains the most popular foreign player ever to wear a Hanshin uniform, and in the years since he has returned regularly as a guest commentator for Hanshin game broadcasts and spokesperson for commercial sales campaigns (Bessatsu Takarajima Editorial Division 2012:6–16). He was the inspiration for the most enduring superstition that has dogged Hanshin fans since that year, known as "the curse of Colonel Sanders." Immediately after the Tigers beat the Lions to win the title, thousands of fans thronged one of the most famous bridges in downtown Osaka, Ebisu Bridge over the Dōtonbori Canal. They chanted the hitting marches of the players, and with each chant a fan who resembled the player dove off the bridge into the canal. There was apparently no one who looked like Randy Bass, the huge, bearded Oklahoman who had won Most Valuable Player honors, so fans absconded with the large statue of Colonel Sanders in front of an adjacent Kentucky Fried Chicken store and tossed it into the canal. The statue was not recovered from the dark and muddy waters, and as the years went by and Hanshin fortunes sank, an urban legend circulated that the team would never win unless Colonel Sanders was recovered. Despite numerous searches, it was not until 2009 that the statue was discovered in the muddy canal bottom. The KFC Company Japan now has it in its Osaka headquarters (although as of 2017, its recovery has not brought a Japan Series title back to Hanshin; Yoshida 2009).

10. The Tigers' "longest day" in 1987. Hanshin was unable to replicate its success the next season and fell even further in 1987, putting Yoshida's managerial position in serious jeopardy. The sports dailies spent the season interpreting signs of discontent among players and even between Yoshida and his coaches. The club announced that it would hold an "emergency" club directors' meeting on October 12, as the season ended, to decide his fate. The meeting began at 9:30 in the morning in the third-floor conference room of the parent company in Umeda, with over fifty print and television reporters monitoring the comings and goings. It is represented in most accounts as a protracted debate between the

five directors from the parent company, led by CEO Kuma, and the two directors from the club, club president Okazaki Yoshihito, and his chief lieutenant, Furuya Shingo. Kuma wanted to keep Yoshida and to continue rebuilding (the common phrase dodai-zukuri was invoked); Okazaki insisted that team morale was so low and relations between Yoshida and the front office so poor that no rebuilding was possible. The meeting dragged on for hours and finally concluded after 5:00 p.m., a nine-hour marathon session that ended with Kuma acceding to Okazaki's position. What is interesting in retrospect is that Okazaki, from such a subordinate position, carried the day. Yoshida would be expected "to resign." The official announcement of the resignation at a press conference that evening has added to the lore of the day. A tight-lipped Okazaki appeared with Yoshida at his side; generally on such occasions, the conclusion is announced first, but Okazaki went on at length about the need for change without hinting at the meeting's decision. Newspaper copy deadlines were nearing, and the reporters were getting irritated; finally, after rambling on, Okazaki raised his voice, "When we look back over the three-year period [whereupon everyone snapped to attention] . . . we are full of appreciation" and then finally "resignation." It was a dramatic moment, as flashbulbs caught the expressions on both men's faces.

Even with a new manager (Murayama was brought in for a second time as manager), Hanshin continued to spiral downward, and further controversies ensued as the 1988 season opened. There was a protracted dispute with Randy Bass, who had to return to the United States in the spring because his son was having critical surgery; this was eventually successful, but mutual recriminations over his absence and paying the medical bills led Kuma to order Bass's dismissal in late June. Players were no happier with Murayama's style than with Yoshida's and the team fell once again to last place.

The worst tragedy was to follow in July, when Furuya, the front office executive who had borne the brunt of the Yoshida struggles the season before and then tried to be an intermediary with Bass, committed suicide while attending baseball meetings in Tokyo. The stories that were then laid out in the press of his protracted anguish personified the intense and ultimately unbearable pressure of a middle manager and go-between being caught in the middle of such contentious and momentous issues.

      o   ·   o

The preceding summaries are, of course, a partial but not unrepresentative set of incidents that one might call historiographical ingredients of

Hanshin history. They (and others) are key moments that are remembered and recalled by many within the Hanshin sportsworld, and they work in that world to give narrative, emotional, and moral depth to its present. This awareness of the past is not just a matter of memory: 286 competing and overlapping histories of the Hanshin past. What happened in the Hanshin past—or rather, what different people thought happened in the Hanshin past—constantly framed their actions and reactions in the present.

Perhaps the old saw is true that those who do not know history are destined to repeat it. The Hanshin sportsworld demonstrates that the opposite can be true as well: those who know their own history are destined to repeat it! The preceding examples are some of the most frequently retold incidents, widely enough recognized that the name of an incident is enough to produce knowing nods, nostalgic smiles, or sharp grimaces. They are not only past highlights and lowlights of the past but also exemplars for the present.

When Fujita Taira refused to resign in September 1995, and the emergency board meeting dragged on into the next morning, the resonance with "Hanshin's longest meeting" over Yoshida in 1987 was within people's horizon of memory. When arguments about releasing foreign players like Mike Greenwell turned sour, actions and reactions were framed by the history of such cases. Kameyama's tantrums in 1995 fit a mold of overindulged young Hanshin stars of the past. At every managerial change, a new version of the factional alignments among ex-players in the OB network was mobilized to push one candidate over another. Every year in late March, when the annual personnel movement was decided, the history of parent company and club relations was reenacted and renegotiated. Every fresh controversy with the Giants (a hard slide, a beanball, a suspect umpire call, a caustic comment to the media) has resonance with and keeps alive a rivalry that has been built upon decades of mutual need, bad blood, hard feelings, and grudging admiration.

And these stories are rehearsed and recycled with an overused and overwrought language: the swings from Fierce Tigers to No-Good Tigers and the suffocating "provincialism" (*haenuki ishiki*) of the club mired in "stagnation" (*teitai*) and embattled by "family squabbles" (oiesōdō) and "internal dramas" (*naibu-geki*), featuring players from "Mr. Tigers" standouts to "problem children" (mondaiji), baited by "crazy Tigers fans" (tora-kichi) fans, and so forth.

The suffocating presence of the past was magnified by the insularity of the Hanshin world. Kuma was head of the parent company and owner of the club for twenty years, from 1984 to 2004. The 1985 championship endowed that year's players and manager with a kind of permanent Kansai celebrity status and club presence. Yoshida of course was to return for another three years in 1996–1999, so that he filled the manager's shoes for three years in each of three decades. Mayumi, Kakefu, and Okada have now had their turns as Hanshin managers as well, and at each moment of vacancy, the sports media emphasize (exaggerate) the candidates' rivalries. The more prominent went on to coaching, managing, and media commentator careers; even Randy Bass, who was released with mutual hard feelings in 1988, returned periodically as a television commentator for Mainichi Broadcasting and product spokesperson. I saw him in person at Kōshien and on billboards throughout Kansai in the late 1990s and from the 2000s to the present.

This self-reinforcing history does not of course exhaust all that is said by those within the sportsworld. Games are about games; players, reporters, and spectators are focused on the action, and subsequent media reports narrate, enumerate, and parse these actions in sometimes excruciating detail. But like most professional spectator sports, baseball is a game with hours of preparation, much airtime between actions, and thus the time and inclination to enrich what is going on, whether on the field or in the offices, by embedding it in shared language and collective memory. For decades, the Tigers were a useful metaphor for Kansai people—for an imagined Osaka character, for the real Osaka economy, and for asserting an Osaka presence in a Tokyo-centric nation.

CONNECTED BY DISCORD

Baseball is an agonistic team sport, our team versus their team, locked in a physically demanding, mentally stressful, and morally charged struggle for victory. The historiography of the Hanshin sportsworld reminds us that there are strong crosscurrents of rivalry and discord within "our team," precisely because everyone cares so much and expresses concern, disappointment, and anger from so many different points of view. The internal, historiographic rivalry between the Fierce Tigers and the No-Good Tigers is as deep-seated as the archrivalry between the Tigers and the Giants.

Manager Yoshida was released in 1999, discouraged by three last-place finishes; the great Nomura Katsuya, hired from the outside, could do no better when he took the helm. At that point, I had been following Hanshin for five years and was still puzzled by a team that was perpetually in last place and under constant duress from the very media and fans that would not give up on it. I suggested to several people, in the front office, in the media, and among academics, that perhaps the source of fascination and support for the Tigers lay with what the noted American scholar of classical Japan, Ivan Morris, labeled "the nobility of failure." Morris found a long line of popular heroes in Japanese history, all of whom had suffered misfortune or defeat but who were celebrated for their sincerity of purpose and indifference to the inevitable outcome. Their failures were a kind of moral masochism. Did this not characterize the emotional and moral compass that sustained those in the Hanshin world over the long stretch of disappointment, as well as the decades of support found in other famous longtime sports losers like the Boston Red Sox and the Chicago Cubs?

The nobility of failure sounded plausible for its historical resonance and logic, but it was roundly rejected by the fans, players, media, and academics I tried it out on.[8] Sports to them was about winning, and there was no nobility in losing, especially losing continually. There was frustration, even a certain resignation as a losing season wore on, but no one found failure to be ennobling. However often the team lost, no one among the players or fans blamed it on giving up.

What engaged them was not the despair of losing or the nobility of failure but the reasons for that failure, that continuing weakness. Failure itself was the point of internal contestation. Was failure to be understood as losing a game despite making efforts to win? Did they fail because they gave up? Did they fail for circumstances beyond their control? How was responsibility to be allocated, and by whom? This is what returns us to the lessons of Tigers history and to the difficulties of what we might call sporting praxis, the practical application of analytical understanding. The Tigers collectively might have deserved the "no-good Tigers" moniker for many years, but just who within that sportsworld was no good, and what was no good about them? How are we to locate and measure responsibility for such a collective enterprise that depends so entirely on coordinated individual effort and talent, both on and off the field? Consider that the enterprise is competitive with multiple other enterprises with the same "allocation of responsibility" problem (Gluckman 1972) and that talent and effort must contend with fortune and misfortune. This is a fundamental conundrum in sports in the recursive actions of doing, supporting, and analyzing sports.

But a proper analysis of the Hanshin Tigers sportsworld must go beyond the generic, as I have in this chapter. The melodramatic swings between celebrating the fierce and castigating the no good were given particular form and meaning by what was happening in the larger society from the 1960s onward. Especially the centralization of population and institutions in Tokyo and the ideological importance placed on corporate culture and workplace organization provided compelling idioms and frames of analysis for coming to terms with the importance and the impotence of Hanshin.

CHAPTER 10

A Sportsworld Transforming

The Hanshin Tigers at Present

The unit of analysis in social science research is both the methodological precondition for an inquiry and, often, its analytical lesson. The game of baseball that has been played at Kōshien Stadium since its opening over ninety years ago is the same game that is played in stadiums, fields, and backyards in countries around the world. In this book I have characterized the Hanshin Tigers as a sportsworld with four key constituent elements: the players; the coaching staff; the front office and its parent corporation, the media; and the fans and other followers. Its spatial coordinates center on Kōshien Stadium, and its cyclical and linear temporal rhythms center on games and seasons. I formulate it as a sportsworld to emphasize that we cannot easily divide those who produce, transmit, and consume Hanshin Tigers baseball. It is difficult to specify precisely the nature of the many links among these people, but it is impossible to ignore their mutual influence. As a game, baseball is played over nine innings by the two teams on the field, but before, during, and after games, the players feel the weight of the club and parent company, the constant media barrage, the force of the fans, and the memories that attach to the stadium itself. And they are continually assessed, narrativized, criticized, and idolized by this human nexus in which they are suspended.

All team spectator sports are regularly occurring, highly visible physical contests between fixed leagues of teams. Beyond that, the particular qualities of baseball (its long seasons, multiple player positions, elaborate statistical measuring, and interval rhythm) enhance the nexus of narratives and numbers, the melodramatic swings of emotional display and experience, the Manichean morality of winning or losing, and the elusive search for accountability.

This is often true to some degree for all sports—even my teenage daughter's softball team was a "coproduction" of girls, coaches, and parents—but it gained a particular density and breadth in the case of the Hanshin Tigers. This is because, as I have tried to show, the structural elements and the historical resonance of Tigers baseball came to dramatize the dynamics of workplace relations and practices in an era when these were of national concern and also because the Tigers' performance relative to its most potent rival, the Yomiuri Giants, reinforced and condensed the growing disparities of Kansai as subordinate to the capital region around Tokyo.

Chapters 8 and 9 identified the likely sources of these distinctive qualities of this Hanshin sportsworld, which go back as far as the beginnings of baseball in Japan. Professional baseball appeared in the 1930s, growing out of long-standing and nationally celebrated schoolboy baseball and inheriting its institutional and ideological struggles. Although baseball coexisted with sumo, golf, pro wrestling, horse racing, and many other sports, it became the overwhelming focus of sports interest, especially after midcentury. It became Japan's national—indeed nationalized—sport. The fully year-round attention given to baseball stunted the growth of other professional sports and prevented most seasonal sharing of spectator interest and emotion. Because baseball is a male-participant sport, it accommodated women as viewers and supporters only on male terms.[1] Both television and the sports dailies were especially potent in baseball's seizing the national sporting limelight.

In the decades since the 1960s, the other Kansai area teams have existed in the deep shadows of the regional media and fan fixation with the Tigers, but across professional baseball, Hanshin itself, along with ten other teams, has existed in the shadow of the Yomiuri Giants. The Yomiuri organization, both the baseball club and its parent media group, created a powerful synergy in the 1960s between preeminence and domination. This seriously deformed baseball as a competitive sport—competitive both on the field and for the consumer yen—but did little to diminish the sport's preeminence. At least that was the condition of NPB when I finished my primary years of fieldwork with Hanshin in 2003 and as I continued to write about them and Japanese sports more generally. In retrospect, however, it is now possible to see 2003 as something of a watershed for the Hanshin sportsworld, something I never anticipated, but which I turn to in this final chapter.

FROM CELLAR DWELLER TO PERENNIAL CONTENDER

On September 15, 2003, the Tigers clinched the Central League championship, their first in eighteen years.[2] After so many years of struggle, the Tigers had a surprisingly easy run to the top that year. They had been in first place from the very beginning of the season and "lit the magic number" with forty-nine games to play, on July 8, the earliest in Central League history. They slipped in the second half of the season and suffered through a typically abysmal August "death road" away from Kōshien, but no other team arose to challenge them. The lack of much suspense during the season did little to dampen regional enthusiasm or growing national attention. If anything, the long, slow march allowed momentum—and marketing—to build steadily through the summer months as it became ever more likely that the Tigers would finally break their long drought. Sales at the Hanshin Department Store grew steadily, the parent company's stock price rose, and the national media took to this emerging feel-good story line.[3] As early as June 9, Asahi's national weekly magazine, *AERA*, featured the Tigers with the headline "Hanshin, the national toy" (Ōta 2003).

However, it was the other Hanshin story in that issue that I found even more symptomatic of the nation's interest in Hanshin that summer. The story's title was "Hanshin Is Becoming Nissan" (Satō 2003), a reference to the dramatic turnaround in that company orchestrated by the Brazilian executive Carlos Ghosn. The French auto company Renault purchased a one-third share interest in Nissan as it languished in the late 1990s and arranged for Ghosn to be Nissan's chief operating officer in 1999; he moved up to CEO in 2001. Renault charged him with restructuring its acquisition, and he orchestrated a draconian but successful recovery for Nissan. Ghosn was lionized in Japan and in the world financial press; in 2002, *Fortune* anointed him "Asia Businessman of the Year." Thus, when Hanshin made its own dramatic turnaround the next year with an outside manager (the equally fiery and competitive Hoshino), the comparison was too obvious to miss.[4] Nissan was second fiddle to Toyota as Hanshin was subordinate to Yomiuri, and both Nissan and Hanshin demonstrated the virtues of new leadership from the outside.

This became a favorite media trope. Newsweek followed with its July 23 cover story asking if Hanshin's victory was a harbinger of the recovery of the Japanese economy; the title of the cover story in the July 4 issue of one of the more respectable weeklies, *Shukan Asahi*, was a statement rather than a question: "Tigers Save Japan." Interestingly, about the only place in the region that seemed immune to "Tigers fever" was the entrance to Hanshin corporate headquarters in downtown Umeda where, Okada (2003:28) noted, they hadn't even put up any Hanshin Tigers posters!

In October 2003, Hanshin met the winners of the Pacific League, the Daiei Hawks, in the Japan Series. Daiei was based in the far western city of Fukuoka but was the successor to the Nankai Hawks, and this recalled for the media and older Kansai fans the famous 1964 Japan Series between Hanshin and Nankai. That Daiei was managed by the Yomiuri Giants great Oh Sadaharu created further frissons in the series because it recapitulated almost a half century of Hanshin encounters with Oh since his rookie year in 1959 and Hanshin's controversial loss to the Giants in the emperor's game.

The Japan Series is played as a best-of-seven format. The first two games were played in Fukuoka, and HT lost. The series then moved to Kōshien for the middle three games, and the Kansai fans mobilized to recover. I was in Osaka at the time, at Kōshien for the third game and around the city for the fourth game. Hanshin rallied in dramatic fashion to win all three games. In the first of the three, Fujimoto homered in the bottom of the ninth inning to squeak by 2–1, and the next night Kanemoto was the hero, again with a final inning walk-off "sayonara" home run.

The third game was less suspenseful, but the outpouring of emotions that overtook the region during those few days as Hanshin recovered and appeared on the verge of claiming "Japan number 1" was clear evidence that wallowing in failure and internal turmoil was not the inevitable basis of Hanshin support. Never had I heard the stadium crowd so loud, nor had I ever felt the rail cars returning to Umeda after the game shake so thoroughly as for that third game. Several times on the return trip, the train staff had to plead with fans over the loud-speaker to stop jumping up and down so they would not cause the cars to tip over!

Alas, they would have to be satisfied with the Central League championship because Hanshin returned to Fukuoka for the final two games, where the team went flat and lost both with little punch. That did not dampen the spirits of the team, the Kansai media, or the region's fans.

The following season was disappointing, but Hanshin roared back again in 2005 to take the Central League championship, although it again fell to the Pacific League champion, Chiba Lotte Marines, in the Japan Series. But with those two championships Hanshin seemed to turn the corner. The Japanese phrase now usually applied to the team is that it is a *jōshō gundan*. The term literally means an invincible corps, but this is hyperbole; in the baseball world, it signifies a team that expects to be competitive for the league title each season. This is the case for Hanshin. In the fifteen years from 2003 to 2017, it finished in A-Class ten times, was twice league champion, and advanced seven times to the Climax Series (see figure 1 in chapter 1). The rhetoric of the Fierce Tigers has largely replaced handwringing about the No-Good Tigers.

ARE THE HANSHIN TIGERS AT THE END OF AN ERA?

One advantage of looking back on my fieldwork now, more than a decade later, is that it is clearer that its two league championships in 2003 and 2005 marked the end of an era, for Hanshin and possibly for Japanese professional baseball. In important respects, the sportsworld that I have depicted in this book no longer exists. Indeed, professional baseball in Japan is facing a decline in popularity and profit that may be irreversible. Together with changes in sumo and soccer, a tectonic shift may be under way that is reshaping the Japanese sportscape. This is what I turn to here in the final chapter.

It may strike readers as rather too neat to treat these two championship years as an endpoint for the Hanshin Tigers world that I witnessed. How convenient to do so when they correspond to the end of my active fieldwork with Hanshin! In fact, many anthropologists do come to believe during their field research and subsequent write-up that they were witnessing the end of an epoch. The changes that we experience loom larger (because we are there), and we sometimes exaggerate their consequences. In my defense, I readily admit that it did not occur to me in 2003, as I ended my active fieldwork, that Hanshin was poised for any significant changes. Subsequent developments have proved me wrong.

It was not the winning itself and the putting an end to several decades of frustration, but rather structural changes in the Hanshin sportsworld, in Japanese professional baseball, and in the wider regional and national society that precipitated a restructuring of that world. Four of these developments are of particular importance:

- There is new club management and new corporate ownership for Hanshin.
- Kōshien Stadium has been renovated, and fan club associations have lost their autonomy and edginess.
- The daily sports newspapers and broadcast television are in steep decline.
- Nippon Professional Baseball is under assault from within and trapped between the growing popularity of soccer and more aggressive recruiting by MLB.

These ongoing changes have rendered the Hanshin sportsworld less vibrant but more profitable than in the 1990s and early 2000s. This is certainly a view that is widely shared among those in the front office, coaching staff, media, and fans with whom I have been able to keep up, and it is a theme in much subsequent commentary. Here I take up each of these changes in some detail.

New Club Management and Corporate Ownership for Hanshin

I visited Kōshien on a game night in June 2016 for a meeting with the former manager, Yoshida, who took me in through the staff entrance to the stadium. I was quite surprised to see, standing inside the entrance, Yotsufuji Keiichirō, who had become club president the previous October. He was engaged in friendly banter and casual conversation with club staff and reporters and took time to come over and introduce himself to me and talk for a while about recent developments. I was even more surprised to go from there into the small stadium restaurant and realize that at the next table was Sakai Shin'ya, the CEO of the parent company, having a quick dinner before going out to watch the game. Only once in all of my years among the Tigers did I see the former CEO, Kuma, at Kōshien (as he moved quickly, surrounded by staff from his car to the owner's room); even Miyoshi and the other club presidents had moved furtively, rarely stopping to engage with anyone. Clearly the tone and transparency of front office management had changed (Okada 2003:166–174).

The management changes were precipitated by Kuma's resignation as designated club owner and corporate director in 2005 in the midst of an NPB scandal. Kuma had been instrumental in bringing in Nomura and then in persuading Hoshino to replace Nomura for the 2002 season. He himself remained in the background, elusive and a lightning rod for widespread criticism. In the wider NPB crises of 2004–2005, which I turn to shortly, he earned the enmity of players, his own club president, and Kansai fans for seeming to side with Giants' owner Watanabe Tsuneo (with whom he had always been close since their wartime years at the University of Tokyo). However, the tipping point came when the sports press revealed that Yomiuri, Hanshin, and Yokohama had made under-the-table payments to a top draft prospect, Ichiba Yasuhiro, in advance of the 2004 draft. Kuma and the Yokohama parent company owner resigned (as did the Giants' Watanabe, but Yomiuri merely elevated him from president to chairman of the board!). It was an ignominious end to a two-decade tenure as owner, but it opened up significant realignment of executives in the front office and the parent company.

It also helped precipitate the most shocking development of all to many in Kansai, when the Hanshin parent corporation itself was bought out by, of all companies, its oldest and foremost rival, Hankyū. This occurred during a decade of corporate mergers and acquisitions spurred by then prime minister Koizumi Jun'ichirō and his administration's push for financial deregulation and privatization of government-run monopolies like the postal service. Onto the scene came a number of flamboyant venture capitalists and merger and acquisition entrepreneurs, both foreigners and Japanese. Two of the most prominent were Horie Takafumi and Murakami Yoshiaki, both of whom saw baseball clubs as poorly run, ripe for takeover, and potential vehicles for their public relations branding. Horie ran an internet service provider called LiveDoor; he set his sights on the Kintetsu Buffaloes and tried to get the parent company to sell him the team in 2004 (Onishi 2004). This and other hostile takeover bids (e.g., Fuji Television) collapsed in 2006, when Horie was arrested and brought to trial for securities fraud.

The investor Murakami was a self-styled shareholder activist and corporate raider. His target, around the same time, was Hanshin Dentetsu, the parent company itself, which he believed to be an underperforming company ripe for takeover. Murakami used one of his investment companies, M&A Consulting, to amass over 40 percent of Hanshin common stock by 2005 and was on the verge of taking control of the corporation, causing panic among the other Kansai regional transportation companies as well as the NPB Owners' Council, which publicly opposed recognizing him as an owner. The upshot of this controversy, which played out in 2004 and 2005, was that in June 2006,

Hanshin Dentetsu was taken over by its century-long rival, Hankyū Railroad.[5]

This is where matters stand in 2018. The group's official English name is Hankyū Hanshin Holdings, Inc. (hereafter Holdings Group). It is composed of several dozen companies organized into six clusters; some companies are wholly owned subsidiaries and others are affiliated companies in which the Holdings Group has majority ownership.[6] The Holdings Group retains the separate identities of the two train lines; Hanshin-marked trains still run out of the Hanshin Umeda Station, and Hankyū-marked trains still operate from the adjacent Hankyū Umeda Station. Initially after the merger, Hanshin Dentetsu retained ownership of the Hanshin Tigers Ball Club as well as the Kōshien Stadium management company. In a Holdings Group reorganization in late 2017, this chain of operation was broken, and the ball club and the stadium company were moved to a different cluster and are under direct management by the Holdings Group. The consequences of this for corporate oversight of the ball club front office are unclear. Headquarters executives sent to the front office are still those of "Hanshin" background, but this could easily change.[7]

The Holdings Group corporate management is much more savvy about public relations, more aggressive with marketing, and more willing to devote financial resources to the team, but two features of club organization remain constant: its preference to find managers from its own ex-player ranks and its impatience with the managers it selects. Hanshin went through four manager changes from 2003 to 2018, and all four have been ex-Hanshin players. Hoshino announced before the end of the season that he would not return because of serious health issues (although he remained as a paid senior consultant to the front office and club owner until 2009). Hanshin then reverted to form in seeking his replacement from among its own ranks. The sports press reported three main contenders for the job, all of whom were longtime Hanshin players: Okada, Kakefu, and Enatsu. The latter two were famous Hall of Fame players and longtime media commentators, and for years they had been touted for the manager position whenever it came open. Okada was younger and had played for Hanshin from 1980 to 1993; he was traded to Orix and played for two more years before retiring and remaining with Orix as a coach. In 1998 he returned to Hanshin and held several positions on the first team and farm staffs from 1999 until his selection as manager. He was much liked by the club president and (the press reported) by Kuma himself, and there was little surprise in the press when he was picked as manager. He lacked the name brand recognition of Kakefu and Enatsu (and Nomura and Hoshino), but it didn't hurt with the front office that he was a graduate of Waseda University, while Kakefu and Enatsu had only high school degrees.

Okada was followed by Mayumi Akinobu, a very popular ex-player also with 1985 season credentials. (Mayumi had not gone to university, but he had played for a championship company team in the industrial leagues after high school before entering the pros.) Failing to lead the team to the play-offs in 2011, his resignation was requested in favor of Wada Yutaka, a seventeen-season veteran who was a rookie in 1985 from the university, had retired in 2001, and worked continuously as a Hanshin coach until his appointment. He served for three seasons as manager; at the time of his replacement at the end of the 2015 season, he had been with Hanshin continuously for thirty-one years. Wada, in turn, was replaced for the 2016 season by Kanemoto Tomoaki, traded from Hiroshima in 2002 to become the team's star during its 2003 league championship season and probably the most well-known player on the team until his retirement in 2012.

Kōshien Stadium's Renovation and Stadium Fan Club Associations' Loss of Autonomy and Edginess

One of the few points of continual consensus over the decades within the Hanshin sportsworld was the historical importance and distinctive atmosphere of Kōshien Stadium, which has a place among the greatest sports stadiums in the world. After seventy-five years, however, it was showing its age, and the Hanshin corporate parent had discussed several plans for renovation since the 1990s. Japan followed the United States at the time in an enthusiasm for covered dome stadiums that included shopping and amusement areas along with the sports ground itself. Nagoya Dome and Osaka Dome both opened in 1997. Hanshin executives were also inclined toward doming Kōshien as part of a larger Hanshin Park project, but with the deteriorating post-bubble economy, conservative Hanshin focused its efforts on finishing its Nishi Umeda zone and put stadium improvements on hold. The 1995 Hanshin earthquake further exacerbated its finances (1996 was the first year in its history that the parent company announced a deficit), and all resources went to emergency repairs to stations, lines, rolling stock, and the stadium itself.[8] The Hanshin Kobe earthquake had the doubly unfortunate impact of hastening the aging of Kōshien and putting a sudden and severe demand on the company's finances.

In the aftermath of the team successes in 2003 and the continued deterioration of the stadium itself, the company again moved to formulate a renovation plan. By now there was a general backlash against domed stadiums, both in Japan and the United States, and Hanshin reaffirmed Kōshien as an open and natural-grass stadium, primarily devoted to baseball. The project proceeded in stages during the off-seasons from 2007 to 2012, and when it was completed, it was a total renovation that nonetheless (like Boston's renovated Fenway Park) preserved the design integrity, sight lines, and aesthetics of the original stadium. The roof, exterior walls, seating, and entrances were all entirely replaced. It now features new practice facilities and modern locker rooms (with showers and Japanese-style baths), new staff offices and an enclosed press box, expanded concession zones, and an expanded Baseball Historical Museum under the outfield grandstands. There is a band of luxury "royal boxes" under the roof and above the infield seating, and solar panels on top of the roof now supply most of the necessary electricity for stadium lighting.[9] In sum, older fans (myself included, not as a fan but as a fieldworker in a now-past era) may claim to pine nostalgically for the old dumpiness, but the new stadium offers a far more comfortable and aesthetically pleasing experience for workers, players, and fans.

Equally striking and much more disconcerting, however, have been changes in the fan club associations. Someone going to the ballpark in 2015 would find the level of fan exuberance and colorful, passionate, orchestrated cheering unchanged from 2003, but under the surface there has been a fundamental shift. The club has long harbored misgivings about the stridently independent fan clubs, the control they exerted over the patterns and rhythms of cheering, and their flouting (at least in their home territories of the outfield bleachers) of many of the stadium's rules. The associations, for their part, took pride in self-policing spectator behavior.

This balance of power lasted for some thirty years, until several incidents occurred in 2002 and 2003 involving the association that was secondary to the main association, the Chūtora Rengō. Chūtora's leadership was long thought to have ties to the Yamaguchi-gumi, one of Japan's largest yakuza organizations and especially powerful in Osaka. There has always been a small undercurrent of violence and petty crime among the fans, and the efforts of the association did not entirely rid the bleachers of criminal elements. The clubs' special access to block sales of tickets attracted several yakuza groups, which could profit from resales, but the team's generally dismal record over the years has kept that from being a lucrative opportunity. However, the team's recent success does seem to have attracted yakuza interest. At least two members of a Yamaguchi-gumi-related crime organization had assumed leadership roles in the Chūtora Rengō by the early 2000s.

The first serious public incident happened on September 24, 2002, the day that Yomiuri clinched the Central League championship. Yomiuri was playing Hanshin at Kōshien and lost the game (which went a hard-fought twelve innings), but it still clinched the title because the second-place Yakult Swallows had lost to Chūnichi in a game that had concluded earlier. The customary celebration on winning a championship is for the players to come out on the field as the game ends and toss the manager in the air three times (*dō-age*). Kōshien Stadium officials had anticipated this and approached the fan clubs before the game to ask them to respect this practice, even it meant watching their bitter rival celebrate on Kōshien soil. This trivial issue grew more serious when the Tigers actually won the game, because now the Chūtora leaders insisted that the clubs go through their game-winning routines (singing the Tigers anthem, etc.) before the Giants were allowed back onto the field to toss their manager. A fierce brouhaha developed in the stands as Chūtora leaders berated stadium officials, threatening to kill them and bury their bodies in the Kōshien outfield if they tried to stop the Hanshin fan celebrations. The stadium officials backed down, and the Giants had to wait, but the Chūtora leaders were subsequently arrested. Then in 2003, during the league championship season, Chūtora clubs became more aggressive in taking over sections of unreserved outfield seating and forcing regular spectators to pay them a seating charge; they illegal sold seventh-inning "rally" balloons and bootleg CD's of hitting marches and became more aggressive with stadium security guards.

Although this behavior was limited to a small number of the several thousand clubs, the Hanshin front office and stadium company saw this as an opportunity for a broad crackdown on the independent associations. Other Chūtora leaders were arrested, the prefectural antivice police were called in, all block sales were terminated, cheerleaders were required to register and have official identification with the stadium, and a code of conduct was drawn up for the cheerleaders and stadium spectators. This was coordinated with other clubs and stadiums, and the overall effect was to bring an end to three decades of autonomous fan organization.

It is still great fun to go to games at Kōshien, and the yellow-jerseyed cheerleaders take the crowd through the hitting marches and other cheers. But for me the most striking sign of the new fan order, on several recent visits, was that spectators were actually paying polite attention to the official scoreboard and to the club's official mascots and "cheer girls" when they performed on the field between innings, and the associations were careful to sit down and defer to them. Written spectator code of conduct signs were everywhere, and the stadium guards moved through the infield and outfield seating alike with more obvious confidence and authority.

Declining Importance of Sports Dailies and Broadcast Television

Even more than the gentrified stadium and the gentled fans was another portentous shift in the Hanshin sportsworld. As I described previously, to ride the subways and local trains in Kansai in the late 1990s was to see a wall of papers, usually sports dailies, that held riders' attention. Even those who had not bought a paper could not help but notice the vivid front pages and be drawn into a sense of what was up with Kansai's team. The scene in 2017 is stunningly different. Riding those same trains and subways, I often find not a single rider with a newspaper; almost everyone is hunched over a cell phone or smart phone, reading manga, on social media, playing games, and so forth (the point is that I have little idea just what they are doing with their phones, unlike the obvious display of newspaper affiliations of the past). Since the early 2000s, the sports daily papers and broadcast television have lost significant revenue, readership, and viewership (and thus teams have lost revenue). Neither has made a successful transition to digital technology and social media.

Overall, Japanese newspaper sales and readership are still the largest in the world per capita, but those totals are declining and mask the fact that almost all sales are home subscriptions, often discounted, often bundled, and actually read less and less (Alford and McNeill 2010; Nippon.com 2015). Between 2000 and 2016, daily circulation of the national general dailies dropped from 47,401,669 to 39,821,106. Sports dailies have been hit much harder than the national dailies; in the same decade and a half, their annual sales have dropped 45 percent, from 6,307,162 to 3,455,041. Whether in Osaka or Tokyo, it is now extremely rare to see the colorful, exploding bouquets of sports papers at platform and street kiosks. Most of the kiosks themselves have been closed, replaced by more vending machines, and the few remaining kiosks devote much less of their counter space to sports dailies and other print media. Convenience stores, too, devote far less of their scarce space to print media than they did ten years ago.[10]

There has also been a decline in mainstream broadcasting of NPB, in broadcast fees, games broadcast, and viewer ratings. Although spectator attendance at NPB ballparks actually increased slightly in 2010, household television viewer ratings have been steadily dropping since 2006. The Yomiuri Giants have been hit hard; according to Video Research, Giants night games had a viewer rating of 23.1 percent in 1994. In 2009, the rating fell to 10 percent, and in 2010, it fell to 8.4 percent, the lowest figure since the company began keeping track in 1989. The low levels are due to a sharp decline in Giants games broadcast since 2006. In 2010, only twenty-seven Giants games were aired. Giants broadcasting rights fees used to bring in about ¥100 million per game, but Yomiuri is now struggling to make money as broadcast fees have decreased. This has a ripple effect across both leagues, because the other eleven teams depend on their Giants games for their top broadcast revenue. Digital satellite broadcasting has moved in to pick up more NPB games, but the rights fees for satellite channels are often only one-third those paid by broadcast channels.

Hanshin has been less affected by this general decline than other teams (Kikkawa 2009). Television viewer ratings for Tigers games have remained healthy relative to other clubs in recent years. The five sports dailies still have large contingents of reporters and photographers attached to Hanshin, although their spot sales have noticeably declined. However, as noted previously, the more significant shift is more difficult to quantify but central to what one might call the public sphere of the Hanshin sportsworld. So much of the knowledge and passion that constituted this sportsworld was conveyed by and through the sports dailies, directly and indirectly (including their deployment every morning on the television "wide shows"), that their disappearance from Kansai public spaces has had devastating consequences.

As in most digital-age societies, the Japanese are not reading and watching less but differently, online, with smartphones. The challenge to baseball is that neither NPB nor the print or broadcasting media have developed an engaged online presence or generated much interest from the online population. There is very limited and expensive online broadcasting of some Tigers games. Newspapers' online publishing is abbreviated, time-consuming to navigate, and expensive to access, with few graphics. This is especially fatal to sports papers; their online statistics are meager, and without the full-page integration of narrative, charts, photos, and diagrams, there is little of interest. The sports dailies are rapidly losing influence as connective tissues of the Hanshin sportsworld.[11]

Nippon Professional Baseball under Assault from Within and Trapped between the Growing Popularity of Soccer and More Aggressive Recruiting by MLB

The years following 2003 were turbulent for Japanese professional baseball generally. The long economic stasis that began with the severe contraction of the speculative bubble economy in the early 1990s took its toll on corporate profits and consumer spending, and companies looked hard at many of their sponsorships. Japan had one of the most extensive programs of corporate sports in the world, which was the route for many of its Olympic competitors; the top corporate baseball teams competed with NPB for graduating talent and in turn were a major source of draftees for NPB. By the early 2000s, there had been massive retrenchment across most sports, including baseball. More directly, a number of NPB team corporate owners reassessed their investments and at least considered selling their clubs. At the same time, several corporate raiders and venture capitalists were eager to invest in baseball for its commercial potential—not for profits, but for name recognition.

Nippon Professional Baseball as a body was ill prepared for these challenges. It was often rumored that Watanabe, the Yomiuri CEO, had long envisioned a compression of NPB into a single league, culling the weaker clubs and identifying eight clubs that would remain. This was confirmed in 2004, when it became public that the two other Kansai region teams, Kintetsu and Orix, had agreed to merge and sought permission from the Owners' Council. Decades of Hanshin dominance had taken their toll. This precipitated a crisis in NPB, as owners clashed with owners, and outrage among the fans. The sharpest response came from the Players Association, which quickly realized that such restructuring would bring a precipitous loss of jobs to its player members. Their deliberations resulted in the first-ever in-season strike by players, who refused to take the field for two days in September near the end of the 2004 season. Despite efforts by the owners to head this off, the strike garnered strong public support, and the owners were forced to negotiate with the players through NPB. Among the items of agreement were inauguration of interleague play between the Central and Pacific Leagues, which allowed Pacific League teams an opportunity to play lucrative games with the Giants during the season; changes in the draft system to have separate drafts for graduating high school players and for college and industrial league players; and some changes in free agency eligibility rules.

Watanabe and his allies (including Kuma, against the advice of his subordinates) backed off from their plans for a one-league restructuring. The merger between the two Kansai Pacific League teams, Orix and Kintetsu, was approved, but to preserve a six-team league, a new team was added, the Tohoku Rakuten Golden Eagles. As the name suggests, it was based in Tohoku, a gesture toward broadening NPB cities, and it was owned by a new internet retail company, Rakuten. Several months later, the Fukuoka Daiei Hawks (who had beaten the Tigers the year before in the Japan Series) were sold to another information technology company, Softbank. Both new owner companies were led by aggressive entrepreneurs, bringing a brashness to marketing that departed from the established owner companies. There was now a club in Tohoku and another in Sapporo on the northernmost island of Hokkaidō, but NPB remained concentrated in the same few metropolitan regions (see map 3). The 2004 strike had exposed deep frictions between the players and owners, but changes in player rights and conditions were minimal and the posting system remained intact. Despite the hiring in 2008 of a new baseball commissioner from the outside, Katō Ryōzō, a former Japanese ambassador to the United States who was deeply knowledgeable about MLB, the Owners' Council gave up none of its powers, which continued to disadvantage almost all clubs in marketing and broadcast rights.[12]

Nippon Professional Baseball's problems are not only a hidebound conservatism about internal reform, but also stem from its wider environment. In particular, it is increasingly trapped between pressures from American MLB and the rising attractions of global soccer. On the one hand, a "bright flight" of baseball talent to professional baseball in the United States has been escalating for twenty years. The increasing success of prominent stars, from Nomo and Ichirō to Matsui, has enhanced the allure of MLB to Japanese players and Japanese fans, who follow the games on ever-widening broadcast, satellite, and internet television coverage in Japan. But while the numbers are still small, another migration is perhaps even more portentous: young Japanese amateur players

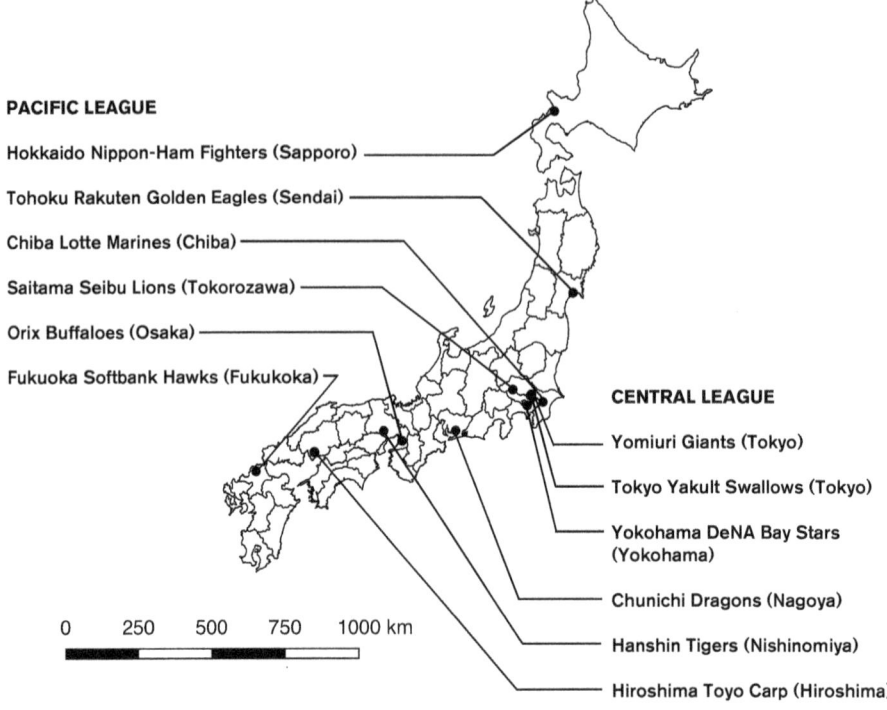

PACIFIC LEAGUE

Hokkaido Nippon-Ham Fighters (Sapporo)

Tohoku Rakuten Golden Eagles (Sendai)

Chiba Lotte Marines (Chiba)

Saitama Seibu Lions (Tokorozawa)

Orix Buffaloes (Osaka)

Fukuoka Softbank Hawks (Fukukoka)

CENTRAL LEAGUE

Yomiuri Giants (Tokyo)

Tokyo Yakult Swallows (Tokyo)

Yokohama DeNA Bay Stars (Yokohama)

Chunichi Dragons (Nagoya)

Hanshin Tigers (Nishinomiya)

Hiroshima Toyo Carp (Hiroshima)

0   250   500   750   1000 km

MAP 3. The home stadium locations of the twelve teams in Nippon Professional Baseball, 2018.

coming out of high school and college who are avoiding NPB altogether for rookie contracts and free agent tryouts with US organizations (Matsushita 2002). There are currently some forty-five Japanese playing in the United States; less than a dozen are on major league rosters, and the rest are riding buses and living off meager meal money in the minor leagues. The Japanese clubs are understandably nervous but relatively impotent to slow the migration; the NPB agreement with MLB has been a poor stopgap measure to regulate the sale of players under contract. The talent pool for Japanese baseball is hollowing out.

The effect of this on Hanshin has been limited thus far. It has lost several of its premier players to MLB teams; in particular Shinjō went to the Mets in 2001, Igawa Kei went to the Yankees in 2007, and Yabu Kei'ichi went to Oakland in 2005 after eleven years with Hanshin. There has been some reverse flow as a few players return for their final years. Most important, Irabu Hideki was signed by Hanshin after an up-and-down career with the New York Yankees and contributed significantly to the 2003 championship season.

Squeezing baseball from the other side is the renewed threat from soccer, both the domestic J.League and growing spectatorship of soccer elsewhere in the world, especially English Premier League and several of the top European leagues. The opening of J.League professional soccer in 1991 scared the baseball establishment, which mobilized to minimize the soccer challenge by dissuading corporate support, keeping J.League teams out of major stadiums, and limiting soccer's access to television and press coverage by the sports dailies. These tactics worked, and the initial "new product" effect of J.League wore off by the mid-1990s. Soccer interests hoped that Japan's cohosting of the World Cup in 2002 would fuel a second soccer boom, but this did not happen despite the publicity, the initial success of the Japanese national team (soon outshone by the South Korea team), and the construction of soccer stadiums across the country.

However, in the current decade, both men's and women's soccer seem to have found a more secure financial footing, fan base, and media exposure (Kelly 2013a, 2013b). For the women, it is the world-class caliber of its national team. For the men, who fare more poorly in global competition, it has been the popularity of the domestic league and the competitive success of the national and club teams in Asian regional competitions. The Asian Football Confederation (AFC) is one of the six world regional bodies that constitute the Federation Internationale de Football Association (FIFA), the global governance organization. The AFC has forty-seven national members, extending from Lebanon and Palestine in the west to Japan in the east, from Australia in the south to Mongolia in the north. Soccer connects Asian nations like no other sport, as it offers the most level playing field for competition. As a counterweight to its orientation to the United States, the Asian geopolitics of soccer has been quite compelling for Japan. This may be the moment when soccer is finally able to challenge and dismantle the hold that baseball has had on Japan for more than a century.

CHANGING WORKPLACES AND A RECEDING SECOND-CITY COMPLEX

To those encountering the Hanshin Tigers in 2018, much looks the same as it did twenty years ago: the game itself at the center of this world; the home stadium on which it is played, evening after evening;

the organization of the team and the hierarchies of club and company; the work routines and rhetoric of the Hanshin media; and the choreographed frenzy of the fans and passions of the followers across Kansai. A closer look, however, reveals the toll that the recent changes outlined above have taken on the world this book has analyzed. Whether professional baseball in Japan is in terminal decline is not a question that interests me even if I had the expertise to answer it. Nor is it properly ethnographic to speculate on the future health of the Hanshin sportsworld. But it is reasonable to conclude, retrospectively, that 2003 and the years following did mark a sharp break for the Hanshin Tigers sportsworld from its key features of the decades from the late 1970s to the early 2000s.

This is not just a matter of the four structural changes just outlined; two broader transitions in the wider society have eroded the fascination with workplace melodrama and second-city insecurity that had been so compelling about Hanshin since the mid-1970s.

Serial recessions since the early 1990s have weakened the prosperity of the world's second-largest economy, and Japan has now slipped into third place behind a surging China. But more consequential for the eroding linkage of workplace dynamics and the Hanshin sportsworld has been the shift in regional and national employment structures. In particular, three changes have radically shifted the orientation of Kansai workers, white collar, pink collar, and blue collar, to their workplaces. The first is the massive casualization of work. Although there were significant inequalities of pay and status in corporate and public workplaces in the decades after 1950, even into the early 1980s, upward of 85 percent of workers at all levels held full-status ("permanent") positions in their companies or agencies. This number started to decline rapidly in the 1990s and early 2000s, to about 60 percent in 2016, with higher numbers for all workers in their twenties and in their sixties and even higher numbers for female employees. There are several categories of nonregular work in Japan at present, but common to all are fixed, short-term contracts; absence of union coverage; limited benefits; and little investment in workplace routines. Second, Kansai was hit especially hard by the hollowing out of domestic manufacturing as operations moved abroad (Cox 2012; Tsukamoto 2011). Third, these two changes have ruptured the predictable chains of contracting between major companies and their tiers of suppliers.

In short, the precarious conditions of employment in an increasingly neoliberal economy (Allison 2013; Osawa, Kim, and Kingston 2013) have been especially evident in the Kansai region. The pervasive job casualization, manufacturing loss, and broken subsidiary chains have all been dissected carefully for their economic and institutional effects (e.g., among many, Baldwin and Allison 2015; Gordon 2015; Matanle and Lunsing 2006; Pilling 2014). What must be emphasized here as having the most direct consequence for the Hanshin Tigers sportsworld is that anxiety about work and job security have now replaced concern for workplace dynamics for many Kansai residents. They are more focused on the prospects and nature of jobs rather than on the social relations of the workplace (to which they have a more transitory and less vested connection), and this erodes the prior fascinations of the Tigers world.

Along with these major changes in employment security and one's relationship to one's workplace, a second societal trend of direct relevance to the Hanshin sportsworld has been an accelerating hyperconcentration in the greater Tokyo region and shrinking populations everywhere else, in Osaka and other major metropolitan regions. Urban concentration has been a fact of the Japanese landscape since the seventeenth century and the beginning of the Tokugawa period, when Edo grew to be the world's largest city and Osaka emerged as the mercantile center. Both continued to expand throughout the nineteenth and twentieth centuries, but I have already noted that the 1960s was the tipping point in their balance of power, when Tokyo became the magnet for population, governmental institutions, business, and culture industries.

So what is happening is not novel in the aggregate, but what is new is that Tokyo is now the country's sole center of growth. As figure 27 shows, Tokyo region in-migration peaked in the speculative bubble years of the mid- to late 1980s and fell sharply by the mid-1990s, but it recovered and has increased significantly every year since. In contrast, the Osaka region never recovered from its early postwar growth and has had steady negative population growth since 1973. The key social point, ironically, is that this has reduced the salience of Osaka as Japan's second city as it falls in line with Nagoya, Fukuoka, Sendai, and Sapporo as the penumbra of cities that are subordinate to the ever-concentrating national capital region (Tsukamoto 2011). I cannot substantiate this claim even though I feel it strongly based on anecdotal evidence. Media commentaries and assertive and controversial Osaka prefectural governors and city mayors like Hashimoto Tōru and Matsui Ichirō have continued to rail against the national bureaucrats and economic might of Tokyo (Johnston 2015, 2016), but the fractious political party wrangling in which these assertions of regional autonomy and Kansai's

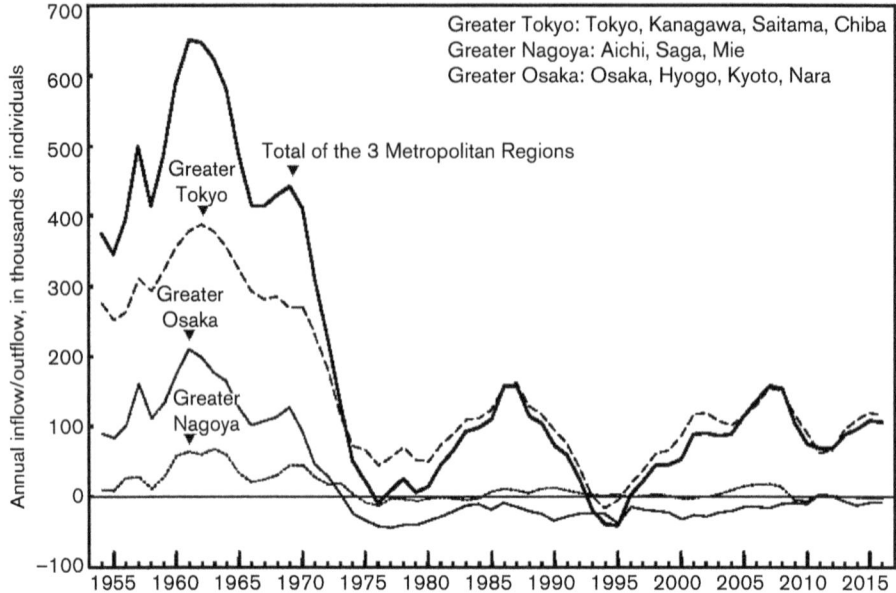

FIGURE 27. Population inflow and outflow in the Greater Tokyo, Osaka, and Nagoya areas, 1955–2015. The zero line marks the break between net inflow (above) and net outflow (below) per year. Data from Ministry of Internal Affairs and Communication (2017).

special status is expressed have actually divided the Kansai population and eroded the symbolic power of the Hanshin Tigers to embody a Kansai resistance.

FROM NATIONAL CHARACTER TO LOCAL SPORTSWORLDS: LESSONS OF THE HANSHIN TIGERS FOR MODERN JAPAN AND SPORTS ANALYSIS

> Because of its slow pace, baseball fits the Japanese character perfectly. The conservative play mirrors the Japanese conservative and deliberate approach to life. Managers and coaches view baseball as a tool to teach loyalty and moral discipline--the same type of loyalty and discipline feudal Japanese lords expected from their soldiers and subjects. This cowboy discipline requires endless hours of training, self-denial, and an emphasis on spirituality. So goes the Japanese approach to baseball. (Howard 1994)

This is the opening narration of a 1994 US television documentary, *Baseball in Japan*, which was broadcast widely on public television in the United States. It is indicative of decades of representations by foreign commentators, reporters, and even scholars, who overwhelmingly apprehend baseball in Japan as Japanese baseball, a radically different version than (normal) American baseball. Journalists filed stories with headlines like "In Japan, Baseball Is the Art of War" (Associated Press 1991); "Japanese Baseball: Throw Till Your Arm Drops off " (*Economist* 1996); "The Japanese Call This Baseball?" (Holtzman 1989); "Japan's Tigers Don't Resemble Baseball's Losers from Detroit" (Kinney 2003); "A Whole Different Ballgame" (Shapiro 1989); and many more. They constitute an orthodox litany about samurai baseball in the "Land of the Rising Fastball": grueling overpractices, abject obedience to coaches and managers, timid game strategies, ignorant owners, mindless fans, and more. It sounds grotesquely simplistic—and it is—but it is omnipresent.

For their part, Japanese too can lapse into a national characterization of the game (e.g., Ikei 2000; Matsuzaki 2001; Sayama 1998; Wakisaka 1989). This is especially evident when teammates, front offices, media, and fans try to make sense of (or make fun of) the few American players in their midst or when they follow anxiously the fates of their few stars who venture across the Pacific to try to make it in MLB. How will a Japanese player fare in the radically different world of American baseball?

As I suggested at the outset, the problem with such national stereotyping of the sport is not that it is wholly wrong—people do talk this way when they are encouraged to formulate national differences—but that it is generally irrelevant in most people's sports experience. It is as far from the actual conditions of playing, managing, and watching baseball in Japan as it is for appreciating and analyzing the sport in the United States (or Cuba, or the Dominican Republic, or anywhere else it is played). Whether coaching a Little League team in a Tokyo park, cheering for one's high school team in a prefectural tournament, or broadcasting a Hanshin Tigers game at Kōshien, broad allegations about national style are of very limited value in understanding and assessing what is going on. Playing, watching, and judging baseball—or any other sport—are intrinsically situational, and there are very few contexts in which putative national styles are relevant.

That is why the concept of sportsworld is so crucial to representing the experiences of sports and why it is so germane to a social science analysis of these sports experiences. The combustible engagements of body, mind, and spirit in physical contests that are freighted with calculation, emotion, and moral mission never occur in a vacuum. They are always suspended in a nexus of meaning, value, and power, and that is precisely what it means to delineate a sportsworld. Players, reporters, and spectators; locations; and occasions—these are never generic but mutually constituted by the moment and all that which has brought them forth. The Hanshin Tigers have been highly unusual as a sportsworld, within Japanese professional baseball, and within sports more generally, for their scale, density, and historical trajectory. This sportsworld is not a representative case, but it is a diagnostic one, presenting us with such an instructive instance of the social grounding of modern sports.

It is diagnostic for appreciating the structures of baseball as a sport that shapes the engagement of all who inhabit such a sportsworld: the long season, league-based competition against a small set of rival teams, the elaborately positional nature of the sport, interval pacing of action and waiting, polyrhythms of circular and linear time lines, and so forth. I have shown how it supports a structure of action and a structure of feeling that are resonant with the genre of soap opera. This was a sportsworld infused with continuous, multiple, overlapping narratives; the melodrama of overflowing emotions, both felt and displayed; the moral imperative of clear-cut contests; the nature of suspense created by the constant oscillations of action and pauses; and the radical uncertainty of accountability. Who deserved credit and who deserved blame when so many were involved in so many ways? The contentious hierarchies of authority among parent company, front office, and team; the central role of the sports dailies; and the unusually assertive independence of associations of fan clubs combined to heighten this compulsive mix of stories, stats, emotions, and moral accountability.

This sportsworld is also diagnostic for understanding some of the key dynamics of change in Japanese society over the last half century. I have argued that central to understanding Hanshin was the fascination of this sportsworld as a workplace to those within it. This was the case, of course, for the players, who saw themselves as professionals seeking to break into and sustain careers that were potentially lucrative but closely monitored, generally short lived, and highly vulnerable to injury. It was the case too for the front office and parent company, which viewed and valued what was going on in terms of personnel, discipline, assessment, selection, budgets, policies, and so forth. However, I have argued here that it was equally true for the media, especially the sports newspapers, whose attention to the course of games and the details of playing the sport was matched by their exposure and analysis of the lines of authority, the rivalries and coalitions, the arguments about accountability, and other manifestations of this sporting workplace. And finally, the fans and spectators shaped this sportsworld as a place of work as much as a place of play, enthusiastically and creatively consuming the media characterizations of the Hanshin world and finding deep resonances between the ambitions, foibles, and interpersonal struggles of that world and those in their own workplaces. Hanshin shows that what draws us to sports is not only the organized physical competition but also the affinities and mutual influence that a sportsworld as a *life*world can have with other dimensions of our everyday existence.

A second theme in the Hanshin Tigers soap opera was an equal source of fascination. By the 1970s Tokyo's eclipse of Osaka was complete, and a pan-Kansai regional identity that was partly defensive, partly defiant found expression against the national center through proud assertions of Kansai dialects, Osaka humor, touristic heritages, and regional cuisines. Above all else, however, given the importance of baseball, the qualities of the sport, the interests of the media, and the structure of the professional leagues, it was the Hanshin Tigers who came to bear the greatest symbolic weight in defining and defending the distinctiveness of the region. In this as well, an analysis of Hanshin as a sportsworld reveals some of the fundamental political-economic changes that have reconfigured Japan in the twenty-first century.

There are many who seek the meaning of modern sports in a single, fundamental quality: conviviality (sports for fun), contest (sports to win), character (sports to mold and test), or commerce (sports for profit). A broad lesson of the Hanshin Tigers sportsworld is that such a reductive search is illusory and misleading. We find all of these qualities present together in the Hanshin experience and, I suspect, in most other sportsworlds. It is precisely this potent and protean mix of motives and meanings that gives sports and the worlds in which they unfold such paramount importance in modern societies.

Endnotes

CHAPTER 1. INTRODUCING HANSHIN TIGERS BASEBALL

1. See the bibliographic essay at http://www.professional.wwkelly.net/ht for other ethnographic analyses that have been particularly helpful to me.

2. Becker wrote that he first began to articulate this concept in 1970, and he published some articles that sketched his formulation in the 1970s (esp. Becker 1974, 1976). His book, *Art Worlds*, was first published in 1982, and in 2008 the University of California Press published a 25th anniversary edition that contains an illuminating new preface (ix–xxxii) and an epilogue (372–386), a dialogue with the French scholar Alain Pessin about the differences between his social world concept and Pierre Bourdieu's notion of field. Becker was not the only one to develop a concept of the art world; the philosopher Arturo Danto (1964) was also concerned to understand the collective creation and negotiation of aesthetic value among artist, critics, curators, and others (see van Maanen 2010 for a very helpful critical history of formulations of the art world). For my analysis, Becker's sociological formulation has been the most directly inspirational.

3. To take a social world as an object of ethnographic analysis is not usual in anthropology or in sports studies. One important exception in Japan studies is Brian Moeran's account of a world of contemporary Japanese ceramics, including the pottery villages, potters organizations, department stores, critics, national shows, arts publications, and others that constitute "folk pottery" as economic commodity, aesthetic object, and social production (e.g., Moeran 1997). He does not reference Becker, but his work is an excellent example of Becker's perspective. Another example within anthropology is Ashley Mears's (2011) ethnography of the high-fashion modeling world, focused insightfully on a crucial but elusive notion of "the look": what it is, who has it, how to find it, how to deploy it on the runway and in fashion photography. As Mears

expresses it: "The look happens through the convergence of strategic work by models, agents, and clients as they collectively grope for the look amid uncertainty" (2011:250).

4. Television scholars have distinguished the soap opera genre from related types like anthology series, in which the host, the tone, and the genre are constant but each episode is unique; episodic series, in which there is a continuing story world but each episode is a self-contained story; and serial narratives, in which the story world and characters develop a single narrative that plays out over a series of episodes. There are other program types that are more or less open ended but filmed and edited, such as news, game shows, reality shows, talk shows, and stand-up comedy.

5. Mittell (2010:240–242), but see the bibliographic essay at http://www .professional.wwkelly.net/ht for the scholarship on soap opera that has been most useful to me.

6. What about gender? Are these baseball contests soap operas for men? This is a seductive binary. We know that the programming intentions of afternoon soap operas elicited overwhelmingly female audiences and that their production codes were built around the distracted attention and multitasking demands of these housewives. We also know that the baseball world is almost entirely male—its players, management, and media—and that spectator sports audiences are largely male (and sometimes brutally misogynistic). Despite this, the matter of baseball's maleness and its masculinity is a bit more complicated, and I touch later on the gender dynamics of Hanshin Tigers fandom (see also Kelly 2013a; Pope 2017; and Swyers 2010).

7. The genre has been discussed in English by Skinner (1979), Matanle, McCann, and Ashmore (2008), and Hirokane (2011).

CHAPTER 2. THE RHYTHMS OF TIGERS BASEBALL: STADIUMS AND SEASONS

1. In the late 1990s and early 2000s, it cost between thirteen and thirty-five dollars to attend a game at Kōshien, a bit lower than pricing at top MLB stadiums. Retaining much of the original atmosphere meant that Kōshien remained rather sparsely attended. The "Alps" sections and outfield bleachers were rising tiers of plastic planks and slab concrete. The iron awning-roof protected the infield seating from most but not all of the rain and sun. Even the most expensive "boxes" behind home plate were rows of plastic, fold-up seats, and Kōshien did not have the tiers of enclosed private luxury boxes that ringed the higher levels of newer stadiums like Green Stadium and Osaka Dome and brought considerable revenue from seasonal corporate rentals.

2. The diamond and the foul lines are the two distinctive features of baseball's playing space. Sports are by definition contests, but there are intriguing differences in how they define the "territory" and the "struggle" over that territory. In football, basketball, soccer, lacrosse, hockey, and similar sports, the terrain is divided into permanent rival territories; both teams are on the terrain in full force all the time, and they mount attacks on and collectively defend the territories. In wrestling, boxing, sumo, and similar "ring" sports, there is a

single bounded, unassigned terrain, over which the contestants range freely, but they are fighting one another and not contesting the territory itself. Baseball and cricket are unusual in that the field is alternately occupied and defended by one full team or the other, and a member of the opposing team "comes to bat" to make forays into and try to successfully return "home" from enemy territory. Where baseball and cricket diverge is in the shape of the field itself; the cricket field is a geometric oval that circumscribes inbounds and out-of-bounds, while the baseball field is a diamond of four bases but with foul lines that stretch infinitely out from home plate along the first- and third-base sides. The baseball field is therefore both enclosed and infinite. Moreover, the infield "diamond" dimensions are precise and uniform, but every stadium's outfield is unique and unspecified (in length, shape, height of walls, etc.). A sports newspaper commentator I worked with had an older brother who played baseball, named Kaname, as in the pivot or kaname of a fan (without which the fan would fall apart); his father actually named him for the catcher in baseball, who is referred to as the "pivot of the infield" (naiya no kaname) because he is the pivot point of the diamond, which looks like a Japanese fan when spread out.

3. These and other data on concessions and vendors come from an interview with the assistant chief of stadium operations on July 29, 1998; from field interviews with vendors and stand operators over several years; and from conversations with reporters who were occasionally tasked with writing small feature articles about Kōshien food and paraphernalia.

4. Unlike American baseball stadiums, Kōshien and other ballparks allowed patrons to bring in their own food and drink (bags were inspected, and bottles were not permitted, but the gate employees kindly poured bottled drinks into paper cups!). This reduced stadium profits but helped with neighborhood relations because it spawned a perimeter of shops and stands that catered to the stadium crowd. The Hanshin Department Store at the Osaka Umeda Station terminus tried to entice stadium goers with special box lunches. In 2002 and 2003 the most popular item was the "Sen-san bentō," named for the popular manager, Hoshino Sen'ichi. It was an assemblage of five items representing the other five teams in the league, so that the fan could feel that by eating the lunch she or he was eating up the Tigers' competition! It had a boiled egg for Yomiuri because its stadium is the Big Egg; a soy-flavored pork cutlet, a Nagoya favorite of the Dragons; a shiitake mushroom for the Swallows because of their fans' umbrellas; Hiroshima-yaki for the Carp; and shumai dumplings for the Bay Stars because their stadium was adjacent to Yokohama's Chinatown.

5. For example, in 1996 there were seventy-five home games, seventy-one of which were played at Kōshien and four at smaller stadiums in the region; sixty-five of the games began at 6:00 p.m., and the remaining games were played on weekend afternoons beginning at 2:00 p.m. The proportions remained the same in 2004: of the sixty games played at Kōshien, fifty-two began at 6:00 p.m., two were scheduled for 4:00 p.m., and six were weekend afternoon games (*Nikkan Sports*, April 9, 2004, 4).

6. Interestingly, the farm team leagues are based on east and west geographical zones to save on travel and hotel expenses. Thus, they mix Pacific League and Central League clubs.

7. With the opening of the domed Osaka Stadium in the center of the city in 1997, the team began playing several home games there, and it played "home" games at several other stadiums in areas where it was trying to sustain local fans (e.g., Kurashiki, Kanazawa, and nearby Nishinomiya). In 1999, for example, the Tigers played their 135 regular season games in sixteen different stadiums. Interleague play between the Central and Pacific League teams started in 2006, so Hanshin now plays twelve games a year in five more stadiums.

CHAPTER 3. ON THE FIELD: PLAYERS, FROM ROOKIES TO VETERANS

1. The corresponding Japanese term, *senshu*, is literally "chosen hands," meaning those who are selected for and play in competitions.

2. More precisely, there are four types of rosters for each Japanese pro club. The first is the organizational roster; each club is limited to seventy players under contract at one time. The second roster is for the first team; each club is limited to forty players who may be called up to play in first-team games during the regular season. Players may only be added or removed from this first-team roster on a few specified dates throughout the season. The third roster is the twenty-eight players registered to be on the first-team bench for game play. Players who are sent to the second team cannot be reactivated for ten days, with two exceptions (players with certain injury status and starting pitchers between starts, both of whom can be kept active and do not require a ten-day delay). The final roster is the twenty-five players chosen by the manager from the twenty-eight-man bench roster to play in a given game (the three players not selected from the twenty-eight may sit in the dugout in uniform).

3. Almost all minor league clubs are owned independently of MLB clubs, but they operate as a sole affiliate of an MLB club. In 2017, there were 19 minor baseball leagues under the MLB umbrella, with 244 member clubs. Firm figures for the total number of minor league players under contract are surprisingly difficult to find, but most media estimates are about five thousand.

4. NFL teams have large player rosters, large coaching staffs, and no minor league affiliates, using "taxi squads" of players under contract who often practice with the regular team and are called up to fill in for injured players.

5. That is, lifetime employment, which was actually an implicit guarantee by companies to provide full-career employment to their regular white-collar and blue-collar employees, generally men, was ideologically dominant but a statistical minority in the second half of the twentieth century. At no point in the last four decades of the twentieth century did the proportion of employees that fit its features ever exceed 35 percent of the national workforce (Kelly and White 2006).

6. I calculated these figures using Hanshin Tigers media guides for 1996 and 1997. Fuller figures and tables are available at https://www.professional .wwkelly.net/ht/.

7. When Nomura took over in 1999, he criticized Nakagomi in the press as having the body of a pro wrestler rather than a pitcher, which led Nakagomi to undertake a crash diet and shed thirty-five pounds. This led to a very poor

season; his arm lost velocity and his record was 8–13. He pitched with Hanshin for another two seasons with little success; after his release at the end of the 2001 season, he pitched and coached with a professional team in Taiwan for three more years.

8. I was never convinced that this reason was so important. More often, I think, it was because many married players had small children, and most games were in the evening. They and/or their wives did not want to interrupt sleeping patterns or homework to bring the kids to the ballpark.

9. For more on the legal status of NPB players, see Nagano (2005) and Tachibanaki (2005).

10. The full Uniform Player's Contract is available at https://www.profess ional.wwkelly.net/ht/.

11. An example is Yu Darvish, who was born in Osaka to an Iranian father and a Japanese mother, who had met at Eckerd College in Florida. Darvish was raised in Japan and was drafted out of high school by the Nippon Ham Fighters. After six years, he moved to the Texas Rangers in the MLB.

12. Baseball insiders use the same idiom, the "narrow gate," that is used for entrance to the most competitive universities like the University of Tokyo.

13. See https://www.professional.wwkelly.net/ht/ for details.

14. The three university graduates were the pitcher Uehara Kōji, the pitcher Yano Eiji, and the infielder Nioka Tomohiro; the high school pitcher was Matsuzaka Daisuke.

15. Nicknames tended to be short versions of names. Who could use a nickname was complicated, and the youngest players tended to show some reserve

16. These figures are calculated from the invaluable *Japan Pro Baseball Fan Handbook and Media Guide* (Graczyk 2000), published annually for over three decades by the late Wayne Graczyk, the dean of Tokyo-based foreign baseball commentators.

17. Year-by-year figures are 1996, four; 1997, five; 1998, seven; 1999, six; 2000, eight; 2001, five; 2002, five; and 2003, five.

18. Most notably, Jeff Williams (Australian), 2003–2009; Lin Wei-Chu (Taiwanese), 2004–2013; Matt Murton, 2010–2015; and Randy Messenger, 2010–2017.

19. This was understandable because most of them were writing for the English-language press in Tokyo or were filing stories for US newspapers. Several of them were knowledgeable reporters and astute commentators on the Japanese game (see my online bibliographic essay), but apart from several of Whiting's books (e.g., 1977b, 1985, 1991) and several by Marty Kuehnart (e.g., 1991, 1998), unfortunately little of their work has been published in Japanese.

20. A couple of the club officials would privately refer to the foreign player condominium as Dejima, the island in Nagasaki harbor where the Dutch merchants and officials were quarantined during the Tokugawa period.

21. I am writing here of retirement, but termination takes other forms as well—in particular, being traded and being released. Trade machinations and the procedures for releasing players are part of the ongoing narrative fabric of the Tigers world, but I do not address the details here.

22. Since the early 2000s, the NPB has negotiated with the amateur associations on conditions under which ex-professionals can return, but so far openings have been scarce.

23. These numbers come from *Nikkan Sports*, November 20, 1996, and Bessatsu Takarajima (2012).

24. Since 2004, the TBS national television network has broadcast a fascinating annual documentary that profiles NPB players who have retired or been released. Some details are available at https://ja.wikipedia.org/wiki/%E3%83% 97%E3%83%AD%E9%87%8E%E7%90%83%E6%88%A6%E5%8A%9B %E5%A4%96%E9%80%9A%E5%91%8A%E3%83%BB%E3%82%AF% E3%83%93%E3%82%92%E5%AE%A3%E5%91%8A%E3%81%95%E3 %82%8C%E3%81%9F%E7%94%B7%E9%81%94. Some of the annual documentaries can be found on YouTube.

25. One of the continuing frictions between players and front offices in the 1990s and early 2000s was the clubs' refusal to allow agents to represent players in their contract negotiations. In the US major leagues, agents have been acceptable for some time, although this was a hard-won right. Japanese clubs often cited a litany of pseudocultural reasons for their continued opposition—most commonly, that Japan is a monoethnic society, unlike the multiethnic, multilingual, and contractual United States, and an agent would disrupt the trust between club and player. Behind that was an economic rationale. As I noted in the text, the US major league clubs drafted a large number of rookies and offered most of them only a small signing bonus and minimal minor league starting salaries. The Japanese clubs, in contrast, drafted only a few players each, paying substantial initial contract bonuses and high salaries during their early years' training before players began to repay the club with actual performance. The Japanese clubs felt they needed time to recoup these investments, and believed that agents would only inflate salary negotiations unreasonably. Club President Miyoshi, among others, termed the players "prior investments" (*senkō tōshi*). The Players Association understandably objected strenuously. The chief argument I read in the papers and heard directly from the players themselves was that the front office staff were not really baseball professionals, especially those in charge of contract negotiations, and agents would force more transparency and more justification in club offers. (Perhaps, therefore, the clubs feared exposing their own inability to defend offers and strike deals.) The clubs' antipathy to player agents is obviously self-serving, although it is yet another feature of the sport that plays against a national stereotype. That is, more conventionally, one finds in Japanese social life rather extensive reliance on third-party brokers for introductions (as in marriage), negotiations, and dispute resolution. In Japan's media and entertainment businesses, for instance, agents (as production/promotion companies) are widely used. They are given minimum salaries and work mostly on commission, drawing a percentage of the earnings for jobs they find for their stables of talent. Recall too that even in baseball, clubs do in fact use third parties at draft time, precisely to generate trust in the drafted player.

26. For starting pitchers, for example, he gave plus points for shutouts, complete games, number of innings without giving up runs, strikeouts, double plays forced, games in which the pitcher lasted more than five innings (regardless of

outcome), and so forth. Points were subtracted for pitching fewer than five innings, walks with runners on base, and so forth. For relief pitchers, he awarded points for number of appearances, the number of innings, runners left on, and so forth.

27. Yet another issue much debated by Ishida and the Hanshin front office was how much weight to give to a player's immediate past season, the longer trajectory of his contributions (the deeper past), and his future prospects (next season when he would be a year older). Miyake Hiroshi, a longtime scout and "scorer" for Hanshin, provides very useful commentary on these issues in two books that he wrote about his career (Miyake 2012, 2013).

CHAPTER 4. IN THE DUGOUT: MANAGER AND COACHES

1. The terms for this position also vary across professional sports. In American football, for instance, the top post is the *coach* and his *assistant coaches*; in NBA basketball, it is the *head coach* with *assistants*; and in the MLB, it is the *manager* with a staff of *coaches*. Japanese pro baseball mixes Japanese and borrowed English terms: the kantoku has a *head coach*, who is his chief assistant, and a number of *coaches*, as well as a farm team *ni-gun kantoku* with another set of *coaches*. Adding further confusion, NPB clubs have another staff position that is called *manager* (*manejā*), but this is what in MLB is called the *traveling secretary*, a staff person who coordinates team logistics. In this book I follow American baseball English and refer to the kantoku as the manager.

2. The managerial changes only involved twenty-two men because two served multiple times. Yoshida was manager three times, and Gotō Tsuguo served in 1969 and again in 1978. The longest tenure was the seven years of Fujimoto Sadao (1961–1968), followed by Nakamura Katsuhiro's six years (1990–1995).

3. Nakanishi Futoshi was appointed midway through 1980 and served through the 1981 season. He had a long career with Nishitetsu in the 1950s and 1960s, one of the strongest teams of those eras; he went on to manage eight different NPB teams, including his brief stint with Hanshin. Kishi Ichirō was more an aberration than an anomaly; he was hired after the 1954 season in the wake of the forced resignation of Matsuki Kenjirō, which stunned the baseball world because no one had ever heard of him. He had had brief experience coaching a high school team, but he knew nothing of professional baseball. Apparently the Hanshin Dentetsu president chose him on a whim. The veteran players would have nothing to do with Kishi and openly defied his commands. After thirty-three games, he took a face-saving medical leave and was replaced by the team's star pitcher, Fujimura Tomio, the hotheaded leader of the opposition, who served out the season and the following one as player-manager.

4. For the following profiles, I have relied on multiple sources: conversations with media and club officials during the managers' years of tenure; daily reading of the sports press; observations of the managers during practices and games; and several books and articles, especially Inoue (2003), Ōtani (2003), Ueda (2003), and Yoshida (2003). Yoshida was the only manager with whom I had extended interviews.

5. More precisely, Fujita's moves created dissent within the front office and between the front office and the parent company about how much autonomy he should be allowed in his decisions. The press personalized this as a split between Miyoshi and Kuma, although the actual encounters remained opaque to everyone beyond the principals.

6. Fujita went back to media commentating, working for Sun Television and the *Daily Sports* newspaper from 1997. In 2005, he got back into managing with a corporate industrial league team.

7. Judging from his writings and media commentary (see, e.g., Nomura 2006), his animosity against Yomiuri ran deep. The Nankai versus Giants rivalry in the 1950s and 1960s was as fierce as that between the Giants and the Tigers, and Nankai frequently got the better of Yomiuri. Nomura was particularly incensed by Yomiuri's constant manipulations to secure an advantage. There were also strong class and personality clashes between the Giants under manager Mihara Osamu and the Hawks under the demanding, working-class Tsuruoka Kazuto. Nagashima Shigeo symbolized the "Keio-boy" image of the metropolitan center. Nomura had a particularly rocky history with Oh Sadaharu, who many thought was favored by the umpires (the "Oh-ball" given by umps). The Oh shift was developed because he always pulled the ball, with the third baseman moving to shortstop and three infielders on the right side. In one game against Nankai, when the Oh shift was set, Oh didn't swing hard but instead bunted down the third baseline, which Nomura found cowardly. Nomura explicitly claimed his "thinking baseball" philosophy was developed to counter the easygoing, intuitive style of Nagashima.

8. Hoshino collapsed while the team was on a final road trip and announced his retirement as soon as the team lost the Japan Series. He retired as what the club called "SD" (for senior director, a sort of consultant to the club president and owner Kuma). Hoshino held that post through 2010, when he returned as manager to a Pacific League team, the Tohoku Rakuten Golden Eagles, leading them to a league pennant. He passed away from pancreatic cancer in January 2018, at age seventy.

9. It is symbolic of their position in the corporate hierarchy that in figure 13, the outgoing manager Hoshino and incoming manager Okada are dressed in business suits, with Hanshin parent company CEO Kuma, discussed in the next chapter, standing between them.

CHAPTER 5. IN THE OFFICES: FRONT OFFICE AND
PARENT CORPORATION

1. One might justifiably criticize MLB naming practices as crass mystification. MLB teams have largely been owned by wealthy businessmen (individually, by a family, or in limited partnerships), and the use of a city name conveniently masks this actual ownership and disguises the often massive subsidies these wealthy owners receive in the form of municipal stadium construction and other inducements. In NPB, all stadiums but Hiroshima's were financed and built by the club owners. (The Hiroshima stadium was a joint project between the city and Mazda Corporation.)

2. See Reaves (1997:ch. 4) for the case of the Chicago Cubs, bled dry by their corporate ownership, the Tribune Company.

3. Nippon Professional Baseball was essentially a two-headed beast, with management vested in both an Owners' Council and the Commissioner's Office. Ultimate authority rested with the Owners' Council. It had several committees, the most important of which was the Implementation Committee, which had four main powers: to select the commissioner and oversee the Commissioner's Office; to manage the franchise system and approve all changes of regional jurisdictions, club names, and stadium rights; to approve any changes to qualifications for membership in NPB; and to approve all changes to the "Baseball Agreement." The NPB Commissioner's Office consisted of the commissioner and, nominally under him, the Central League and Pacific League directors. These three met to discuss all significant matters affecting both leagues. The third and fourth components of the NPB structure were the Players' Union and the umpires.

4. The hierarchy at the top was finely graded and not transparent. The directors themselves were of several types; for instance, a few of the directors were "representative directors," which is to say they could legally represent the company. A managing director sounds important, but he was a cut below those with representative status. As in most Japanese companies, Hanshin directors were internal appointments from senior management rather than outside appointments. Most of the top executives (at the senmu and jōmu levels) and some, though not many, division heads (buchō), were made board members. By Japanese commercial code, a crucial legal quality of directors is that they are contract employees. Their nominal terms are for two years, and they usually serve two terms, but they formally work under a series of one-year contracts, just like the Hanshin ball players. Thus, they can be released without cause at any point, and because directors are the figures of responsibility—the ones who take the fall if something goes wrong—this does happen, for baseball club matters as well as other causes.

5. The fact that corporate image was involved in Japanese team ownership certainly added to management intrusions and concerns with player behavior. This was true for the Yomiuri Giants as well. In a highly entertaining memoir of his playing years with the Giants that he wrote with Robert Whiting, Warren Cromartie offered many details of how tightly the company controlled the team and how thoroughly the coaching staff managed the players (through constant meetings, minute regulations, 24/7 scheduling, etc.); see Cromartie (1991:32–33). Like Hanshin, Yomiuri was hugely concerned with its image in a sport so thoroughly covered by the media. However, Cromartie was inconsistent in his stories. For instance, he noted that all younger players were required to live in the team dormitory and observe a 10:00 p.m. curfew: "One of the dormitory residents, a 19-year-old pitcher named Mizuno, got caught breaking curfew and drinking beer with a girl who was also a minor (the legal age in Japan is 20). For that, he was fined $10,000—about a third of his annual pay! He was also suspended and confined to his dormitory quarters for a month" (84). Five pages later, Cromartie regales us with stories about Shinozuka Toshio, then the Giants second baseman and a great singles hitter and smooth fielder: "Shinozuka had

fast hands in other ways too. In the course of his career, he compiled an impressive set of statistics with members of the opposite sex. He got engaged to one of the girls who always hung around the Tamagawa practice field, then broke the engagement when he became involved with a nightclub hostess. Later on, he had an affair with a well-known actress, which supposedly continued even on his way to two subsequent marriages and one divorce" (89). And later: "My teammates, I was beginning to discover, liked to go to hostess bars—both in Roppongi and the Ginza—even though the Giants did not approve" (117). At best, surveillance was incomplete and evasion was pervasive.

CHAPTER 6. IN THE STANDS: FANS, FOLLOWERS, AND FAIR-WEATHER SPECTATORS

1. For more lyrics to hitting marches and audio recordings of hitting marches and other fan songs and chants, see https://professional.wwkelly.net/ht.

2. An example of chant messages from the gods was the fire warning (hi no yōshin), which was called out with clappers by the watchmen who made the rounds of urban neighborhoods at night.

3. These are available at https://professional.wwkelly.net/ht.

4. Kosugi (2013:18) sensitized me to a more subtle form of jeering. Hanshin players are usually cheered by name, but if someone is playing poorly they will start calling him out by number ("hey you, number 6!"); even worse, they will start referring to him as "hey you, in the Hanshin uniform."

5. As I mentioned previously, when I asked players and front office people why so few of the players' wives attended Hanshin games, they very often voiced concern that the wives would be upset by the booing and jeering. I am still skeptical of this explanation because most heckling couldn't be heard from the backstop box seats in which wives and other favored guests sat and because the wives themselves more often cited the difficulties of bringing young children to night games. Still, I didn't doubt the sensitivity of the team to jeering.

6. This figure is the cover of a book by Ōtani Kōichi, a well-known Osakan writer and critic, author of over two dozen books on literary topics and Kansai culture. This delightful cover renders a Tigers fan sitting at home on a cushion watching the evening's game on television, dressed in his favorite player's jersey, a megaphone in his left hand and a beer in his right hand. His tiger-striped cat is at his side, as the television announcer screams that Yano has just cleaned up the bases with a three-run home run to give Hanshin a massive 12–1 lead. Most interesting about the illustration is the shrine altar to the left of the television, with candles and incense burning to the fan's god of supplication, who is none other than Colonel Sanders of Kentucky Fried Chicken. See chapter for the story of how the KFC founder became a central figure in Hanshin fan-lore.

7. Probably the non-Kansai team with the largest fan base in the region was the Hiroshima Carp, largely because so many people from Hiroshima had relocated to Kansai for work. There was a notable Yomiuri Giants fan presence in Kansai, too, although they were less visible and audible. There was a real difference, though, in the attitudes of local Hiroshima fans and local Giants fans toward the Tigers. Both Hanshin and Hiroshima fans saw one another as close

and friendly rivals, sharing much in fan organization and passion. Both sets of fans had stronger enmity toward Giants fans, who returned the disdain in equal measure.

8. One of the jeers recorded in the 1994 collection was "Hanshin fans are first class! The Tigers team is second class! The parent company is third class!" (Hanshin Taigāsu ni nekkyō suru yaji-kenkyūkai 1994:65).

9. Stevens (2004) and Yano (2002) are especially astute in analyzing the dynamics of ittaikan in music concert scenes.

CHAPTER 7. IN THE PRESS BOX: SPORTS DAILIES AND MAINSTREAM MEDIA

1. For their part, many reporters had been lobbying for years to enclose the press seating and modernize their facilities, complaining that the noise, the rain, and the midsummer heat and late autumn cold made it difficult to work. Neither Hanshin nor the Asahi Newspaper Corporation, which was concerned to preserve "the traditional Kōshien" experience for its high school tournament, was sympathetic.

2. The standard Japanese news manuscript page is a 20-by-20 grid of boxes for 400 characters, or very roughly, 150 words.

3. Of these, most important were the three national general dailies, the five sports dailies, the two wire services, four Kansai television stations, and two regional radio stations.

4. An example of a full morning edition may be found at www.professional .wwkelly.net./ht.

5. The three largest papers tended to color-code their front-page masthead logos for distinctiveness. *Nikkan* favored blue (see the upper left-hand corner of figure 20), *Supo-Nichi* used cinnabar, and *Hōchi* used green.

6. In the early 2000s, this group was reorganized into four separate operations and editions: Tokyo, Hokkaido, Nishi Nihon (covering Osaka, Nagoya, and Fukuoka), and Okinawa. Each was, legally, a newspaper corporation.

7. In 2006, for example, ABC broadcast twenty-five Hanshin home games, Yomiuri TV carried twenty games, and MBC and Kansai TV each were given fourteen (*Asahi Shimbun*, August 5, 2006). The details could be even more complicated. For example, Asahi ABC would sometimes buy a game to broadcast in its 7:00–8:30 p.m. time slot and resell the first hour and the conclusion to Sun TV.

CHAPTER 8. BASEBALL AS EDUCATION AND ENTERTAINMENT

1. How the Meiji-era samurai ideology and imagery were adopted into baseball and have continued to influence the sport up to the present has been the subject of a rich Japanese scholarship, principally Abe (2006); Ariyama (1997); Inoue (2004); Ishizaka (2002, 2003; Kiku (1993); Kusaka (1985); Saeki (2004):ch. 4; Sakaue (2001); and Sugano (2003). Key contributions to foreign commentary and debate include Blackwood (2008); Hayford (2007, 2008); Kelly (2009); Roden (1980a); and Whiting (2006, 2008).

2. A few of the key sources in English are Benesch (2014); Berry (2005); Friday (1994); and Hurst (1997). Robert Sharf puts it succinctly: "As Japan experienced a series of stunning military victories in Asia, notably the defeat of the Chinese in 1895 and the Russians in 1905, and as Japan pushed farther into Korea, Manchuria, and Taiwan, the military and cultural accomplishments of the Japanese nation came to be explained with reference to Bushidō or 'the way of the warrior.' This supposedly ancient 'samurai code,' exemplified by the heroes of countless popular legends and myths, comprised an ethos of self-discipline, self-sacrifice, single-mindedness, unhesitating obedience to one's lord, and utter fearlessness in the face of death. The proponents of kokutai proffered these qualities as the birthright of all Japanese–Bushidō and as the expression of 'Japaneseness' itself. The fact that the term Bushidō itself is rarely attested in pre-Meiji literature did not discourage Japanese intellectuals and propagandists from using the concept to explicate and celebrate the cultural and spiritual superiority of the Japanese" (1993:6). The parallels to cowboy imagery are not coincidental. The samurai were dominant for centuries and the cowboy only for a few decades, but both were pushed aside around the same time, in the 1860s and 1870s. The modern nostalgia about the cowboy began after his demise at the end of the nineteenth century, simultaneously with the celebration of the samurai. Owen Wister's novel *The Virginian* (1902) is credited with beginning the popular cowboy boom. What C. Wright Mills, the noted American sociologist, wrote about his Texas background and its reverence for cowboys might well be applied to Japanese celebrations of samurai, in baseball and elsewhere: "My God, what men they are. Or were. Or must have been. Or might have been. There was no movie like a cowboy movie" (Mills 2000:25).

3. The sport also attracted participation outside of school. In 1919 Suzuka Sakae invented a soft, hollow rubber baseball and introduced it at the Kyoto Youth Baseball Tournament. Being cheap and safe, rubber baseball was not only immediately successful with elementary school kids, but it also enabled adult recreational leagues. Baseball fever also spread into major companies, which began forming their own teams from 1918. The following year, a Tokyo tournament attracted thirty-six corporate team entries. Nonetheless, middle school and university baseball really defined the sport in the 1910s and 1920s.

4. Predating this, the earliest ensen baseball field was at Kōroen, a leisure park that Hanshin had opened along its trunk line in 1907. Three years later, the University of Chicago sent its team to Japan to play a series against Waseda University, and the Osaka Mainichi newspaper company wanted to stage several of the games in Kansai. It could not find a proper baseball field and asked Hanshin to construct one within Kōroen. Two weeks in the making, the result apparently was not much of a field; there were no spectator stands, and a portion of the first base side ran up a hill, while the left side of the outfield sloped dangerously away from the infield (Kiku 1994). Still, it remained in use for over three years.

5. For details on these government efforts, see Nakamura (2007), Onose (2001), Sakaue (2001), Tashiro (1996), and others noted in the Bibliographic Essay at https://www.professional.wwk.net/ht.

6. It is doubtful that any Japanese squad could have provided strong competition to these American All-Stars, but as a result of the 1932 Ministry of Educa-

tion regulations, Shōriki was not allowed to recruit college players or to match university teams against the American pros. Instead, he had to put together a team of college alumni or high school stars (who had to give up their college eligibility). This led to a telling incident with the White Russian émigré and star schoolboy pitcher Victor Starfin. See Thompson and Ikei (1987–1988) on the heavy recruiting pressures on Starfin by Yomiuri. Starfin wanted to lead his Hokkaidō school in his senior season, but Yomiuri threatened to have the family deported. Starfin joined the team late in the series and had only one, undistinguished outing. The other memorable story on the Japanese side is that of another teenage pitcher, Sawamura Eiji. He was beaten badly in two outings, but in his third outing he struck out Babe Ruth three times, and at one point he struck out Charley Gehringer, Babe Ruth, Jimmy Foxx, and Lou Gehrig in succession. Sawamura became an instant hero. He stayed with the new Giants, and in September 1936 he became the first pro pitcher to pitch a no-hit game (against the Hanshin Tigers). He repeated that feat against the same Tigers in May 1937, a season in which he went 33–10. He was conscripted into the Imperial Army in 1943 and died in the Battle of Okinawa in 1944. The Japanese equivalent of the Cy Young Award is named for him (Fitts 2012).

7. The inaugural teams and their owners were the Tokyo Giants (Yomiuri Newspaper Company), the Osaka Tigers (Hanshin Electric Railroad Company), the Tokyo Senators (Musashino Electric Railroad Company), Hankyū (Hankyū Electric Railroad Company), Dai Tokyo (Kokumin Newspaper Company), the Nagoya Golden Dolphins (Aichi Newspaper Company), and Nagoya (New Aichi Newspaper Company).

8. Fujimura Fumio was another pitcher who went on to greatness. He had been planning to attend Hōsei University. but his father signed him to Hanshin without his knowledge. His signing bonus went to pay off his brother's debts, and he was expected to give ¥40 of his ¥100 monthly salary to his parents.

CHAPTER 9. WORKPLACE MELODRAMAS AND SECOND-CITY COMPLEX

1. The expansion of secondary education in the 1950s meant that almost all children moved from middle school to high school. Schoolboy baseball reorganized correspondingly, and the spring and summer national tournaments at Kōshien were now held at the high school level. NHK began broadcasting the full ten-day tournament schedules, which enormously enhanced the prestige of high school baseball and its association with Kōshien Stadium.

2. By far the most popular wrestler of the era was Rikidōzan, and his matches, especially those against the American Smith brothers, became the most widely watched television. The irony about Rikidōzan was that this heroic defender of Japanese honor in the ring was in fact Korean born (Okamura 2008; Thompson 1986).

3. Pro baseball teams are used by companies both for product advertising and PR and for internal purposes: to provide benefits for employees (tickets, etc.) and as an incentive for recruiting new employees. Although baseball was the most prominent sport with corporate involvement, most major companies

developed extensive company sports programs at both the recreational and elite competitive levels. Corporate teams had appeared even before the war, in the 1920s, but they expanded rapidly in the 1950s and 1960s. In the absence of national sports programs for elite athletes, they were integral to national Olympic development, recruiting both Japanese and foreign athletes as employees. The most famous in the early postwar was the Kanebo women's volleyball team, which supplied most of the 1964 Tokyo Olympic gold-medal-winning team (Arata 2013; Tagsold 2011)

4. It is intriguing that Mōko, or Fierce Tigers, is a Chinese-character compound, pronounced in the more formal on-yomi, while dame-tora, or No-Good Tigers, was written as a Japanese-syllabary compound, pronounced in the less formal kun-yomi. And "dame," a very common colloquial utterance, can sometimes carry an implicit qualifier, as in dame da kedo . . . sho ga nai (no good, but we/you can't do anything about it) or dame da kedo—gambatta (it turned out poorly—but we tried our best).

5. For this history, I have used Inoue (2001), Matsuki and Okui (1992), *Nikkan Sports Newspaper*, Western Japan(2016), Nishii (1995), Nishizawa (2014), Ōtani (2003), Tamaki (1991), Ueda (2003), Yamada (2009), and Yoshida (2003).

6. A short news clip of the final moments may be viewed at https://www.youtube.com/watch?v=ErOkGVziuN8. Nagashima had been drafted by the Giants in 1957 as the top university prospect and was in his second year. The Giants then drafted Oh Sadaharu, the top high school prospect, the following year, in 1958. Nagashima had already homered in the fifth inning, and Oh had tied the game in the seventh inning with his own two-run home run. This added further significance to the game; it was the first of many times that the two stars had home runs in the same game, which the press dubbed *abekku-hōmu ran* (from the French *avec*, with).

7. It has also been a blight on Japanese baseball more generally and is taken by some as proof of a national prejudice against foreigners. This is a complex matter, difficult to resolve definitively. There is neither universal support for nor universal enmity toward foreign players by teammates, front office, fans, or media, as we have seen here. They can be unfairly targeted but also justifiably criticized. There are two points specific to the Bass case. First, for many commentators, it was less about his being American and more about the long-standing bad blood between the Tigers and the Giants, involving Oh and other players. Second, this particular record—the single-season home run record that Oh set in 1964—took on a particular symbolic importance beyond other records. Tuffy Rhodes in 2001 also had fifty-five home runs with four games remaining in the regular season and was denied fair pitches after that; the following year, Alex Cabrera reached fifty-five home runs and he too was pitched away from. It wasn't until 2013 that the Curaçaoan Vladimir Balentien finally broke the barrier, with sixty home runs (some fans at Kōshien told me that they were happy that his fifty-sixth and fifty-seventh home runs were against Hanshin; I heard no claims that it was done deliberately, but Tigers fans were pleased that a Giants player's record was erased). Of course a further irony of this long-running melodrama is that Oh himself is Taiwanese Japanese, has never taken

Japanese citizenship, and was subject to considerable slights by the Yomiuri organization and its fans as a player and manager.

8. These include fans like Fujita; manager Yoshida; the trainers; Terao from *Nikkan Sports*; and academics like Sugimoto Atsuo, Tom Blackwood, and Okamoto Jun.

CHAPTER 10. A SPORTSWORLD TRANSFORMING: THE HANSHIN TIGERS AT PRESENT

1. In the case of both schoolboy and professional baseball, we can distinguish between participation and spectatorship. Despite occasional attempts to organize a women's league, women are almost always excluded from participation at organized school and professional levels; instead, they are relegated to the parallel sport of softball (where they do quite well; the women's national softball team has had greater success than the men's national baseball team in international tournaments over the last three decades). As spectators in the Hanshin sportsworld (and as nonsports workers in the front office, parent company, fan club alliance, and concessions), they are marginalized, with limited advancement pathways. And yet, in talking with many of them over the years, I have found that their knowledge and passion for the features and fortunes of Hanshin can be fully the equal of their male counterparts. (See Cohen 2009; Esashi 1994; Kelly 2013a; Takai 2006; and Tsuchiya 1996.)

2. See Okada (2003:14) for a firsthand account of what occurred at the stadium that day.

3. The 2003 league championship and Japan Series loss resurrected the most well-known urban legend in the Hanshin sportsworld, that of Colonel Sanders of Kentucky Fried Chicken fame. Osaka's central city region is bisected by natural rivers and artificial canals that have been important transportation arteries for centuries. Dotonbori Canal is a section of this waterway network that runs through one of the most vibrant nightlife areas, and as fans gathered in October 1985 to celebrate the Tigers' Japan Series victory, many jumped off the bridge and streets into the canal. Some were dressed in the garb of the players. The story spun by the media was that no one looked like the big, burly, and bearded American star, Randy Bass, so some exuberant fans grabbed the statue of Colonel Sanders (a bearded white man) that stood in front of the nearby Kentucky Fried Chicken store and chucked it into the canal. It was not subsequently located, and when the Tigers fell precipitously the next year, an urban legend quickly spread that the Tigers would not win again until Colonel Sanders was found and dredged up. Teams of divers periodically searched the relatively shallow but quite muddy canal, but the statue was not recovered. The "curse of the Colonel" grew in local imagination over the next twenty years, and when the Tigers finally did win the Central League title in 2003 and again in 2005, local wags claimed the curse was still in force because in neither year did they go on to take the Japan Series. (KFC store managers nevertheless took no chances and made sure to bring their statues inside in both years on the evenings that the Tigers clinched their league title!) Finally, in March 2009, construction workers stumbled upon the top half of the statue, and a few days later they found the

lower half. With great fanfare, the statue was restored and put on display outside the KFC outlet near the Kōshien Stadium railroad station. In 2013 KFC Japan moved it to corporate headquarters in Tokyo, where it greets visitors. The bridge over the Dotonbori Canal, meanwhile, has become a frequent spot of contention between excited and often inebriated Hanshin fans, who try to jump off the bridge in celebration, and local police, who are concerned about the injuries that frequently ensue. Barriers have been erected and arrests made.

4. As Hoshino took over in the off-season between 2002 and 2003, twenty-four players left or were dismissed and twenty-six players were added, the largest turnover in club history.

5. More precisely, HK Holdings, the umbrella company for Hankyū Railroad, bought out all of Murakami's Hanshin Railroad shares, gaining sufficient control that Hanshin Dentetsu became a subsidiary of Hankyū Holdings. Even this did not sit well with the other NPB owners, who were still suspicious of Hankyū because of its sale of the Hankyū Braves to Orix in 1989. The Owners' Council initially demanded that HK Holdings post a ¥30 million bond guarantee to NPB. Hankyū Holdings objected, and the amount was rather quickly adjusted downward to a mere ¥1 million, along with an unusual written internal agreement between the holding corporation and Hanshin Dentetsu that the holding corporation would not involve itself in the management of the ball club.

6. The six are urban transport, real estate, entertainment and communications, travel, international transportation, and hotels (Hankyū Hanshin Holdings 2017).

7. In 2017, Sakai Shin'ya remained designated owner of the Tigers club. Sakai joined the Hanshin Dentetsu in 1970 when he graduated from Kobe University, then rose through the parent company ranks. He became CEO in 2006 and moved up to become chairman of the board in 2013. Sakai had handled the contentious negotiations with Murakami and then Hanshin's acquisition by Hankyū. To the reporters I talked with, he was clearly the most powerful and respected figure among top Hanshin executives. He resigned as chairman of the board early in 2017 but remains a club director and designated owner. In effect, Hanshin used the opportunity of Kuma's retirement to separate more clearly the corporate presidency and responsibility for ball club operations. Sakai gained his position for his corporate business savvy and not his baseball acumen, which is one reason that Hoshino was kept on as his "special director" consultant.

8. On January 17, 1995, an earthquake of 6.8 magnitude rocked the port and downtown neighborhoods of Kobe, with major damage spreading eastward toward Osaka (Edgington 2010). It was Japan's second largest earthquake in the twentieth century. In much of the foreign press, this was known as the Kobe earthquake. "Gambarō Kobe" (Let's Fight Kobe) was the catch phrase of recovery, and support was taken up by the Orix team. During my first year of field research in 1996, Orix team uniforms carried this phrase, and there were game events and charitable outings to raise attention and money for local recovery efforts. In fact, it was Hanshin, the company, the port areas of Kobe, and the coastal neighborhoods along the Hanshin corridor that were hardest hit by the earthquake and its aftermath. Hanshin rail lines, roadways leading to

Kōshien, and the stadium itself sustained far more damage than the western sections of Kobe that were close to Orix's Green Stadium. In Japanese, the quake is generally known as the "Great Hanshin Earthquake Disaster." It was a substantial financial brake on Hanshin's development plans.

9. One small detail: The project used the occasion of redoing the massive centerfield scoreboard to change the display from the long-standing Japanese order of Strikes-Balls-Outs to the US order of Balls-Strikes-Outs.

10. Circulation figures are from http://www.pressnet.or.jp/data/circulation /circulation01.php (accessed September 14, 2017). Not surprisingly, newspaper reading is strongly correlated with age and inversely related to digital use. Hayashi (2013) reports research by NHK that sixty- to sixty-nine-year-old males reported daily newspaper reading of forty-four minutes and personal online time of fourteen minutes; for males twenty to twenty-nine, online time was sixty-eight minutes and newspaper reading was three minutes per day (see also Dentsū 2017; Villi and Hayashi 2017). More data are available at http:// www.professional.wwkelly.net/ht.

11. The Hanshin club has a digital publishing and social media section and a busier club website than ten years ago, but it is impossible to determine traffic. Facebook is much less developed in Japan than in other countries; it tends to be deployed more for corporate and organizational use than for individual social communication, which is done much more through mobile messaging (LINE, Instagram, and Twitter are overwhelmingly the major mobile messaging plat-forms). A consequence of such a digital landscape is that it is much harder to develop the broad fan community of shared concern and knowledge that had been so characteristic of the Hanshin sportsworld over the decades. I have no reliable data to cite, but in four research stays at Tokyo's Waseda University between 2010 and 2017, totaling eleven months, I only encountered one stu-dent who used social media or mobile messaging for baseball topics.

12. Another development of the early 2000s was enthusiasm for hiring American managers. Bobby Valentine had enormous success with Chiba Lotte (leading them to a Japan Series title over Hanshin in 2005), and his popularity with fans and corporate sponsors helped overcome barriers against US manag-ers (Jenks and Pettigrew 2008). By 2007, four of the twelve teams had Ameri-can managers. Nonetheless, by 2011 all of these managers were gone, replaced by Japanese counterparts. The circumstances varied, and some separations were mutually amicable, but the six years do seem in retrospect to have been excep-tional. Again, the foreign sports press is apt to interpret this as another instance of Japanese prejudice and parochialism, but that is a rash and simplistic analy-sis. As we saw in chapter 4, there are multiple expectations placed on the NPB manager, and there is also a huge pool of domestic candidates for the position. Both of these factors work against hiring an unknown foreigner.

Appendix: A Note on the Research and Writing

The method of doing anthropological research that became conventional in the early twentieth century was based on spending a year or so with a small group of people; sharing to some degree their conditions of life; observing that life; and talking with them in their own language about their lives, formally (in interviews) and informally (in daily conversation). Anthropologists called it doing fieldwork, and we have debated its utility and its ethics among ourselves for decades. Everyone who does fieldwork lives through and deals with personal difficulties, moral dilemmas, and epistemological doubts. We have coined odd phrases to capture our borderline position. We see ourselves as marginal natives or inside outsiders, doing participant-observation in an intersubjective mode. We have generated a huge literature about doing fieldwork, from memoirs to bitter critiques. (The reader by Robben and Sluka [2007] is a representative sample; for Japan, Bestor, Steinhoff, and Bestor [2003] is a very instructive collection.)

I began this fieldwork in the mid-1990s after two decades of experience in the anthropology of Japan, but I had no special expertise in sports studies. Colleagues often suspect that I took it up as a fun way at midcareer to indulge the personal love of sports that all American males are suspected to harbor. However, apart from a lifelong emotional attachment to and marginal membership in the Boston Red Sox Nation, rooted mostly in childhood nostalgia and sibling rivalry, the sport of baseball held no special interest for me. Rather, what motivated me was the growing realization that sports did matter very much to Japan, and among them, baseball may have mattered the most over the century and a quarter of modern Japan's existence.

As a sports ethnography, this book is based on my observations of Hanshin Tigers professional baseball for about ten years, primarily from mid-1996 through 2003, with some follow-up through 2005. Even now, I continue to follow news and literature about Hanshin and to visit Kōshien and the club occasionally for interviews and observations. Over that time, I spent many long days and evenings at ballparks, watching practices and games and talking with players, coaches, front office staff, stadium employees, spectators and fans, and the omnipresent media. I watched several hundred games in eleven different stadiums: in the stands, the press boxes, and the bleachers, as well as in bars and homes. I was equally fortunate to be allowed to attend Tigers spring training in Shikoku, away games in other parts of Japan, several of the fall training camps in Shikoku and Kōshien, numerous farm team games, and even the Japan Series in 2003. I had opportunities to interview executives of the parent company, reporters, editors, photographers, commentators, bar owners, and fan club officers. I was able to observe newsrooms, broadcast booths, and player dormitories, and I could participate in the activities of several fan clubs. Although the Hanshin Tigers became the focus of my time and energy, I also came to know something about comparable sites and individuals with the Orix BlueWave and the Kintetsu Buffaloes through more occasional although continuing visits, interviews, and reading.

Professional baseball is an unusual field site for an anthropologist, and it required careful thinking about matters of gaining access to places and people, protecting sources, dealing with the volume of publicity and reporting, and so forth. As I have argued in this book, the connections among and between players, coaching staffs, company employees, media professionals, and fans and Kansai residents were as indirect and tenuous as they were the essential lineaments of the Hanshin Tigers sportsworld. They also posed very different problems and possibilities for an inquiring anthropologist. Hanshin players were generally quite polite and accommodating but guarded in formal exchanges. Most were well practiced in dealing with the media, and they knew the media's voracious need to *shuzai*—to gather any and all tidbits of information and collect quotes for their daily stream of stories and commentaries. Moreover, the media relations staff of the front office tightly managed media access to players throughout the season, and I followed their procedures when seeking formal interviews. At the same time, quick, informal conversations could happen spontaneously, especially when we were sitting around the trainers' rooms at Kōshien or Tiger Den or at the hotels during the preseason. Initially it was not clear to the players how I might be different from the reporters they dealt with daily, but those whom I interacted with over a number of years appreciated my aims and shared some fascinating experiences and reflections about the club and their careers.

My interactions with front office staff and corporate employees also ranged widely. They too were unfailingly polite, though many were reserved when our conversations turned to details of policy and internal club procedures. I became rather close with a half dozen or so of them (and remain in touch today), but all are sensitive to the club's and company's anxieties about publicity. They expressed their opinions freely to me, but with the understanding that I would protect their identities and avoid direct quotes.

My fieldwork with Hanshin also reversed the normal relationship between anthropologist and journalists. In many parts of the world, it is the anthropologist who makes a long-term commitment to a local world and to a linguistic expertise and deep knowledge. We can be rather dismissive of those journalists who drop by with their translators for a short visit and a few quotes. In my case, however, the dynamics were reversed, to my discomfort! With Hanshin and the other clubs, it was the press corps—the beat reporters and ex-player commentators—whose experience and expertise vastly outweighed mine. Many of them had been around every day for years; they had cultivated contacts in many places, they were fluent in the lingo of baseball, and they knew the lineages of Hanshin personnel. It was I who was the neophyte, and it was I who learned much from them.

As one might assume, the fans were usually the most uninhibited, indeed enthusiastically sharing their Tigers passion and its place in their lives and identities. Interacting with them was the opposite dynamic from working with front office staff. They really embraced me and assumed—indeed expected—me to be a fan and to act like a fan, dressing in fan garb and cheering madly along with them.

Was I? Did I become fan? Well, I did come to care deeply about the fans in this sportsworld, especially those who opened up to me and drew me in. I earnestly wanted to understand them and their felt attachments to the Hanshin Tigers—in the same way that I wanted to understand the players and their careers, the front office and its anxieties, and the media and its pressures—all of which together constituted this sportsworld. I socialized, I observed, I sympathized—probably empathized, given my own attachments from childhood with the Boston Red Sox—but I never really become a fan. And frankly, for that reason, I think I understood better what it meant to invest so much of oneself in being a Hanshin fan than I would have if I had given myself over to the possibilities and perils of Hanshin fandom.

Beyond the challenge of finding distinctive ways of relating to the various members of the Hanshin Tigers sportsworld, the scheduling of the research was also unusual. My personal circumstances and my university obligations dictated that I could not conduct the field research in the conventional manner, by which the anthropologist spends an extended period of continuous field research (most of us think one to two years is ideal), followed by an equally concentrated period of "writing up." I never had more than four months at a stretch available for fieldwork, and several times I could only manage a few weeks. Altogether, my time "in the field" totaled about thirteen months, spread over eight trips:

1996: July through November (midseason through fall postseason camp)

1997: February–March (spring training), May–June (early season)

1998: July (midseason)

1999: March (exhibition season)

2001: July–August (midseason)

2002: March (exhibition season)

2003: January (preseason), July–August (midseason), and October (Japan Series)

I was initially disappointed and unnerved by the interval nature of my research because it violated anthropologists' preference for a long, intensive, uninterrupted stay "in the field." but I came to appreciate several advantages of such a schedule. I was able to situate my direct observations and interviews about Hanshin baseball during this seven-year period by keeping up with the daily sports press; listening to internet broadcasts of games; continuing email communications with individuals in the Tigers front office, the news media, and fan clubs; and studying the primary and secondary literature on Hanshin baseball and the sport more generally. I could gradually build up familiarity and knowledge with and between each stay. The Hanshin Tigers world was constantly in my head for years and years, even when I was not physically "there," in its multiple locations. Being able to (i.e., forced to) to follow Tigers baseball over multiple years also gave me a better appreciation for career structures, rhythms of competition, and structural transformations that I would not have understood in a single year of intensive study.

Since those years of active, if periodic, fieldwork, I have continued occasional follow-up inquiries and long-distance monitoring, and this too has given me an unusual perspective on the significance of those years. Usually we come back and try to "write up" as soon as possible, with no sense of what in fact will transpire after the research. My early articles on Kansai and Hanshin baseball were written with just such a presentist view. Now, however, I do know what has happened over a decade and more—to Hanshin, to Kansai, and to Japanese baseball—and that has allowed me to situate those years of contemporary fieldwork not only with what had led up to and produced that world but also with what has become of that world subsequently.

It is these unusual circumstances of the research that leads to a final note on the verb tenses I have used in this book. To most readers perhaps, verb tense in writing is a straightforward matter of style and syntax, but in social science writing, especially in anthropology, it bears methodological and theoretical significance as well. In our ethnographic writing, we anthropologists tend to use the simple present tense of English grammar, for which we have a special term, the ethnographic present. This goes back to the style of our founding ethnographers in their early twentieth-century writing. One of the most famous, Bronislaw Malinowski, wrote his five-hundred-page monograph on the overseas kula expeditions of the Trobriand Islanders of Melanesia using sentences like, "A few days before the appointed date of the departure of the Kula expedition there is a great stir in the villages. Visiting parties arrive from the neighbourhood, bringing gifts mostly of food, to serve as provisions for the journey" (1922:150).

The simple present tense as ethnographic present is enticing; it tempts the reader to imagine that the events are occurring even as he or she reads the anthropologist's words—it creates a copresent for readers, author, and subjects. This is always a kind of time travel; in Malinowski's case his ethnography was published in London in 1922, but he wrote it in the Canary Islands in 1918–1919 based on his fieldwork and notes from Melanesia in 1914–1917! Anthropologists have long debated the intentions behind this ethnographic present and its effects on readers. Critics charge that it conveys a false timelessness of the subjects' lifeworld, removing it from history. Defenders interpret it as the extended moment when the anthropologist is "in the field," so that we can ground our analysis in our personal research experience; at best, it is a necessary and transparent acknowledgment of the limits of our data.

I raise this issue here because I have written this book in the past tense, or what I would call the ethnographic past. The fieldwork on which this book is largely based was done in 1996–2003. There are enduring features of the Hanshin Tigers and of Japanese baseball (the rule book hasn't changed!), but from the perspective of over fifteen years, there have also been consequential changes to the Hanshin Tigers that reveal important shifts in Japanese baseball and Japanese society. To be able to see what the Tigers had been in the early decades after their formation, what they were in the 1990s and early 2000s, and what they are now allows me to place this ethnographic fieldwork, and the concept of sportsworld itself, in an instructive historical framework, before, during, and after.

Glossary of Key Japanese Terms

Note: The following are Japanese character renderings of key terms in the text that may not be familiar to all Japanese-speaking readers. Throughout, I have tried to avoid excessive use of Japanese terms and used English glosses after first use. Baseball, however, has an extensive vocabulary, and interested readers are referred to the following online site, where I have posted a far larger glossary that I developed over my years of fieldwork: https://professional.wwkelly.net/ht.

chīmu	チーム	team
Dame Tora	ダメ虎	the No-Good Tigers
dodai-zukuri	土台作り	foundation building
furonto	フロント	front office
gaijin senshu	外人選手	foreign player
genba	現場	the field of play
gōken na seishin	剛健な精神	manly spirit
haenuki ishiki	生え抜き意識	provincialism
Hanshin Kōshien Kyūjo	阪神甲子園球場	Hanshin Kōshien Stadium
Hanshin Taigāsu kyūdan	阪神タイガース球団	Hanshin Tigers baseball club
Hanshin Taigāsu shisetsu ōendan	阪神タイガース私設応援団	Private Alliance of Hanshin Tiger Fan Clubs

horyū senshu	保留選手	holdout (player in salary negotiations)
jishu tore	自主トレ	(preseason) independent preseason training
jōshō kyūdan	常勝球団	regularly winning ball club
kaimakusen	開幕戦	opening day game
kantoku	監督	manager (of baseball team)
kenzen na taikaku	健全な体格	healthy physique
ki-jāji kumi	黄ジャージ組	the yellow-jersey squad
Kintetsu Bafarōzu	近鉄 バファローズ	Kintetsu Buffaloes
kogaisha	子会社	subsidiary company, child company
kōhakusen	紅白戦	intrasquad scrimmage
kyūdan	球団	ball club
kyūsaisha	救世主	savior
ma no rōdo	魔のロード	"road of misfortune"
makenai ishiki	負けない意識	resolve not to lose
Mōko	猛虎	Fierce Tigers
mondaiji	問題子	problem child
naibu-geki	内部劇	internal drama
oiesōdō	お家騒動	family squabble
Orikkusu Burūwēvu	オリックスブルーウェーブ	Orix BlueWave
Orikkusu Bafarōzu	オリックスバファローズ	Orix Buffaloes
osawagase otoko	お騒がせ男	troublemaker
oyagaisha	親会社	parent company
seishin yakyū	精神野球	spiritual baseball
senpon nokku	千本ノック	thousand-fungo drill
senshu	選手	player
setsu	節	one-week unit of baseball season

shi no rōdo	死のロード	"death road
shuzai	取材	collecting information for a news story
taishingi	体心技	body, spirit, and technique
teuchi renjū	手打ち連中	handclapping (fan) club
tora-kichi	トラキチ	Tiger-crazy
teitai	停滞	stagnation
waidoshō	ワイドショウ	morning TV variety show
yakyū gaidokuron	野球害毒論	"Dispute about the Evils of Baseball"
yakyū-dō	野球道	the Way of Baseball
yōchi asagake	夜討ち朝駆け	"night raid and dawn attack" (referring to journalists' overnight stakeout)

References

Note: The following list includes only those references cited in the text. Readers interested in more scholarship on sports and baseball in Japan and on Kansai and the Hanshin Tigers may consult my longer bibliographic essay on primary sources and secondary materials at https://www.professional.wwkelly.net/ht. To provide better reference for Japan-language scholars, article and book titles are given in original Japanese characters, not in Romanized transliteration, which is meaningless to those who do not read Japanese and unhelpful to those who do. English glosses are provided for all Japanese titles except for the rare instance in which a book or journal title has an original English title.

Abe Ikuo 阿部生雄. (2006). "Muscular Christianity in Japan: The Growth of a Hybrid." *International Journal of the History of Sport* 23(5): 714–738.

Abe Ikuo 阿部生雄. (2009). 近代スポーツマンシップの誕生と成長 [The birth and growth of modern sportsmanship]. Tokyo: 筑波大学出版会.

Abe Ikuo and J. A. Mangan. (2002). "'Sportsmanship'—English-Inspiration and Japanese Response: F. W. Strange and Chiyosaburō Takeda." *International Journal of the History of Sport* 19(2–3): 99–123.

Abe Masahiko 安倍昌彦. (2009). スカウト [Scout]. Tokyo: 日刊スポーツ出版社.

Alford, Peter, and David McNeill. (2010). "Stop the Press? The Sankei and the State of Japan's Newspaper Industry." *Japan Focus: An Asia-Pacific E-Journal*, March 8. Accessed March 9, 2010. http://japanfocus.org/products/details/3318.

Allen, Robert C. (1983). "On Reading Soaps: A Semiotic Primer." In *Regarding Television: Critical Approaches—An Anthology*, edited by E. Ann Kaplan, 97–108. Frederick, MD: University Publications of America.

Allison, Anne. (2013). *Precarious Japan*. Durham, NC: Duke University Press.

Alt, John (1983). "Sport and Cultural Reification: From Ritual to Mass Consumption." *Theory, Culture & Society* 1(3): 93–107.

Arata Masafumi 新雅史. (2013). 「東洋の魔女」論 [Debates about the "Witches of the Orient"]. Tokyo: イースト・プレス.

Ariyama Teruo 有山輝雄. (1994). "マスメディアイベントとしての甲子園野球" [Kōshien baseball as mass-media event]. メディ史研究 [Journal of media history research] 1: 102–119.

Ariyama Teruo 有山輝雄. (1997). 甲子園と日本人：メディアのつくったイベント [Kōshien and the Japanese: A media-made event]. Tokyo: 吉川弘文館.

Asahi Newspaper Editorial Department 朝日新聞編集部. (1991). "付録：野球とその害毒" [Appendix: Baseball and its evils]. In 貧困なる青春 日記 [Journal of a poor youth], edited by Honda Katsuichi 本多勝一, 175–221. Tokyo: 朝日新聞社.

Associated Press. (1991). "In Japan, Baseball Is the Art of War." *Los Angeles Times*, April 21. Accessed September 15, 2015. http://articles.latimes.com /1991-04-21/sports/sp-906_1_japanese-baseball.

Baldwin, Frank, and Anne Allison, eds. (2015). *Japan: The Precarious Future*. New York: Social Science Research Council and New York University Press.

Becker, Howard S. (1974). "Art as Collective Action." *American Sociological Review* 39(6): 767–776.

Becker, Howard S. (1976). "Art Worlds and Social Types." *American Behavioral Scientist* 19(6): 703–719.

Becker, Howard S. (2008). *Art Worlds: 25th Anniversary edition, Updated and Expanded*. Berkeley and Los Angeles: University of California Press.

Benesch, Oleg. (2014). *Inventing the Way of the Samurai: Nationalism, Internationalism, and Bushido in Modern Japan*. Oxford: Oxford University Press.

Berry, Mary Elizabeth. (2005). "Samurai Trouble: Thoughts on War and Loyalty." *Journal of Asian Studies* 64(4): 831–847.

Besnier, Niko, Susan Brownell, and Thomas F. Carter. (2017). *The Anthropology of Sport: Bodies, Borders, Biopolitics*. Oakland: University of California Press.

Bessatsu Takarajima Editorial Division 別冊宝島編集部. (2012). 元阪神 424人の今 [424 former Hanshin players: Where they are now]. Tokyo: 宝島社.

Bessatsu Takarajima Editorial Division 別冊宝島編集部. (2015). プロ野球パーフェクトデータ2015 選手名鑑 [Professional baseball perfect data: The 2015 player directory]. Tokyo: 宝島社.

Bestor, Theodore C., Patricia G. Steinhoff, and Victoria Lyon Bestor, eds. (2003). *Doing Fieldwork in Japan*. Honolulu: University of Hawai'i Press.

Blackwood, Thomas Stephen. (2008). "Bushido Baseball? Three 'Fathers' and the Invention of a Tradition." *Social Science Japan Journal* 11(2): 223–240.

Blomberg, Catharina. (1991). "The Vicissitudes of Bushidō." In *Social Sciences, Ideology, and Thought*, edited by Adriana Boscano, Franco Gatti, and Massimo Raveri, 318–323. Sandgate, Folkstone, Kent: Japan Library Limited.

Carter, Thomas F. (2008). *The Quality of Home Runs: The Passion, Politics, and Language of Cuban Baseball*. Durham, NC: Duke University Press.

Chun, Jayson Makoto. (2007). *"A Nation of a Hundred Million Idiots"? A Social History of Japanese Television, 1953–1973*. New York: Routledge.

Cohen, Marilyn. (2009). *No Girls in the Clubhouse: The Exclusion of Women from Baseball*. Jefferson, NC: McFarland.

Condry, Ian. (2006). *Hip-Hop Japan: Rap and the Paths of Cultural Globalization*. Durham, NC: Duke University Press.

Connery, Donald S. (1962). "A Yank in Japan." *Sports Illustrated*, June 25, 60–73.

Cox, Wendell. (2012). "The Evolving Urban Form: Osaka-Kobe-Kyoto." *NewGeography*, March 28. Accessed May 30, 2018. http://www.newgeography.com/content/002750-the-evolving-urban-form-osaka-kobe-kyoto.

Cromartie, Warren (1991). *Slugging It Out in Japan: An American Major Leaguer in the Tokyo Outfield*. Tokyo and New York: Kodansha International.

Dai-ichi kōtōgakkō kōyū kai 第一高等学校校友会. (1897). 野球部史 [A history of the baseball club]. Tokyo: 前川文栄堂.

Danto, Arturo C. (1964). "The Art World." *Journal of Philosophy* 61(19): 571–584.

Dentsū 電通, ed. (2017). 日本新聞年鑑 [Japan newspaper annual]. Tokyo: 電通.

Douglass, Mike. (1993). "The New Tokyo Story: Restructuring Space and the Struggle for Place in a World City." In *Japanese Cities in the Global Economy: Restructuring and Urban-Industrial Change*, edited by Fujita Kuniko and Richard Child Hill, 83–119. Philadelphia: Temple University Press.

Economist. (1996). "Japanese Baseball: Throw Till Your Arm Drops Off." 340(7985): 104.

Edgington, David W. (2000). "City Profile: Osaka." *Cities* 17(4): 305–318.

Edgington, David W. (2010). *Reconstructing Kobe: The Geography of Crisis and Opportunity*. Vancouver: University of British Columbia Press.

Edo-Tokyo Museum 江戸東京博物館, Yukiyoshi Shōichi 行吉 正一, and Yoneyama Jun'ichi 米山 淳一, eds. (2014). 東京オリンピックと新幹線 [The Tokyo Olympics and the Shinkansen]. Tokyo: 青幻舎.

Esashi Shōgo 江刺正吾. (1994). "甲子園とジェンダー" [Gender and Kōshien]. In 高校野球の社会学：甲子園を読む [The sociology of high school baseball: Reading Kōshien], edited by Esashi Shōgo 江刺正吾 and Komuku Hiroshi 小椋博, 63–82. Tokyo: 世界思想社.

Fitts, Robert K. (2005). *Remembering Japanese Baseball: An Oral History of the Game*. Carbondale: Southern Illinois University Press.

Fitts, Robert K. (2008). *Wally Yonamine: The Man Who Changed Japanese Baseball*. Lincoln: University of Nebraska Press.

Fitts, Robert K. (2012). *Banzai Babe Ruth: Baseball, Espionage, & Assassination during the 1934 Tour of Japan*. Lincoln: University of Nebraska Press.

Flüchter, Winfried, (2012). "Urbanisation, City, and City System in Japan between Development and Shrinking: Coping with Shrinking Cities in Times of Demographic Change." In *Urban Spaces in Japan: Social and Cultural Perspectives*, edited by Christoph Brumann and Evelyn Schultz, 15–36. London and New York: Routledge.

Friday, Karl F. (1994). "Bushido or Bull? A Medieval Historian's Perspective on the Imperial Army and the Japanese Warrior Tradition." *The History Teacher* 27(3): 339–349.

Fukuda Takuya 福田拓哉. (2011). "わが国のプロ野球におけるマネジメントの特徴とその成立要因の研究" [Research on distinctive features and formative causes of management practices in our professional baseball]. 立命館経営学研究 [Ritsumeikan business review] 49(6): 135–159.

Geraghty, Christine. (1991). *Women and Soap Opera: A Study of Prime Time Soaps*. London: Polity Press.

Geraghty, Christine. (2005). "The Study of the Soap Opera." In *A Companion to Television*, edited by J. Wasko, 308–323. Malden, MA, and Oxford: Blackwell Press.

Gluckman, Max. (1972). "Moral Crises: Magical and Secular Solutions." In *The Allocation of Responsibility*, edited by Max Gluckman, 1–50. Manchester, UK: Manchester University Press.

Gmelch, George. (2006). *Inside Pitch: Life in Professional Baseball*. Lincoln: University of Nebraska Press.

Gmelch, George, and J.J. Weiner. (1998). *In the Ballpark: The Working Lives of Baseball People*. Washington, DC: Smithsonian Institution Press.

Gordon, Andrew. (2015). "Making Sense of the Lost Decades: Workplaces and Schools, Men and Women, Young and Old, Rich and Poor." In *Examining Japan's Lost Decades*, edited by Funabashi Yōichi and Barak Kushner, 77–100. Abingdon, Oxon: Routledge.

Gordon, Dan. (2000). "An Invitation to See the Hanshin Tigers: Japanese Baseball as Seen through the Eyes of a Female Fan." *Nine: A Journal of Baseball History and Culture* 9 (1–2): 248–252.

Graczyk, Wayne. (2000). *Japanese Pro Baseball Fan Handbook and Media Guide*. Tokyo: JapanBall.com.

Grossberg, Lawrence. (1992) "Is There a Fan in the House? The Affective Sensibility of Fandom." In *The Adoring Audience: Fan Culture and Popular Media*, edited by Lisa A. Lewis, 50–68. London and New York: Routledge.

Guttmann, Allen. (1978). *From Ritual to Record: The Nature of Modern Sport*. New York: Columbia University Press.

Hanes, Jeffrey E. (2002). *The City as Subject: Seki Hajime and the Reinvention of Modern Osaka*. Berkeley and Los Angeles: University of California Press.

Hankyū Hanshin Holdings. (2017). "Hankyū Hanshin Holdings Group Guide." Accessed November 15, 2017. http://www.hankyu-hanshin.co.jp/en/.

Hanshin denki tetsudō K.K. 阪神電気鉄道株式会社. (1985). 阪神電気鉄道八十年史 [The 80-year history of the Hanshin Electrical Railroad Company]. Osaka: 阪神電気鉄道.

Hanshin Taigāsu 阪神タイガース. (1991). 阪神タイガース 昭和のあゆみ [The Showa era advance of the Hanshin Tigers]. Osaka: 阪神電気鉄道.

Hanshin Taigāsu 阪神タイガース. (1996). 阪神タイガース *Media Guide* [Hanshin Tigers media guide]. Osaka: 阪神タイガース.

Hanshin Taigāsu ni nekkyō suru yaji kenkyūkai 阪神タイガースに熱狂するヤジ研究会, ed. (1994). 甲子園のヤジ [Jeers at Kōshien]. Tokyo: 同文書院.

Hanshinkan modanizumu ten jikko iinkai 「阪神間 モダニズム」展 実行 委員 会, ed. (1997). 阪神 間 モダニズム [Hanshin-kan modernism]. Kyoto: 淡交 社.

Hara Takeshi 原武史 (1998). 「民都」大阪対「帝都」東京：思想としての関 西私鉄 [Osaka, the people's city, versus Tokyo, the imperial city: Kansai private railroads as thought]. Tokyo: 講談社.

Harrington, C. Lee, and Denise B. Bielby. (1995). *Soap fans: Pursuing Pleasure and Making Meaning in Everyday Life*. Philadelphia: Temple University Press.

Hata Mahito 秦真人. (1993). "1911 年における野球論争の実証的研究 (4) -大 正期における「全国優勝野球大曾」の地方大会主催者に関わる考察" [An empirical study of the 1911 baseball controversy 4: Discussion relating to the sponsorship of regional qualification tournaments for the National Baseball Championships in the Taisho period]. 総合保健体育科学 [Nagoya journal of health, physical fitness, and sports] 16(1): 29–43.

Hata Mahito 秦真人 and Kaga Hideo 加賀秀雄. (1990). "「野球害毒論争」 (1911年)の実相に関する実証的検討―新聞各紙の論調分析を通じて" [An empirical study of the reality of the 1911 dispute about the evils of baseball: Through an analysis of the tone of each newspaper's coverage]. 総合保健体 育科学 [Nagoya journal of health, physical fitness, and sports] 13(1): 19–31.

Hata Mahito 秦真人 and Kaga Hideo 加賀秀雄. (1991a). "1911 年における野 球論争の実証的研究 (I):「野球と其害毒」をめぐって" [Empirical research on the 1911 dispute about the evils of baseball 1: Focusing on "baseball and its evils]. 総合保健体育科学 [Nagoya journal of health, physical fitness, and sports] 14(1): 25–31.

Hata Mahito 秦真人 and Kaga Hideo 加賀秀雄. (1991b). "1911年における野 球論争の実証的研究 (2):「東京朝日新聞」及び「大阪朝日新聞」の編集 内容の相違をめぐって" [Empirical research on the 1911 dispute about the evils of baseball 2: Focusing on the differences in editorial content between Tokyo Asahi Newspaper and Osaka Asahi Newspaper]. 総合保健体育科学 [Nagoya journal of health, physical fitness, and sports] 14(1): 33-38.

Hata Mahito 秦真人 and Kaga Hideo 加賀秀雄. (1992). "1911年における野球 論争の実証的研究 (3):「野球論争」から「第一回全国優勝野球大会」開 催に至る朝日新聞の動向，及び同紙にあらわれた学生野球観について" [Empirical research on the 1911 dispute about the evils of baseball 3: Concerning trends in the Asahi Newspaper from the baseball and its evils dispute to the opening of the first National Baseball Tournament and the newspaper's views of schoolboy baseball]. 総合保健体育科学 [Nagoya journal of health, physical fitness, and sports] 15(1): 39–48.

Hayashi Kaori. (2013). "Japan's Newspaper Industry: The Calm before the Storm." *Nippon.com*, November 6. Accessed November 1, 2016. https:// www.nippon.com/en/currents/d00097/.

Hayford, Charles. (2007). "Samurai Baseball vs. Baseball in Japan." *Asia-Pacific Journal: Japan Focus* 4(5). Accessed April 3, 2007. https://apjjf.org /-Charles-W.-Hayford/2398/article.html.

Hayford, Charles. (2008). "Response to 'Samurai Baseball vs. Baseball in Japan—Revisited'." *Asia-Pacific Journal: Japan Focus* 4(5). Accessed April 3, 2007. https://apjjf.org/-Charles-W.-Hayford/2765/article.html.

Hill, Richard Child, and Kuniko Fujita. (1995). "Osaka's Tokyo Problem." *International Journal of Urban and Regional Research* 19(2): 181–193.

Hirai Hajime 平井肇. (1983). "日本プロ野球の組織論的アプローチ：選手は野球人か球団人か？" [The organizational approach of Japanese professional baseball: Are players baseball men or ball club men?] 体育科教育 [Japanese journal of physical education] 48(3): 45–64.

Hirai Takashi 平井 隆司. (2016). 阪神タイガース「黒歴史」 [A dark history of the Hanshin Tigers].Tokyo: 講談社.

Hirokane Kenshi. (2011). "Advice from Japan's Most Popular CEO." In *Reimaging Japan: The Quest for a Future That Works*, edited by McKinsey and Company, 255–262. San Francisco: VIZ Media.

Hiyama Shinjirō 桧山進次郎. (2011). 生え抜き: タイガースから教わったこと [Native-Born: Things I learned from the Tigers]. Tokyo: 朝日新聞出版社.

Holtzman, Jerome. (1989). "The Japanese Call This Baseball? What in the World Is Going on Over There?" *Chicago Tribune*, July 21, sports sec., 3.

Honda Katsuichi 本多勝一. (1991). "新版 ”野球とその害毒” [New edition: Baseball and its evils]. In 貧困なる精神: 悪口雑言罵詈讒謗集 [Impoverished spirit: A collection of slander, abuse, vilifications, and libel], 108–156. Tokyo: すずさわ書店.

Howard, Tony. 1994. *Baseball in Japan* (documentary). Bowling Green, Ohio: WBGU-TV, Bowling Green State University.

Huffman, James L. (1997). *Creating a Public: People and Press in Meiji Japan*. Honolulu, University of Hawai'i Press.

Hurst, G. Cameron, III. (1997). "The Warrior as Ideal for a New Age." In *The Origins of Japan's Medieval World: Courtiers, Clerics, Warriors, and Peasants in the Fourteenth Century*, edited by Jeffrey P. Mass, 209–233. Stanford, CA: Stanford University Press.

Hye, Allen F. (2004). *Religion in Modern Baseball Fiction*. Mercer, GA: Mercer University Press.

Ikari Seiya 猪狩誠也. (1987). "スポーツ：國際化と大衆化" [Sports: Internationalization and popularization]. In 昭和文化, *1925–1945* [Shōwa culture: 1925–1940], edited by Minami Hiroshi 南博 and Shakai shinri kenkyūjo 社会心理研究所, 504–527. Tokyo: 勁草書房.

Ikei Masaru 池井優. (1991). 野球と日本人 [Baseball and the Japanese]. Tokyo: 丸善.

Ikei Masaru 池井優. (2000). "Baseball, bēsubōru, yakyū: Comparing the American and Japanese games." *Indiana Journal of Global Legal Studies* 8: 73–79.

Imao Kensuke 今尾謙典恵介. (2017). 関西 *(1)*: 阪神・阪急・京阪 [Kansai (1): Hanshin, Hankyū, and Keihan] Tokyo: 白水社.

Ino Sumie 井野澄恵. (2015). *プロ野球パーフェクトデータ：選手名鑑 2015* [Professional baseball perfect data: The 2015 player directory]. Tokyo: 寶島社.

Inoue Hiroshi. (2006). "Osaka's Culture of Laughter." In *Understanding Humor in Japan*, edited by Jessica Milner Davis, 27–36. Detroit: Wayne State University Press.

Inoue Shōichi 井上章一. (2001). 阪神 タイガース の 正体 [The true nature of the Hanshin Tigers]. Tokyo: 太田出版.

Inoue Shōichi 井上章一. (2003). 「あと一球っ!」の精神史：阪神ファンとして生きる意味 [A spiritual history of "just one more pitch!" The living truth according to Hanshin fans]. Tokyo: 太田出版.

Inoue Shun. (1998). "Budō: Invented Tradition in the Martial Arts." In *The Culture of Japan as Seen through Its Leisure*, edited by Sepp Linhart and Sabine Fruhstuck, 83–94. Albany: State University of New York Press.

Inoue Shun 井上俊. (2004). 武道 の 誕生 [The birth of the Way of the Warrior]. Tokyo: 吉川 弘文館.

Ipponmatsu Mikio 一本松幹雄. (1999). 王者猛虎軍の栄光と苦悩 [The glory and anguish of the ruling Fighting Tigers team]. Tokyo: 南雲堂.

Ishii Renzō 石井連蔵. (1980). "飛田穂洲の思い出" [Reflections of Tobita Suishū]. In スポーツ記者の視座 [The viewpoint of sports reporters], edited by Asahi shimbun 朝日新聞, 2:59–77. Tokyo: 朝日ソノラマ.

Ishizaka Yuji 石坂友司. (2002). "学歴エリートの誕生とスポッツ：帝国大学ボート部の歴史社会学的研究から" [Sports and the birth of the academic elite: Based on historical sociological research on crew clubs at the imperial universities]. スポーツ社会学研究 [Japanese journal of sport sociology] 10: 60–71.

Ishizaka Yuji 石坂友司. (2003). "「野球害毒論争」（1911年）再考" [Reconsidering the 1911 dispute about baseball and its evils]. スポーツ社会学研究 [Japanese journal of sports sociology] 11: 115–126.

Itō Ayumi 伊藤歩. (2010). "プロ野球ビジネスは生き返るか" [Will the business of professional baseball revive?]. *AERA* 朝日新聞ウィークリー [AERA, the Asahi Newspaper weekly], November 29, 44–47.

Iwai Hiroshi 岩井洋, Hirosawa Toshimune 広沢 俊宗, and Inoue Yoshikazu 井上 義和. (2006). "プロ野球ファンに関する研究 (VI)：阪神ファンと巨人ファンのイメージ" [A study of professional baseball fans: Images of Hanshin fans and Yomiuri fans]. 関西国際大学地域研究所叢書 [Kansai University of International Studies Institute of Area Studies research series] 3: 41–48.

Iwakawa Takashi 岩川 隆. (1984a). "The Mystique of the Yomiuri Giants." *Japan Echo* 11(3): 60–64.

Iwakawa Takashi 岩川 隆. (1984b). "日本人と巨人軍 (1): 犠打の精神" [The Japanese and the Giants 1: The spirit of the sacrifice bunt]. 文芸春秋 [Bungei shunjū] 62(6): 132–148.

Iwakawa Takashi 岩川 隆. (1984c). "日本人と巨人軍 (2): GY マークの大和魂" [The Japanese and the Giants 2: The Yamato spirit of the GY logo]. 文芸春秋 [Bungei shunjū] 62(9): 168–184.

Jenks, Andrew, and Jonah Quickmire Pettigrew, dirs. (2008). *The Zen of Bobby V*. Throwback Pictures and ESPN Films.

Johnson, Sally, and Frank Finlay. (1997). "Do Men Gossip? An Analysis of Football Talk on Television." In *Language and Masculinity*, edited by Sally Johnson and Ulrike Hanna Meinhof, 130–143. Oxford and Cambridge: Blackwell.

Johnston, Eric. (2015). "Is Tokyo Killing the Rest of Japan? The Overconcentration of People and Resources in Tokyo Could Be Holding Back the Remainder of the Country." *Japan Times*, November 28. Accessed November 29, 2015. https://www.japantimes.co.jp/life/2015/11/28/lifestyle/tokyo-killing-rest-japan/.

Johnston, Eric (2016). "Osaka Ishin in Existential Crisis as Election Looms." *Japan Times*, May 22. Accessed May 23, 2016. https://www.japantimes .co.jp/news/2016/05/22/national/politics-diplomacy/osaka-ishin-existential -crisis-election-looms.

Kahn, Roger (1972). *The Boys of Summer*. New York: Harper and Row.

Kanda Junji 神田順治. (1985). 飛田穂洲 [Tobita Suishū]. In 言論は日本を動か す [Discussion inspires Japan], edited by Mitani Taichirō 三谷太一郎, 127–158. Tokyo: 講談社.

Kanno Kakumyō 菅野覚明. (2004). 武士道の逆襲 [The counterattack of the Way of the Warrior]. Tokyo: 講談社.

Katō Hidetoshi. (1972). "Service-Industry Business Complexes: The Growth and Development of Terminal Culture." *Japan Interpreter* 7(3/4): 376–382.

Katō Hidetoshi. (1987). "Oh, Curry Rice!" *LOOK Japan*, June, 36–37.

Kawauchi Atsurō 河内 厚郎, ed. (1994). 阪神学 事始 [The beginnings of Hanshin-ology]. Kobe: 神戸新聞総合出版センター.

Kelly, William W. (1997). "An Anthropologist in the Bleachers: Cheering a Japanese Baseball Team." *Japan Quarterly* 44(4): 66–79.

Kelly, William W. (1998a). "Blood and Guts in Japanese Professional Baseball." In *The Culture of Japan as Seen through Its Leisure*, edited by Sepp Linhart and Sabine Fruhstuck, 95–112. Albany: State University of New York Press.

Kelly, William W. (1998b). "Learning to Swing: Oh Sadaharu and the Pedagogy and Practice of Japanese Baseball." In *Learning in Likely Places: Varieties of Apprenticeship in Japan*, edited by John Singleton, 265–285. New York and Cambridge, UK: Cambridge University Press.

Kelly, William W. (1999a). "Caught in the Spin Cycle: An Anthropological Observer at the Sites of Japanese Professional Baseball." In *Lives in Motion: Composing Circles of Self and Community in Japan*, edited by Susan Orpett Long, 137–150. Ithaca, NY: East Asia Program, Cornell University.

Kelly, William W. (1999b). "愛すべき阪神タイガース応援団：文化人類学的 アプローチ" [Lovable Hanshin Tiger fan clubs: A cultural anthropological approach]. In プロ野球観戦学 [The study of watching professional baseball], edited by Usami Yō 宇佐美陽, 21–28. Tokyo: 時事通信社.

Kelly, William W. (2000). "The Spirit and Spectacle of School Baseball: Mass Media, Statemaking, and 'Edu-tainment' in Japan, 1905–1935." In *Japanese Civilization in the Modern World XIV: Information and Communication*, edited by Umesao Tadao, William W. Kelly, and Kubo Masatoshi, 105–116. Senri: National Museum of Ethnology.

Kelly, William W. (2002). "Failure in Sport: Accepting Disappointment in Japanese Professional Baseball." *IIAS Newsletter* (28): 10.

Kelly, William W. (2004a). "Introduction: Locating the Fans." In *Fanning the Flames: Fans and Consumer Culture in Contemporary Japan*, edited by William W. Kelly, 1–16. New York: State University of New York Press, Albany.

Kelly, William W. (2004b). "Sense and Sensibility at the Ballpark: What Fans Make of Professional Baseball in Modern Japan." In *Fanning the Flames: Fans and Consumer Culture in Contemporary Japan*, edited by William W. Kelly, 79–106. New York: State University of New York Press.

Kelly, William W. (2006). "Japan: The Hanshin Tigers and Japanese Professional Baseball." In *Baseball without Borders: The International Pastime*, edited by George Gmelch, 22–42. Albany: State University of New York Press.

Kelly, William W. (2007a) "Is Baseball a Global Sport? America's 'National Pastime' as Global Field and International Sport." *Global Networks* 7(2): 187–201.

Kelly, William W. (2007b). "Men at Work or Boys of Summer? The Workplaces of Professional Baseball in Contemporary Japan." In *This Sporting Life: Sports and Body Culture in Modern Japan*, edited by William W. Kelly, 247–262. New Haven, CT: Council on East Asian Studies, Yale University.

Kelly, William W. (2009). "Samurai Baseball: The Vicissitudes of a National Sporting Style." *International Journal of the History of Sport* 26(3): 429–441.

Kelly, William W. (2011a). "Kōshien Stadium: Performing National Virtues and Regional Rivalries in a 'Theatre of sport'." *Sport in Society* 14(4): 481–493.

Kelly, William W. (2011b). "The Sportscape of Contemporary Japan." In *Handbook of Japanese Culture and Society*, edited by Theodore C. Bestor and Victoria Lyon Bestor, 251–262. New York and London: Routledge.

Kelly, William W. (2013a). "Adversity, Acceptance, and Accomplishment: Female Athletes in Japan's Modern Sportsworld." *Asia Pacific Journal of Sport and Social Science* 2(1): 1–13.

Kelly, William W. (2013b). "Japan's Embrace of Soccer: Mutable Ethnic Players and Flexible Soccer Citizenship in the New East Asian Sports Order." *International Journal of the History of Sport* 30(11): 1235–1246.

Kelly, William W. (2015). "Sport Fans and Fandoms." In *Routledge Handbook of Sports Sociology*, edited by Richard Giulianotti, 313–322. London: Routledge.

Kelly, William W. (2017). "Japan: Professional Baseball in 21st-Century Japan." In *Baseball without Borders: The International Pastime*, edited by George Gmelch and Daniel A. Nathan, 183–201. Lincoln: University of Nebraska Press.

Kelly, William W., and Merry I. White. (2006). "Students, Slackers, Singles, Seniors, and Strangers: Transforming a Family-Nation." In *Beyond Japan: The Dynamics of East Asian Regionalism*, edited by Peter J. Katzenstein and Takashi Shiraishi, 63–82. Ithaca, NY, and London: Cornell University Press.

Kennedy, Eileen. (2004). "Talking to Me? Televised Football and Masculine Style." In *British Football and Social Exclusion*, edited by Stephen Wagg, 147–166. London and New York: Routledge.

Kikkawa Takeo 橘川武郎. (1997). "阪神タイガ-ズの経済学" [Economics of the Hanshin Tigers]. 週刊ダイヤモンド [Weekly diamond], September 27, 128–129.

Kikkawa Takeo 橘川武郎. (2004). "プロ野球 阪神タイガース「連覇」を組織論で占う" [Forecasting successive championships for the Hanshin Tigers with organizational theory]. エコノミスト [Economist], April 6, 49–51.

Kikkawa Takeo 橘川武郎. (2009). "プロ野球の危機と阪神タイガース: ファンの懸念" [The Hanshin Tigers and the crisis of professional baseball: A fan's concern]. 一橋ビジネスレビュー [Hitotsubashi business review] 56(4): 62–73.

Kiku Kōichi 菊幸一. (1993). "近代プロスポーツ"の歴史社会学：日本プロ野球の成立を中心に [A historical sociology of "modern professional sports": Centered on the rise of Japanese professional baseball]. Tokyo: 不昧堂出版.

Kiku Kōichi 菊幸一. (1994). "物的文化装置としての甲子園スタジアム" [Kōshien Stadium as a material cultural apparatus]. In 高校野球の社会学：甲子園を読む [Sociology of high school baseball: Reading Kōshien], edited by Esashi Shōgo 江刺正吾 and Komuku Hiroshi 小椋博, 83–111. Tokyo: 世界思想社.

Kinney, Pat. (2003) "Japan's Tigers Don't Resemble Baseball's Losers from Detroit." *The Record (Bergen County, NJ)*, September 28.

Kitaya Yukio 北矢行男. (1992). プロ野球の経営学 [Management studies of professional baseball]. Tokyo: 東洋経済新報社.

Klein, Alan M. (1997). *Baseball on the Border: A Tale of Two Laredos*. Princeton, NJ: Princeton University Press.

Kobayashi Itaru 小林至. (2002). プロ野球ビジネスの仕組み [The organization of the professional baseball business]. Tokyo: 宝島社.

Kosugi Nangin 小杉なんぎん, ed. (2013). 阪神ファンの流儀 [The style of Hanshin fans]. Tokyo: KKベストセラーズ.

Kōzu Masaru 高津勝. (1995). "一九三　年代の都市新中間階層とスポーツ" [Sports and the new urban middle classes of the 1930s]. In 日本近代スポーツ史の底流 [Undercurrents of modern Japanese sports history], 238–292. Tokyo: 創文企画.

Kuehnart, Martin P. (1991). 「Yes」と言えなかった大リーガー――来日ガイジン選手200人の告白 [Major leaguers who couldn't say "yes": Confessions of 200 foreign players in Japan]. Tokyo: ベースボール・マガジン社.

Kuehnart, Martin P. (1998). 愛すべき助っ人たち [The lovable foreign players]. Tokyo: ベースボール・マガジン社.

Kuma Shunjirō 久万俊二郎. (1994). "阪神タイガーズの六十年" [60 years of the Hanshin Tigers]. In 阪神学 事始 [Beginnings of Hanshin-ology], edited by Kawauchi Atsurō 河内 厚郎, 43–75. Kobe: 神戸新聞総合出版センター.

Kunisada Kōichi 国定浩一. (2002). 阪神ファンの経済効果 [The economic effects of Hanshin fans]. Tokyo: 角川書店.

Kusaka Yūkō 日下裕弘. (1985). "明治期における『武士』的、『武士道』的野球信条に関する文化社会学的研究" [A cultural sociology study of "samurai" and "way of the samurai" creeds of baseball in the Meiji era]. 体育・スポーツ社会学研究 [Studies in physical education and sports sociology] 4: 23–44.

Kusaka Yūkō 日下裕弘. (2006). "The Emergence and Development of Japanese School Sport." In *Japan, Sport and Society: Tradition and Change in a Globalizing World*, edited by Joseph Maguire and Nakayama Masayoshi, 19–34. London and New York: Routledge.

Light, Richard L. (1999). "Regimes of Training, Seishin and the Construction of Masculinity in Japanese University Rugby." *International Sport Studies* 21(2): 39–54.

Love the Title-less Tigers Club 優勝しないタイガースを愛する会, ed. (2003). 阪神タイガースよ、優勝しないでくれ！ [Hey, Hanshin Tigers! Please don't win!]. Tokyo: 長崎出版.

Magazine, Roger. (2007). *Golden and Blue Like My Heart: Masculinity, Youth, and Power among Soccer Fans in Mexico City*. Tucson: University of Arizona Press.

Malinowski, Bronislaw. (1922). *Argonauts of the Western Pacific*. London: Routledge and Kegan Paul.

Matanle, Peter C.D., and Wim Lunsing, eds. (2006). *Perspectives on Work, Employment and Society in Japan*. Basingstoke, UK, and New York: Palgrave Macmillan.

Matanle, Peter C.D., Leo McCann, and Darren Ashmore. (2008). "Men under Pressure: Representations of the "Salaryman" and his Organization in Japanese Manga." *Organization* 15(5): 639–664.

Matsudaira S. (1984). "Hiiki renchū (Theatre Fan Clubs) in Osaka in the Early Nineteenth Century." *Modern Asian Studies* 18(4): 699–709.

Matsuki Kenjirō 松木 謙治郎. (1982). タイガースの生い立ち―阪神球団史 [Tigers upbringing: A history of the Hanshin baseball club]. Tokyo: 恒文社.

Matsuki Kenjirō 松木 謙治郎 and Okui Shigekazu 奥井 成一. (1992). 大阪タイガース球団史 [A history of the Osaka Tigers baseball club]. Tokyo: ベースボールマガジン社.

Matsushita Kayo (2002). "We Gotta Have Fun: Japanese Baseball Players Seek Freedom in the American Major Leagues" (master's thesis, School of Journalism, Columbia University).

Matsuzaki Yoshinori 松崎仁紀. (2001). "野球とフットボール、掛け持ち選手の系譜: 日米の差異を事実で語る「文化人類学」" [A genealogy of two-sport athletes in baseball and football: Cultural anthropology that relates the real differences between Japan and the US]. ベースボーロジ: 野球文化學會論叢 [Baseball-ology: Papers of the Society for the Study of Baseball Culture] 2: 128–165.

Mears, Ashley. (2011). *Pricing Beauty: The Making of a Fashion Model*. Berkeley and Los Angeles: University of California Press.

Miki Masafumi. 三木理史 (2003). 水の都と都市交通：大阪の20世紀 [Water, metropolis, and urban transportation]. Tokyo: 成山堂書店.

Miki Masafumi 三木理史. (2005). "The Origins of Commutation in Japan." *Geographical Review of Japan* 78(5): 247–264.

Miki Masafumi 三木理史. (2010). 都市交通の成立 [The establishment of urban transportation]. Tokyo: 日本経済評論社.

Mills, Kathryn, ed. (2000). *C. Wright Mills: Letters and Autobiographical Writings*. Berkeley: University of California Press.

Ministry of Internal Affairs and Communications, Statistics Bureau 総務省統計局. (2017). 住民基本台帳人口移動報告: 平成28年 （2016年） 結果 [Report on internal migration in Japan for 2016]. Tokyo: Ministry of Internal Affairs and Communications.

Mittell, Jason. (2010). *Television and American Culture*. New York: Oxford University Press.

Miyake Hiroshi 三宅博. (2012). 虎の 007: スコアラー室から見た阪神タイガースの戦略 [A Tiger 007: Strategies of the Hanshin Tigers as seen from the scorers' room]. Tokyo: 角川マガジンズ.

Miyake Hiroshi 三宅博. (2013). 「プロ」の野球観戦術：虎のスコアラーが教える [Strategies for watching baseball like a pro: What a Hanshin scorer can teach]. Tokyo: 祥伝社.

Miyamoto Ken'ichi. (1993). "Japan's World Cities: Osaka and Tokyo Compared." In *Japanese Cities in the World Economy*, edited by Fujita Kuniko and Richard Child Hill, 53–82. Philadelphia: Temple University Press.

Modleski, Tania. (1983). "The Rhythms of Reception: Daytime Television and Women's Work." In *Regarding Television: Critical Approaches—An Anthology*, edited by E. Ann Kaplan, 67–75. Frederick, MD: University Publications of America.

Modleski, Tania. (2008). *Loving with a Vengeance: Mass-Produced Fantasies for Women*. New York: Routledge.

Moeran, Brian. (1997). *Folk Art Potters of Japan: Beyond an Anthropology of Aesthetics*. Richmond, Surrey: Curzon Books.

Morse, Margaret. (1983). "Sport on Television: Replay and Display." In *Regarding Television: Critical Approaches—An Anthology*, edited by E. Ann Kaplan, 44–66. Frederick, MD: University Publications of America <in association with American Film Institute>.

Nagai Yoshikazu 永井良和. (1997). つくられるスポーツファン：企業の経営戦略とプロ野球 [The constructed sports fan: Professional baseball and corporate management strategies]. In スポーツファンの社会学 [The sociology of sports fans], edited by Sugimoto Atsuo 杉本厚夫: 世界思想者, 51–70. Kyoto: 世界思想社.

Nagai Yoshikazu 永井良和 and Hashitsune Shin'ya 橋爪 紳也. (2003). 南海ホークスがあったころ──野球ファンとパ・リーグの文化史 [When the Nankai Hawks were here: A cultural history of baseball fans and the Pacific League]. Tokyo: 紀伊國屋書店.

Nagano Hideo 永野秀雄. (2005). "プロスポーツ選手の労働者性" [Professional baseball players as laborers]. 日本労働研究雑誌 [Japanese journal of labor studies]. (537): 20–22.

Nagatani Osamu 永谷修. (2005). 野村・星野・岡田 復活の方程式──阪神タイガースを変えた男たち [The comeback equations of Nomura, Hoshino, and Okada: The men who changed the Hanshin Tigers]. Tokyo: イーストプレス.

Nakagawa Yūsuke 中川 右介. (2016). 阪神タイガース 1965-1978 [The Hanshin Tigers, 1965–1978]. Tokyo: 角川書店.

Nakamaki Hirochika 中牧弘允. (1997). "経営人類学にむけて：会社の「民族誌」とサラリーマンの「常民研究"」 [Toward the anthropology of administration: Companies' "ethnographies" and salaryman "common people research"]. In 経営人類学 ことはじめ [Toward an anthropology of administration], edited by Nakamaki Hirochika 中牧弘允 and Hioki Kōichirō 日置 弘一郎, 13–29. Osaka: 東方 出版.

Nakamura Tetsuya 中村哲也. (2007). "「野球統制令」と学生野球の自治: 1930年代における東京六大学野球を中心に" [The baseball regulation ordinance and the self-governance of schoolboy baseball: Focusing on the Tokyo six-university league in the 1930s]. スポーツ史研究 [Japan journal of sport history] 20: 81–94.

Nakamura Tetsuya 中村哲也. (2008). "明治後期における「一高野球」像の再検討: 一高内外の教育をめぐる状況に着目して" [Reconsidering the late Meiji era image of Ichikō baseball: Attending to the conditions surrounding education inside and outside Ichikō]. 一橋大学スポーツ研究 [Hitotsubashi University sports research] 28: 27-34.

Nakamura Tetsuya 中村哲也. (2010). 学生野球憲章とはなにか—自治から見る日本野球史. [What is the schoolboy baseball charter? Looking at Japanese baseball history through self-governance]. Tokyo: 青弓社.

Nakata Jun 中田 潤, Yazaki Ryōichi 矢崎 良一, Hashimoto Tokiyoshi 橋本 清, Ikeda Hiroaki 池田 浩明, and Nakabashi Yasuyuki 高橋 安幸. (2004). 元・阪神: 謎のトレード・突然のFA・不可解な解雇・12の理由 [Hanshin before: Puzzling trades, sudden free agency, baffling releases, and 12 reasons]. Tokyo: 竹書房.

Nakatsugawa Akiko 中津川詔子. (2004). "応援すると負ける" [When we support them, they lose]. *AERA* 朝日新聞ウィークリー [AERA, the Asahi Newspaper weekly], November 1, 94.

Nikkan Sports Newspaper, Western Japan 日刊スポーツ新聞西日本, ed. (2016). 猛虎の80年: 喜怒哀楽の歩み [80 years of the Fierce Tigers: Moving along with joy, anger, pathos, and humor]. Tokyo: 日刊スポーツ出版社.

Nippon.com. (2014). "Newspaper Circulation in Japan: Still High but Steadily Falling." December 5. Accessed January 17, 2016. https://www.nippon.com/en/features/h00084/

Nippon.com. (2015). "Japanese Publishing in Free Fall." January 21. Accessed May 30, 2018. https://www.nippon.com/en/features/h00092/.

Nishihara Shigeki 西原茂樹. (2004). "東京・大阪両都市の新聞社による野球（スポーツ）イベントの展開過程—1910〜1925年を中心に—" [The developmental process of baseball (sports) events sponsored by Tokyo and Osaka newspapers in the period 1910-1925]. 立命館産業社会論集 [Ritsumeikan social sciences review] 40(3): 115-134.

Nishihara Shigeki 西原茂樹. (2006). "1910〜30年代初頭の甲子園大会関連論説における野球（スポーツ）の教育的意義・効果に関する所説をめぐって--『大阪朝日』『大阪毎日』社説等の分析から" [About assertions that baseball (sports) has educational significance and effects, as offered in editorials about the Kōshien Tournament from the 1910s through the early 1930s: An analysis of editorials in the Osaka Asahi Newspaper and the Osaka Mainichi Newspaper]. 立命館産業社会論集 [Ritsumeikan social sciences review] 41(4): 65-83.

Nishihara Shigeki 西原茂樹. (2009). "関西メディアと野球—戦時下の甲子園大会を中心に" [Kansai media and baseball: Focusing on the Kōshien Tournament during wartime]. In 幻の東京オリンピックとその時代 : 戦時期のスポーツ・都市・身体 [The phantom Tokyo Olympics and its era: Wartime sports, cities, and bodies], edited by Sakaue Yasuhiro 坂上 康博 and Takaoka Hiroyuki 高岡弘幸, 379-404. Tokyo: 青弓社.

Nishii Teiichi 西井禎一. (1995). なにわタイガース学 [Studies of the Naniwa Tigers]. Osaka: 一番出版.

Nishizawa Akira 西澤 暗. (2014) 阪神戦・実況 32年: 甲子園の放送席から見続けたタイガースの真実 [32 years of live broadcasting Hanshin games:

The reality of the Tigers from continuous viewing in the broadcast booth]. Tokyo: 講談社.

Nitobe Inazō 新渡戸稲造. (1969). *Bushido: The Soul of Japan*. Rutland, VT: Charles E. Tuttle.

Nomura Katsuya 野村克也. (2006). 巨人軍論：組織とは，人間とは，伝統とは [A treatise on the Yomiuri Giants Club: Its organization, its personnel, its traditions]. Tokyo: 角川書店.

Nomura Shūhei 野村周平. (2009). さらば阪神の「赤い彗星」 [Farewell, Hanshin's red comet]. *AERA* 朝日新聞ウィークリー [AERA, the Asahi Newspaper Weekly], December 28, 27.

Ogawa Isao 小川功. (1995). "阪神電気鉄道：阪神間の遊園地・都市開発に果たした役割" [Hanshin Electric Railroad Company: Its role in urban development and amusement parks in the Hanshin corridor]. In 民鉄経営の歴史と文化〈西日本編〉 [The history and culture of private railroad management: Western Japan volume], edited by Uda Tadashi 宇田 正, Takechi Kyōzō 武知京三, and Asaka Katsusuke 浅香 勝輔, 167-188. Tokyo: 古今書院.

Ogawa Isao 小川功. (1998). "History of Amusement Park Construction by Private Railway Companies in Japan." *Japan Railway and Transport Review* (15): 28-34.

Okada Hisao 岡田久雄. (2003). 阪神電鉄物語：球団経営に成功した鉄道会社 [The story of the Hanshin Electrical Railroad: A railroad company that succeeded in baseball club operations]. Tokyo: JTB.

Okamoto Satoru 岡本さとる. (1996). 阪神ファンの変態的快楽 [The perverse pleasures of Hanshin fans]. Tokyo: 飯倉書房.

Okamura Masashi 岡村正史. (2008) 力道山 [Rikidōzan]. Kyoto: ミネルヴァ書房.

Okazaki Mitsuyoshi 岡崎満義. (1982). "V9 巨人軍の「戦争」" [The wars of the V9 Giants]. 文芸春秋 [Bungei shunjū] 60(4).

Onishi Norimitsu. (2004). "Forget the Fans: It's Bean Ball in the Boardroom." *New York Times*, August 25, Section A, 4.

Onose Tsuyoshi 小野瀬剛志. (2001). "昭和初期におけるスポーツ論争—「日本的スポーツ観」批判をめぐって" [Sports controversies in the early Showa era: Focusing on criticisms of a "Japanese sports viewpoint"]. スポーツ社会学研究 [Japan journal of sport sociology] 9: 60-70.

Onose Tsuyoshi 小野瀬剛志. (2002). "野球害毒論争 (1911年) に見る野球イデオロギー形成の一側面" [An aspect of the process of making baseball ideology through the 1911 baseball and its evils controversy"]. スポーツ史研究 [Japan journal of sport history] 15: 61-72.

Osawa Machiko, Kim Myoung Jung, and Jeffrey Kingston. (2013). "Precarious Work in Japan." *American Behavioral Scientist* 57(3): 309-334.

Ōta Satoru 太田サトル. (2003). 阪神という国民のおもちゃ [The Hanshin Tigers, the people's toy]. *AERA* 朝日新聞ウィークリー [AERA, the Asahi Newspaper weekly], June 9, 12-15.

Ōtani Kōichi 大谷 晃一. (1999a). 大阪学：世相 [Osaka studies: Social conditions]. Tokyo: 経営書院.

Ōtani Kōichi 大谷 晃一. (1999b). 阪神タイガース学 [Hanshin Tigers studies]. Tokyo: ザ・マサダ.

Ōtani Kōichi 大谷 晃一. (2003). 大阪学: 阪神タイガース編 [Osaka studies: Hanshin Tigers volume]. Tokyo: 新潮社.

Ozaki Moriteru 尾崎盛光. (1967). 就職: 商品としての学生 [Finding employment: University students as commercial goods]. Tokyo: 中央公論社

Painter, Andrew A. (1996). "Japanese Daytime Television, Popular Culture, and Ideology." In *Contemporary Japan and Popular Culture*, edited by John Whittier Treat, 197–234. Honolulu: University of Hawai'i Press.

Partner, Simon. (1999). *Assembled in Japan: Electrical goods and the making of the Japanese consumer*. Berkeley and Los Angeles: University of California Press.

Pilling, David. (2014). *Bending Adversity: Japan and the Art of Survival*. London: Allen Lane.

Pope, Stacey. (2017). *The Feminization of Sports Fandom: A Sociological Study*. Abingdon, Oxon: Routledge.

Popick, Barry. (2012). "Entry from October 27, 2012: 'Sports is the toy department of life.'" *The Big Apple* (blog). Accessed June 1, 2018. https://www.barrypopik.com/index.php/new_york_city/entry/sports_is_the_toy_department_of_life/.

Rashad, Ahmad. (1982). "Journal of a Plagued Year: Part I." *Sports Illustrated*, October 18, 43–58.

Reader, Ian, and George J. Tanabe Jr. (1998). *Practically Religious: Worldly Benefits and the Common Religion of Japan*. Honolulu: University of Hawai'i Press.

Reaves, Joseph A. (1997). *Warsaw to Wrigley: A Foreign Correspondent's Tale of Coming Home from Communism to the Cubs*. South Bend, IN: Diamond Communications.

Robben, Antonius C. G. M., and Jeffrey A. Sluka, eds. (2007). *Ethnographic Fieldwork: An Anthropological Reader*. Malden, MA: Blackwell Publishers.

Roden, Donald F. (1980a). "Baseball and the Quest for National Dignity in Meiji Japan." *American Historical Review* 85(3): 511–534.

Roden, Donald F. (1980b). *Schooldays in Imperial Japan: A Study in the Culture of a Student Elite*. Berkeley: University of California Press.

Rokusaisha henshūbu 鹿砦社編集部, ed. (1996). なんとかせんかいタイガース！！ [Well, whatever, Tigers!]. Nishinomiya: 鹿砦社.

Rokusaisha henshūbu 鹿砦社編集部, ed. (1997). しっかりせんかいタイガース！！ [Get tough, Tigers!]. Nishinomiya: 鹿砦社.

Rokusaisha henshūbu 鹿砦社編集部, ed. (1999). 野村は笑い、虎は泣く！野村タイガースの舞台裏 [Nomura laughs and the Tigers cry: Behind the scenes of the Nomura Tigers]. Nishinomiya: 鹿砦社.

Rokusaisha henshūbu 鹿砦社編集部, ed. (2004). 阪神タイガースおっかけマップ [A map for Hanshin Tiger groupies]. Nishinomiya: 鹿砦社.

Rose, Ava, and James Friedman. (1994). "Television Sports as Mas(s)culine Cults of Distraction." *Screen* 35(1):22–35

Saeki Shin'ichi 佐伯真一. (2004). 戦場の精神史: 武士道という幻影 [A spiritual history of the battlefield: The illusion that is the Way of the Warrior]. Tokyo: NHK 出版.

Sakai Yasuhiro 酒井康広. (2004). "戦前期における電鉄会社系野球場と野球界の変容" [Baseball stadiums operated by electric train companies and changes in the baseball world during the wartime years]. スポーツ社会学研究 [Japan journal of sport sociology] 12: 71–80.

Sakaue Yasuhiro 坂上 康博. (2001). にっぽん野球の系譜学 [A genealogy of Japanese baseball]. Tokyo: 青弓社.

Sakudō Yōtarō 作道洋大郎. (1995). "阪急電鉄：その経営と沿線文化の開発" [Hankyū Electric Railroad: Its management and the development of its route culture]. In 民鉄経営の歴史と文化: 西日本編 [The history and culture of private railroad management: Western Japan volume], edited by Uda Tadashi 宇田 正, Takechi Kyōzō 武知京三, and Asaka Katsusuke 浅香 勝輔, 143–166. Tokyo: 古今書院.

Sankei Shimbun Sports Department 産経新聞運動部. (2011–2012). "阪神タイガース事件史" [A history of Hanshin Tiger incidents]. 産経新聞 [Sankei Newspaper]. Special series, December 11, 2011–March 12, 2012.

Satō Osami 佐藤修史. (2003). "阪神は日産になる" [Hanshin will become Nissan]. AERA 朝日新聞ウィークリー [AERA, the Asahi Newspaper weekly] 16: 8–11.

Sayama Kazuo 佐山和夫. (1998). ベースボールと日本野球：打ち勝つ思考、守り抜く精神 [Baseball and Japanese yakyū: Aggressive thought, defensive spirit]. Tokyo: 中央公論社.

Sayama Kazuo 佐山和夫. (2007). 日本野球はなぜベースボールを超えたのか「フェアネス」と「武士道」 [Why did Japanese yakyū overcome baseball? "Fairness" and "The Way of the Warrior"]. Tokyo: 彩流社.

Shapiro, Michael. (1989). "A Whole Different Ball Game." Japan Society Newsletter, June, 2–5.

Sharf, Robert H. (1993). "The Zen of Japanese Nationalism." History of Religions 33(1): 1–43.

Shaughnessy, Dan. (2011). "Riveting Drama at Fenway Theater." Boston Globe, October 16. Accessed June 30, 2018. https://www.bostonglobe.com/sports/2011/10/16/red-sox-providing-riveting-drama-fenway-theater/MmXdFQKs7hgf7wU6HnOoYN/story.html.

Shimada Akira 島田 明, ed. (2001). 明治 44 年慶應野球部アメリカ横断実記 [A record of the U.S. transcontinental trip by the Keio Baseball Club in 1911]. Tokyo: ベースボールマガジン社.

Shimoda Masami 真銅正宏, ed. (2006). 大阪のモダニズム [Osaka modernism]. Tokyo: ゆまに書房.

Shinbō Nobunaga 新保 信長. (1999). タイガースファンという生き方 [The way of life of Tiger fans]. Tokyo: メディアファクトリー.

Shiozawa Yukito 塩澤 幸登. (2012). 死闘: 昭和三十七年 阪神タイガース [Struggle to the death: The 1962 Hanshin Tigers]. Tokyo: 河出書房新社.

Shōji Tatsuya 庄司達也, ed. (2008). 郊外住宅と鉄道 [Suburban housing and the railroads]. Tokyo: ゆまに書房.

Skinner, Kenneth A. (1979). "Sararīman Manga." Japan Interpreter 12(3–4): 449–457.

Smith, Henry D., II. (1980). "The Paradoxes of the Japanese Samurai." In Learning from Shogun: Japanese History and Western Fantasy, 86–98. Santa Barbara: Program in Asian Studies, University of California.

Spence, Louise. (2005). *Watching Daytime Soap Operas: The Power of Pleasure*. Middletown, CT: Wesleyan University Press.

Spielvogel, Laura. (2003). *Working Out in Japan: Shaping the Female Body in Tokyo Fitness Clubs*. Durham, NC: Duke University Press.

Stanka, Jean, and Joe Stanka. (1989). *Coping with Clouters, Culture and Crisis*. Wilmington, DE: Dawn Press.

Starn, Orin. (2012). *The Passion of Tiger Woods: An Anthropologist Reports on Golf, Race, and Celebrity Scandal*. Durham, NC: Duke University Press.

Stevens, Carolyn S. (2004) "Buying Intimacy: Proximity and Exchange at a Japanese Rock Concert." In *Fanning the Flames: Fans and Consumer Culture in Contemporary Japan*, edited by William W. Kelly, 59–78. Albany: State University of New York Press.

Stocker, Joel Floyd. (2002). "The 'Local' in Japanese Media Culture: Manzai Comedy, Osaka, and Entertainment Enterprise Yoshimoto Kogyo." PhD diss., University of Wisconsin, Madison.

Sugano Shinji 菅野真二. (2003). ニッポン野球の青春―武士道野球から興奮の早慶戦へ [The springtime of Japanese baseball: From samurai baseball to the exciting Waseda-Keio series]. Tokyo: 大修館書店.

Sugimoto Atsuo 杉本厚夫. (2006). "阪神タイガースファンにみる大阪文化--なぜ、350万人も甲子園球場に行くのか?" [Osaka culture as seen through Hanshin Tiger fans: Why do 3,500,000 people go to Kōshien Stadium?]. フォーラム 現代 社会学 [Kansai sociological review] 5: 69–76.

Sugimoto Naotsugu 杉本尚次. (1989). "野球をめぐる文化地理学的考察" [Cultural geographical inquiries about baseball]. In 日本人と遊び [The Japanese and play], edited by Moriya Takeshi 守屋毅, 28–52. Tokyo: ドメス出版.

Suzuki Akira 鈴木明. (1982). "一九四五年のプレボール" ["Play ball" in 1945]. In 焼け跡に流れるりんごの歌 [The apple song flows in the ruins of war], edited by Gakushūsha Editorial Department 学習社編集部, 168–173. Tokyo: 学習研究社.

Suzuki Akira 鈴木明. (1987). セ・パ分裂 プロ野球を変えた男たち [The separation of the Central and Pacific Leagues: The men who changed professional baseball]. Tokyo: 新潮社.

Swyers, Holly (2010). *Wrigley Regulars: Finding Community in the Bleachers*. Urbana: University of Illinois Press.

Tachibanaki Toshiaki 橘木俊詔. (2005). "プロ野球と労働市場" [Professional baseball and labor markets]. 日本労働研究雑誌 [Japan journal of labor research] (537): 14–16.

Tachibanaki Toshiaki 橘木俊詔. (2016). プロ野球の経済学 [The economics of professional baseball]. Tokyo: 東洋経済新聞社.

Tada Michitarō (1988). "Osaka Popular Culture: A Down-to-Earth Appraisal." In *The Japanese Trajectory: Modernization and Beyond*, edited by Gavan McCormack and Sugimoto Yoshio, 33–53. Cambridge, UK: Cambridge University Press.

Tada Michitarō 多田道太郎, Kawauchi Atsurō 河内厚郎, and Asahi Shimbun Mirai Tankentai 毎日新聞未来探検隊, eds. (1993). 阪神観:「間」の文化快楽 [Hanshin perspectives: The cultural pleasures of the "Kan"]. Osaka: 東方出版.

Tagsold, Christian. (2011). "Remember to Get Back on Your Feet Quickly": The Japanese Women's Volleyball Team at the 1964 Olympics as a 'Realm of Memory'." *Sport in Society* 14(4): 444–453.

Takahashi Hidesato 高橋豪仁. (1994). "広島市民球場におけるプロ野球の集合的応援に関する研究" [Research on the collective cheering for professional baseball at the Hiroshima city stadium]. スポーツ社会学研究 [Japanese journal of sport sociology] 2: 54–66.

Takahashi Hidesato. (2007). "The Conviviality of Cheering: An Ethnography of Fan Clubs in Professional." In *This Sporting Life: Sports and Body Culture in Modern Japan*, edited by William W. Kelly, 263–280. New Haven, CT: Council on East Asian Studies, Yale University.

Takahashi Hidesato 高橋豪仁. (2011). スポーツ応援文化の社会学 [The sociology of sports supporters' culture]. Kyoto: 世界思想社.

Takai Masashi 高井昌茨吏. (2006). 女子マネージャーの誕生とメディア―スポーツ文化におけるジェンダー形成 [Media and the birth of girl managers: Gender formation in sports culture]. Kyoto: ミネルヴァ書房.

Takashima Kō 高嶋航. (2012). 帝国日本とスポーツ [Imperial Japan and sports]. Tokyo: 塙書房.

Takemura Tamio 竹村民郎 and Suzuki Sadami 鈴木貞美, eds. (2008). 関西モダニズム再考 [Reconsidering Kansai modernism]. Kyoto: 思文閣出版.

Tamaki Masayuki 玉木正之. (1988). タイガースへの鎮魂歌（レクイエム）[Requiem for the Tigers]. Tokyo: 朝日新聞社.

Tamaki Michio 玉置道夫. (1989). 一億八千万人の甲子園：青春のメッカ昔と今 [180,000,000 people at Kōshien: The Mecca of youth, then and now]. Tokyo: オール出版.

Tamaki Michio 玉置道夫. (1991). これがタイガース：阪神タイガース研究 [These are the Tigers: Hanshin Tiger research]. Tokyo: 創英社.

Tashiro Masayuki 田代正之. (1996). "中等学校野球の動向からみた「野球統制令」の歴史的意義" [The historical significance of the regulatory law on baseball, as seen from tendencies in middle school baseball]. スポーツ史研究 [Japan journal of sport history] 9: 11–26.

Terao Hirokazu 寺尾博和. (2004). "阪神の真相：久万オーナーの思想と現実" [The truth about Hanshin: The reality and thought of owner Kuma]. In 日刊スポーツ大阪版 [Nikkan sports newspaper, Osaka edition]. 15-part daily series, January 7–January 21.

Terao Hirokazu 寺尾博和. (2011). Legend 伝説：川上哲治―巨人不滅のV9 [Legendary stories: The immortal V-9 of the Kawakami Tetsuharu Yomiuri Giants]. 日刊スポーツ大阪版 [Nikkan sports newspaper, Osaka edition]. 15-part daily series, January 25–February 12.

Thompson, Lee Austin. (1986). "Professional Wrestling in Japan: Media and Message." *International Review for the Sociology of Sport* 21(1): 65–82.

Thompson, Lee Austin. (2011). "The Professional Wrestler Rikidōzan as a Site of Memory." *Sport in Society* 14(4): 532–541.

Thompson, Stephen I. (1991). "Baseball and the Heart and Mind of Japan: The Randy Bass Case." In *Baseball History: An Annual of Original Baseball Research*, edited by Peter Levine, 39–50. Westport, CT: Meckler.

Thompson, Stephen I., and Ikei Masaru. (1987–1988). "Victor Starfin: The Blue-Eyed Japanese." *Baseball History* 2(4): 4–19.

Tobita Suishū 飛田穂洲. (1972). 飛田穂洲の高校野球入門 [Tobita Suishū's introduction to high school baseball]. Tokyo: ベースボール・マガジン社.

Todeschini, Maya Morioka. (2011). "'Webs of Engagement': Managerial Responsibility in a Japanese Company." *Journal of Business Ethics* 101(S1): 45–59.

Torigoe Norio 鳥越規央. (2013). 本当は強い阪神タイガース [The Hanshin Tigers really are strong]. Tokyo: 筑摩書房.

Tsuchiya Reiko 土屋礼子. (1996). "創刊期のスポーツ紙と野球イベント：女子プロ野球と映画人野球" [Baseball events and the beginnings of the sports newspapers: Women's pro baseball and movie company baseball]. In 戦後日本のメディア・イベント [1945–1960] [Media events of postwar Japan, 1945–1960], edited by Tsuganesawa Toshihiro 津金澤聰廣, 47–70. Kyoto: 世界思想社.

Tsukamoto Takashi. (2011). "Devolution, New Regionalism and Economic Revitalization in Japan: Emerging Urban Political Economy and Politics of Scale in Osaka–Kansai." *Cities* 28(4): 281–289.

Uda Tadashi 宇田 正, Takechi Kyōzō 武知京三, and Asaka Katsusuke 浅香 勝輔, eds. (1995). 民鉄経営の歴史と文化: 西日本編 [The culture and history of private railroad company management: Western Japan volume]. Tokyo: 古今書院.

Ueda Ken'ichi 上田賢一. (2003). 猛虜伝説：阪神タイガースの栄光と苦悩 [Legends of the Fierce Tigers: The glory and the anguish of the Hanshin Tigers]. Tokyo: 集英社.

Ushigome Tadahiro 牛込惟浩. (1993). サムライ野球と助っ人たち：横浜球団スカウトの奮闘記 [Samurai baseball and foreign players: A record of the hard struggles of a Yokohama baseball club scout]. Tokyo: 三省堂.

van Maanen, Hans. (2010). *How to Study Art Worlds: On the Societal Functioning of Aesthetic Values*. Amsterdam: Amsterdam University Press.

Villi, Mikko, and Hayashi Kaori. (2017). "'The Mission Is to Keep This Industry Intact'." *Journalism Studies* 18(8): 960–977.

Wada Yutaka 和田豊. (2003). 虎の意地: 和田コーチの野球日記 [The spirit of the Tigers: The baseball diary of coach Wada]. Tokyo: 集英社.

Wakisaka Akira 脇阪昭. (1989). 野球はベースボールに勝てるか: 日米文化の根本的ギャップを探る [Is yakyū beating baseball? Exploring the fundamental gap between U.S. and Japanese culture]. Tokyo: 學生社.

Watanabe Kentarō 渡辺謙太郎. (2003). "自分史的ラジオ実況論" [A personal history of radio broadcasting]. ベースボーロジ: 野球文化學會論叢 [Baseball-ology: Papers of the Society for the Study of Baseball Culture] 4: 128–165.

Watanabe Toru 渡辺融. (1976). "明治期の横浜における外国人スポーツ・クラブの活動と日本のスポーツ" [Japanese sports and the activities of the foreigners' sports clubs in Meiji-era Yokohama]. Supplement, 東京大学教養学部体育学紀要 [Proceedings of the Department of Sports Sciences College of Arts and Sciences, University of Tokyo] 10: 1–33.

Watanabe Toru 渡辺融. (1982). "ベースボールから野球へ：中馬庚の仕合規則に見られるベースボールの日本化" [From baseball to yakyū: The Japanization of baseball viewed from Chūma Kanoe's playing rules]. 比較文化研究 [Comparative study of cultures] (21): 1–54.

Watanuki Yoshinori 綿貫慶徳. (2001). "近代日本における職業野球誕生に関する史的考察―新聞社主権による野球イベントの分析を中心として" [Historical inquiries relating to the birth of professional baseball in modern Japan]. スポーツ史研究 [Japan journal of sport history] 14: 39–54.

Westney, D. Eleanor. (1987). *Imitation and Innovation: The Transfer of Western Organizational Patterns to Meiji Japan*. Cambridge, MA: Harvard University Press.

Whannel, Garry. (1992). *Fields in Vision: Television Sport and Cultural Transformation*. London and New York: Routledge.

Whiting, Robert. (1977a). *The Chrysanthemum and the Bat: Baseball Samurai Style*. New York: Dodd, Mead & Company.

Whiting, Robert. (1977b). 菊とバット：プロ野球にみる日本スタイル [The chrysanthemum and the bat: Japanese style as seen in professional baseball]. Tokyo: シムル出版会.

Whiting, Robert. (1985). 日本野球は永久に不滅 [Japanese baseball, eternally indestructible]. Tokyo: 筑摩書房.

Whiting, Robert. (1989). *You've Gotta Have Wa: When Two Cultures Collide on the Baseball Diamond*. New York: Macmillan.

Whiting, Robert. (1991). ベースボールジャンキー [Baseball junkie]. Tokyo: 朝日新聞社.

Whiting, Robert. (2006). "The Samurai Way of Baseball and the National Character Debate." *Studies on Asia*, ser. 3, 3(2): 104–122.

Whiting, Robert. (2008). "Samurai Baseball vs. Baseball in Japan—Revisited." *Asia-Pacific Journal: Japan Focus* 6(5). Accessed May 4, 2008. https://apjjf.org/-Robert-Whiting/2764/article.html.

Whiting, Robert. (2009). *You've Gotta Have Wa: When Two Cultures Collide on the Baseball Diamond*. 2nd ed., rev. New York: Vintage.

Will, George F. (1990). *Men at Work: The Craft of Baseball*. New York: Macmillan.

Williams, Raymond. (1977). "Structures of Feeling." In *Marxism and Literature*, by Raymond Williams, 128–135. Oxford: Oxford University Press.

Yamada Takamichi 山田隆道. (2009). 阪神タイガース 暗黒のダメ虎史: あのとき虎は弱かった [A history of the hapless Tigers in the dark ages of the Hanshin Tigers]. Tokyo: ミリオン出版.

Yamamuro Hiroyuki 山室 寛之. (2010). 野球と戦争 [Baseball and war]. Tokyo: 中央公論新社.

Yano Akihiro 矢野燿大. (2011). 阪神の女房 [Hanshin wife]. Tokyo: 朝日新聞出版社.

Yano, Christine R. (2002). *Tears of Longing: Nostalgia and the Nation in Japanese Popular Song*. Cambridge, MA: Harvard University Asia Center.

Yoshida Reiji. (2009). "Colonel Stages a Comeback in Osaka" *Japan Times*, March 11. Accessed June 13, 2013. https://archive.is/20130218132853/http://info.japantimes.co.jp/text/nn20090311a3.html.

Yoshida Yoshio 吉田義男. (2003). 阪神タイガース [Hanshin Tigers]. Tokyo: 新潮社.

Yoshimi Shun'ya 吉見俊哉. (1996). "メディア・イベント概念の諸相" [Aspects of the concept of media event]. In 近代 日本 の メディア・イベント [Media events in modern Japan], edited by Tsuganesawa Toshihiro 津金澤 聰廣, 3–30. Kyoto: 同文舘.

Yoshimi Shun'ya. (2003). "Television and Nationalism: Historical Change in the National Domestic TV Formation of Postwar Japan." *European Journal of Cultural Studies* 6(4): 459–506.

Yoshimi Shun'ya. (2005). "Japanese Television: Early Development and Research." In *A Companion to Television*, edited by Janet Wasko, 540–557. Malden, MA, and Oxford: Blackwell Press.

Index

CPSIA information can be obtained
at www.ICGtesting.com
Printed in the USA
LVHW010119231118
597980LV00003B/616/P